Professional Selling

C. Shane Hunt
Idaho State University

George D. Deitz
The University of Memphis

John D. Hansen
The University of Alabama at Birmingham

PROFESSIONAL SELLING

Published by McGraw Hill LLC, 1325 Avenue of the Americas, New York, NY 10121. Copyright ©2022 by McGraw Hill LLC. All rights reserved. Printed in the United States of America. No part of this publication may be reproduced or distributed in any form or by any means, or stored in a database or retrieval system, without the prior written consent of McGraw Hill LLC, including, but not limited to, in any network or other electronic storage or transmission, or broadcast for distance learning.

Some ancillaries, including electronic and print components, may not be available to customers outside the United States.

This book is printed on acid-free paper.

2 3 4 5 6 7 8 9 CPI 26 25 24 23

ISBN 978-1-260-59775-2
MHID 1-260-59775-X

Cover Image: *Djomas/Shutterstock; Ranta Images/Shutterstock; Syda Productions/Shutterstock*

All credits appearing on page or at the end of the book are considered to be an extension of the copyright page.

The Internet addresses listed in the text were accurate at the time of publication. The inclusion of a website does not indicate an endorsement by the authors or McGraw Hill LLC, and McGraw Hill LLC does not guarantee the accuracy of the information presented at these sites.

mheducation.com/highered

BRIEF CONTENTS

About the Authors iv
Dedications vi
Preface vii
Acknowledgments xiv
Detailed Contents xv

PART ONE Finding Customers and Developing Relationships

1. Everyone Is a Salesperson 2
2. Prospecting and Qualifying 22
3. Engaging Customers and Developing Relationships 46

PART TWO Using Strategies and Tools to Meet Client Needs

4. Social Selling 72
5. Sales-Presentation Strategies 98

PART THREE Finding and Negotiating Solutions for Customers

6. Solving Problems and Overcoming Objections 120
7. Negotiating Win-Win Solutions 148
8. Profitology: Pricing and Analytics in Sales 174

PART FOUR Achieving Success in a Sales Career

9. Sales Compensation and Career Development 196
10. The Psychology of Selling: Knowing Yourself and Relating to Customers 216

Glossary 240
Name Index 246
Subject Index 249

ABOUT THE AUTHORS

Hello, my name is...

Shane Hunt

C. Shane Hunt

Dr. Shane Hunt received his Ph.D. in Marketing from Oklahoma State University, where he was an AMA-Sheth Foundation and National Conference in Sales Management Doctoral Fellow. Shane is the recipient of the 2010 National Inspire Integrity Award from the National Society of Collegiate Scholars; the 2010 Lt. Col. Barney Smith Award as Professor of the Year at Arkansas State University; the 2015 Honors Professor of the Year Award at Arkansas State University; and the 2019 National Teaching Innovation Award from the Association of Collegiate Marketing Educators.

Prior to teaching, Shane used his MBA from the University of Oklahoma working for a Fortune 500 company in Tulsa. He spent eight years as a pricing analyst, product manager, and business development manager overseeing numerous mergers and acquisitions initiatives. Shane's research has appeared in *The Journal of Personal Selling and Sales Management* and *The Journal of Business Logistics*. He has been invited to present to numerous organizations including the American Marketing Association and the National Conference in Sales Management. In addition to his role as a professor and dean, Shane also serves as a consultant, speaker, and board member for businesses and nonprofit organizations across the country.

Today, Shane serves as the dean of the College of Business and a professor of marketing at Idaho State University. He lives in Pocatello, Idaho, with his wife Jenifer; they have two children, Andrew and Sarah.

George D. Deitz

George D. Deitz

Dr. George D. Deitz is the George Johnson Professor of Marketing and founding director of the Customer NeuroInsights Research Lab (C-NRL) at The University of Memphis. He received his Ph.D. in marketing from The University of Alabama, where he was recognized as the Fred Bostick endowed fellow and was selected to participate in the 2004 AMA-Sheth Consortium. His research has appeared in a variety of leading marketing journals, including the *Journal of the Academy of Marketing Science*, *Journal of Service Research*, *Journal of Business Research*, *Journal of Advertising Research*, *Journal of Business Logistics*, and *Journal of Business Venturing*.

George grew up in the Panama Canal Zone and completed his undergraduate and graduate degrees at West Virginia University. Soon after, he began a decade-long career in professional selling in the healthcare financial management software sector.

George and his wife, Kristine, live in Memphis, home to the world's best BBQ and the birthplace of rock and roll. They have three children, Luke, Mark, and Koren, and a lovely daughter-in-law, Rachel.

John D. Hansen

John Hansen

Dr. John D. Hansen is an associate professor of marketing and director of the Center for Sales Leadership at the University of Alabama at Birmingham (UAB). He previously served on the faculty at the University of Southern Mississippi and at Northern Illinois University, and received his Ph.D. from the University of Alabama. Prior to entering academe, he held numerous positions in industry for a Fortune 500 company.

John focuses on research issues related to salesperson and frontline employee performance in the business and consumer contexts. His research has been accepted for publication in the *Journal of Personal Selling and Sales Management, Journal of Business Research, Journal of Business Venturing, Journal of Business Logistics, Journal of Services Marketing,* and *Industrial Marketing Management*. His research has been included in several refereed conference proceedings, and his submissions to the National Conference in Sales Management and Society for Marketing Advances annual conferences were recognized as best papers.

John received the Award for Excellence in Teaching by a Doctoral Student while at the University of Alabama and the President's Award for Excellence in Teaching at UAB.

John lives in Birmingham, Alabama, and has two children, Samuel and Mary Elizabeth.

DEDICATIONS

To the R. M. "Bob" Wood Family, who have provided extraordinary support for sales education through the establishment of the Wood Sales Leadership Center. Thank you, Mark, Lisa, Jill, and Peggy, for your investment in me and toward the goal of producing the next generation of great salespeople.

Shane Hunt

To my children, Mark, Koren, Luke, and Rachel: Thank you for your love and support. You are the light of our lives. If you have learned anything from me (or from reading this text), I hope it is understanding the rewards that accompany providing valued service to others as well as the importance of following your dreams with passion and a fun-loving spirit.

George Deitz

To my children, Samuel and Mary Elizabeth, for helping me keep in perspective those things that matter most. This book is dedicated to you both.

John Hansen

PREFACE

The role of selling in our economy and our lives continues to grow. Numerous textbooks and sales courses introduce students to the best practices and importance of sales professionals to every organization. **Students and professors want—and deserve—learning and teaching experiences that engage and empower them to appreciate and choose selling as a profession.**

At conferences and teaching symposia across the country, and through surveys of students in the professional selling course at several universities, we have gathered feedback about products available for the professional selling course. Three themes emerged:

1. In a field in which digital resources are becoming more central to the selling process, instructors want **digital resources** that will help familiarize students with the processes and tools they will need in their careers.
2. **Textbooks need to be right-sized**—only long enough to provide content needed by the instructor and the student.
3. **Content must relate to students' goals and lives** to engage their interest. It should be closely woven, avoiding random use or needless repetition of sales terms and topics.

Our text and its accompanying digital resources aim to meet the challenges and needs of instructors as well as students. Its goal is to deliver the most relevant content, in the most engaging format possible, with a complete set of digital resources, to help students from all backgrounds and all career aspirations learn the science—and art—of selling. Along the way, students will come to appreciate that sales is essential to their careers and businesses and to society as a whole.

Professional Selling Is for Students

Your students will find that this text is:

- **Logically designed for student engagement.** Most existing sales texts present the subject matter as various selling "silos." Ours, instead, follows a logical sequence of chapters: Chapter 1 sets the stage by showing that *everyone* in every organization is in sales. Often, students who feel little affinity for sales are taking the course only because they "have to." Chapter 1 shows students, from the very first day of class, the relevance of sales to them—strengthening their personal engagement with the text and the course. Chapters 2 through 7 then follow a structured, logical flow of the selling process, taking students through the steps successful salespeople will use in today's marketplace. Chapter 8, "Profitology," addresses pricing and the use of analytics in sales. Chapters 9 and 10 address related aspects of achieving success in a sales career: how salespeople are compensated (Chapter 9) and the psychology of selling (Chapter 10). Also, rather than covering ethics as a stand-alone chapter, we integrate this critical concept into every aspect of professional selling, reflecting the reality of this issue in the lives of salespeople.
- **Value-oriented.** This text provides students with a powerful toolkit of sales knowledge that will help them and the organizations they work for. It combines the most current research with practical examples. In addition, we have built the text to work seamlessly with McGraw Hill Connect® in a way that no sales product on the market can match: We have developed examples, exercises, and role plays at the same time as the text, and they are integrated into every chapter.

- **Focused on multiple sales roles.** The bulk of the content shows the importance of sales in for-profit businesses. But we also include content relating to fund-raising sales roles in not-for-profit organizations. In addition, we emphasize that career success will be partially determined by how well students tell their personal narrative and *sell themselves* to employers, investors, and graduate schools.

As students learn how to apply selling skills to their own lives, they will be more engaged to understand the discipline for all that it has to offer. They will finish the text and the course with a thorough understanding that professional selling is essential to organizational success, whatever one's role in an organization.

Professional Selling Is for Instructors

Instructors will find that our text is:

- **Right-sized for various course settings.** The first thing you'll notice when you look at the Contents listing (page XV) is that there are fewer chapters than is the case with most other products for the professional selling course. Our text contains 10 chapters—a length that instructors we surveyed consistently voted as the most desirable number. The 10-chapter length makes the content very manageable for instructors to cover in various course settings: traditional 15-week semester, 10-week quarter, 7-week online, or 5-week summer course formats.
- **Readable and relevant.** To promote engagement, we have written for today's students in a casual but business-professional style. The chapters consistently provide examples of how theory interacts with practice in organizations that are interesting and relevant to today's students. Many chapters include examples of scripted dialogues, which give students the flavor of a salesperson's voice and approach.
- **A potential recruiting tool.** With this text, you will give students content that will encourage them to learn the best practices, strategies, and careers that are part of professional selling. We've seen in our own experiences that the text's content, combined with interesting online materials, ultimately will lead to more sales majors and minors and to increased student credit hours.
- **Fully integrated with online support materials.** The text's authors themselves have carefully developed chapter content in conjunction with related online support materials. This fully integrated package, delivered on MHE's Connect platform, is a significant step up from the current sales-course standard in terms of teaching and support materials for the classroom. For those who are teaching online courses of professional selling, our product provides an unprecedented amount of Connect exercises and content. This wealth of material dramatically increases the instructor's ability to engage students regardless of physical location.

In sum, this new text for the professional selling course represents sales in a fresh, practical way. It illustrates to students the impact of sales skills on their lives and careers in all types of businesses. It shows that sales is not just a core business activity but is an **essential business skill** for every organization and individual—relevant for students in any major.

Chapter Features

The pedagogical features in our chapters are crafted around teaching and learning preferences in today's classroom:

- **Executive Perspective.** Each chapter begins with a senior manager's perspective on the role of sales to his or her business. We have recruited highly successful senior managers from a wide range of backgrounds outside of sales, including finance, operations, accounting, publishing, and politics. They represent a variety of industries and sales situations—insurance, telecommunications, building materials manufacturing and supply, the wine and spirits industry, healthcare, and nonprofit fundraising. The perspectives of these executives illustrate the need for successful leaders—from any background and in any organization—to be effective salespeople who can lead and achieve their firm's goals.

- **Today's Professional Perspective.** Each chapter also contains a profile of a recent (within five years) college graduate. These dynamic and diverse young professionals provide on-the-ground details of their work in a sales career. They also emphasize for students the utility of using on-campus job fairs, networking events, and internships to find first jobs in sales. Their profiles provide an engaging contrast with the Executive Perspectives boxes and resonate with students.
- **In-chapter Connect Assignments.** Three Connect Assignments per chapter provide immediate online opportunities for students to review and practice content they've just learned. These exercises appear at the end of key content sections in each chapter.
- **Ethics coverage.** Ethics is an essential element in professional selling as well as in AACSB assessment requirements. Every chapter of the text includes real-world discussion and examples of business ethics, highlighting how ethical issues permeate selling decisions.
- **Career Tips.** Each chapter ends with advice that can help students master the sales process. These career tips from leading sales executives and sales instructors will help students develop skills that will be beneficial throughout their professional lives.
- **Standard learning format.** Chapters are structured around a standard learning format: *Learning Objectives, Chapter Summaries,* and *Key Terms*. The learning objectives, using Bloom's taxonomy verbs, break chapter content into manageable chunks and give students and instructors concrete goals for learning.
- **Rich end-of-chapter assignment material.** Each chapter ends with a rich set of review and assignment material: *Discussion Questions* help students expand their thinking just a bit past the chapter content, putting their learning into context. An *Ethical Challenge* presents a situation related to chapter content that asks questions to help students think through ethical issues involved in selling decisions. The *Role Play* sets up a situation in which students practice being either the seller or the buyer and then reflect on the situation and provide feedback to the class. The *Sales Presentation* is available in Connect and typically asks students to provide a short (three- to five-minute) sales presentation. All end-of-chapter assignment material has been written and developed by the text's authors.

Supplements Package

HDH *Professional Selling* is committed to having the *best supplements package* in the professional selling text arena. It offers a total learning experience that integrates text content, Connect exercises, and social media throughout the life of the product.

- **Instructor's Manual**
- **PowerPoint Presentations**
- **Test Bank and Quizzes**
- **Video Library**
- **Connect Content Matrix:** Looking to see a listing of all of the assignable assets available for a particular chapter or learning objective? Look no further than the Connect Content Matrix, found in the Instructor Resources listing to the left.

- **Marketing Insights Podcast Series:** Go beyond the text! Our Marketing Insights Podcast Series connects you to sales content intended to inform, educate, entertain, and inspire. Updated regularly with timely topics, these seven- to ten-minute podcasts were created by marketing and sales professionals with you in mind. Available on iTunes, Spotify, Google Play, and Stitcher to go with you wherever you go.
- **Weekly Article Recommendations from the Textbook Authors via Social Media:** Go to our website, huntmello.com, or follow author Shane Hunt on Twitter @drshanehunt.

Conclusion

We strongly believe that sales is at the heart of modern business. Understanding and using the aspects of sales in order to improve for-profit businesses, not-for-profit organizations, and students' career prospects is a critical educational activity. Such an understanding is relevant to any undergraduate student, regardless of their functional area of academic focus.

Our goal is to introduce the first professional selling text that captures the importance and opportunities of sales in a way that is fully relevant to today's business students and business professionals. We want this product to enable professional selling instructors to have accomplished these three key objectives by the end of the course:

- Provide knowledge leadership in the area of professional selling, with content that is high quality and socially responsible.
- Engage students through modern and relevant examples and leave them with the understanding of the critical role sales plays in their lives.
- Integrate the themes of a traditionally organized sales text with cutting-edge digital resources to help students develop a deep, thorough understanding of this complex discipline.

We are very excited about the future of sales and grateful for the opportunity to help colleges and universities throughout the world develop the next generations of great salespeople. We have worked carefully to produce an integrated print and digital experience for you and your students. We trust that it will help inspire students to explore and apply the marketing experiences they need in order to leave your course prepared for their future coursework and careers. It is our sincere hope that this new product, *Professional Selling,* will engage your students and demonstrate the universal importance of professional selling . . . *because everyone is a salesperson!*

C. Shane Hunt
Idaho State University

George D. Deitz
The University of Memphis

John D. Hansen
University of Alabama at Birmingham

Instructors: Student Success Starts with You

Tools to enhance your unique voice

Want to build your own course? No problem. Prefer to use our turnkey, prebuilt course? Easy. Want to make changes throughout the semester? Sure. And you'll save time with Connect's auto-grading too.

65% Less Time Grading

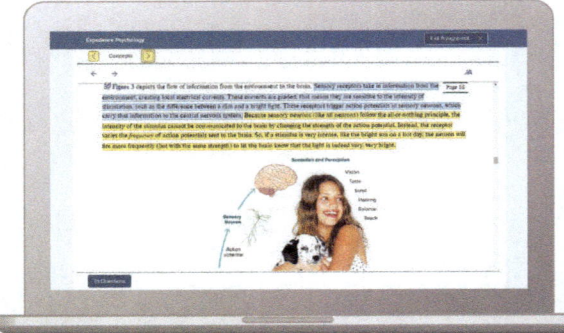

Laptop: McGraw Hill; Woman/dog: George Doyle/Getty Images

Study made personal

Incorporate adaptive study resources like SmartBook® 2.0 into your course and help your students be better prepared in less time. Learn more about the powerful personalized learning experience available in SmartBook 2.0 at **www.mheducation.com/highered/connect/smartbook**

Affordable solutions, added value

Make technology work for you with LMS integration for single sign-on access, mobile access to the digital textbook, and reports to quickly show you how each of your students is doing. And with our Inclusive Access program you can provide all these tools at a discount to your students. Ask your McGraw Hill representative for more information.

Padlock: Jobalou/Getty Images

Solutions for your challenges

A product isn't a solution. Real solutions are affordable, reliable, and come with training and ongoing support when you need it and how you want it. Visit **www.supportateverystep.com** for videos and resources both you and your students can use throughout the semester.

Checkmark: Jobalou/Getty Images

Students: Get Learning that Fits You

Effective tools for efficient studying

Connect is designed to make you more productive with simple, flexible, intuitive tools that maximize your study time and meet your individual learning needs. Get learning that works for you with Connect.

Study anytime, anywhere

Download the free ReadAnywhere app and access your online eBook or SmartBook 2.0 assignments when it's convenient, even if you're offline. And since the app automatically syncs with your eBook and SmartBook 2.0 assignments in Connect, all of your work is available every time you open it. Find out more at **www.mheducation.com/readanywhere**

> "I really liked this app—it made it easy to study when you don't have your textbook in front of you."
>
> - Jordan Cunningham, Eastern Washington University

Everything you need in one place

Your Connect course has everything you need—whether reading on your digital eBook or completing assignments for class, Connect makes it easy to get your work done.

Calendar: owattaphotos/Getty Images

Learning for everyone

McGraw Hill works directly with Accessibility Services Departments and faculty to meet the learning needs of all students. Please contact your Accessibility Services Office and ask them to email accessibility@mheducation.com, or visit **www.mheducation.com/about/accessibility** for more information.

Top: Jenner Images/Getty Images. Left: Hero Images/Getty Images. Right: Hero Images/Getty Images

ACKNOWLEDGMENTS

Special Thanks to Our Reviewers

We send special thanks to the reviewers who provided feedback that was essential to the development of this product:

Sterling Bone
Utah State University Logan

Brian K. Collins
Virginia Polytechnic Institute and State University

Cristina Connolly
California Polytechnic State University

Diane Edmondson
Middle Tennessee State University

Jeffrey Hoyle
Central Michigan University

Robert Leach
Atlanta Technical College

David Lehman
Kansas State University

Patrick Pallentino
Florida State University

Joel Petry
Southern Illinois University Edwardsville

Ian J. Scharf
University of Miami

Amanda Stoecklein
State Fair Community College

Del Wakley
Milwaukee Area Technical College

In addition, this product would not have been possible without the effort and expertise of many people. First and foremost, we recognize and thank the entire editorial and marketing teams at McGraw Hill Education who have made this product possible. We thank Meredith Fossel, who surrounded us with the best team in all of higher-education publishing. We also thank our development editor, Haley Burmeister, for keeping us on track and focused on all of the integrated aspects of the product, and Nicole Young, a truly amazing marketing manager, whose vision was instrumental in communicating the message of our product. We especially thank our content editor Ann Torbert, whose incredible efforts, guidance, and support made every page of this product better and more student-focused.

We also thank Maria McGreal, Keri Johnson, Jacob Sullivan, Kristin Piljay, and all of the talented people McGraw Hill assembled, whose guidance and feedback made the product much better. It has been our pleasure and privilege to work with these incredibly talented and skilled professionals who have shaped the final product that you are about to read.

A special thank you to Cortney Kieffer, who was Shane's first McGraw Hill field sales representative when he became a professor. Cortney was our first exposure to McGraw Hill, and her professionalism, dedication to our students, and friendship made us want to be part of the McGraw Hill family.

We also thank our colleagues at Idaho State University, the University of Memphis, and the University of Alabama at Birmingham. It is an honor every day to work with brilliant people who genuinely and passionately care about the education of our students. Their support and friendship is priceless, and we feel very thankful to be part of these truly world-class institutions.

We thank our families for their love, support, and patience while we developed this product. In addition, we thank the great faculty members at Oklahoma State University and the University of Alabama for the training and knowledge they gave us during our doctoral programs. We also thank our many outstanding colleagues in the private sector, who provided us with experiences that sharpened our focus on the practical applications of sales and the need to prepare our students for today's competitive job market.

Finally, we thank our students. Teaching the sales course is one of the best jobs in the world because of the students we get to educate, help, and learn from. The students at Idaho State University, the University of Memphis, the University of Alabama at Birmingham, as well as those throughout the country and the world, drove our decision to create this product. Professional selling is an extremely important topic for their careers and their lives, and we hope we have developed a product to help them succeed and achieve their dreams.

Shane Hunt, George Deitz, John Hansen

DETAILED CONTENTS

PART ONE Finding Customers and Developing Relationships 1

1 EVERYONE IS A SALESPERSON 2
Executive Perspective 3

The Importance of Sales 4
Challenges of Personal Selling 5
Advantages of Personal Selling 5

The Strategic Role of Personal Selling and Sales Analytics 6
Factors That Influence the Use of Personal Selling 6
Sales Analytics 7
Connect Assignment 1-1: Sales Analytics 8

Personal Selling in the Digital Era 8
Connect Assignment 1-2: Social Selling 9

Career Opportunities in Sales 11
Types of Sales Roles 11
Sales Roles in Nonprofit Organizations 13
"Am I Cut Out for Sales?" 13

Today's Professional 14

Ethics in Personal Selling 15
Standards of Professional Conduct in Sales 15
Connect Assignment 1-3: Sales Ethics 16

Selling Yourself 16

Chapter Summary 17 | Key Terms 19 | Discussion Questions 19 | Ethical Challenge 19 | Role Play 20 | Sales Presentation 20 | Career Tips 20 | Chapter Endnotes 21

2 PROSPECTING AND QUALIFYING 22
Executive Perspective 23

An Introduction to Prospecting 24
The Importance of Prospecting 24
The Challenges Associated with Prospecting 24
Why Salespeople Are Hesitant to Prospect 25
Connect Assignment 2-1: The Challenges of Prospecting 26

Matching Personal Strengths to Prospecting Roles 26
Hunting and Farming Sales Orientations 27
The Role of Inside Sales in Prospecting 27

The Prospecting Process 28
- Lead Generation 29
- Lead Prioritization 30
- Lead Qualification 30
- Prospect Prioritization 32
- Sales-Call Planning 33

Connect Assignment 2-2: The Prospecting Process 34

Lead-Generation Methods 34
- Virtual Networking 34
- Traditional Networking 35
- Referrals 35
- Trade Shows 36
- Cold-Calling 36
- Websites 36
- Sales Directories 37
- Centers of Influence 37
- Noncompeting Salespeople 37
- Marketing 37

Connect Assignment 2-3: Lead-Generation Methods 38

Formulating a Prospecting Strategy 38
- Develop a Prospecting Plan 39
- Allocate Time 39
- Track Results 39
- Evaluate Lead-Generation Methods and Prospecting Processes 39
- Maintain a Positive Attitude 40

Ethics in Prospecting 40

Today's Professional 41

Chapter Summary 42 | Key Terms 43 | Discussion Questions 43 | Ethical Challenge 43 | Role Play 44 | Sales Presentation 44 | Career Tips 45 | Chapter Endnotes 45

3 ENGAGING CUSTOMERS AND DEVELOPING RELATIONSHIPS 46

Executive Perspective 47

Relationship Selling 48
Engaging Customers 49
Different Purchase Types 50
- New-Task Purchases 50
- Straight-Rebuy Purchases 51
- Modified-Rebuy Purchases 51
- How Purchase Types Affect Buying Teams 52
- How Purchase Types Affect Decision Making 54

Connect Assignment 3-1: Purchase Types 55

Differences in Customer Relationships 55
- Differences Based on Relationship Level 55

Differences Based on Relationship Type 56
Differences Based on Relationship Life Cycle 57
Connect Assignment 3-2: Customer Loyalty 58

Building Trust 58
The Importance of Character 59
The Importance of Competence 61
Connect Assignment 3-3: Trust 64

Salesperson Ethics 64
Research on Salesperson Ethics 65
Specific Ethics Challenges 65

Today's Professional 66

Chapter Summary 67 | Key Terms 68 | Discussion Questions 68 | Ethical Challenge 68 | Role Play 69 | Sales Presentation 69 | Career Tips 69 | Chapter Endnotes 70

PART TWO Using Strategies and Tools to Meet Client Needs 71

4 SOCIAL SELLING 72

Executive Perspective 73

Understanding Social Selling 74
Social Selling Versus Traditional Sales 75
Social Buyers, Social Sellers 76
Creating Value for B2B Buyers 77

Using Social Media to Enhance Salesperson Credibility 78
Developing a Buyer-Centric Social Profile 78
Connect Assignment 4-1: Salesperson Credibility 81

Creating a Prospect-Rich Social Network 81
Tracking New Activity 81
Building a Revenue-Generating Social Network 82
Socially Surrounding Your Buyer 83

Curating and Sharing Relevant Content 84
Benefits of Content Curation 85
Sharing Curated Content 85
What Content Do Buyers Want? 86
Connect Assignment 4-2: Developing Content 90

Measuring Social-Selling Performance 90
Measure What Matters! 91
Establishing Social-Selling KPIs 91
Connect Assignment 4-3: Measuring Social-Selling Performance 92

Today's Professional 93

Chapter Summary 94 | Key Terms 95 | Discussion Questions 95 | Ethical Challenge 95 | Role Play 96 | Sales Presentation 96 | Career Tips 96 | Chapter Endnotes 97

5 SALES-PRESENTATION STRATEGIES 98

Executive Perspective 99

Types of Sales Presentations 100
Memorized Sales Presentations 100
Formula Sales Presentations 100
Need-Satisfaction Sales Presentations 101

Connect Assignment 5-1: Sales Presentations 102

Preparing the Sales Presentation 102
Identify the Customer Problem 102
Plan What You Want the Customer to Remember 103
Consider a Product Demonstration 103
Provide "Slick" Data 103
Practice Through Role Play 104

Why Sales Presentations Fail 105
Technical Problems 105
Poor Presentation Skills 105
Irrelevant Information 106
Unethical Behaviors 106
International and Intercultural Communication Challenges 106

Connect Assignment 5-2: Unethical Sales-Presentation Practices 107

Nonverbal Communication in Sales Presentations 108
Eye Contact 108
Posture 108
Facial Expressions 108

Connect Assignment 5-3: Nonverbal Communication 109

Virtual and Team-Sales Presentations 109
Virtual Presentations 109
Team Selling 111

Today's Professional 112

Storytelling in Sales Presentations 113
Benefits of Storytelling in Sales 113
Selling Yourself with Stories 114

Chapter Summary 114 | Key Terms 115 | Discussion Questions 115 | Ethical Challenge 115 | Role Play 116 | Sales Presentation 116 | Career Tips 117 | Chapter Endnotes 117

PART THREE Finding and Negotiating Solutions for Customers 119

6 SOLVING PROBLEMS AND OVERCOMING OBJECTIONS 120
Executive Perspective 121

Solving Customer Problems 122
  The Salesperson as Problem Solver 122

Skills Needed in Solving Customer Problems 124
  Questioning 124
  Listening 126
  Creativity 128
Connect Assignment 6-1: Spin Selling 129

Gaining Commitment 129
  Customer-Oriented Approach to Gaining Commitment 130
  Techniques for Gaining Commitment 131

Types of Customer Objections 133
  No-Need Objection 134
  Source Objection 134
  Time Objection 134
  Product Objection 135
  Price Objection 135

Overcoming Objections 135
  The Process of Overcoming Objections 136
  Techniques for Overcoming Objections 138
Connect Assignment 6-2: Overcoming Objections 140

Ethics in Gaining Commitment 140
  Ethics and Objections 141
  Manipulative Closing Techniques 141

Today's Professional 142
Connect Assignment 6-3: Ethics in Gaining Commitment 143

  Chapter Summary 143 | Key Terms 144 | Discussion Questions 145 | Ethical Challenge 145 | Role Play 145 | Sales Presentation 146 | Career Tips 146 | Chapter Endnotes 147

7 NEGOTIATING WIN-WIN SOLUTIONS 148
Executive Perspective 149

Basic Negotiation Concepts 150
  Basic Elements of Negotiation 151
Common Negotiation Styles 153
  Accommodators 154
  Avoiders 154

Collaborators 155
Competitors 155
Compromisers 156
Connect Assignment 7-1: Negotiation Styles 156

Planning for Formal Negotiations 156
Gathering Information 157
Profiling Your Negotiating Partner 157
Formalizing Goals and Objectives 158
Agreement on Broad Principles 160
Setting an Agenda 160
Choosing a Location 160
Team Negotiation 160
Online Negotiation 161
Connect Assignment 7-2: Planning for Negotiations 162

Conducting the Negotiation Session 162
Defining the Problem 162
Generating Alternatives 163
Making Timely Concessions That Matter 164

Ethical Considerations in Sales Negotiations 164
Questions of Ethical Conduct 165
Ethically Ambiguous Tactics 165
How to Deal with Deception 166

Today's Professional 167

Connect Assignment 7-3: Ethics in Sales Negotiations 168

Chapter Summary 168 | Key Terms 169 | Discussion Questions 170 | Ethical Challenge 170 | Role Play 171 | Sales Presentation 171 | Career Tips 171 | Chapter Endnotes 172

8 PROFITOLOGY: PRICING AND ANALYTICS IN SALES 174

Executive Perspective 175

The Role of Pricing in Sales 176

What Is Profitology? 177
Challenges of Traditional Markup Pricing 178
Connect Assignment 8-1: Markup Pricing 179

Strategic Pricing 179
How Salespeople Can Contribute to Strategic Pricing 180
Connect Assignment 8-2: Strategic Pricing 181

Predictive Analytics and the Science of Sales Productivity 181
Use of AI in Sales 182

Legal and Ethical Issues in Pricing 184
Price Discrimination 184
Price Fixing 185
Predatory Pricing 185
Deceptive Pricing 186
Pricing Issues for Nonprofit Fundraising 186

Connect Assignment 8-3: Pricing Laws 187

CRM and Strategic Pricing 187

Today's Professional 189

Chapter Summary 190 | Key Terms 191 | Discussion Questions 191 | Ethical Challenge 192 | Role Play 192 | Sales Presentation 192 | Career Tips 193 | Chapter Endnotes 193

PART FOUR Achieving Success in a Sales Career 195

9 SALES COMPENSATION AND CAREER DEVELOPMENT 196

Executive Perspective 197

Elements of a Sales Compensation Plan 198
- Base Salary 198
- Commissions 198
- Bonuses 199
- Non-Core Elements of Sales Compensation Plans 199

Connect Assignment 9-1: Elements of Sales Compensation 200

Types of Sales Compensation Plans 201
- Salary-Only Compensation 201
- Commission-Only Compensation 201
- Base Salary Plus Commission 202
- Base Salary Plus Bonus 203
- Absolute and Relative Commission Plans 203
- Straight-Line Commission 203
- Gross Margin Commission 204
- Comparison of Sales Compensation Plans 204

Connect Assignment 9-2: Types of Sales Compensation Plans 204

Designing Sales Compensation Plans 207
- The Dangers of Complex Compensation Plans 208
- The Problem with Capping Sales Compensation 208

Today's Professional 209

Career Paths in Sales and Sales Management 210
- What to Look For 210
- Salesperson Motivation, Training, and Performance Management 210
- Careers in Sales Management 211

Connect Assignment 9-3: Career Paths in Sales 212

Chapter Summary 212 | Key Terms 213 | Discussion Questions 213 | Ethical Challenge 213 | Role Play 214 | Sales Presentation 214 | Career Tips 214 | Chapter Endnotes 215

10 THE PSYCHOLOGY OF SELLING: KNOWING YOURSELF AND RELATING TO CUSTOMERS 216

Executive Perspective 217

True Grit: Salesperson Persistence and Resilience 218
Developing Grit in Sales Organizations 219

Self-Confidence: Overcoming Fears and Building Trust 220
The Cost of Fear in Sales 220
Improving Self-Confidence in Sales 221
Self-Affirmation 222
Alter-egos 222
Body Language and Confidence 223
Dress for Success 223
Belief in What You Are Selling 224

Connect Assignment 10-1: Overcoming Salesperson Fear 224

Emotional Intelligence in Sales 224
Perspectives on Decision Making 225
Emotions in Decision Making 225
Sales EQ 226
What Can Salespeople Do to Strengthen Sales EQ? 226
Empathy: Stepping into Customers' Shoes 229

Connect Assignment 10-2: Emotional Intelligence 230

Time Management 230
Work from a List 230
Prioritize Activities and Accounts 231
"Time-Chunk": Using the Pomodoro Technique 231
Automate Administrative Tasks 232
Stop Multitasking 232
Minimize Distractions 233

Connect Assignment 10-3: Time Management 233

Today's Professional 234

Chapter Summary 235 | Key Terms 236 | Discussion Questions 236 | Ethical Challenge 236 | Role Play 237 | Sales Presentation 237 | Career Tips 238 | Chapter Endnotes 238

Glossary 240
Name Index 246
Subject Index 249

Part ONE

Finding Customers and Developing Relationships

Tom Merton/Caiaimage/Getty Images

Chapter 1
Everyone Is a Salesperson

Chapter 2
Prospecting and Qualifying

Chapter 3
Engaging Customers and Developing Relationships

Chapter 1

Everyone Is a Salesperson

Learning Objectives

After reading this chapter, you should be able to:

LO 1-1 Describe the importance, challenges, and unique advantages of personal selling.

LO 1-2 Explain the strategic role of personal selling and sales analytics in modern organizations.

LO 1-3 Describe the impact of digital technology and social selling on personal selling.

LO 1-4 Explain the appeal of sales as a career and the different types of sales positions.

LO 1-5 Describe ethical issues in personal selling.

LO 1-6 Describe the foundational skills necessary for sales success.

Executive **Perspective** ... because everyone is a salesperson

Randy Hoggard
Managing Director
Northwestern Mutual

Randall P. Hoggard

Describe your job.

I am the managing director of Northwestern Mutual, a company that has been helping clients for over 160 years with a variety of products, including life insurance, disability income, long-term care insurance, annuities, investments, and investment advisory services. We help people understand financial security and give them the tools to help achieve it. Financial security has four main objectives: protecting income, retirement planning, debt reduction, and savings. Our insurance agents work with customers to help them attain all four.

How did you get your job?

I did an internship with Northwestern Mutual during my senior year in college. When I experienced the opportunity to affect people in a way that would outlast me, I knew this career was for me. I joined Northwestern Mutual after graduation and worked my way through various positions, up to managing director.

What has been most important in making you successful at your job?

I believe in and practice what we encourage our clients to do. Even at the age of 22, I had no doubt that the people I was working with would be better off because of our conversations. Now when I give advice, it's from experience. Belief in the products and process is key, and has resulted in a career that I love.

What advice would you give future graduates about a career in sales?

Oh, I have lots of advice:

- If you want job security, be in sales and be excellent at it.
- Sales are the beginning of all business; nothing happens unless there is a transaction of money for goods or services.
- Sales are not limited to the traditional sales career. Now, *everyone* is in sales—physicians, attorneys, bankers, professors, and so on.
- If you don't believe in what you're selling, move on to another opportunity.
- Internships allow you to test-drive a career.

What is the most important characteristic of a great salesperson?

This is a great question because I believe that everyone is a salesperson! I would say there are two important characteristics: First is the ability to ask great questions and then ask great follow-up questions. I like the phrase "seek first to understand." Second is the ability to communicate in simple terms. People don't care how smart you are if they don't understand what you're saying.

THE IMPORTANCE OF SALES

LO 1-1
Describe the importance, challenges, and unique advantages of personal selling.

Virtually everything we do in the course of the day—from the trivial to the truly miraculous—is a direct result of someone selling something to someone else. The range of personal selling activity is wide:

- A jeweler showing a heart-shaped diamond to a young man seeking to buy an engagement ring for his fiancée.
- A pharmaceutical representative advocating the benefits of a new drug to a group of physicians at a hospital.
- A sales team from Boeing working diligently over the course of several years to secure a $200 billion bid for a new fleet of fighter jets.
- A single inside sales representative at a Delta Airlines call center in Atlanta spending 15 minutes to help a grandmother in Memphis schedule a round-trip flight to visit her grandchildren in Tampa.
- A development director at your university asking a donor to permanently endow a scholarship benefitting students like you.

Despite such different situations, a number of common factors highlight the importance of personal selling as a marketing activity. We'll explore those commonalities throughout this text.

Sales are at the heart of modern business. Every other function in an organization exists in some way to support sales. Without sales, an organization does not generate revenue; without revenue, there is no need to hire financial analysts, human resource managers, or engineers. The importance of sales to organizations of all sizes is the highest it has been in our economic history, and organizations need great salespeople.

The title of this text, *Professional Selling,* indicates two things about sales: First, selling is a profession that requires skills that can be learned, practiced, and perfected. Second, the more that salespeople know and practice sales techniques and skills, the more effective and successful—the more "professional"—they become. As we'll describe later in this chapter, sales as a profession has great appeal for many. But whether or not you choose sales as your profession, as you move forward in your career, developing *personal selling skills* will benefit you in countless ways.

What is **personal selling**? It is the two-way flow of communication between a buyer and a seller, paid for by the seller and seeking to influence the buyer's purchase decision. Personal selling takes many forms. It can be someone trying to sell you insurance for you and your family. It can be someone selling business software that will be used in each of your firm's stores. It can even be the person behind the fast-food counter trying to get you to upsize your order.

Organizations promote their goods or services—and themselves—through what is called the promotion mix. The promotion mix consists of four main elements of marketing communication: advertising, sales promotion, personal selling, and public relations. Advertising is typically one-directional; it communicates the seller's message to the buyer. Personal selling, in contrast, consists of the *two-way* flow of communication between a buyer and a seller. The salesperson and customer share information and feedback, often face-to-face. Personal selling is the interpersonal arm of the promotional mix. The interpersonal aspect of personal selling helps companies create and maintain strong customer relationships. As a result, personal selling is often a much more effective tool than are advertising or sales promotion in complex purchase situations.

Despite economic and technological changes, salespeople often serve as the critical link between the firm and the customer. They are the eyes and ears of the organization; they help marketers understand what customers like and dislike and what changes are happening within an industry.

personal selling
The two-way flow of communication between a buyer and a seller, paid for by the seller and seeking to influence the buyer's purchase decision.

Challenges of Personal Selling

Organizations in all industries face several major challenges with professional selling, including cost and message consistency. For one thing, personal selling is expensive. The average cost of a sales call varies across industries but almost always averages several hundred dollars per visit. Costs mount when you consider that, for most products, one sales call will not result directly in an order. In general, though, sales investments are highly profitable for businesses. According to the Marketing Science Institute, firms on average gain a $31 increase in sales revenue for every $100 in increased sales expenditures.[1] Wise firms view the costs of an accomplished sales team as investments. It is critical that salespeople develop skills to make sure that their organizations are getting a satisfactory return on this investment.

Another challenge for personal selling has been message consistency. Organizations need to ensure that each salesperson communicates a message that is consistent with that of other salespeople as well as with the full-integrated marketing-communications strategy. Inconsistent messaging is the equivalent of a firm having as many marketing strategies as it does salespeople. Firms can overcome this challenge by offering information and training to the sales force.

Advantages of Personal Selling

Despite its cost and the possibility of message inconsistency, personal selling offers two unique advantages over the other promotional elements: immediate feedback and relationship selling.

First, personal selling results in immediate feedback from the customer. The salesperson can *see* the nonverbal communication that might give insight into the customer's mindset and the likelihood that he or she will buy. In addition, the salesperson can listen directly to the customer's feedback, objections, and concerns. This face-to-face interaction allows the salesperson to adjust the sales presentation accordingly and to provide detailed and customized solutions that can generate more sales.

Second, personal selling enables the firm to develop a personal relationship with the customer. **Relationship selling** is a sales approach that involves building and maintaining customer trust over a long period of time. Relationship selling is increasingly important; very few firms would expect to survive on the profits generated from one-time transactional sales.

relationship selling
A sales approach that involves building and maintaining customer trust over a long period of time.

At the level of the individual firm, personal selling activities play a crucial role in driving competitive advantage and superior financial performance. Salespeople serve as the critical link between the firm and the customer. For many buyers, their assigned salesperson is more than simply the face of the company; that salesperson *is* the company. As such, salespeople represent the firm to customers and also often represent the interests of customers within the firm.

As the eyes and ears of the organization, salespeople gather information about customer likes and dislikes and share it with marketers and product designers. In most organizations, salespeople play one of the most important roles in marketing research by providing market feedback on competitors and trends in the macro-environment. At the macro-economic level, selling is an engine of economic growth for vast sectors of the economy.

Monkey Business Images/Shutterstock

LO 1-2

Explain the strategic role of personal selling and sales analytics in modern organizations.

THE STRATEGIC ROLE OF PERSONAL SELLING AND SALES ANALYTICS

For years, the dominant view of the sales mission involved some or all of the following:

- *To enhance the firm's cash flow* by communicating value to customers about basic goods and services. In this view, *value creation* was largely the domain of the marketing and research and development (R&D) units, through their branding and product innovation efforts.
- *To increase the volume of sales transactions.* In this view, the firm set an overall revenue target that managers distributed across territories and individual salespeople. Many organizations and salespeople viewed attainment of sales objectives as a "numbers game."
- *To close deals.* Sales performance was thought to derive primarily from the amount of effort put in by sales personnel to create new opportunities and close deals.

Some organizations continue to hold these traditional views. Over time, though, changes in the selling environment have led to a fundamental rethinking of the *strategic nature* of the salesperson's role. For one thing, the selling environment has become increasingly complex. Globalization has brought greater competition to many markets. As sellers leapfrog each other with innovations to attract buyers, the number and complexity of product features can overwhelm customers. This is especially true when multiple features require the customer to make trade-off decisions. In addition, customers' use of web-based and social technologies has brought greater transparency with respect to price, product quality, and customer service.

Today, many leading firms are reorganizing their business processes—including sales—around the lifetime value represented by their most important accounts. **Customer lifetime value (CLV)** focuses on the net present value of a customer's business over the span of its relationship with an organization. (Don't worry if you're not familiar with the concept of net present value from other business courses—we'll discuss it fully in a later chapter.) Customer lifetime value emphasizes keeping customers for long periods. To do that, firms focus on *customer relationships*.

As a result, relationship selling is the core of all modern selling strategies. It involves building and maintaining customer trust over a long period of time—not just meeting periodic sales quotas. Because it costs several times more to acquire new customers than it does to retain them, firms see the business necessity of developing long-term, consulting-type relationships with downstream partners and critical customers.

customer lifetime value
A sales approach that focuses on the net present value of a customer's business over the span of its relationship with an organization.

Factors That Influence the Use of Personal Selling

Personal selling often is the foundation for successful relationship selling. When you think about personal selling, you might have in mind the relationship between salesperson and customer that exists when you are buying something like a pair of high-end sneakers or a new computer. Personal selling also is arguably the most important decision factor in the large, complex sales that are common in *business-to-business (B2B)* settings. There are many parallels between selling products to consumers and to businesses. Both center on helping customers resolve problems, and both follow a similar sequence of steps. There are, though, a couple of important differences in the two types of selling:

- B2B sales are often much larger financially and take longer to complete.
- There are often multiple decision makers in B2B sales. In many cases, B2B buyers possess extensive information about the product and are experienced, professional negotiators.

Given the importance of personal selling, is it effective in all sales situations? No. In practice, it turns out that personal selling is more effective for some products than for others. New goods and services tend to enjoy higher elasticity levels than do existing goods and services. That is, firms can increase demand for new products more than they can for existing products by making changes in the market conditions relating to the new product. Price is, of course, one of those market conditions. Also, promotional-mix components such as advertising and public relations are market conditions that can increase demand. When launching and establishing new products, companies may be better off making significant investments in direct sales force resources such as hiring new salespeople to visit with potential customers across a territory, and then shifting to other means of marketing communications as the product matures.[2]

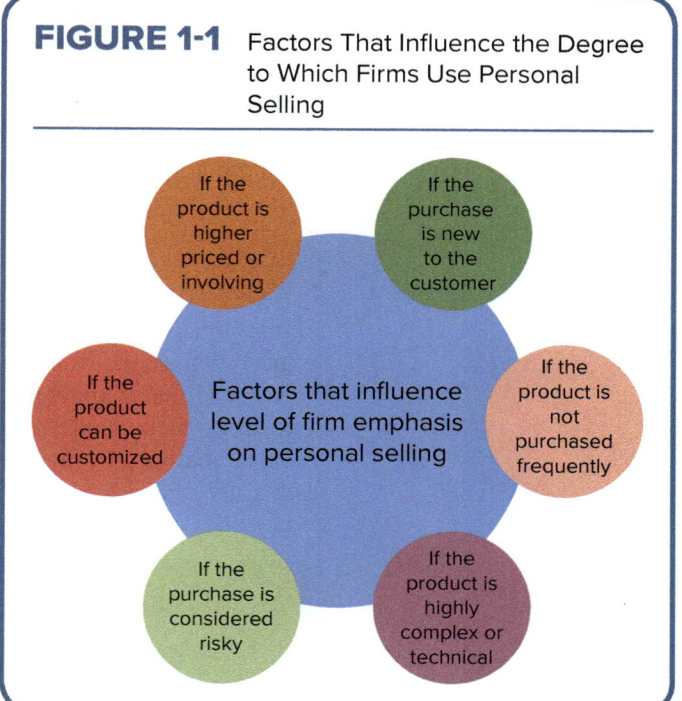

FIGURE 1-1 Factors That Influence the Degree to Which Firms Use Personal Selling

Figure 1-1 shows several factors that influence the degree to which a firm would use personal selling. Personal selling is more effective when the good or service is:

- New-to-the-world (such as a self-driving vehicle).
- Infrequently purchased (a young couple buying a new home).
- Highly technical or complex (the purchase of an advanced communications satellite by the U.S. Department of Defense). Such products often require the services of a specialized salesperson to educate customers on product benefits and proper use.
- Viewed as risky (such as investing in an emerging-markets mutual fund). Purchases of high-priced or high-involvement items typically elevate buyers' risk perceptions. In such cases, salespeople often play a critical role in helping to build customers' trust in the firm and its products.
- Customizable (such as a university medical center buying and implementing a new telecommunications system). Customizable products may require the assistance of sales personnel to properly configure the offering to match customer needs. (See the Today's Professional Perspective interview of Candence Brooks featured later in this chapter.)

Because the selling environment—and products themselves—are becoming increasingly complex, the need for personal selling remains strong. Businesses need knowledgeable sales professionals to guide buyers through sometimes-complex decision processes. Such salespeople are able to bring together resources from across their extended organization to craft a solution aimed at meeting customer needs. Their overall aim is to establish mutually beneficial long-term relationships with customers.

Sales Analytics

An emerging trend in personal selling is the increasing use of sales analytics. **Sales analytics** is the practice of generating insights from sales data, trends, and metrics to set targets and forecast future sales performance.

Sales analytics represents different things to different sales teams. In one company, it could mean simply gathering and analyzing hard data about sales each day. In

sales analytics
The practice of generating insights from sales data, trends, and metrics to set targets and forecast sales performance.

another, it could involve the numbers and information assembled through the company's customer relationship management system. As we'll discuss more fully in a later chapter, *customer relationship management (CRM)* is a technology for managing all of a company's relationships and interactions with customers and potential customers.[3] The goal is simple: to improve business relationships. A CRM system can enable the selling company and the salesperson to see everything in one place—a customer's previous history with you, the status of their orders, any outstanding customer service issues, and more. When people talk about CRM, they are usually referring to a CRM system like Salesforce.

An effective sales analytics program can yield benefits for all types of organizations. Organizations hire people with advanced skills in statistics and sales analytics—experts who can translate the insights into actions for the field. Employers are looking for sales analytics professionals and will continue to do so in the decades ahead. In each chapter in this textbook, you will have the opportunity to complete a sales analytics Connect assignment that will give you some practice in data analytics use and skills.

connect Assignment 1-1

Sales Analytics

Please complete the Connect exercise for Chapter 1 that focuses on sales analytics. By understanding and interpreting the data provided by CRM systems, you as a salesperson can better serve your clients and drive successful results for your organization.

PERSONAL SELLING IN THE DIGITAL ERA

LO 1-3 Describe the impact of digital technology and social selling on personal selling.

"In a world in which anybody can find anything nearly instantly with just a few keystrokes, who needs salespeople?" Every few years, some new business guru boldly asks this question. Such comments herald the approaching decline, or even death, of personal selling as a cost-effective tool for communicating business value.

Yet sales remains the second-largest occupational category (behind office and administrative workers) in the U.S. workforce—as it has for decades. According to the U.S. Bureau of Labor Statistics (BLS), each day more than 15 million people earn their living trying to convince others to make purchases.[4] That's one out of every nine American workers. The chances are that if you are not a sales professional yourself, you are related to one or you know one quite well. What's more, the BLS projects that the economy will add more than 2 million *new* sales jobs in the next few years. The good news for people in sales is that the digital transformation of advanced economies has not erased the need for salespeople.

However, the scope and nature of personal selling activities are changing. In his book *To Sell Is Human: The Surprising Truth about Moving Others,* Daniel Pink observes that the very technologies that some thought would make salespeople obsolete have in fact *transformed more people into sellers.* According to his research, people spend roughly 40 percent of their work time—24 minutes out of every hour—persuading, influencing, and convincing others in ways that don't involve making a purchase.[5] Pink calls these activities *non-sales selling.* What's more, people consider this aspect of their work most crucial to their professional success.

Television shows and movies like *Mad Men, The Wolf of Wall Street,* and *Love & Other Drugs* depict images of fast-talking, do-anything-for-the-buck salespeople. In general, that era is long past. Today's trained sales professional is much more likely to adopt an approach that fosters a long-term, *consultative relationship* with customers, working with them to solve problems. In fact, in many B2B and services contexts, world-class salespeople are among the most highly trained and regarded professionals within their industries.

Today's trained sales professional also is likely to use available digital technologies to find and foster business. We call this new approach **social selling.** It is the process of developing, nurturing, and leveraging relationships online to sell products or services. Social selling is affecting organizations of all sizes in the modern sales environment. For example, Pitney Bowes, a global technology company, started a social-selling program to reach buyers who were actively using LinkedIn to network and find useful information. The company piloted with a small group of sales team members and helped to build their credibility as subject matter experts on LinkedIn. They then shared a combination of original and third-party content with their networks. The initial group saw an increase in opportunities within the first days of the pilot. Social selling has now been rolled out across every business line in Pitney Bowes globally.

social selling
A sales approach that develops, nurtures, and leverages relationships online to sell products or services.

Social selling involves meeting buyers on the social-network platforms where they are already conducting product research and due diligence online. It is a broad strategy that includes various online activities: sharing relevant content with leads and prospects, interacting directly with potential buyers and customers, personal branding, and social listening. **Social listening** is the monitoring of your brand's social media channels for any customer feedback and direct mentions of your brand or discussions regarding specific keywords, topics, competitors, or industries, followed by an analysis to gain insights and act on those opportunities.

social listening
The monitoring of a brand's social media channels for customer feedback or discussion regarding specific keyword, topics, competitors, or industries, followed by analysis to gain insights and act on opportunities.

Figure 1-2 shows the percentage of revenue influenced by social selling across 14 leading industries. While these industries serve very different customers and parts of the global economy, over half of revenue in each of them is influenced by social selling.

Over the last few years, several studies have showcased the increasing value of social selling. One example is that social sellers gain 57 percent higher return on investment from social selling compared to a 23 percent return using traditional sales tactics.[6]

A foundation of social-selling success is to be active on the same platform(s) as potential customers are. It's why salespeople in fashion excel on Pinterest, and why B2B sales reps generate leads from LinkedIn. Figure 1-3 shows social media use by demographic group. YouTube and Facebook have the lion's share of social platform use of all age groups. Forrester Research has found that the decision makers who make most B2B decisions primarily use LinkedIn for business purposes.[7] So if you're selling products that appeal to teenagers, you should use Facebook and Instagram for social selling. If you sell products or services aimed toward business decision makers, then use LinkedIn or Twitter for social selling.

McGraw Hill Connect Assignment 1-2

Social Selling

Please complete the Connect exercise for Chapter 1 that focuses on factors that influence personal selling. Match salespeople with the business challenge where they are most needed to better understand how to deploy sales resources to provide customer solutions.

FIGURE 1-2 Revenue in Various Industries Attributable to Social Selling

Source: Ethan Andrianos. "Investigating the Truth About Social Selling by Industry." LinkedIn, September 20, 2017. https://business.linkedin.com/sales-solutions/blog/proof-month/2017/investigating-the-truth-about-social-selling-by-industry.

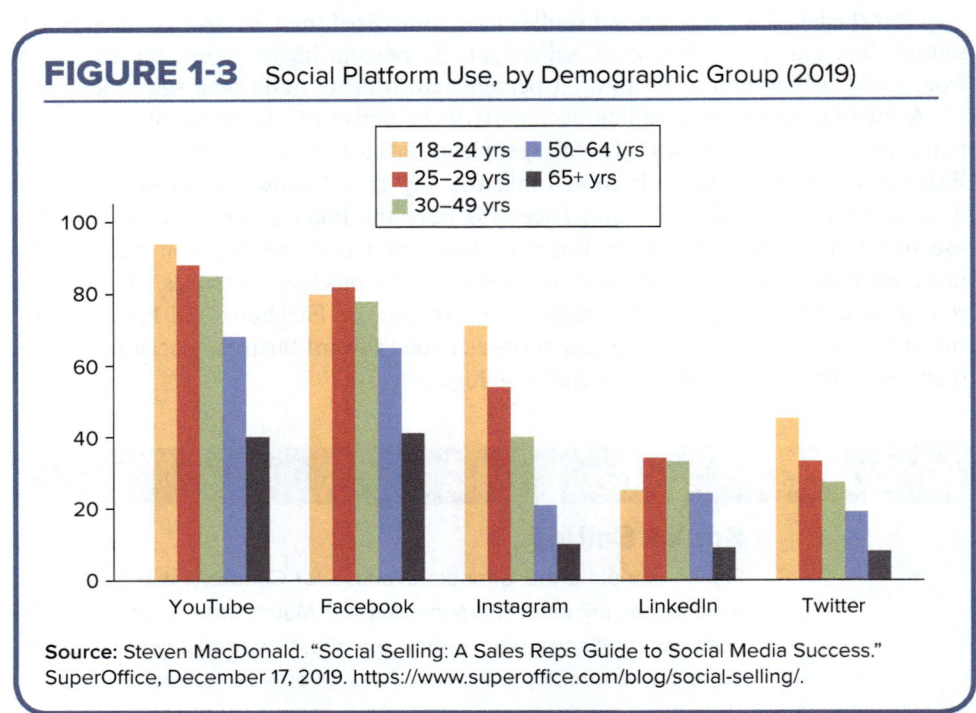

FIGURE 1-3 Social Platform Use, by Demographic Group (2019)

Source: Steven MacDonald. "Social Selling: A Sales Reps Guide to Social Media Success." SuperOffice, December 17, 2019. https://www.superoffice.com/blog/social-selling/.

CAREER OPPORTUNITIES IN SALES

What are the career opportunities in professional selling? There are many attractive choices. Job listings for entry-level sales representatives are among the most plentiful. Typically, the first job of more than 50 percent of college graduates is in sales. Recent studies report that more than 88 percent of marketing majors start their careers in sales.[8] Many firms, of all sizes and across various industries, actively recruit on university campuses in search of new sales talent.

In response, more universities are introducing sales-related degree programs. These courses are designed to give students a head start in developing the basic skills, knowledge, and experience for entry-level sales positions. According to research from the Baylor University Center for Professional Selling, students in sales programs, nationally, each average 2.8 job offers *before* graduation.

Salespeople are also in demand in almost every market, of any size, in the United States. If your life takes you to a major city or a small town for personal or professional reasons during your career, there is a great likelihood that organizations in that community will be actively looking to hire sales professionals. Many new graduates find that this career path provides a tremendous amount of flexibility and freedom.

Rest assured that professional selling can be a financially rewarding career. This is true for new hires as well as experienced reps, particularly in B2B settings. The national average salary for an entry-level sales position in 2019 was over $56,000 per year.[9] High-performing salespeople earn incomes far above that national average. (See more about sales salaries in the next section.) Excellent salespeople also enjoy great visibility within the organization. Within many firms, high-performing salespeople tend to move quickly into higher-level sales- and marketing-management roles.

Sales positions also offer qualities that appeal to many millennials: autonomy, rewards linked to personal effort, and the opportunity to interact with a variety of people. Many people find that the selling process requires a high level of innovativeness and creativity. Many are self-directed, with little day-to-day supervision. Even though sales roles often require a fair amount of travel, many sales representatives work out of their homes or virtual offices. Such arrangements offer flexibility and contribute to a work-family life balance and high job satisfaction.

LO 1-4 Explain the appeal of sales as a career and the different types of sales positions.

Types of Sales Roles

What are the major types of sales roles available to those looking for a professional selling career? Here, we briefly describe the main types of sales roles. Table 1-1 provides details of national average sales salaries by job title and across different major markets in the United States. As you read this section and look at possible sales salaries, keep in mind that almost every job—from that of part-time retail staff to CEO to the manager of a nonprofit organization—has some aspects of professional selling in it.

Inside Sales
Inside salespeople are those who perform selling activities at the employer's location, typically using email and the telephone. Inside sales is the dominant sales model for sales reps in many B2B companies and a variety of business-to-consumer (B2C) industries. This type of job routinely involves high-touch transactions over the phone and through email. Unlike telemarketers (who typically have little professional sales training and often read from a script), inside salespeople are highly skilled and knowledgeable. Thanks to advances in communications technology, inside sales reps give presentations, conduct demos, and perform most of the functions traditionally handled by sales representatives in the field.

inside salespeople Salespeople who perform selling activities at the employer's location, typically using email and telephone.

Sales Representative
Sales representatives are typically entry-level, customer-facing or business-to-business sales positions. In this job, your primary goal is to sell

sales representatives Entry-level, customer-facing or business-to-business sales positions.

TABLE 1-1 Sales Salaries by Job Title, Across Major U.S. Markets

Sales Job Title	National	Chicago	Atlanta	Austin	L.A.	Boston
Inside sales	$39,584	$36,500	$38,000	$41,625	$37,120	$46,736
Sales representative	39,300	39,300	40,010	28,273	42,672	48,575
Account executive	56,000	45,000	47,409	45,720	49,679	52,000
Sales analyst	60,000	61,575	57,270	58,183	58,781	60,128
Sales manager	59,715	64,725	58,877	54,206	66,139	67,583
District sales manager	74,509	82,467	91,357	79,248	74,765	81,280
Sales engineer	87,633	79,571	85,601	91,834	72,720	95,505
Regional sales manager	105,290	92,655	88,729	85,000	88,381	88,318
Vice president of sales	149,854	158,811	n/a	n/a	134,961	n/a

Source: Data from Glassdoor.com, https://www.glassdoor.com/Salaries/entry-level-sales-salary-SRCH_KO0,17.htm.

the company's products, whether you work from a storefront or cover a territory. The term *sales rep* covers different types of entry-level sales jobs. For example:

- Sales reps who work "in the field," calling on customers at the customers' places of business, are called **field reps.** Field reps typically work for B2B and wholesale organizations whose sales processes rely on relationship-building and long-term contracts.
- Many sales representatives are **new-business salespeople,** responsible primarily for finding new customers and securing their business. Typically, the sales prospect is likely to be a client of a competing firm.

Within the range of sales-rep positions, you can advance to a leadership position, with some supervisory responsibility.

field reps
Sales reps who work "in the field," calling on customers at their places of business.

new-business salespeople
Salespeople responsible primarily for finding new customers and securing their business.

account executives
Sales position that offers increasing responsibility above the sales rep job.

Account Executive The position of **account executive** offers increasing responsibility above the sales rep job. Duties often involve establishing relationships with new clients and managing the needs of existing clients. In many businesses, account executives are **order-taker salespeople,** sales representatives who primarily process orders that a customer initiates.

order-taker salespeople
Sales representatives who primarily process orders that a customer initiates.

sales analysts
Salespeople responsible for the collection and analysis of sales data.

Sales Analyst **Sales analysts** are responsible for the collection and analysis of sales data. Their goal is to increase sales productivity and customer satisfaction as well as to reduce sales barriers and low revenue levels. They create standardized and customized reports that analyze everything from quantitative data to sales-funnel flows to future needs forecasts.

Sales Support Nonmanagerial *sales-support roles* are typically found in high-tech sectors like aerospace and enterprise software. They usually require educational backgrounds in fields like engineering, computer science, or physics. These technical specialists are often referred to as **sales engineers.** In complex sales settings, sales engineers are an integral part of the selling team. They commonly interact with counterparts within the customer's buying center to address technical question and issues that arise over the course of the entire sales process.

sales engineers
Technical specialists who sell in high-tech sectors like aerospace and enterprise software.

sales managers
Sales positions with managerial oversight of selling efforts at varying levels of the organizational hierarchy.

Sales Manager The final category of sales positions is sales management. **Sales managers** have oversight of selling efforts at varying levels of the organizational hierarchy. Sales managers work with human resource personnel to recruit, select, train, supervise, and evaluate sales employees. They often work directly in the field with their assigned reps. They establish sales objectives, and they forecast and develop annual sales quotas for their assigned territories. They serve as conduits for information received from the front lines to senior management about ongoing market trends and competitive actions. A typical career path in sales management is sales manager, district sales manager, regional sales manager, and vice president of sales.

Sales Roles in Nonprofit Organizations

"Nonprofit" and "sales" are two words that rarely appear in the same sentence. But that's changing—and for good reason. A growing number of nonprofit organizations are discovering that without a sales team, their programs struggle to reach large numbers of intended beneficiaries.[10]

What, exactly, are nonprofits? **Nonprofit organizations** (also called *not-for-profit organizations*) are those whose motive is something *other than* to make a profit for owners. Nonprofits generally are organized to further a social cause or advocate for a point of view. They include hospitals, charities, universities, zoos, and churches. Funds gathered by a nonprofit are put to the purpose for which the nonprofit was organized rather than being distributed to owners or shareholders.

nonprofit organizations (*not-for-profit organizations*) Organizations whose motive is something *other than* to make a profit for owners.

In order to accomplish its mission and to grow, a nonprofit must continually bring in new donors and workers (typically volunteers). To do that, nonprofits need to sell themselves. Nonprofits are finding that utilizing sales and CRM tools can help them raise money. With those funds, nonprofits can have dramatic impacts on our society—from lowering the cost of college through scholarships, to curing forms of cancer through donations to medical research, and beyond. If your passion is to one day work for a nonprofit organization, sales will be a critical aspect in helping that organization help people in your community.

"Am I Cut Out for Sales?"

At this point, you may be asking yourself if a career in sales is right for you. As attractive as a sales career sounds to many people, some college students think sales is not for them. Even the authors of this textbook, when they were in college, were hesitant to consider careers in sales, fearing they did not have the skills to be successful at selling for a living.

Such feelings raise the question: *Are great salespeople born or made?* That is, to what extent is sales success influenced by deeply ingrained traits, like personality? To what extent can qualities that lead to sales success be taught or gained through experience? Sales managers and researchers have long debated such questions. It is true that individuals with certain personality characteristics, such as extroversion, may indeed be more drawn to selling careers. Yet a comprehensive analysis of research has shown the relationship between personality and sales performance to be negligible.[11] At the same time, differences in other individual characteristics—like positive attitude and high motivation—can have a tremendous impact on long-term sales success. Fortunately, those attributes can be established and improved by virtually anyone through proper training, experience, and personal discipline.

In sales, marketing, or any other career field, fear and self-doubt are almost always the greatest enemies of human potential. These issues can manifest themselves in various ways; within the sales context, the most common warning sign is procrastination. In fact, research suggests nearly 85 percent of all salespeople, regardless of experience or age, regularly experience some degree of reluctance before they contact a potential customer.[12] This finding underlines the extreme importance of strong self-belief and positive attitude to the achievement of personal success in the field of sales.

Today's **Professional Perspective**... because everyone is a salesperson

Candence M. Brooks
Realtor
Westbrook and Reeves Real Estate

Candence M. Brooks

Describe your job. I am a licensed real estate agent. My specialty is residential real estate. I work with buyers and sellers. I especially love to work with first-time homebuyers.

How did you get your job? I have always had an interest in real estate. After passing my real estate exam, I visited with a few brokers to decide what company would be the most suitable for me. A friend mentioned an office that was just starting, so I set up a meeting with the owners. Their personalities, beliefs, and business ethic were the most attractive. I knew that this was the place I would like to work.

What has been most important in making you successful at your job? What has made me successful is knowing who I am and being comfortable with it. Although I am affiliated with a company, I still represent myself. Whenever meeting new people or working with clients, self-confidence is key. We can set daily, monthly, and annual goals, but if we don't have the self-confidence to motivate us to push forward, the goals are just good intentions with no follow-through.

What advice would you give future graduates about a career in sales? My advice is to follow your own path. Be creative with your degree and do what you love. Don't be down on yourself if your first job after graduation fails your expectations or is not what you want to do in life. Learn from the experience and take what you have learned to the next venture. Every job I have had has given me the experience that helps me to be successful today. I would also strongly encourage every student to consider a career in sales, as the opportunities are limitless.

What is the most important characteristic of a great salesperson? Great salespeople are savvy, quick witted, and passionate. These traits shine through in one's work ethic and in personal relationships. Also, although one's brand may continue to evolve, great salespeople always stay true to themselves.

ETHICS IN PERSONAL SELLING

LO 1-5
Describe ethical issues in personal selling.

Historically, sales careers were often depicted negatively in movies and television: a salesperson who shades the truth (or even lies), a salesperson who pressures you to buy, a salesperson who sells a product that doesn't meet the customer's needs. We've all seen (and maybe experienced) examples. What's missing from these unfortunate situations is ethics. **Ethics** are moral standards expected by a society—and they are an essential element in a successful sales career. Salespeople should clearly understand the norms and values expected of them and act in a way that puts their company, their profession, and themselves in a positive, ethical light.

ethics
Moral standards expected by a society.

The potential for ethical and legal issues pervades nearly all areas of business. Such concerns are often spotlighted within personal-selling contexts, due to the one-to-one nature of salesperson-customer interactions. From the poor ethical decisions of selling homes to buyers who could not afford them before the Great Recession, to the opening of unauthorized accounts at Wells Fargo, the past two decades of business history have been filled with ethical issues in personal selling and sales management. With the rising use of social media networks among consumers and business buyers, sellers' ethical infractions can become highly visible to external stakeholders—including prospective customers and financial investors. These have the potential to cause significant damage to corporate reputations. Conversely, research has shown that maintaining high ethical standards on the part of sales personnel is a critical driver of sales force performance: It affects the firm's capacity to (1) build relationships with customers and (2) develop a positive work environment for employees.

Standards of Professional Conduct in Sales

How can firms promote ethical behavior? Many do so by emphasizing core organizational values and strictly enforcing codes of ethics. Yet reports of damaging transgressions among sales and marketing employees remain commonplace. One study found that more than 50 percent of sales and marketing executives believe their salespeople have lied on a sales call. Nearly 75 percent of respondents in the survey agreed that the pressure to meet sales goals encourages salespeople to lose focus on customers' needs.[13]

Another common area of ethical concern involves salespeople's behaviors toward their own firm, such as improper use of expense accounts or misreporting account information. Conversely, illegal or unethical behavior, such as buyer solicitation of bribes, favors, or gifts in exchange for lower prices, faster delivery schedules, or other types of preferential treatment, may be initiated by others toward the salesperson.

Many companies invest in training programs to better prepare employees to make good decisions when confronted with a potentially unethical situation. In addition, trade organizations such as Sales and Marketing Executives International (SMEI) and the Canadian Professional Sales Association (CPSA) have incorporated ethical codes of conduct into their sales and marketing certification programs. Salespeople must abide by these codes of conduct in order to maintain their certification. The SMEI code of conduct begins with three pledges that serve as excellent guides for all sales professionals:

Antonio Guillem/123RF

> **SMEI Code of Conduct**
>
> 1. **I hereby acknowledge** my accountability to the organization for which I work and to society as a whole to improve sales knowledge and practice and to adhere to the highest professional standards in my work and personal relationships.
> 2. **My concept of selling** includes as its basic principle the sovereignty of all consumers in the marketplace and the necessity for mutual benefit to both buyer and seller in all transactions.
> 3. **I shall personally maintain** the highest standards of ethical and professional conduct in all my business relationships with customers, suppliers, colleagues, competitors, governmental agencies, and the public.[14]

Today's business environment calls for transparency and customer-oriented behaviors. Deviating from these norms in pursuit of short-term gains will ultimately prove detrimental to an individual's—and an organization's—reputation for sales and marketing professionalism.

In each chapter in this textbook, you will have the opportunity to complete a Connect assignment that focuses on ethics. There also is an Ethical Challenge assignment in the end-of-chapter materials. These resources are intended to give you opportunities to think about potentially unethical situations and how to deal with them if they come up in your career.

McGraw Hill connect Assignment 1-3

Sales Ethics

Please complete the Connect exercise for Chapter 1 that focuses on ethics. Applying the SMEI code of conduct to actual scenarios will provide insight into how to evaluate ethical challenges and the potential risks involved when an ethical approach is not selected.

SELLING YOURSELF

LO 1-6 Describe the foundational skills necessary for sales success.

Whether or not you currently intend to work in sales, it is important to understand personal-selling processes and the skills necessary for sales success. Why? Because in a few short years, regardless of your major, you will be "selling" employers on how your unique talents and experiences will contribute to the success of their organization. Once you start your career, your professional achievement and advancement hinge on your ability to introduce new ideas to customers, peers, and managers in a persuasive and convincing manner. Ultimately, "selling yourself" means communicating your value—a beneficial skill for everyone.

Specific skills needed to be a great salesperson, and ones that will also benefit you throughout your professional career, are as follows:

- *Active listening* Most of us operate in an increasingly distracted and distracting world. People can usually tell if you're really listening to them rather than just thinking about what you'll say next—and most people appreciate a good listener.

Good listening skills can help reps empathize with prospects to learn more about their business and pain points. With that knowledge, reps can then sell more effectively and offer a better solution.

- *Communication* Strong communication skills are important for any career that you pursue after graduation, but they are essential for sales success. Remember that it not just *what* you say, but also how you deliver it—from tone to emphasis. Equally important is when you choose to stay silent and let the client talk. Effective communication is a salesperson's best tool, but it takes time to perfect.
- *Time management* Salespeople who are the most effective are able to make the most of their time, with more connections and customer time than other reps manage. The key to being highly productive is managing your time. You need to know how to sort through leads to find the most promising ones and not waste time on deals that aren't going anywhere. It's vital to make the most of the hours in the day to bring in more deals.
- *Solution development* Great salespeople find ways to solve problems for their clients. By thinking, researching, and working hard, salespeople can develop solutions that save their clients money, make their business more efficient, or open up new worlds of potential customers. These same principles apply as you apply for jobs, by the way: Research what a potential employer is looking for and meet their requirements with your own skills and achievements.
- *Attention to detail* The difference between excellence and mediocrity in sales is almost always a matter of attention to detail. Sometimes little things really count and will set you apart from your competitors. This is especially true when you are working on a competitive bid; you need to perform each tiny task with precision. Every little thing you do will be used to measure the worth of your product.

Thomas Barwick/Getty Images

We hope this textbook helps you develop these skills and enhances your ability to "sell yourself" in a positive, ethical, and successful way that will benefit you throughout your professional career.

CHAPTER SUMMARY

LO 1-1 Describe the importance, challenges, and unique advantages of personal selling.

Sales are at the heart of modern business. Revenue generated by sales makes possible a company's other activities. The need for great salespeople is high. Developing your personal-selling skills will benefit you in countless ways in your professional career.

Personal selling is the two-way flow of communication between a buyer and a seller that is paid for by the seller and seeks to influence the buyer's purchase decision. Personal selling differs from the other tools of the promotion mix because messages flow directly from the salesperson to the customer, often face to face. Despite economic and technological changes, the role of personal selling is important.

Organizations in all industries face a couple of major challenges with professional selling: cost and message consistency. Personal selling is expensive, but wise firms view the costs of an accomplished sales team as investments.

Personal selling offers two unique advantages over the other promotional elements: immediate feedback and relationship selling. Personal interactions with customers allow salespeople to adjust the sales presentations and to provide solutions that can generate more sales. Personal selling also enables *relationship selling,* a sales approach that involves building and maintaining customer trust over a long period of time. Very few firms can survive only on the profits generated from one-time transactional sales.

LO 1-2 Explain the strategic role of personal selling and sales analytics in modern organizations.

Over time, the changing selling environment has led to a fundamental rethinking of the strategic nature of the salesperson's role. Today, many leading firms are reorganizing their business processes—including sales—around the *lifetime value* represented by their most important accounts. Personal selling is an important aspect of building long-term customer relationships, including *B2B selling.*

In practice, personal selling is more effective for some products than for others. Personal selling is most effective when products are new, infrequently purchased, highly technical or complex, viewed as risky, and customizable.

Sales analytics is the practice of generating insights from sales data, trends, and metrics to set targets and forecast future sales performance. In many organizations, a first step in data analytics involves assembling numbers and information about interactions with customers and potential customers in a customer relationship management (CRM) system. A sales analytics program can yield benefits for organizations of all types.

LO 1-3 Describe the impact of digital technology and social selling on personal selling.

Sales remains the second-largest occupational category in the U.S. workforce. The digital transformation of advanced economies has not erased the need for salespeople. *Social selling* is the process of developing, nurturing, and leveraging relationships online to sell products or services. Social selling is about meeting buyers on the social-network platforms where they're already conducting due diligence online.

LO 1-4 Explain the appeal of sales and different types of sales positions.

Professional selling offers attractive career choices. Job listings for entry-level sales representatives are among the most plentiful. Professional selling can be a financially rewarding career for new hires as well as experienced reps. Sales positions offer qualities that appeal to millennials: autonomy, creativity, rewards linked to personal effort, the opportunity to interact with a variety of people, self-direction, and flexibility that contribute to a work-family life balance.

There are various types of sales positions: *Inside salespeople* perform selling activities at the employer's location, typically using email and the telephone. *Sales reps* are typically entry-level, customer-facing or business-to-business sales positions, whose primary goal is to sell the company's products, whether from a storefront or as *field reps* in a sales territory. Many sales reps are *new-business salespeople,* responsible primarily for securing business from new customers. *Account executives* have increasing responsibility above the sales-rep job. Some account executives are *order-taker salespeople,* who primarily process orders that a customer initiates.

Sales analysts collect and analyze sales data and produce standardized and customized reports. Nonmanagerial *sales-support roles* are typically found in high-tech sectors; these technical specialists are often referred to as *sales engineers.* Finally, *sales managers* have oversight of selling efforts at varying levels of the organizational hierarchy. A typical career path in sales management is sales manager, district sales manager, regional sales manager, and vice president of sales.

Nonprofit organizations are organizations whose motive is something *other than* to make a profit for owners. A growing number of nonprofit organizations are discovering the importance of professional selling to attract funding and volunteers that will help them accomplish their mission and grow.

Research shows that qualities that lead to sales success can be taught or gained through experience. Positive attitude and high motivation can have a tremendous impact on long-term sales success.

LO 1-5 Describe ethical issues in personal selling.

The potential for ethical and legal issues is often spotlighted within personal-selling contexts. Many firms promote ethical behavior by emphasizing core organizational values and strictly enforcing codes of ethics. Many invest in training programs to better prepare employees to make good decisions in potentially unethical situations. Trade organizations have incorporated ethical codes of conduct into their sales certification programs.

LO 1-6 Describe the foundational skills necessary for sales success.

Throughout your career, you will have numerous opportunities to sell your ideas, solutions, and the reasons why a company should hire you. Ultimately, "selling yourself" means communicating your value. The foundational skills needed to be a great salesperson—active listening, communication, time management, solution development, and attention to detail—will also benefit you throughout your career.

KEY TERMS

personal selling (p. 4)
relationship selling (p. 5)
customer lifetime value (p. 6)
sales analytics (p. 7)
social selling (p. 9)
social listening (p. 9)

inside salespeople (p. 11)
sales representatives (p. 11)
field reps (p. 12)
new-business salespeople (p. 12)
account executives (p. 12)
order-taker salespeople (p. 12)

sales analysts (p. 12)
sales engineers (p. 12)
sales managers (p. 12)
nonprofit organizations (p. 13)
ethics (p. 15)

DISCUSSION QUESTIONS

1. Identify an outstanding salesperson with whom you have come in contact in your life, and describe what made your sales experience with him or her so positive.
2. Think about products you have purchased over the last five years. Name three of them for which a salesperson was especially important or valuable to your purchase. What is it about those products that made the salesperson more important?
3. Of the social media platforms that you have used, which one do you think is the most valuable to salespeople? Explain your answer.
4. What do you think is the top reason you would consider a role in sales after graduation? What is the top reason you might *not* consider a role in sales? Find someone in your family or community who works in sales and ask that person to describe what he or she likes most and least about working in sales.
5. Illustrate each of the three SMEI Code of Conduct pledges as they relate to a salesperson attempting to sell you a house.

ETHICAL CHALLENGE

Over the course of four years, at least 5,000 Wells Fargo employees opened more than a million fake bank and credit card accounts on behalf of unwitting customers. Although many of these bank accounts were deemed "empty" and closed automatically, employees sometimes transferred customer funds to the new accounts, triggering overdraft fees and hurting customers' credit ratings. The Consumer Financial Protection Bureau (CFPB) cited Wells Fargo with several major violations including:

- **Opening deposit accounts and transferring funds without authorization:** According to the bank's own analysis, employees opened roughly 1.5 million deposit accounts that might not have been authorized by consumers. Employees then transferred funds from consumers' authorized accounts to temporarily fund the new, unauthorized accounts. This widespread practice gave the employees credit for opening the new accounts, allowing them to earn additional compensation and to meet the bank's sales goals. Consumers, in turn, were sometimes harmed because the bank charged them for insufficient funds or overdraft fees because the money was not in their original accounts.
- **Applying for credit card accounts without authorization:** According to the bank's own analysis, Wells Fargo employees applied for roughly 565,000 credit card accounts that might not have been authorized by consumers. On those unauthorized credit cards, many consumers incurred annual fees as well as associated finance or interest charges and other fees.
- **Issuing and activating debit cards without authorization:** Wells Fargo employees requested and issued debit cards without consumers' knowledge or consent, going so far as to create PINs without telling consumers.
- **Creating phony email addresses to enroll consumers in online banking services:** Wells Fargo employees created phony email addresses not belonging to consumers to enroll them in online banking services without their knowledge or consent.

These sales ethics problems led to billions of dollars in fines and losses in market value for Wells Fargo.

Questions

Think about ethical issues from your own role as a future salesperson or as a future executive by answering the following questions:

1. What would you have done as a salesperson if you were pressured to open accounts for customers who did not authorize them? Why do you think so many salespeople at Wells Fargo acted the way they did?
2. How could a deeper organizational commitment to the standards of professional sales conduct, discussed earlier in this chapter, have helped Wells Fargo avoid this costly and embarrassing situation?
3. Think about a company at which you would like to be an executive in the future. What could that company do to make sure its salespeople acted ethically even when unethical actions could lead to greater short-term rewards?

Source: https://www.consumerfinance.gov/about-us/newsroom/consumer-financial-protection-bureau-fines-wells-fargo-100-million-widespread-illegal-practice-secretly-opening-unauthorized-accounts/.

ROLE PLAY

This role play will give you experience in selling the college that you are currently attending. For this role play, half of your class will be college recruiters responsible for selling potential students as to why they should attend your institution. The other half of the class will be the prospective students. The students can raise issues they have experienced or heard of that might make them hesitant to choose to take classes at this college.

The salesperson should anticipate the potential objections the prospective students might have and develop answers to those objections. In addition, the salesperson should ask questions of the prospective students and use their active listening skills to match the qualities of the college to the needs and goals of those particular students.

At the end of the role play, both the recruiter and the prospective student should reflect on what made the biggest positive or negative impact and what they would suggest a college recruiter should do when selling a school to future students.

SALES PRESENTATION

For the Connect assignment in Chapter 1, students will get practice selling themselves to a specific company they want to work for after graduation. In two minutes or less, provide an "elevator pitch" presentation selling the company you choose on why it should hire you.

CAREER TIPS

Shane Hunt

Dean and Marketing Professor
Idaho State University

Using Sales Skills to Drive Early Career Success

Most salespeople have at one time or another struggled to meet goals. There may be a variety of external causes for lower-than-desired performance. Before placing blame elsewhere, it's important for a salesperson to take a closer look at his or her own lifestyle, work habits, and belief systems.

Personal selling is a mentally demanding and highly competitive field. A sales rep who keeps late nights or is not conscious of healthy eating and drinking habits will soon feel insufficiently prepared, physically drained, and at a decided disadvantage to his or her competitors. Individuals in sales roles often work without regular direct supervision. Without the proper discipline, it is very easy for salespeople (inexperienced as well as experienced) to fall into poor work habits such as getting to work late or not spending enough time qualifying prospects or preparing for sales calls.

Students often face similar challenges when they are seeking entry-level employment after graduation, or even later, as they pursue career advancement. If you are facing struggles in your school work or in finding the right internship or job, before placing blame elsewhere, you should ask yourself: *Am I getting enough sleep? Am I eating well and getting enough exercise? Am I really doing all I can do to become the best in my field?*

Whether you are seeking to sell a product, a service, or yourself, if you cannot comfortably answer "yes" to these types of questions, then it is critical that you proactively seek ways to correct the issue. Experts offer a few helpful tips:

- Hang around positive, successful people.
- Start your day an hour before everyone else.
- Talk to some of your best customers, friends, professors, or a mentor and ask them to evaluate your situation.
- Rearrange your work space.
- Set activity goals.
- List five things you could do to work harder *and* smarter to achieve your goals.

Ultimately, the best way to get out of a rut is to accept the fact that it is temporary and believe in your ability to change it. After all, if you don't believe that you are the best person to fulfill the opportunity you are applying for (or to supply the product you are selling), then it will be exceedingly difficult to convince someone else that you are!

CHAPTER ENDNOTES

1. D. M. Hanssens, ed., *Empirical Generalizations about Marketing Impact: What We Have Learned from Academic Research,* 2nd ed. (Cambridge, MA: Marketing Science Institute, 2015).
2. S. Albers, M. K. Mantrala, and S. Sridhar, "Personal selling," in *Empirical Generalizations about Marketing Impact,* 2nd ed., ed. D. M. Hanssens (Cambridge, MA: Marketing Science Institute, 2015).
3. Salesforce.com, "CRM 101: What Is CRM?," n.d., https://www.salesforce.com/crm/what-is-crm/.
4. Bureau of Labor Statistics, "Sales Occupations," *Occupational Outlook Handbook,* n.d., http://www.bls.gov/ooh/sales/home.htm.
5. D. H. Pink, *To Sell Is Human: The Surprising Truth about Moving Others* (New York: Penguin, 2012).
6. https://www.salesforlife.com/the-ultimate-guide-to-social-selling).
7. https://go.forrester.com/blogs/13-07-17-in_business_everybody_uses_social_media_for_work_the_question_is_how/.
8. https://salesfoundation.org/who-we-serve/.
9. https://www1.salary.com/Sales-Representative-I-salary.html.
10. https://ssir.org/articles/entry/how_some_nonprofits_build_sales_teams_on_a_budget.
11. Murray Barrick, Michael Mount, and Timothy Judge, "Personality and Performance at the Beginning of the New Millennium: Where Do We Go Next?" *Journal of Selection and Assessment* 9, no. 1 (2001): 9–30.
12. G. W. Dudley and S. L. Goodson, *The Psychology of Sales Call Reluctance: Earning What You're Worth in Sales* (Dallas, TX: Behavioral Sciences Research Press, Inc., 1999).
13. E. Strout, "To Tell the Truth," *Sales and Marketing Management* 154 (July 2002): 40–47.
14. Sales & Marketing Executives, International, *Sales & Marketing Creed: The International Code of Ethics for Sales and Marketing,* https://www.smei.org/?16.

Design elements: Marketing Insights Podcast: vandame/Shutterstock

Chapter 2

Prospecting and Qualifying

Learning Objectives
After reading this chapter, you should be able to:

LO 2-1 Describe the importance of prospecting, the challenges associated with prospecting, and why many salespeople are hesitant to prospect.

LO 2-2 Contrast the hunting and farming sales orientations, and explain the role inside sales can play in prospecting.

LO 2-3 List the steps in the prospecting process and the necessary requirements for a lead to be qualified as a prospect.

LO 2-4 List common lead-generation methods.

LO 2-5 Explain the activities involved in formulating a prospecting strategy.

LO 2-6 Explain the importance of salesperson ethics in prospecting for new customers.

Executive **Perspective** ... because everyone is a salesperson

George E. Hayes

George E. Hayes
Co-Owner
Southern Grit

Describe your job.

Currently, I am the co-owner of Southern Grit, a concrete-coating startup located in Birmingham, Alabama. We specialize in concrete coatings as well as polishing concrete for the residential and commercial markets.

How did you get your job?

I attended the University of Alabama, and the first job I landed out of college was with a finance company. Looking back, I don't know why they hired someone with a general management degree to manage accounts and conduct internal-account audits. I must have done a good job selling them on myself.

A few years into this position I discovered that I didn't love what I was doing. I looked at my manager's position and on up the continuum to the vice president's position, and I didn't have the desire to do any of their jobs.

One day, during lunch with a coworker, I was introduced to someone who worked for DEWALT. I couldn't believe that I was sitting in an office looking at numbers and *he* was driving around to accounts in a cool-looking yellow DEWALT truck, selling power tools. The passion and enthusiasm that he had when describing his job to me were contagious. Instantly I knew that this was something that I would love to do! I did everything in my power to figure out how to secure a job with DEWALT. Several months later I got an interview and had an offer letter for a sales-rep position calling on The Home Depot in Birmingham, AL.

This position was a perfect fit. It was the first time I could say I truly loved what I was doing. I enjoyed the people, culture, and products, and I was learning something new every single day. Over the next several years I moved with DEWALT from Birmingham to Houston, ultimately landing at the corporate office in Towson, Maryland.

During my tenure at DEWALT, I was promoted through the organization—from sales representative to territory manager, operations manager, and marketing manager roles. And, yes, I loved every single position I had. While I was a marketing manager in Towson, my wife and I decided to try to move back to the Southeast to be closer to our families. To this day, deciding to leave Towson was the hardest professional decision I've made. I put out some feelers and landed a pharmaceutical sales position with Eli Lilly and Company back in Birmingham. Calling on physicians to drive demand in the pharmaceutical industry wasn't very different from selling to The Home Depot. I was in sales, learning new products in a new industry, and facing new challenges.

One evening I received a call from Newell Rubbermaid asking me to come to Atlanta to discuss an opportunity they had open at The Home Depot. I took a trip over to Atlanta and was ultimately offered the position of Strategic Account Manager of Hardware & Home Improvement Sales at Newell Rubbermaid. This was a wonderful career opportunity, and the people and culture at Newell Rubbermaid were a perfect fit.

Upon accepting the offer, we packed our bags and moved the family to Atlanta. I loved working with Newell Rubbermaid and, once again, loved what I was doing. Over the course of the ten years I was in Atlanta, I made a few career changes, ultimately working with Bradshaw Home Products as Vice President of sales, running the Hardware & Home Improvement division. I continued to love what I was doing. During my last few years at Bradshaw Home Products, Laura and I were very fortunate to be able to relocate back to Birmingham so we could be close to our families and continue to raise our family of five.

After being back in Birmingham for a few years, I decided to partner with a friend, Brett Hubbard, who had recently sold a family business. The timing was perfect for the next chapter in my career. We launched Southern Grit, a startup company focusing on concrete coatings and polishing concrete. We love what we do!

What has been most important thing in making you successful at your job?

Love what you do.

What advice would you give future graduates about a career in sales?

Take your time and do your due diligence when making a career decision. Make a list of pros and cons as well as a five-year plan supporting your career decision. Don't get distracted by chasing a title. Try your hardest, do your best, and the VP, GM, or CEO title will come to you. When you get the title, you will realize that the title isn't important—it's what you did to get there that is important. Also, value the people and experiences throughout your career.

What is the most important characteristic of a great salesperson?

Don't be afraid to make mistakes. You will fail and make mistakes during your career. If you don't, you're not trying hard enough. Learn from your mistakes and leverage them to make you a better person. With this being said, don't make the same mistake twice.

AN INTRODUCTION TO PROSPECTING

LO 2-1 Describe the importance of prospecting, the challenges associated with prospecting, and why many salespeople are hesitant to prospect.

prospecting
The process through which salespeople identify and engage with new customers or new areas of business with existing customers.

Prospecting is the process through which salespeople identify and engage with new customers or new areas of business with existing customers. It is one of the more challenging tasks that salespeople are asked to perform. For most, it is not the most enjoyable part of the job, partly because it is not easy and the potential for rejection is high. Yet, many would argue that prospecting is one of the most important things—if not *the* most important thing—that salespeople do.

The Importance of Prospecting

Why is prospecting so important? Why does it play a critical role in determining sales success? First and foremost, there can be no sale if there is no customer. In this way, prospecting is the lifeblood of the sales organization. It is the process that produces a continuous flow of organizational customers and business opportunities. Without this flow, the organization and its sales force would cease to exist. There would be no need for either.

Moreover, at the individual salesperson level, salespeople must prospect to help ensure the attainment of their sales goals. In most sales positions, salespeople are given a **quota**, or a quantifiable sales goal for a given time period. Many factors can affect whether salespeople achieve their quotas. At its core, though, the sales role ultimately requires that salespeople be able to sell more to their existing customers *while also* identifying and engaging new customers. Experienced salespeople will tell you that consistent goal attainment requires both of these things—you cannot focus on one to the neglect of the other. Just as salespeople must be able to manage their existing customer relationships, they must also be able to prospect for new ones.

quota
A quantifiable sales goal for a given time period.

Think, for example, about your university. Countless individuals work in development, where they focus on fundraising to support capital campaigns. These individuals understand the importance of prospecting; they will cultivate relationships with potential donors for extended periods of time before ever making a request. For them, the ability to identify the right people as donors plays a critical role in determining their individual success—and the success of your university.

Thus, sales success requires an ability to prospect for new business. Salespeople who assume that they will be able to attain their goals by simply selling more to all of their existing customers are not being realistic. This will not happen. While they may have some customers who buy more over time, they will also lose some customers due to *attrition*, a reduction or decrease in number. There are a variety of reasons for this attrition. For example, customers may be dissatisfied, they may hit a rough patch or go out of business, or they may cease operations in the category the salesperson sells in. Whatever the reason, a certain level of attrition is inevitable and to be expected. As a result, a certain level of prospecting is required. Through new customers and growth opportunities, prospecting can help offset the challenges customer attrition will inevitably present.

This chapter focuses on the prospecting process. Understand that while some may think of prospecting in terms of new customers only, prospecting also occurs when salespeople sell new products or services to their existing customers. That said, our focus in this chapter is on the process through which salespeople identify and engage new customers. In the following section, we discuss the challenges associated with prospecting.

The Challenges Associated with Prospecting

The things that are most important in a job are often the most difficult. Such is the case with prospecting in sales. It is not easy and, for most, it is not fun. In fact, many salespeople will tell you that prospecting is the most challenging thing they are asked to do in their job.

Why is this? Why can prospecting be such a daunting task? First, prospecting can be a very inefficient activity compared to others performed by salespeople. In fact, in some instances, salespeople are happy with a success rate of 10 percent when prospecting. This may mean that only 1 out of 10 prospects is receptive to a meeting, or that it takes 10 attempts to secure a meeting with a particular prospect. At this rate, salespeople invest a great deal of time against what can seem like minimal returns. This challenge has only become more pronounced with the recent onset of the global coronavirus pandemic. Buyers have become even more difficult to reach, and those operating in economic sectors that have slowed are hesitant to invest given the uncertainty that looms in their businesses.

SDI Productions/iStockphoto/Getty Images

One reason for prospecting inefficiency also contributes to the overall challenge that prospecting can present: Buyers are often hesitant to explore the possibility that they have a need for the product or service. Think about your own interactions with salespeople who have attempted to sell you something in the past. Perhaps at first you did not think you needed what the salesperson was selling. You were skeptical, in part because you did not want to dedicate the time that a conversation would have required. Although professional buyers are seeking to enhance the effectiveness and efficiency of the companies they work for, they are subject to this same thinking. Buyers are not only inundated with requests for meetings from salespeople but also limited by time constraints and therefore not able to accept all of these requests. As their time is valuable, they have to make decisions about which salespeople they are or are not going to meet with.

Moreover, the consultative-type sales approach also plays a role: Salespeople are anxious to talk with prospects about the problems the prospects are facing in their business. But because most buyers already have a long list of problems to address, it is only natural that they will be hesitant to engage in conversations about additional problems. In fact, experienced salespeople often state that the greatest objection they must overcome when prospecting stems from this issue. *It simply is easier for a buyer to do nothing than to do something.* Indeed, we are often comfortable accepting the status quo as long as we do not believe that there are any grave consequences associated with doing so. Given this human inclination, it is important that salespeople attempt to quantify the **opportunity costs**, or the costs associated with doing nothing or with other alternatives, for the buyer. In many instances, these costs are much greater than the costs associated with implementing a solution.

opportunity costs
For the buyer, the costs associated with doing nothing or with other alternatives.

A final point: Salespeople may have to overcome issues based on the company they sell for or the products and/or services they sell. Perhaps the buyer has never heard of the selling company. Perhaps the buyer has had a negative experience with the selling company in the past. Perhaps the buyer favors a different product or solution instead. Perhaps the buyer has a strong personal relationship with a different salesperson. Whatever the reason, issues such as these can make the prospecting process very challenging.

Why Salespeople Are Hesitant to Prospect

Taken in their totality, all of these factors contribute to the fact that the rejection rates when prospecting can be very high. Many people believe salespeople to be immune to rejection, but this is typically not the case. Most of us do not like to hear "no." Rejection wears on us, and it carries an emotional toll than can be demoralizing.

call reluctance
An avoidance of customer interactions.

Because of this, some salespeople can become hesitant to engage in the prospecting process. Salespeople may even struggle with **call reluctance**—an avoidance of customer interactions—when prospecting.

Experienced salespeople who have grown accustomed to the prospecting process and its challenges will tell you that prospecting success requires repetition. It requires consistency and a strong persistence. Moreover, salespeople have to stay mindful of the fact that rejection is not personal. It is business, and a natural part of the prospecting process that must be dealt with.

Salespeople may also be hesitant to prospect because they feel it will take too much time away from their existing customer relationships. Given the heightened service requirements salespeople must now meet in order to effectively manage these relationships, this concern is legitimate. Customer retention takes time and effort, and salespeople have to avoid becoming complacent and taking their relationships for granted. Because of this, some are wary of allocating too much time to customer acquisition.

This time allocation imbalance is shown in Figure 2-1. The time required to manage existing relationships often far exceeds the time allocated to customer acquisition. This is a slippery slope, however: Some customer attrition is to be expected even when salespeople are doing all they can to ensure the continued development of their existing customer relationships. Thus it is important that salespeople strike the right balance when managing the amount of time they invest in their existing relationships against the time they spend prospecting.

To help ensure an adequate focus on these two activities (customer acquisition and retention) at the organizational level, sales leaders have begun differentiating sales roles based on activities performed. We discuss this in the following section, with a particular focus on the hunting and farming sales orientations. We also discuss the explosive growth seen in inside sales, a function that in recent year is often tasked with prospecting.

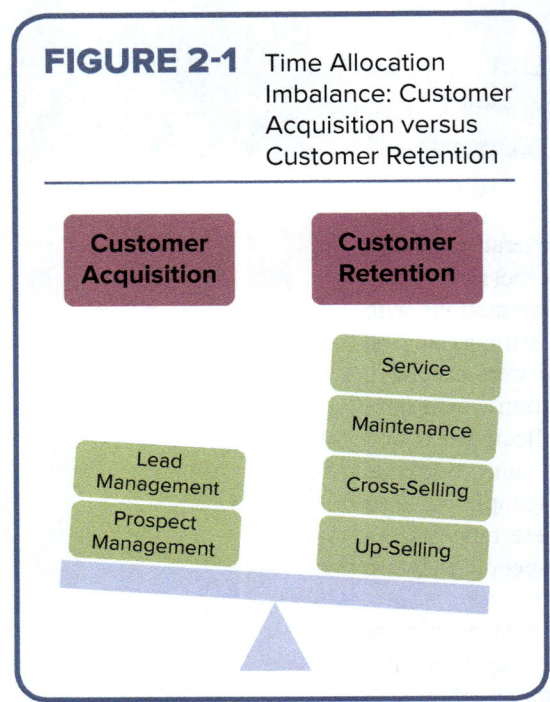

FIGURE 2-1 Time Allocation Imbalance: Customer Acquisition versus Customer Retention

Connect Assignment 2-1

The Challenges of Prospecting

Please complete the Connect exercise for Chapter 2 that focuses on the challenges associated with prospecting. By understanding why salespeople struggle with prospecting, you will gain insight into how salespeople can be more focused and reduce call reluctance.

LO 2-2
Contrast the hunting and farming sales orientations, and explain the role inside sales can play in prospecting.

MATCHING PERSONAL STRENGTHS TO PROSPECTING ROLES

We have seen a dramatic evolution in sales over the past decade. For one thing, salespeople have assumed the role of trusted advisors in the relationship-development process. For another, the sales field has also evolved in its understanding of the different skills required for success across the different types of sales roles that exist. There has been a growing realization that, to enhance organizational effectiveness and efficiency, salespeople should focus on those activities at which they are most proficient. In fact, many now believe that sales success is a function of fit between the salesperson and sales role. Not surprisingly, salespeople are far more likely to succeed when placed in roles that fit their strengths.

Hunting and Farming Sales Orientations

As it relates to prospecting, different salespeople have different orientations that make them more or less likely to succeed when seeking out new customers. Specifically, researchers have identified two orientations: hunting and farming.[1]

- A salesperson with a **hunting orientation** tends to focus more on securing new customers through lead generation, prospecting, pre-call planning, and delivering sales presentations.
- In contrast, a salesperson with a **farming orientation** tends to focus more on selling to existing customers by building long-term relationships.

> **hunting orientation**
> A focus on securing new customers through lead generation, prospecting, pre-call planning, and delivering sales presentations.
>
> **farming orientation**
> A focus on selling to existing customers by building long-term relationships.

In essence, hunters excel at identifying and engaging new business; farmers are more adept at managing existing relationships.

Some salespeople are inherently oriented to both types of activities. Others tend to favor one orientation over the other. This is fine. Neither orientation is better than the other—both are needed for the firm to succeed. The key lies in salespeople knowing their own strengths, and management placing them in roles that leverage these strengths.

One way to discover your strengths as a salesperson is through a professional assessment. GrowthPlay (www.growthplay.com) is a sales consulting firm that assists firms with this process. Specifically, GrowthPlay provides an assessment designed to assist both the firm and the salesperson in understanding what role best fits the salesperson. Similar in nature to the hunting and farming orientations, GrowthPlay's assessment differentiates *new-business developers* from *account managers*. New-business developers, like hunting-oriented salespeople, uncover new opportunities. They promote company offerings, focus on prospect-conversion processes, develop a presence in competitive markets, and expand coverage beyond the existing customer base. On the other hand, account managers, like farming-oriented salespeople, increase purchases and expand sales to current customers. They are proactive in strengthening existing customer relationships, focus on meeting existing customer needs, and assume the responsibility of handling special requests to solve existing customer problems. The GrowthPlay assessment provides firms a means through which they can practically differentiate the hunting and farming sales orientations, ensuring that the right people are assigned to the right sales roles.

The Role of Inside Sales in Prospecting

From a functional perspective, another trend in recent years involves the explosive growth in use of inside salespeople. As discussed in Chapter 1, **inside salespeople** perform selling activities at the employer's location. They differ from their traditional outside counterparts in that they interact with customers only remotely, though phone, email, text, social media, the internet, or some other form of remote technology. Thus, while outside salespeople visit their customers onsite, inside salespeople do not. Inside sales forces are most effective when they work closely with the outside sales force. Indeed, in some instances, inside salespeople prospect to identify potential new customers, who are then handed off to an outside counterpart to further develop the relationship. In most instances, one inside salesperson will support multiple outside salespeople (e.g., one inside salesperson may work with three outside salespeople).

> **inside salespeople**
> Salespeople who perform selling activities at the employer's location, typically using email and telephone.

antonioguillem/123RF

The use of an inside sales force has become increasingly common for several reasons. First, inside salespeople, compared with their outside counterparts, are incredibly cost-efficient. Inside reps are able to interact with a large number of customers without the expenses typically associated with travel. Second, many firms have come to understand that using inside as well as outside sales forces allows for a better division of labor. Inside salespeople can handle certain sales responsibilities while outside salespeople handle others. If these responsibilities are allocated correctly, the firm can not only become more efficient but also ensure effective management of the overall sales process.

As an example, a firm could differentiate customers based on sales and profitability potential, and have inside salespeople interact with lower-potential customers while outside salespeople interact with higher-potential customers. Or, as was previously noted, the firm could differentiate the various steps in the sales process and have inside salespeople handle certain steps while outside salespeople handle others.

From a prospecting perspective, inside salespeople will often perform the activities required to initiate a relationship. They will, for example, contact potential customers via phone or email and engage in an initial qualifying conversation. If sales potential does indeed exist, the inside salesperson will transfer the prospect to an outside salesperson for an onsite meeting.

Many companies have now established inside sales positions as an introductory role for newly hired salespeople. New hires will begin in an inside sales position, learning more about the company and customer base, and will eventually transfer to an outside sales position when performance merits a promotion. Inside salespeople tasked with generating leads may be alternately referred to as **sales-development representatives**.

sales-development representatives
Inside salespeople tasked with generating leads.

We have seen significant growth in the use of inside sales forces in recent years. In fact, the U.S. Department of Labor has estimated that 750,000 new inside sales positions will be created between 2013 and 2020.[2] The American Association of Inside Sales Professionals (www.aa-isp.org), which was created in 2009 as a support mechanism for inside salespeople, now has over 12,000 members. The association has approximately 60 chapters that span the globe, staffed by individuals who volunteer to keep those in the industry abreast of the latest trends and best practices in inside sales.

THE PROSPECTING PROCESS

LO 2-3 List the steps in the prospecting process and the necessary requirements for a lead to be qualified as a prospect.

Throughout this chapter, we have referred to prospecting as a process. This process is depicted in Figure 2-2. As shown, the process begins with *lead generation*. As not all leads are created equal, salespeople must *prioritize the leads* and then *qualify* them to determine which are actual sales prospects. From there, to ensure effective time management, salespeople should *prioritize their prospects* based on importance. Last, once they then have a list of prospects that are ranked by importance, salespeople should *plan calls*—taking the necessary steps to ensure they are prepared to meet with the sales prospects.

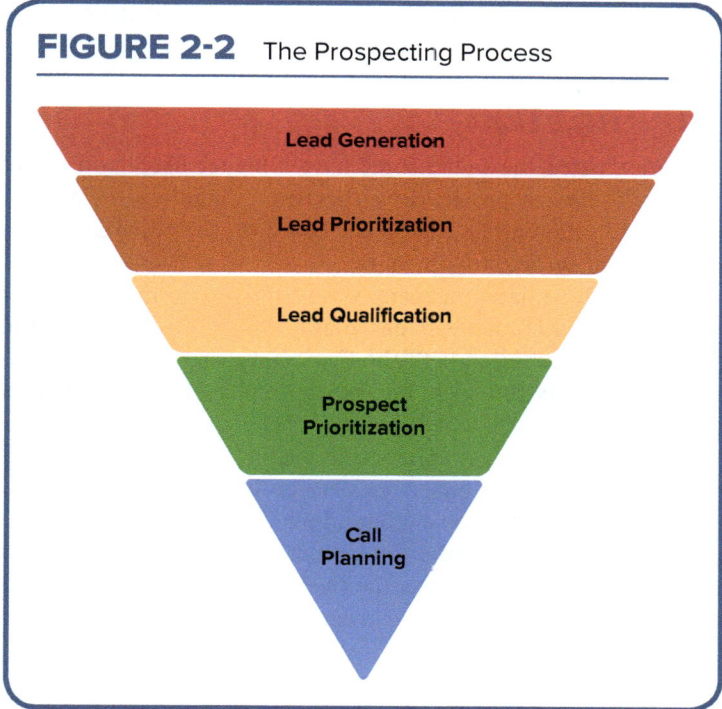

FIGURE 2-2 The Prospecting Process

Most people in sales view the prospecting process as a funnel through which the number of prospects dwindles as the process unfolds. Salespeople can pursue two schools of thought in the prospecting process:

1. Salespeople should generate as many leads as possible, making the funnel very wide at the top, to transition an adequate number of leads into prospects.
2. The very-wide funnel is an inefficient form of prospecting. People who hold this view argue that a wide funnel causes salespeople to waste time and effort working through many leads that do not have potential. Those with this perspective argue instead that it's better to be effective at the various steps contained in the funnel, as opposed to simply loading the funnel with as many leads as possible at the top. Obviously, the second approach is more efficient, but it requires more skill on the part of the salesperson.

Whichever the technique, the end goal is the same: to generate an adequate level of new business. In the following sections, we discuss in greater detail each step of the prospecting funnel.

Lead Generation

A **lead** is an individual or organization that exhibits characteristics similar in nature to those exhibited by current customers. Thus, leads possess characteristics that would indicate the possibility that the individual or organization may be qualified as a prospect. For example, a firm may possess organizational demographics that are similar in nature to other firms who currently purchase from the organization. Obviously, those characteristics in no way guarantee that the firm will have a need for the product or service being offered. It simply means that similarities exist and that the firm may meet the requirements needed for designation as a prospect. As lead generation is the starting point in the prospecting process, later in the chapter we

lead
An individual or organization that exhibits characteristics similar in nature to those exhibited by current customers.

will spend more time on this step, looking at the different methods through which leads can be generated.

Lead Prioritization

Not all leads are created the same; some have a higher likelihood of benefiting from the products and services provided by the firm. Therefore, to enhance efficiency, salespeople need to differentiate their leads based on the potential to ensure a greater return on the time they invest with them.

Leads can be differentiated in many ways. One of the most common ways is the inbound-lead versus outbound-lead designation. **Inbound leads** are those in which the lead initiates the interaction with the firm. **Outbound leads** are those in which the firm proactively contacts the lead. For example, if a buyer contacts the firm based on the recommendation of a colleague, the buyer and the organization he or she represents would be classified as an inbound lead. Conversely, if an inside salesperson proactively contacts this same buyer, with no initiation on the part of the buyer, the buyer would be categorized as an outbound lead.

Often, organizations have different processes in place for the management of inbound and outbound leads because the likelihood of success is much higher in the case of inbound leads. These leads are given a higher priority and are therefore acted upon more quickly.

The distinction between hot leads and cold leads is similar. A **hot lead** is an individual or organization that has shown some level of interest in the product or service being offered. A **cold lead** has yet to demonstrate this interest. Thus, inbound leads are a type of hot lead; outbound leads are but one type of cold lead.

Salespeople tasked with following up on leads need to know how the leads came—whether they are inbound or outbound, hot or cold. With that knowledge, they will be able to ensure that they are targeting the right leads in order to maximize efficiency in their prospecting activities.

Lead Qualification

Lead qualification refers to a process that is designed to differentiate leads from prospects. A **prospect** is an individual or an organization that:

- Demonstrates a need for the product or service being offered.
- Possesses the authority and the ability to purchase.
- Demonstrates both organizational potential and purchasing alignment.

For a lead to be qualified as a prospect, salespeople must be able to answer "yes" to the questions shown in Figure 2-3.

The first of these questions is easily the most important. Without a *need*, there is no reason for the salesperson to pursue the lead. Indeed, when prospecting, everything should begin with a determination of whether a need exists. Needs are the basis from which everything begins in the sales process—they provide a necessary foundation from which the sales process can unfold.

That said, buyers may sometimes be unaware of underlying, latent needs. In these situations, the salesperson can question the buyer to help develop a mutual understanding of the need. In complex buying situations, the need-identification process can extend for a considerable amount of time. It may take numerous interactions for the selling and buying organizations to reach a final determination of the need at hand, and often multiple people will be involved on both the selling and buying sides.

---

inbound leads
Leads initiated by the potential buyer.

outbound leads
Leads in which the selling firm proactively contacts the lead (the potential buyer).

hot lead
An individual or organization that has shown some level of interest in the product or service being offered.

cold lead
An individual or organization that has yet to demonstrate interest in the product or service being offered.

lead qualification
A process designed to differentiate leads from prospects.

prospect
An individual or organization that demonstrates a need for the product or service being offered, possesses the authority and ability to purchase, and demonstrates both organizational potential and purchasing alignment.

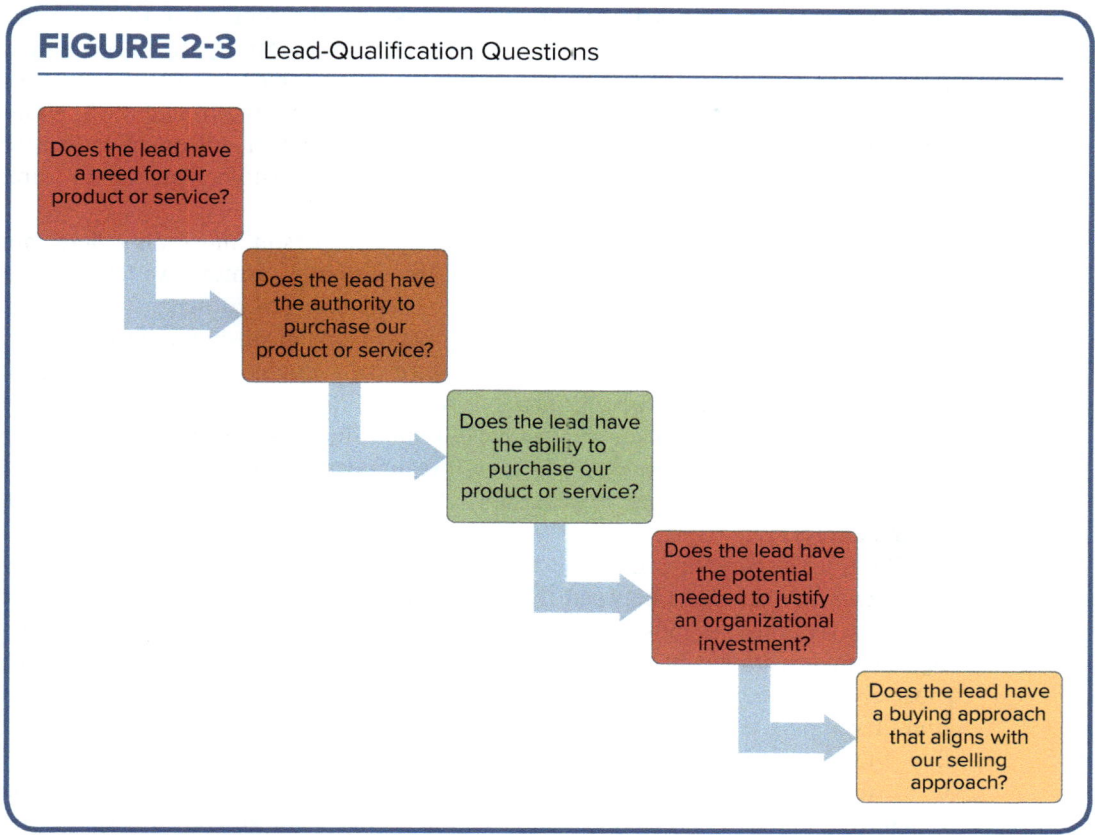

FIGURE 2-3 Lead-Qualification Questions

Beyond the need, it is also important the lead have both the *authority* and the *ability* to purchase. Salespeople should focus on two issues when addressing purchasing authority:

- Am I dealing with a decision maker?
- From a channel-management perspective, is the lead eligible to purchase?

With respect to the first question, there is nothing more frustrating for a salesperson than finding that he or she has been having conversations with someone within the buying organization who does not have the authority to purchase. Salespeople must ensure that this person does indeed have the authority ultimately to authorize a purchase. While individuals who do not have purchasing authority may play a role in the decision-making process, they cannot be the sole point of contact for the salesperson. Salespeople must determine who the ultimate decision makers are and bring these individuals into the conversation at a very early point. This is critically important as it will help ensure efficiency through effective time management.

With respect to the second question, salespeople must also be aware of how a potential customer will be categorized from a channel-management perspective. What does this mean? In instances where selling organizations have different salespeople selling to different types of customers within the same geographic region, salespeople have to be careful to ensure that they are funneling the customer through the proper channel. There may be instances in which the customer does not have the authority to purchase through the channel a particular salesperson represents.

In these instances, the salesperson must transition that customer to the proper channel. As a simple example, let's say there are two salespeople in a geographic region. One of these salespeople sells only to those customers who buy direct from the company; the other sells only to those customers who buy through a wholesaler. To understand which salesperson should sell to a particular customer, both salespeople would have to make a determination of how that customer purchases (direct or through a wholesaler).

Once authority has been established, the salesperson must also determine whether the customer is able to purchase. In the consumer context, we tend to think of this in terms of the customer having the money required to make the purchase. This issue may also arise in the business context: smaller business customers may not have the financial resources a large investment requires. Even more common, however, are instances in which budgetary constraints limit an ability to purchase. In these instances, the customer may have limited financial resources due to major expenditures already planned. It is therefore important that the salesperson ask about planned expenditures, to determine their importance in relation to the need being addressed.

The final lead-qualification questions focus on the *potential* a lead possesses and the *alignment* that exists between the selling and buying organizations. In terms of potential, salespeople must understand that the prospecting process can require a significant investment at the individual salesperson and organizational levels. The most obvious example of this is time: Salespeople may have to spend considerable time developing and maintaining a relationship with the customer. This time is not free; there are opportunity costs in the form of forgone time investments that could be made elsewhere. From an organizational perspective, salesperson time is extremely valuable, given the costs associated with sales force management. As such, there may be instances in which leads meet the first three criteria (a need, along with the authority and ability to purchase), but just do not show the potential required to justify the resource expenditures needed to establish and maintain a relationship.

Salespeople should also seek to understand what type of approach the buying organization favors when working with suppliers, to determine whether this approach aligns with that of their company. As an example, there may be instances in which a salesperson comes to realize that the buying organization is very transactional in nature; in such a case, it may favor an arms-length approach and a reliance on power and an accompanying sense of supplier dependence to ensure desirable relationship outcomes. This buying approach might be perilous for the selling company, in which case the salesperson may think it best to focus on other prospects. Obviously, when making this decision, the salesperson would also have to take into account customer potential.

Prospect Prioritization

prospect prioritization
A process through which salespeople rank-order prospects based on their desirability.

ideal customer profile
A profile of organizational characteristics shared by current, highly desirable customers

Given their time constraints, salespeople should next seek to prioritize the prospects they have identified. **Prospect prioritization** refers to a process through which salespeople can rank-order prospects based on their desirability.

One of the ways to prioritize prospects is through the use of an **ideal customer profile**—a profile of organizational characteristics shared by current highly desirable customers. Salespeople can use this information to identify which prospects are most similar to these highly desirable customers. The prospects who are similar in nature to these customers would be given the highest priority. Thus an ideal customer profile provides yet another tool through which salespeople can ensure prospecting efficiency.

Sales-Call Planning

Once all prospects have been prioritized, salespeople should begin preparing for the sales call. There may be multiple salespeople involved in this planning process, particularly if an inside salesperson has identified and qualified the prospect. In these situations, the inside salesperson will have information about the prospect that should be shared with the outside salesperson. In complex sales situations, where team-based selling is more common, all sales team members must be provided this information. Communication across team members is key to ensure a shared understanding of the customer and situation.

Pre-call information can be organized in many ways. Figure 2-4 shows one example: the SPIN call-planning template. As we will discuss in Chapter 6, SPIN is a sales methodology designed to assist salespeople in developing a questioning process that focuses on four question types: Situational questions, Problem questions, Implication questions, and Need-Payoff questions. The SPIN call-planning template provides an organizing document that salespeople can use to ensure adequate meeting preparedness. The template forces salespeople to think through their primary and alternative call objectives, customer-oriented purpose statement, anticipated questioning strategy, and relevant organizational capabilities.

The template also requires that the salesperson gather information to ensure an understanding of the situation confronting the customer. Figure 2-5 provides examples of relevant buyer-level and organizational-level questions that salespeople should address when planning for the sales call.

FIGURE 2-4 SPIN Call-Planning Template

Sales Call-Planning Template
Customer: Call Date:
Contact Name: Call Time:
Customer History (Relevant Notes):
Call Objectives:
Specific, **M**easurable, **A**ctionable, **R**ealistic, **T**ime-Based
Primary Call Objective:
•
Secondary Call Objective:
•
Anticipated Needs:
Value Proposition (How do we meet these needs?):
•
•

SPIN Questioning Strategy	
Potential **S**ituational Questions	Potential **P**roblem Questions
•	•
•	•
•	•
Potential **I**mplication Questions	Potential **N**eed-Payoff Questions
•	•
•	•
•	•

Post-Call Follow-Up		
Task:	Responsibility:	Date:
•	•	•
•	•	•
•	•	•
Meeting Notes:		

FIGURE 2-5 Call-Planning Questions

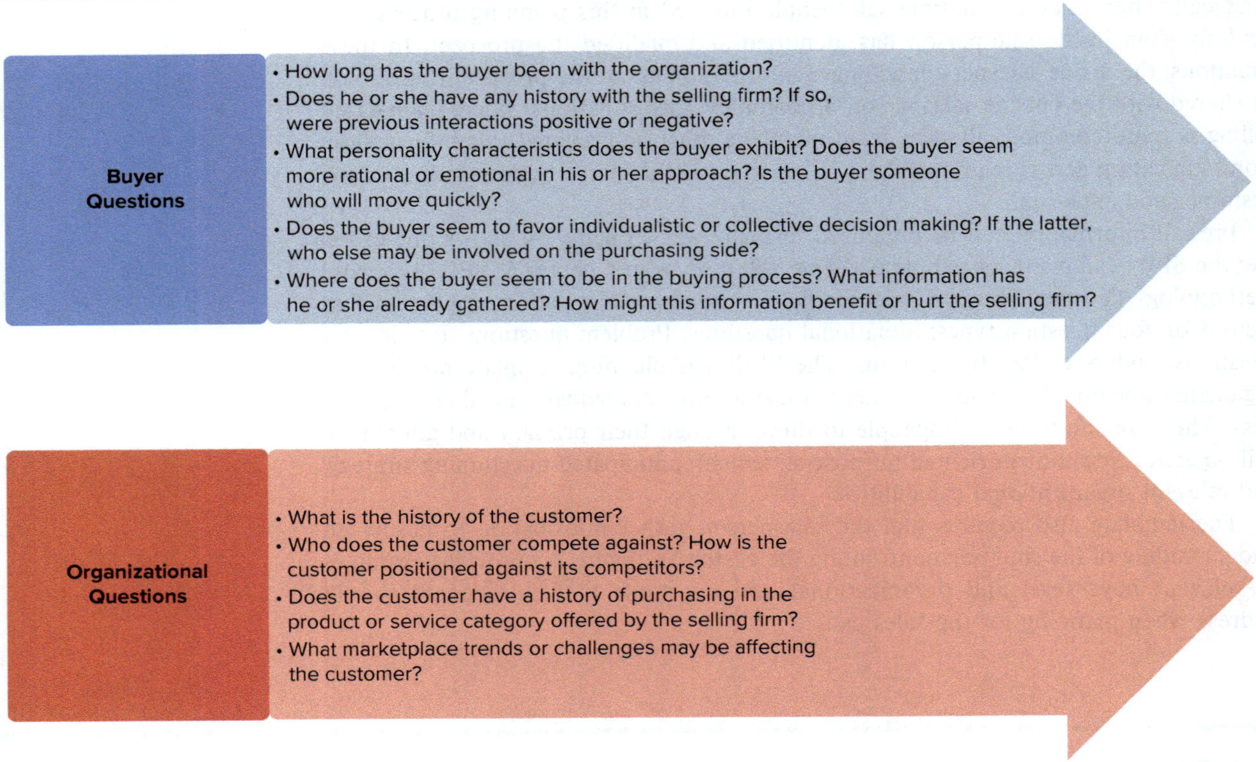

Buyer Questions
- How long has the buyer been with the organization?
- Does he or she have any history with the selling firm? If so, were previous interactions positive or negative?
- What personality characteristics does the buyer exhibit? Does the buyer seem more rational or emotional in his or her approach? Is the buyer someone who will move quickly?
- Does the buyer seem to favor individualistic or collective decision making? If the latter, who else may be involved on the purchasing side?
- Where does the buyer seem to be in the buying process? What information has he or she already gathered? How might this information benefit or hurt the selling firm?

Organizational Questions
- What is the history of the customer?
- Who does the customer compete against? How is the customer positioned against its competitors?
- Does the customer have a history of purchasing in the product or service category offered by the selling firm?
- What marketplace trends or challenges may be affecting the customer?

McGraw Hill Connect Assignment 2-2

The Prospecting Process

Please complete the Connect exercise for Chapter 2 that focuses on the prospecting process. By better understanding the prospecting process, salespeople can better match their personal strengths to prospecting roles that increase their likelihood for success.

LEAD-GENERATION METHODS

LO 2-4 List common lead-generation methods.

We've seen that the overall prospecting process begins with lead generation. It therefore is important that salespeople identify and understand the different lead-generation methods they may use. Here, we present some common lead-generation methods. Because social selling has come to assume a more prominent role in sales in recent years, we begin with a discussion of virtual networking via social media.

Virtual Networking

networking
Activities through which individuals communicate to strengthen their professional and/or social relationships.

virtual networking
Networking activities that take place via social media.

Networking refers to activities through which individuals communicate to strengthen their professional and/or social relationships. When we say **virtual networking**, we are referring to instances when these activities take place via social media. As you can probably attest, we live in a virtual world. Many of us now spend more time managing our virtual relationships than we do managing our traditional relationships. While social media usage has created opportunities and challenges in society, it has also altered the way salespeople prospect for new customers.³

Social selling, defined in Chapter 1 as the process of developing, nurturing, and leveraging relationships online to sell products or services, can be beneficial throughout every stage of the selling process.⁴,⁵ Prospects today are sharing incredibly valuable information on their social channels. Salespeople can use information about customer needs and wants, detailed on public profiles, to send communications that are personalized, relevant, and helpful. Building a strong personal brand and network through social media channels allows salespeople to seek out introductions to new prospects through existing mutual connections.

social selling
A sales approach that develops, nurtures, and leverages relationships online to sell products or services.

How should you go about building this personal brand? First, whenever you meet someone interesting offline, extend an invitation to connect with them digitally. With more than 600 million users worldwide, LinkedIn (www.linkedin.com) represents the most important social platform for business networking. Although LinkedIn has generic invitation messages you can use, you will be much more successful if you personalize your outreach. Your new acquaintances will be more likely to accept your invitation to connect if it's personalized. Also, their perceptions of your authenticity and professionalism will be much higher if you make an effort to connect on an individual level. For example, you might include details relating to your association and potential benefits for them from establishing an online relationship.

Roman Pyshchyk/Shutterstock

One of the biggest advantages of LinkedIn lies within its groups—of which there are currently more than 1.8 million. In most instances, salespeople can review the profiles of existing or prospective customers to see what interest groups they are active in. As an example, if the ideal target customer is a small-business owner, then the salesperson should search for groups relating to small businesses. Conversely, if the organization sells customer-service software, then salespeople should search for groups that are dedicated to customer-service managers. By advancing conversation within a group in a professional and helpful manner, the salesperson can effectively build credibility and recognition among group members, eventually resulting in new sales opportunities.

Traditional Networking

Traditional networking refers to face-to-face communications that are designed to strengthen an individual's professional and/or social relationships. Because individual relationships can often provide the foundation for business relationships, traditional networking has long been a valuable lead-generation method in sales. Moreover, as is the case with virtual networking, traditional networking provides salespeople a means through which they can spread their individual and company brand awareness.

traditional networking
Face-to-face communications that are designed to strengthen an individual's professional and/or social relationships.

Referrals

A **referral** is a lead provided by an existing customer, based on a belief that the potential buyer may benefit from the products or services provided by the selling firm. Because potential customers are typically more receptive to salespeople who are reaching out based on the suggestion of another customer, referrals are incredibly beneficial in sales. Moreover, existing customers are often most adept at identifying other businesses who might benefit from the products or services offered by the selling firm.

referral
A lead provided by an existing customer, based on a belief that the potential buyer may benefit from the products or services provided by the selling firm.

Adriano Castelli/Shutterstock

trade shows
Industry-specific events designed to bring selling companies and customers to the same location.

cold-call
An unsolicited call or visit by a salesperson.

As a result, conversion rates (a measure of the rate or number of leads that become actual customers) from referrals are usually higher than conversion rates from other lead-generation methods. It is important that salespeople remember that customers are staking their reputations to the referrals they provide. Thus, salespeople must be factual in the way they represent any information provided by the referring customer.

Trade Shows

Trade shows are industry-specific events designed to bring selling companies and customers to the same location. Thus, customer interactions at trade shows differ from those at traditional sales meetings that are conducted via phone or on-site with the customer. Further, in most instances, selling companies will offer trade-show promotions to encourage customer purchases. Some customers will purchase almost exclusively at trade shows in order to take advantage of these promotions and their access to so many selling companies in one place.

Equally important is the fact that prospects will often approach selling companies at trade shows. These prospects are lucrative in that they are proactively approaching the selling company—they are initiating contact. This willingness to make contact usually indicates a belief on the part of the customer that a need or problem exists. Because of this, conversion rates for prospects who initially make contact at trades shows are often higher than what is seen for other prospecting methods.

Cold-Calling

A cold-call is an unsolicited call or visit by a salesperson. While many have criticized cold-calling due to its inefficiency, sales organizations still use it as a means to identify new customers. In fact, as mentioned, many organizations now have inside salespeople handling cold-calls to enhance overall sales force efficiency.

You may think of cold-calling in terms of those bothersome phone calls you receive from telemarketers at the most inopportune times, but cold-calling is an accepted practice in many B2B contexts. In fact, even today, some organizations report higher than normal success rates in this context, particularly when there is a strong need for the product or service. That said, in relation to what we have seen historically, the percentage of firms now relying on cold-calling as their sole lead-generation method has dropped significantly.

Websites

Another significant change in sales in recent years is that buyers are now proactively beginning their search process minus any salesperson involvement. To do so, buyers frequently interact with sales websites as they attempt to gather information. While company websites are not new, the fact that buyers are willing to rely on them almost entirely as they begin their search process is. When this occurs, selling firms can capture the buyer's information and forward it to the appropriate salesperson to be acted upon. The buyer would be qualified as a hot lead, given that he or she initiated the search process.

However, at the same time, many selling firms have found that these buyers are significantly advanced in their decision-making process by the time any interaction occurs between the salesperson and the buyer. Salespeople should move quickly on leads generated through a company website, to ensure continuing interest and involvement.

Sales Directories

Sales directories are lists of leads that are typically compiled by third parties. Some of these lists are free to the public, but many third parties sell the lists. While the lists are beneficial in providing a large number of leads, salespeople will often complain that the conversion rates for these lists are quite low. As a result, salespeople may spend a great deal of time working through a list to identify potential customers. Moreover, with advances in technology, many sales organizations and individual salespeople can now compile their own lists and do not have to outsource the process to a third party.

sales directories
Lists of leads that are typically compiled by third parties.

Centers of Influence

A **center of influence** is someone who is both connected to and respected by a group of prospects. Salespeople who are able to build relationships with individuals who hold influential positions are often able to leverage the relationship to gain access to the group. In exchange, the salesperson may have to sponsor an event, financially support the group, or do something else to justify being granted access. However, particularly in instances when the center of influence has a wide reach and is able to draw a large number of prospects, such support may be an investment that is easily recouped. As an example, woodworking communities comprise individuals who create items from wood. Within these communities, woodworking experts will emerge and lead educational meetings. Salespeople representing companies that manufacture woodworking products will partner with these experts, sponsoring meetings in an attempt to build relationships with all attendees.

center of influence
Someone who is both connected to and respected by a group of prospects.

Noncompeting Salespeople

One of the things new salespeople quickly realize is that there is a bond among salespeople, particularly those who do not compete in the same category directly against one another. *Noncompeting salespeople* can be a valuable resource through which leads are generated. Typically, this occurs when the noncompeting salesperson is selling to the same *types* of customers, but to customers who are not currently purchasing in the category sold by the salesperson seeking the lead. In these instances, there is an expectation that this favor will be returned—that the salesperson seeking the lead will extend the same courtesy when the roles are reversed.

Marketing

Many of the lead-generation methods discussed in this chapter are also performed by marketing personnel. Historically, however, there has been friction between the two functions as it relates to this activity.[6,7] Marketers can grow frustrated over the fact that the sales force does not act on the leads they provide. Similarly, salespeople can become frustrated over what they perceive to be a lack of quality leads. Because of this, salespeople are often slow to act on the leads their marketing counterparts provide.

It is important that the marketing and sales functions work together to better understand lead-generation issues and the factors contributing to these issues. For instance, if salespeople find that a very low percentage of leads generated by marketing are being converted into customers, the two sides need to talk so as to identify problematic patterns leading to the low conversion rate.

In some larger companies, both the chief marketing officer (CMO) and chief sales officer (CSO) report to a chief revenue officer (CRO). The CRO has the task of driving company revenues while also ensuring coordinated efforts across the two functions. While this is happening at the higher levels of the organization, salespeople should understand that marketers can be a valuable source of leads in the prospecting process.

---

connect Assignment 2-3

Lead-Generation Methods

Please complete the Connect exercise for Chapter 2 that focuses on lead-generation methods. By better understanding how to generate leads, salespeople will be better prepared to begin the prospecting process and ultimately close more sales.

LO 2-5

Explain the activities involved in formulating a prospecting strategy.

FORMULATING A PROSPECTING STRATEGY

Although it is important for salespeople to understand different lead-generation methods, it is perhaps even more important to develop an overall prospecting strategy. We talk about such a strategy in the following discussion, highlighting key issues that salespeople should be mindful of in their prospecting efforts. Consistent with Figure 2-6, we focus on four strategic imperatives that salespeople should address in sequence:

1. Develop a prospecting plan.
2. Allocate adequate time to the prospecting process.
3. Track results.
4. Evaluate lead-generation methods and overall prospecting processes.

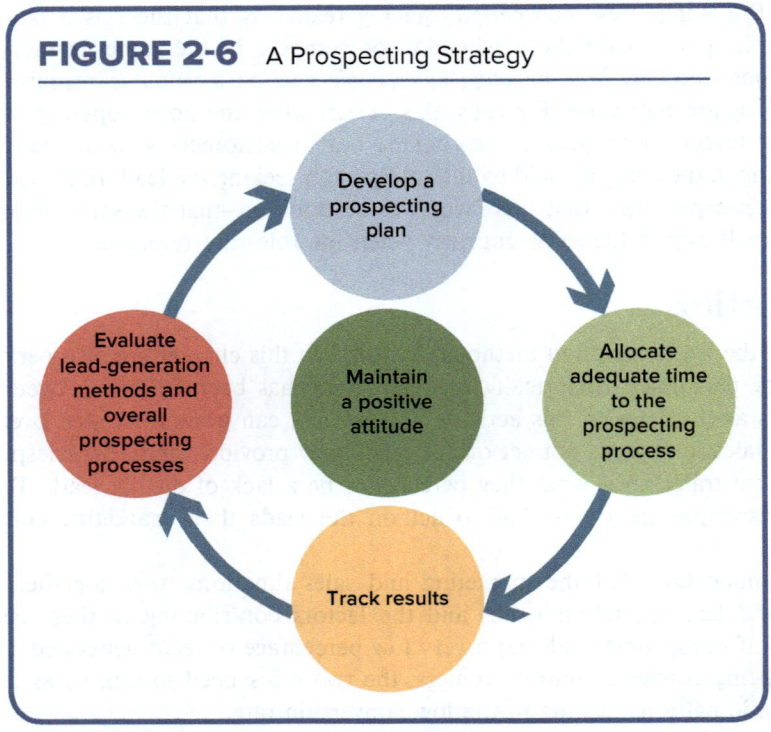

FIGURE 2-6 A Prospecting Strategy

We also discuss the importance of salespeople maintaining a positive attitude as they prospect for new customers.

Develop a Prospecting Plan

We've said that planning plays a critical role in determining success on sales calls. In addition, salespeople also need to develop a *prospecting plan* for their overall sales territory or, in the case of a key or strategic account manager (KAM or SAM), key customer. Part of this plan should be a strategy for developing new business through prospecting. Any prospecting plan should address questions such as:

- What percentage of my existing customer base might I lose through attrition?
- What percentage of business do I anticipate earning through new customers in the planning period?
- On which prospects do I anticipate focusing my efforts?
- What resources do I need to transition these prospects into customers?
- What tactics will I employ to ensure that this happens?

The Power of Prospecting

From there, the salesperson should review the prospecting plan with his or her manager so that both agree on it. Equally important, the salesperson must regularly revisit the prospecting plan to ensure that he or she is taking the necessary steps required for success. A good sales manager will also hold the salesperson accountable to the plan and ask for periodic updates on it. In the absence of a prospecting plan, it is unlikely that the salesperson will do what is required to acquire new business.

Allocate Time

Converting accounts from the competition or working with them as they make the decision to invest in a new product category can be an arduous and time-consuming process. One of the challenges with prospecting is that salespeople are often hesitant to allocate adequate time to prospecting. As they set an overall prospecting strategy, salespeople must therefore decide how much time to spend seeking out new business.

As an example, a salesperson managing a territory may decide to spend one day per week handling paperwork, three days per week servicing and growing existing customers, and one day per week prospecting for new business. With this decision, the salesperson is planning to allocate 20 percent of the time to prospecting. The salesperson and sales manager could then discuss the adequacy of this time allocation against the amount of new business the salesperson needs to generate.

Track Results

"How am I doing?" Salespeople need to know, via a results-tracking system, how they are doing numerically in meeting their prospecting goals. They then can focus on the most efficient methods and make better use of the time allocated to prospecting. Fortunately, technologies such as customer relationship management (CRM) software provide salespeople a means through which this can now be done in a timely manner.

Evaluate Lead-Generation Methods and Prospecting Processes

Salespeople who track their prospecting results can evaluate the different lead-generation methods they employ and their overall prospecting processes. Just as salespeople seek to identify the most effective and efficient lead-generation methods, they also look to refine their overall prospecting process. That is, through repetition, salespeople will seek to master an overall process for interacting with potential new customers. As an example, salespeople may have a script they use when cold-calling. By evaluating various cold-calling scripts, a salesperson can work toward developing a script that has the most impact when reaching out to prospects.

Maintain a Positive Attitude

Maintaining a positive attitude throughout the prospecting process is crucial (as highlighted by its position in the middle of Figure 2-6). As noted at the beginning of this chapter, prospecting is one of the more challenging activities salespeople perform. Rejection rates when prospecting are high, even for experienced salespeople. Yet prospecting is a necessary part of the job, and those who maintain a positive attitude not only make the job more enjoyable but also enhance the likelihood of prospecting success. As so many in sales will attest, your attitude toward a job plays a critical role in determining how well you will perform in that job.

ETHICS IN PROSPECTING

LO 2-6 Explain the importance of salesperson ethics in prospecting for new customers.

Ethical salesperson behavior is prerequisite for the development of any customer relationship, including throughout the prospecting process. Even the slightest hint of unethical behavior will undermine any prospecting activities; customers will not willingly enter into a relationship with someone they believe to be of questionable ethical character. Salespeople should focus on four key ethical standards when prospecting.

First, as the initial step in the lead-qualification process, salespeople must be honest in their assessment of whether a need truly exists. If there is no need, the process must stop. Attempting to sell a product or service to a customer when there is no need is unethical. There can be no gray area on this. A salesperson should never manufacture a need to gain a customer.

Second, when initially interacting with prospects, salespeople must be factual in their communications. When first meeting a new salesperson, it is difficult for the prospect to know whether the salesperson and organization he or she represents can deliver on the promises the salesperson makes. Uncertainty is high. Because of this, salespeople should avoid setting unrealistic expectations when communicating with prospects. Seasoned salespeople will tell you that honesty is always the best policy, particularly when first communicating with a potential customer.

Third, salespeople should be factual when providing information about the competition. Often, when salespeople are attempting to convert a prospect from a competitor, the customer will ask questions or make comments about the competitor. While it may be tempting to disparage the competition, salespeople should tread lightly. As is the case when describing what their firm can provide, salespeople should be factual in sharing information about the competition. If the prospect were to find that the salesperson fabricated competitive information in an attempt to win the business, the prospect would likely, in the future, question the integrity of the salesperson.

Fourth, salespeople must be careful to manage the integrity of the referral process when prospecting. When an existing customer provides a referral, he or she assumes that the salesperson will use the referral as intended. For instance, if a customer willingly provides a referral for a prospect, the referral should be used only with that prospect and not with others. Moreover, if the customer makes specific comments in support of the referral (for example, "Joe said that he thought you might benefit from our products or services as well, based on . . ."), the referral should be limited only to what the customer said. To embellish these comments or use a referral on additional prospects beyond those intended by the referring customer is unethical; it represents a breach of trust.

Today's **Professional Perspective** ...because everyone is a salesperson

Darrious Duffin
Sales Operations Analyst
Ritter Communications

Describe your job. I'm a sales operations analyst at Ritter Communications, a communications provider that offers business, residential, and wholesale customers internet, phone, video, and cloud services. My main responsibility is to provide our executive team with information to help them make data-driven decisions that increase sales and improve efficiency. I partner with our sales leadership to create and implement strategies that generate new sales leads, close more deals, shorten the sales cycle, and grow the overall enterprise sales channel. I inform and advise management on current business trends, risks, and opportunities.

Darrious Duffin

Describe how you got your job. During my senior year in college, I had an internship with Ritter Communications. Through my internship, I was part of a sales-strategy team that bid on two multi-million-dollar opportunities to provide data service. Although I wasn't the one who closed the deal, the team recognized me as a young, eager, and driven student whose talents and personality aligned with the needs of the company. Five years later, I have been afforded the opportunity to learn and grow my skill set in a variety of ways. I'm happy to still call Ritter Communications home.

What has been most important in making you successful at your job? I've benefited from several opportunities to grow my business acumen and put my education to work, but my people skills have also been vital to my success. We are an extremely team-oriented company. I try to be open to new ideas and learn from others. I work very closely with people who identify the same goals and finish line but have different ideas on how to get there. I have the ability to adapt to new situations and find common ground with people to achieve an objective.

What advice would you give future graduates about a career in sales? Don't focus on finding the perfect job. Pay, location, and job responsibilities are unlikely to be glamorous at first. Focus on landing a sales job with a company that will allow you to test your abilities, expose you to all parts of the business, and most important, make mistakes. With humility, realize you must start at the bottom and will hear a lot of no's that first year. Your first professional sales opportunity will springboard you into many other ones if you are doing the right things. My biggest advice would be: don't get discouraged—you are likely to find an exciting and rewarding career in sales if that is where your passion is.

What is the most important characteristic of a great salesperson? I think great salespeople help leaders understand problems and possible routes to be successful in a positive and honest way. While I'm invested in my own career, the success of those I work with is even more important than that of my own. I was trained to be service minded, and I try to provide information and options to my clients. I've worked to develop winning strategies that benefit employees and customers, and I was raised to be humble and never forget where I came from. I'm very team oriented, and I want those around me to enjoy working with me. I think focusing on client problems and being someone others want to work with has helped me to be respected. I want to be a great salesperson who consistently uses my talent, experiences, and the lessons I have learned to make a difference in the lives of others.

CHAPTER SUMMARY

LO 2-1 Describe the importance of prospecting, the challenges associated with prospecting, and why many salespeople are hesitant to prospect.

Prospecting is the lifeblood of the organization; it provides a continuous flow of new customers and new business opportunities. Without the customer, there is no need for the organization. Salespeople must prospect on a regular basis to offset customer attrition.

That said, prospecting is one of the more challenging tasks of salespeople. Buyers are often resistant when approached by salespeople they do not currently purchase from. The rejection rates typically experienced when prospecting can be quite high. Because of this, many salespeople are hesitant to prospect. They view prospecting as an inefficient activity in relation to those activities that are focused on retaining current customers and may even avoid prospecting due to a fear of rejection.

LO 2-2 Contrast the hunting and farming sales orientations, and explain the role inside sales can play in prospecting.

There has been a growing realization that salespeople should focus on those activities they are most proficient at to enhance organizational effectiveness and efficiency. The hunting and farming sales orientations capture this: Salespeople who have a *hunting* orientation excel at identifying and engaging new business; those salespeople who have a *farming* orientation are more adept at managing existing relationships.

Many firms are acting on information about salespersons' individual strengths by developing both inside and outside sales forces. Inside salespeople interact with the customer only remotely, through phone, email, text, social media, the internet, or some other form of remote technology. Often, inside salespeople handle the initial steps contained within the prospecting process, eventually handing a qualified prospect off to an outside salesperson. Inside salespeople, who often are new hires, may also be referred to as sales-development representatives.

LO 2-3 List the steps in the prospecting process and the necessary requirements for a lead to be qualified as a prospect.

The prospecting process should be thought of as a funnel consisting of the following steps: (1) lead generation, (2) lead prioritization, (3) lead qualification, (4) prospect prioritization, and (5) sales-call planning. The number of leads and/or prospects dwindles as salespeople successively move through each step.

The lead-qualification process is perhaps the most important step in the prospecting process; it differentiates leads from prospects and ensures that salespeople maximize their prospecting efficiency by focusing on the right customers. For a lead to be qualified as a prospect, salespeople must be able to determine that the lead has: a need for the product or service; the authority to purchase; the ability to purchase; the potential needed to justify an organizational investment; and a buying approach that aligns with the company's selling approach.

LO 2-4 List common lead-generation methods.

Because the prospecting process begins with lead generation, salespeople need to understand the different lead-generation methods. Popular lead-generation methods are virtual networking, traditional networking, referrals, trade shows, cold-calling, websites, sales directories, centers of influence, noncompeting salespeople, and marketing.

Of these, virtual networking has exploded in popularity in recent years due to the rise in use of social media. Further, the marketing department often assumes the responsibility of generating sales leads through use of one or more of the methods presented in the chapter. There is a need for marketing and sales to have a strong relationship within the organization and for salespeople to act on the leads their marketing counterparts provide them.

LO 2-5 Explain the activities involved in formulating a prospecting strategy.

Prospecting success requires a strategy. There are four key activities when formulating an overall prospecting strategy: (1) develop a prospecting plan; (2) allocate adequate time to prospecting; (3) track the results; and (4) evaluate the effectiveness and efficiency of the different prospecting activities. Finally, and critically, salespeople must also work to maintain a positive attitude as they prospect for new business, given the challenges prospecting can present.

LO 2-6 Explain the importance of salesperson ethics in prospecting for new customers.

Ethical salesperson behavior is prerequisite for the development of any customer relationship, including during the prospecting process. If prospects have any questions regarding the ethics of a salesperson in their initial interactions with the salesperson, they will not willingly enter into a relationship with the salesperson. When prospecting, ethical salespeople will only: (1) Attempt to sell their product or service if a need truly exists. (2) Be factual in their communications regarding what the salesperson and selling firm can provide. (3) Be factual in their communications related to the competition. (4) Use referrals in the manner intended by the referring customers.

KEY TERMS

prospecting (p. 24)
quota (p. 24)
opportunity costs (p. 25)
call reluctance (p. 26)
hunting orientation (p. 27)
farming orientation (p. 27)
inside salespeople (p. 27)
sales-development representatives (p. 28)

lead (p. 30)
inbound leads (p. 30)
outbound leads (p. 30)
hot lead (p. 30)
cold lead (p. 30)
lead qualification (p. 30)
prospect (p. 30)
prospect prioritization (p. 32)
ideal customer profile (p. 32)

networking (p. 34)
virtual networking (p. 34)
social selling (p. 35)
traditional networking (p. 35)
referral (p. 35)
trade shows (p. 36)
cold-call (p. 36)
sales directories (p. 37)
center of influence (p. 37)

DISCUSSION QUESTIONS

1. Prospecting can be a challenging activity in sales because of the high rejection rates salespeople experience when prospecting. Think of instances when you have experienced rejection in your life. How were you able to overcome this rejection? How might the lessons you learned through these experiences benefit you if dealing with rejection in a sales role?

2. We differentiate the hunting and farming orientations in the chapter. Considering how these orientations were described, do you think that you have more of a hunting orientation or a farming orientation? Why do you feel this way? What specific characteristics do you possess that would cause your thinking on this issue?

3. If you were to begin a career in sales following graduation, what benefits would you see in starting in an inside sales position? How might experiences gained in this position benefit you in the future?

4. Think about some of the things you are currently doing to build your network via social media. Might you be able to do some of these same things if you were attempting to build a virtual network in a sales role? Which virtual-networking activities can be applied in both your personal and professional life? Conversely, are there some things you do when building your personal network via social media that should be avoided when building a professional network? If so, why?

ETHICAL CHALLENGE

Although not as popular as it once was as a lead-generation method, many firms still use cold-calling when prospecting for new customers. While some business customers are accepting of unsolicited sales calls, such calls are a source of immense frustration for consumers. Because of this, the Federal Trade Commission (FTC) amended the Telemarketing Sales Rule (TSR) in 2003 and created a Do Not Call Registry.[8] Although that registry now includes nearly 230 million telephone numbers,[9] illegal robocalls remain a problem. They constantly disturb consumers' privacy and are frequently used to deceive and defraud consumers.[10] In fact, in 2017 alone, the FTC received more than 4.5 million robocall complaints.[11]

Alliance Security (www.alliancesecurity.com) has been a particularly egregious perpetrator. The company, which installs home-security systems, cold-calls when prospecting for customers of the systems and associated monitoring services. The FTC recently filed a complaint alleging that since 2014 Alliance has made or helped others make at least two million cold-calls that violate the TSR, including more than a million calls to numbers on the Do Not Call Registry.[12] Some consumers were reportedly so frustrated by the volume of calls that they scheduled an installation just to plead in person for the calls to stop.[13]

Questions

1. Clearly, the decision by Alliance and its leadership team to prospect in this manner represents a serious ethical breach. That cannot be debated. Why, though, would Alliance do this? What do you think would cause a company to act so egregiously?

2. How does it make you feel about the company? How would you react if a company were treating you in that manner? Would you ever purchase from the company?

ROLE PLAY

While role plays are critical in helping you develop your sales skills, understand that simply having someone assigned to you as a customer in a role play is not realistic. Instead, in real life, you will prospect in order to find customers. This is often the greatest challenge salespeople face. Indeed, the success rates most achieve when prospecting are much lower than the success rates typically seen on actual sales calls.

This role play exercise will give you an opportunity to practice cold-calling skills. For the role play, you will be able to set the scenario. You should select the company that you are representing and the company and individual you are cold-calling. The class should be divided into teams of three. Each student within each team should first develop a cold-calling script that he or she will use during the role play. Your script should:

1. Identify the salesperson and the selling firm.
2. Establish initial rapport.
3. Provide a value statement to motivate interest.
4. Be customer-oriented.
5. Respectfully request action on the part of the prospect.

An example of a script is shown below. Numbers correlating with each of the criterion listed above indicate where that criterion is met.

SAMPLE PROSPECTING SCRIPT

Hi [Prospect Name], my name is [Seller Name]. I am a local representative with the [Seller Company] **[1]**. *How are you today?* **[2]**

Great, I was referred to you by John Doe at the XYZ Corporation. John and I have been working together for a number of years, and he suggested you as someone who might benefit from the types of products and services we provide **[3]**. *Do you have a few moments to spare?*

Thanks. I know you are busy so I will be sure to respect your time.

First, rest assured that my intent in this conversation is not to sell you anything. What I would like to do, with your permission, is set up a meeting to see if there might be some level of fit between our companies, and to see if we might be able to help you address some of the issues you face **[4]**. *For example, John has told me time and again that one of his goals as a retail buyer is to increase sales, and over the past two years we have generated approximately two million dollars in additional sales at his account* **[3]**. *Again, however, my goal for this meeting would simply be to determine whether a fit exists between our companies. I will not attempt to sell you anything. Such meetings usually last 30 minutes. Might there be a time that works well for you?* **[5]**

For each of the role plays, one student acts as the seller, another acts as the prospect, and the third critiques both the script and the quality with which it was delivered. Students should exchange roles for each successive role play.

SALES PRESENTATION

For the Connect assignment in Chapter 2, students will get practice prospecting for companies who might purchase a product or service they currently use.

First, think of a product or service you use on a regular basis. Next, use one of the lead-generation methods presented in the chapter to develop a list of at least five companies that would potentially benefit from the product or service. Most of you will probably use social media or the web to generate the list.

You should be prepared to discuss exactly how you conducted your research and what organizational characteristics were important in leads being included on your list.

CAREER TIPS

John Hansen

John Hansen
Marketing Professor
University of Alabama—Birmingham

How Much Prospecting Will I Do?

Although you may not know it yet, many of you will accept jobs in sales following graduation. While the goal is to have multiple job offers from which you can choose, deciding between sales jobs can be difficult. There are many factors to consider, including one that is the focus of this chapter—the amount of prospecting that will be required.

Most outside sales roles require territory management, where the salesperson manages customer relationships within a given geographic territory. When examining job opportunities, it is important you know how much prospecting is going to be required in a territory. In some instances, a territory will have a strong "book of business"—an existing set of established customer relationships. In other cases, there may be very few existing relationships within the territory. Obviously, if you acquire a territory where this is the case, you are going to have to prospect for new business in order to grow the territory. Although you will likely have prospecting goals in an established territory as well, you are likely to spend more time managing relationships that have previously been established.

Is one type of territory better than the other? Not necessarily, although most graduates would prefer to step into a situation in which they are working with existing customers. That said, and as was discussed in the chapter, the key lies in knowing who you are: What do you excel at? What do you need to improve upon? If you excel at activities that require a farming orientation, you would be better served in a territory that has an established book of business. Conversely, if you exhibit characteristics that align with a hunting orientation, you may excel in a territory that requires a great deal of prospecting.

Because this is an important decision, you should also talk with your professors, as they will able to provide additional insight based on their knowledge of the hiring company.

CHAPTER ENDNOTES

1. T. E. DeCarlo and S. K. Lam, "Identifying effective hunters and farmers in the sales force: A dispositional–situational framework," *Journal of the Academy of Marketing Science* 44, no. 4 (2016.): 415–439.
2. M. Mayberry, "The amazing evolution and power of inside sales," *Entrepreneur* (2015).
3. M. Ahearne and A. Rapp, "The role of technology at the interface between salespeople and consumers," *Journal of Personal Selling & Sales Management* 30, no. 2 (2010): 109–118.
4. J. M. Andzulis, N. G. Panagopoulos, and A. Rapp, "A review of social media and implications for the sales process," *Journal of Personal Selling & Sales Management* 32, no. 3 (2015): 305–316.
5. K. J. Trainor, et al., "Social media technology usage and customer relationship performance: A capabilities–based examination of social CRM," *Journal of Business Research* 67, no. 6 (2014): 1201–1208.
6. P. Kotler, N. Rackham, and S. Krishnaswamy, "Ending the war between sales and marketing," *Harvard Business Review* 84 (July 2006): 68–78.
7. D. Rouziés, et al., "Sales and marketing integration: A proposed framework," *Journal of Personal Selling & Sales Management* 25, no. 2 (2005): 113–122.
8. L. Greisman, "Abusive robocalls and how we can stop them," in *United States Senate Committee on Commerce, Science and Transportation,* 2018.
9. *Do not call registry data book 2017: Who is using the do not call registry.* 2017.
10. L. Greisman, "Abusive robocalls and how we can stop them," in *United States Senate Committee on Commerce, Science and Transportation,* 2018.
11. *Do not call registry data book 2017: Who is using the do not call registry.* 2017.
12. Federal Trade Commission, *FTC charges recidivist telemarketer for millions of illegal calls pitching home security systems and monitoring services to consumers* (2018).
13. Ibid.

Design elements: Marketing Insights Podcast: vandame/Shutterstock

Chapter 3

Engaging Customers and Developing Relationships

Learning Objectives

After reading this chapter, you should be able to:

LO 3-1 Explain the importance of trust in a relationship selling approach.

LO 3-2 Explain what customer engagement is and how technology is affecting the way salespeople and customers interact.

LO 3-3 Describe how different purchase types affect the buying team and decision-making process.

LO 3-4 Summarize differences in customer relationships based on relationship level, relationship type, and customer-relationship life cycle.

LO 3-5 Explain the importance of trust and the role character and competence play in establishing trust.

LO 3-6 Summarize the importance of ethics and the challenges associated with salesperson ethics.

Executive Perspective ... because everyone is a salesperson

Zach King
District Sales Manager
Fastenal

Zach King

Describe your job.

As a district sales manager at Fastenal, an industrial supply company that sells an array of products and seeks to help customers streamline their supply chain operations, I wear many hats, but the most important are hiring the right applicants and putting them in the right spot to grow. To me, growth has three aspects: monetary income, career pathway, and taking market share. I'm also responsible for teaching my team how to manage a business for maximum profitability as well as executing sales strategies.

How did you get your job?

Throughout its history, Fastenal has proved that it will reward employees who take ownership of a job. I was very green early in my career as a sales associate, but the company gave me the training as well as leadership I needed to succeed. I proved I could develop my employees so they could advance in their career pathways, hit the KPIs (key performance indicators) set by management, and be innovative about how my business unit went to market. Achieving these goals gave me the opportunity to become a district manager (DM), in the hope that I could take that same approach with multiple business units.

What has been most important in making you successful at your job?

Understanding early on that success is not just about me—it's about the people who surround me in each business unit. The most important part of my job is finding and hiring the best person for the job. As a DM, you have to trust employees to make decisions that ultimately help our organization. Recruiting at local universities is key. Each employee is a reflection of my values and of the market we serve.

Please discuss the importance of customer relationships at Fastenal.

With over 2,100 public stores and 900 onsites (physically located within the customer's site), we are able to get closer to our customers than most competitors are. When I hire the right team member for a market, it's amazing how fast our customers start to buy into what we are selling.

What role does trust play in these relationships?

At the end of the day, our customers want to buy from good people whom they can trust to take care of their supply chain. In most cases we are managing thousands of parts for a customer on any given day. Our customers trust us to make sure that parts are there when they need them, whether it is a maintenance-related item or a production-related item. It can take months, if not years, to build trust with some customers. I teach my team members that 99 percent of the problems in our business happen if we didn't do what we said we were going to do. You may get only one shot to break through for a customer. It can be the start of something great, or it can crash and burn.

We hear a lot about ethics in sales. Why is ethical behavior so important in sales today?

As a sales rep, you never want a customer to question your integrity or professionalism. That can destroy any momentum you may have built in a market. Doing the right thing when nobody is watching is a trait I always try to find in my team members. Are they making as many calls as they can per day? Do they understand the product and solutions that they are selling? Are they a great representation of their store, myself, and Fastenal?

What, in your opinion, are the top three things customers desire out of their relationships with Fastenal?

- A sales rep who continuously brings solutions that help drive cost savings in the customer's supply chain.
- The best TCO (total cost of ownership) on the products they are procuring.
- Bringing in vendors who can introduce new products and services that make their products or distribution more efficient.

What advice would you give future graduates about a career in sales?

Start networking immediately! At career fairs I often meet people who have already graduated. Many tell me they never went to career fairs during school, nor did they network when they saw employers recruiting on campus. The longer you wait, the longer it takes for you to find a company that fits your values.

What is the most important characteristic of a great salesperson?

I push my sales team to understand the customer *prior* to the sales call. This helps us understand which solution fits the customer. It also allows us to close the sales cycle much faster. The best salespeople understand this and are always at the top when it comes to KPI metrics.

RELATIONSHIP SELLING

LO 3-1 Explain the importance of trust in a relationship selling approach.

relationship selling
A sales approach that involves building and maintaining customer trust over a long period of time.

As discussed in Chapter 1, we have entered a new era in sales—one in which the focus has shifted from singular customer transactions to long-term customer relationships. Many organizations have adopted **relationship selling**, a sales approach whose primary strategy is building and maintaining customer trust over a long period of time. In this approach, salespeople are responsible for guiding customers through the relationship-development process. Their personal interactions and ongoing efforts to build and maintain the relationship largely determine the level of value and the satisfaction provided the customer.

Relationship selling is a worthy goal, though salespeople and selling firms often fall short of achieving it. Examples of those who do things that jeopardize their customer relationships are far too common. One such example involves Pilot Flying J, the largest operator of travel centers in North America, with more than 750 locations in 44 states and 6 Canadian provinces (www.pilotflyingj.com). The company sells over a billion gallons of fuel on an annual basis, managing relationships with a large number of trucking firms.

However, in a highly publicized case, the FBI accused numerous Pilot Flying J employees of engaging in a scheme to withhold customers' rebates and discounts in order to enhance company profitability and increase individual sales commissions. The investigation began when FBI agents learned that Brian Mosher, director of sales for national accounts at Pilot Flying J, had advised salespeople to target customers too unsophisticated to realize that their rebates were incorrect. When learning of the salespeople alleged by the FBI to have been involved in the scheme, Paul Weick, president and CEO of one such customer, Western Express, noted, "A lot of those folks that are mentioned in the affidavit are people that I know, that I trusted."[1]

trust
The belief that another person will act with integrity on a reliable basis.

Can you blame a customer for responding this way? Would you feel the same way? Moreover, would you ever want to work with, much less partner with, the company again? Most of us would say no; actions like those in the Pilot Flying J example cut at the core of any relationship. They violate our **trust**, or our belief that another person will act with integrity on a reliable basis. Without trust, there can be no relationship. Trust provides the necessary foundation for our personal and business relationships.

Salespeople place their customer relationships at risk when they engage in behaviors that undermine trust. These behaviors often have disastrous consequences. In all, investigators estimated that the scheme cost Pilot Flying J customers $56.5 million in rebate payouts and resulted in guilty pleas or convictions for 17 former employees. Company leadership ultimately confessed criminal responsibility and agreed to pay $92 million in criminal penalties and $85 million in civil settlements. It is difficult to monetize the true harm done to the company's customer relationships.[2]

It's tempting to focus on companies and salespeople who have done the wrong things. In fact, though, there are many more salespeople out there doing the right things. These salespeople understand how important trust is and how critical it is to their success. In sales today, given the focus on relationship selling, it is impossible to succeed if your customers do not feel they can trust you. Trust is an imperative; it must be there for the relationship to develop and ultimately endure.

In this chapter, we focus on how salespeople establish trust and build customer relationships. The first step is to engage customers by understanding their unique purchasing processes. Throughout the selling process, displays of competence and ethics from salespeople will result in customer trust and long-term relationships.

ENGAGING CUSTOMERS

Customer engagement refers to the connection that exists between the salesperson, the selling firm, and the customer. This connection is a necessary starting point in developing a relationship. To engage with customers, salespeople must align their selling processes to their customers' purchasing preferences. In other words, salespeople must sell in a manner that is consistent with how their customers want to buy.

Selling firms have come to realize that customers are changing the way they interact with salespeople. In years past, firms have focused on their own selling processes and ways through which they can optimize these processes. Today, firms are now focused on better aligning *their* sales processes with *customers'* purchasing processes. Technology has been a major contributor to this change, particularly as it relates to when and how the customer and salesperson first interact.

Historically, salespeople have been involved in their customers' purchasing processes from the onset. The salesperson was the primary provider of information required to begin the process. This is no longer the case. Today, customers do much of their initial search electronically. Think of the number of items you've researched online for just your own buying needs. Then imagine the number of individuals and firms doing the same for their purchasing needs. Buyers are making decisions regarding which potential suppliers they are interested in, often unbeknownst to the suppliers.

This digital-search behavior presents challenges and opportunities from a selling perspective. Many customers engage salespeople and selling firms much later in their purchasing process. They gather information on their own via the internet and bring in a select group of potential suppliers based on the information they gather. In some instances, potential suppliers are eliminated from contention without so much as a conversation. In others, suppliers have seen significant success based on their ability to provide the type of information desired by the customer early in the sales process. Many suppliers have also come to rely more heavily on inside sales forces for this purpose. Providing information for online search will continue to be an area of focus for selling firms and salespeople in the years to come.

In addition to differences in their purchasing-process preferences, customers will also differ in the decision-making processes they employ, based on the type of purchase situation they are confronting. For example, a customer who is confronting a decision that will have a significant impact on the organization is more likely to employ an extended decision-making process. Doing so lessens the risks associated with the purchase. In contrast, a customer who is confronting a routine decision with minimal consequences will typically employ an abbreviated decision-making process. It is important for salespeople to understand the decision-making process being used when deciding how to best interact with the customer.

Sales success is partly predicated on the salesperson's ability to make the purchasing process as easy and convenient as possible for the customer. Salespeople who are adept at engaging with customers via technology will have a tremendous advantage over those who are not. Thus, salespeople must understand the dynamics underlying their customers' purchase situations. Accordingly, in the sections that follow, we delve more deeply into each of the following issues:

- What type of purchase is being made?
- Who will be involved in the purchasing decision?
- How will the customer make the decision?

LO 3-2

Explain what customer engagement is and how technology is affecting the way salespeople and customers interact.

customer engagement
The connection that exists between the salesperson, the selling firm, and the customer.

DIFFERENT PURCHASE TYPES

LO 3-3 Describe how different purchase types affect the buying team and decision-making process.

In your personal experience, you know that not all purchases are the same; the way you buy a gallon of milk is quite different from how you buy a smartphone. So, too, do situational differences drive variations in terms of how customers approach purchases. Customer purchases can be thought of as existing on a continuum, as shown in Figure 3-1. *New-task purchases* and *straight-rebuy purchases* anchor either end, with *modified-rebuy purchases* somewhere in the middle. We differentiate these three purchase types in this section.

New-Task Purchases

As the name suggests, **new-task purchases** are new to the purchasing organization. Because of this, the customer has no history to draw from when making the decision. New-task purchases require a significant amount of time and energy on the part of the customer. In these situations:

- The level of importance associated with the purchase is high.
- The information needs for the customer are high.
- The dollar volume associated with the purchase may be high.
- Many participants may be involved in the purchase decision.
- There is an extended timeline.

new-task purchases Purchases that are new to the purchasing organization, typically involving high information needs, a high number of purchasing participants, and an extended timeline.

Given these dynamics, there are often many people involved on the selling side when the customer is facing a new-task purchase.

An extreme example of a new-task purchase can be seen through the Mine-Resistant Ambush Protected (MRAP) program launched by the U.S. Department of Defense (DOD) in 2007. The program was initiated in response to the high number of casualties resulting from improvised explosive device (IED) attacks during the Iraq War. The goal of the program was the development of light tactical vehicles capable of withstanding the effects of these IED attacks. Specifically, MRAP vehicles employed V-shaped hulls designed to deflect explosive forces emanating from IEDs detonated below the vehicle, thereby protecting passengers. Ultimately, the MRAP program deployed approximately 24,000 vehicles in Iraq and Afghanistan, with an average approximate cost of $1,000,000 per vehicle.[3]

The MRAP program highlights all the characteristics typically associated with a new task purchase:

- It is hard to quantify the importance of the program; in Iraq alone, 63 percent of all casualties between 2003 and 2007 were attributable to IEDs.[4] In response, Secretary of Defense Robert Gates noted in 2007 that the acquisition of MRAPs was the DOD's highest priority.[5]

FIGURE 3-1 Types of Customer Purchases and Their Characteristics

New-Task Purchase	Straight-Rebuy	Modified-Rebuy
• No history • High importance • High information needs • High dollar volume • High number of purchasing participants • Extended timeline	• Significant history • Low information needs • Less important • Lesser dollar volumes • Low number of purchasing participants • Short timeline	• Some history • Moderate information needs • Varying importance • Moderate dollar volume • Moderate timeline • Varying number of purchasing participants

- The information needs associated with the purchase were quite high given this importance and the implementation of new, blast-deflecting technologies.
- The program was incredibly expensive, with a price tag ultimately estimated at $50 billion.[6]
- There were thousands of civilian and military personnel involved in the project, with a total of nine firms submitting formal bids.
- Even though every effort was made to hasten the delivery of the new vehicles, a decision of this magnitude required an extended timeline.

Terry Moore/Stocktrek Images/Getty Images

Although the project had its detractors, it was estimated to have reduced casualties by 30 percent between 2000 and 2010, saving thousands of lives. Incredibly, in 2011, the Pentagon estimated that the MRAP program had ultimately saved 40,000 lives.[7]

Straight-Rebuy Purchases

In contrast, **straight-rebuy purchases** are purchases the customer makes on a frequent basis. The customer has a significant history to rely upon for these purchases. In fact, in many cases, there is no formal decision to be made. In these situations:

- The information needs for the customer are low.
- The decisions are less important.
- The dollar volumes associated with individual purchases are typically low.
- Very few participants are involved in the purchase decision.
- The timeline is short and little energy is required.

straight-rebuy purchases
Purchases the customer makes on a frequent basis, involving low information needs and a short timeline.

Straight-rebuy purchases are often automated based on parameters agreed upon between the buyer and the seller. A subscription for monthly coffee delivery by mail is an example: the seller will send the buyer the same order each month unless the buyer changes the order.

Electronic data interchange (EDI) provides a mechanism through which many straight-rebuy purchases are transacted, especially in B2B settings. **EDI** is a technology designed to integrate the computer systems of supplier and buyer firms, allowing for the accurate and reliable exchange of data between the firms. For example, in situations where manufacturers sell to retailers, EDI allows for automated ordering with the goals of enhanced communications, more accurate accounting, better inventory management, and reduced cost. In many instances, EDI eliminates the need for human interaction in the transaction. Instead, the entire process is automated, thereby allowing for enhanced efficiencies.

electronic data interchange (EDI)
A technology designed to integrate the computer systems of supplier and buyer firms.

Modified-Rebuy Purchases

Modified-rebuy purchases combine elements of both new-task purchases and straight-rebuy purchases. In these situations:

- The information needs for a modified-rebuy purchase are not as high as they are for a new-task purchase. There is some history for the customer to rely upon when making the purchase.
- As is seen with new-task purchases, modified-rebuys are often important purchases for the organization.
- The dollar volume can range from moderate to high.
- The timeline is moderate, though many participants can be involved.

modified-rebuy purchases
Purchases that combine elements of both new-task purchases and straight-rebuy purchases, involving moderate information needs, a moderate timeline, and moderate dollar volume.

An example of a modified-rebuy purchase can be seen in what are called *line reviews* that retailers conduct with their suppliers. Typically, straight-rebuy purchases are used to handle the daily transactions between a supplier and a retailer. Once a year, retailers will engage in a formal *line review* to decide which products they will regularly stock in the coming year. In doing so, retailers will typically examine the history for that product category over the previous year. A formal line review differs from the automated orders that are handled through straight rebuys; the consequences associated with decisions made during the line review are more consequential. In the modified-rebuy purchase that results from the line review, there is a heightened sense of importance, there are more individuals involved in the decision, and the dollar volumes can be significant because the decision is implemented for an extended period of time.

How Purchase Types Affect Buying Teams

Much as salespeople need to understand the type of decision facing the customer, they also need to know who will be involved in the decision process. Experienced salespeople will tell you that few things are more frustrating than to find out late in the sales process that the person with whom you have been communicating does not have the authority to make the decision. Whenever this occurs, the salesperson must go back and ask questions to determine which individuals the buying team comprises. This is particularly important: In sales today, **buying teams**—groups of individuals who ultimately have a voice in the purchase decision—have become increasingly common. Often, multiple individuals will represent the selling organization as well, typically led by the salesperson who manages the account.

In some instances, formal titles will dictate the purchasing role assumed by an individual. For example, the salesperson will spend significant time dealing with the *buyer* or *purchasing agent*. However, it can be difficult to know exactly what role an individual is playing based on title alone. For instance, it could be that someone who will be using the product in the production process has tremendous say in the final decision but is not in a "formal" position in which that influence would be obvious. It is therefore important for salespeople to ask questions about the decision-making process within the organization, to better understand who is involved and in what role.

Buying teams have historically been examined in terms of five different types of individuals: initiators, users, influencers, deciders, and purchasers. We'll look at each briefly.

buying teams
Groups of individuals who ultimately have a voice in the purchase decision.

initiator
The individual or group of individuals on a buying team who first recognizes the customer's need.

Monkey Business Images/Shutterstock

Initiator The **initiator** is the individual or group of individuals who first recognizes the customer's need. This could be an employee who uses a product in the production process and recognizes a shortcoming. Or it could be a frontline employee who interacts with customers on a regular basis and learns from conversations with customers of a need not being addressed.

Regardless of how the need surfaces, the initiator is very important in the purchase process. Recognizing a need, the initiator sets in motion the search for potential solutions. It is important the salesperson knows who the initiator is, as he or she will often serve as a champion for the salesperson as the sales process unfolds.

Product User As you might expect, initiators frequently also are **product users**—individuals who use the product or service in their daily activities. For instance, if your university was considering the adoption of new classroom technology, it would likely form a committee of faculty (and maybe students) for discussion on the needs that must be addressed in purchasing the new technology. Users often focus on the functionality of the offering, as this is important to them in their role.

> **product users**
> Individuals on a buying team who use the product or service in their daily activities; because of their involvement, they often focus on product functionality.

Influencer Consistent with the name, **influencers** help determine the priorities to be addressed when making the purchase decision and express their opinions regarding potential solutions. These individuals play an important role in the customer decision-making process. In some instances, influencers affect the final purchase decision. In others, they may affect some facet of the purchase decision.

For instance, in retail and wholesale sales situations it is common to interact with both a buyer and an inventory manager. While the *buyer* will make decisions about what products are being stocked (what will be purchased), the *inventory manager* will have influence over inventory levels. In such situations, the salesperson would need to work not only with the buyer but also with the inventory manager to determine acceptable order quantities. Therefore, as is the case with initiators, it is very important the salesperson understand who the influencers are; their voices are pivotal in determining what the customer ultimately decides to do.

> **influencers**
> Individuals on a buying team who help determine the priorities to be addressed when making the purchase decision and express their opinions regarding potential solutions.

Decider **Deciders** make the *actual choice* of a product or service for purchase, although they typically rely on other individuals on the buying team when making their decision. The title of this individual within the buying organization is typically a function of purchase importance. For instance, in new-task purchase situations, the CEO may assume responsibility for the decision. For straight-rebuy purchase situations, a purchasing agent or buyer may be the final decision maker. Regardless, it is extremely important the salesperson understand who this person is, given the authority the decider has over the final decision.

> **deciders**
> Individuals on a buying team who make the *actual choice* of a product or service for purchase.

Purchaser **Purchasers** are individuals within the buying organization who negotiate final terms and make the actual purchase. These individuals interact with salespeople on a regular basis. In some instances, particularly when purchasing items of low importance, the same person might be both decision maker and purchaser.

Purchasers may also assume other roles on the buying team. For instance, the decider may consult with the purchaser to better understand which of the potential selling companies is easiest to work with from a purchasing perspective. Because of the possible mashup of roles, it is important the salesperson understand exactly how the purchasing process unfolds in the buying organization, to help the purchaser make the process as easy as possible.

> **purchasers**
> Individuals within the buying organization who negotiate final terms and make the actual purchase.

Gatekeeper Last, **gatekeepers** control access to the buying-team members and have influence over the communication the salesperson is able to have with these members. The gatekeeper is typically not a formal member of the buying team.

Historically, the gatekeeper has been someone who serves in an administrative-assistant-type position. In many instances today, technology now serves the gatekeeper role. For example, many individuals screen communications that come in via email or phone message. Salespeople often have to communicate with buying-team members via technology, and in some instances the technology serves as a gatekeeper, preventing full access for the salesperson. Because of this, salespeople must be adept at developing communications that spark an interest among members of the buying team, motivating them to engage.

> **gatekeepers**
> Individuals within the buying organization who control access to the buying-team members; typically not part of the buying team.

How Purchase Types Affect Decision Making

Just as purchase type affects the composition of the buying team, so too will it affect the extensiveness of the decision-making process. A typical five-step decision-making model is presented in Figure 3-2. Salespeople who understand the decision-making process being employed will be able to use strategies at each step within the process to help educate the customer and ensure success.

problem recognition
Phase of the decision-making process in which the customer first recognizes a need.

latent needs
Needs that are undetected or of which the customer is unaware.

Problem Recognition
The customer first recognizes a need during **problem recognition**, which occurs when a customer recognizes that a need or problem exists. Often, the salesperson identifies **latent needs**—that is, needs that are undetected or of which the customer is unaware—and brings them to the attention of the customer. In some instances the salesperson may even challenge the customer on the problems associated with accepting the status quo (that is, doing nothing). Once the problem is identified, the customer will assemble an appropriate buying team based on the magnitude and scope of the issue.

information search
Phase of the decision-making process in which the customer gathers information and identifies potential suppliers.

Information Search
The customer gathers information and identifies potential suppliers during an **information search**. In this step, the customer will gain focus on the actual nature of the problem and the requirements that must be fulfilled in a solution. This step has historically required assistance from salespeople; customers are now able to gather a great deal of information on their own via the internet. The salesperson needs to stay engaged with the customer, though, to ensure that the customer is receiving the appropriate information needed to make a decision.

evaluation of alternatives
Phase of the decision-making process in which the customer assesses the competing solutions, weighing their decisions based on criteria that are most important in the decision.

Evaluation of Alternatives
During the **evaluation of alternatives**, the customer assesses the competing solutions. In most instances, customers will weight their decisions based on those criteria that are most important in their decision. The salesperson must therefore assist the customer in developing these weights to ensure that the right factors receive an appropriate level of attention. Where appropriate, the salesperson may suggest that additional criteria be considered as well.

Once the weights are established, the customer will rank the competing solutions on the varying criteria to determine which perform best. Here again, the salesperson should work to educate the customer to ensure accurate perceptual assessments.

supplier-solution decision
Phase of the decision-making process in which the customer actually chooses a vendor from which to buy.

Supplier-Solution Decision
With the results of the evaluation of alternatives in hand, the customer will make a **supplier-solution decision**. As the name suggests, at this point in the decision-making process the customer actually chooses a vendor from which to buy. This step represents a significant shift for the salesperson: the focus shifts from which solution will be chosen to how the solution will be implemented. The purchaser for the customer will work closely with the salesperson to ensure a seamless purchasing process. The scope of this process will be determined by the magnitude of the purchase.

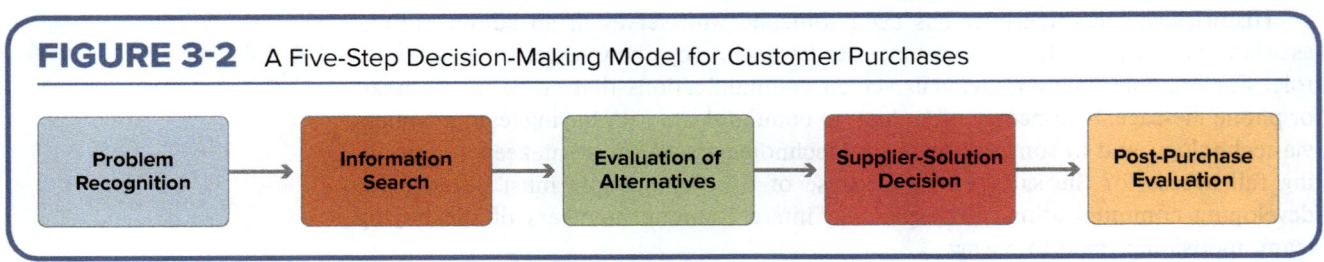

FIGURE 3-2 A Five-Step Decision-Making Model for Customer Purchases

Post-Purchase Evaluation Finally, when the solution has been implemented, the customer will engage in some form of **post-purchase evaluation**. Here, the customer assesses how well the solution-implementation process promised by the salesperson and selling firm actually unfolded.

Interestingly, research suggests that when conducting this evaluation, customers differentiate the *core offering* (the actual product or service purchased) from the *service offering* provided by the vendor.[8] While the core offering addresses the functionality and performance of the product or service that was purchased, the service offering addresses the intangible elements, such as responsiveness and communication, that determine the customer's overall satisfaction. In most instances, the salesperson is responsible for the service offering. Remarkably, research indicates that 61 percent of the variance seen in customers' post-purchase satisfaction assessments is attributable to the service offering.[9] The remaining 39 percent is a function of the core offering. This finding once again highlights the important role salespeople play in ensuring customer satisfaction.

> **post-purchase evaluation**
> Phase of the decision-making process in which the customer assesses how well the solution-implementation process promised by the salesperson and selling firm actually unfolded.

---

connect Assignment 3-1

Purchase Types

Please complete the Connect exercise for Chapter 3 that focuses on different purchase types. Understanding the purchase types and how they affect the buying team will help you develop the best sales strategy for different situations.

DIFFERENCES IN CUSTOMER RELATIONSHIPS

Selling firms desire mutually beneficial, long-term customer relationships. They expect their salespeople to establish, develop, and maintain such relationships. This is no easy task: Salespeople must provide their customers with a reason to enter into and remain in a relationship. It is therefore important that salespeople understand what the relationship means to the customer and what will motivate the customer to remain in the relationship. For a 360-degree perspective of customer relationships, we can look at them based on relationship level, relationship type, and relationship life-cycle phase.

> **LO 3-4**
> Summarize differences in customer relationships based on relationship level, relationship type, and customer-relationship life cycle.

Differences Based on Relationship Level

First, it is important to note that customers differentiate the relationship they have with the salesperson from the relationship they have with the selling firm. Sometimes the customer has similar feelings toward the salesperson and the selling firm, but this is not always the case. In some situations the customer has a strong relationship with the salesperson but not the selling firm, or vice versa.

What happens in these situations? Will the customer remain in the relationship if he or she feels strongly about the salesperson but not the selling firm? Or will the customer instead focus more on the selling firm as a whole and look for another selling firm (and salesperson)? Obviously, answers to these questions may differ based on context. Research examining this issue has found that most customers believe the salesperson relationship is more important than the firm relationship. Specifically, researchers attribute this outcome to **salesperson-owned loyalty**, defining it as the loyalty directed toward an individual salesperson as opposed to the selling firm.[10] Indeed, research has found that salesperson-owned customer loyalty is usually more important

> **salesperson-owned loyalty**
> The loyalty directed toward an individual salesperson as opposed to the selling firm.

than selling-firm-owned loyalty in determining whether the relationship will continue if the salesperson leaves. That is, if the salesperson leaves, the customer is more likely to follow the salesperson than to stay with the selling firm.

This finding makes sense in light of previous research on customers' buying motivations. In a long-term study of nearly 80,000 professional buyers, the salesperson emerged as the dominant factor buyers focus upon when making purchasing decisions. Loyalty to the salesperson easily outdistanced product quality and price.[11] Nearly 40 percent of the respondents in the study identified salesperson competence as the primary determinant of their purchasing decisions.

Certainly, this is not to say that product and price are unimportant. Rather, it suggests that differentiation through either of these two variables alone is becoming increasingly difficult. Competing firms can quickly copy product advancements and quickly match pricing deals. The ability to build and maintain successful customer relationships is a differentiating factor that allows firms to achieve long-term success.

Differences Based on Relationship Type

Another way to understand customer relationships is through the different types of customer loyalty they may exhibit. It is easy to assume that repeat purchases demonstrate a true sense of loyalty on the part of the customer, but this is not always the case. Think of some of the companies you purchase from on a regular basis: Do you purchase from the company because you feel a strong sense of loyalty? Or are you just purchasing out of habit? Even worse, are you locked into a contract that you cannot escape from?

Salespeople need to ask these same type questions of their customer relationships to understand the customer's type of loyalty. Customers may exhibit three types of loyalty: *constrained loyalty*, *affective loyalty*, and *spurious loyalty*. Across all of these, the customer is repurchasing from the firm. However, their motivations for doing so are different.

constrained loyalty
The loyalty that exists when the customer is constrained to the relationship, usually by a contractual obligation.

Constrained Loyalty
Constrained loyalty exists when the customer continues to purchase from the selling firm because he or she is constrained to the relationship. In most instances, this constraint comes in the form of a contractual obligation. For example, the customer might be locked into a contract with the selling firm and therefore required to purchase from the selling firm even though the customer would rather purchase elsewhere.

affective loyalty
The loyalty that exists when the customer feels a strong attitudinal connection and true attachment with the salesperson and/or selling firm.

Affective Loyalty
In contrast, affective loyalty exists when the customer feels a strong attitudinal connection with the salesperson and/or selling firm. The customer feels a strong sense of loyalty, a true attachment to the selling firm, and desires to maintain the relationship deep into the future. From the perspective of the salesperson, affective loyalty is a highly desirable state; in these instances the customer is unlikely to defect to the competition even if the competition offers a lower price.

spurious loyalty
The loyalty that exists when the customer continues to purchase only out of habit.

Spurious Loyalty
Last, spurious loyalty exists when the customer continues to purchase only out of habit. There is no strong attitudinal connection, but the customer is not constrained to the relationship. Spurious loyalty may exist because the customer does not feel that purchases made in the product category are particularly important (the supplier is not of strategic importance) or because the customer simply does not have the time to seek out alternative suppliers. The customer continues to purchase from the supplier out of convenience and there is no impetus for change.

It is important for selling firms as well as salespeople to know what kind of loyalty exists in their customer base. If salespeople can develop a strong sense of attitudinal loyalty among their customers, there is a high likelihood of future success. Such relationships are insulated against competitive threats. In contrast, if salespeople are able to maintain relationships only because of contractual obligations, they are in a very precarious situation; at some point, those contractual obligations will end. Thus, the goal for most salespeople is the development of a true sense of attitudinal loyalty in their customer base.

Differences Based on Relationship Life Cycle

Customer relationships also are evolutionary in nature. They change as they develop over time. These changes can bring important differences in how the customer views the relationship and what he or she desires from it. This means that salespeople should manage customer relationships differently based on their level of development.

The **customer-relationship life cycle** identifies the distinct phases through which customer relationships evolve as they develop: awareness, exploration, expansion, commitment, and dissolution.[12] Not all relationships proceed through these phases. In some instances, phases may be bypassed; in other instances, the relationship may regress to an earlier phase due to the actions of the salesperson or customer. Figure 3-3 visually depicts each of the relationship life-cycle phases.

Awareness Phase
In the **awareness phase** of the relationship, the customer recognizes a need and begins seeking out selling firms that may potentially be able to solve a problem or fulfill a need.

Exploration Phase
In the **exploration phase** of the relationship, the customer engages in initial prospecting activities to determine the desirability of a long-term relationship with a particular selling firm. Typically, it is in this phase when the

> **customer-relationship life cycle**
> The distinct phases through which customer relationships evolve as they develop: awareness, exploration, expansion, commitment, and dissolution.
>
> **awareness phase**
> Phase in the customer-relationship life cycle in which the customer recognizes a need and begins seeking out selling firms that may potentially be able to solve a problem or fulfill a need.
>
> **exploration phase**
> Phase in the customer-relationship life cycle in which the customer engages in initial prospecting activities to determine the desirability of a long-term relationship with a particular selling firm.

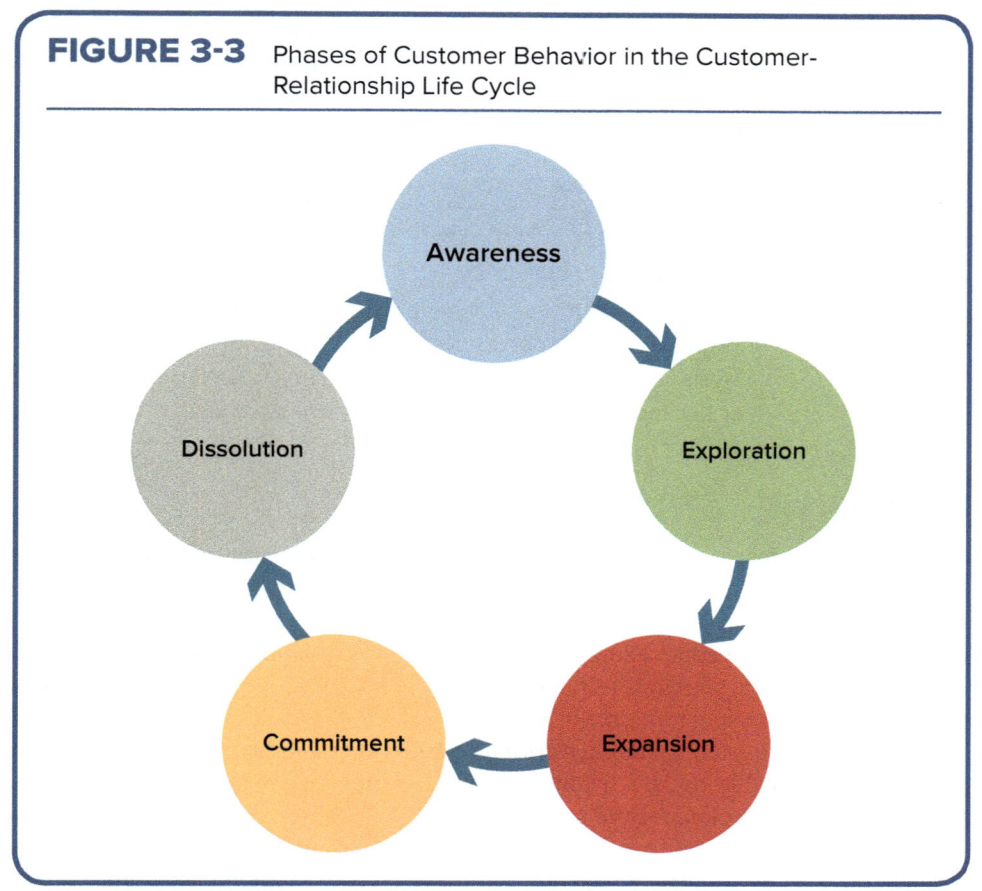

FIGURE 3-3 Phases of Customer Behavior in the Customer-Relationship Life Cycle

salesperson and customer first interact. The customer assesses whether the selling firm will be able to deliver the necessary level of benefits needed to justify a long-term relationship.

Expansion Phase In the **expansion phase** of the relationship, the customer receives increasing benefits and becomes increasingly dependent on the salesperson and the selling firm. The customer invests money, time, and effort to expand or strengthen the relationship.

Commitment Phase In the **commitment phase**, the customer has decided to continue the relationship with the salesperson and the selling firm. Commitment is the most advanced of the customer-relationship life-cycle phases. Here, the customer is receiving a level of benefits and satisfaction that would be difficult for other firms to match. This life-cycle phase is very desirable for the salesperson: the customer is paying little or no attention to offers from competing firms.

Dissolution Phase In sharp contrast, the **dissolution phase** of the customer-relationship life cycle is characterized by a customer's desire to end the relationship. In some instances, dissolution is scripted—for example, the relationship may be contractually designed to end. In others, dissolution occurs due to dissatisfaction.

It is important for salespeople to know where their relationships are within the relationship life cycle. Just as a couple celebrating their first wedding anniversary differs from a couple celebrating their fiftieth, or a relationship between a parent and an infant differs from one between a parent and an adult child, a developing sales relationship differs from one that is late in the life cycle. With these differences come important differences in what the customer desires. Salespeople must manage their sales relationships differently depending on their level of development.

Successful salespeople look at their customer relationships in the three ways described in this section: level, type, and life-cycle phase. Keep in mind the main goal, which is to build trust, the essential factor in long-term customer relationships.

Connect Assignment 3-2

Customer Loyalty

Please complete the Connect exercise for Chapter 3 that focuses on the different types of customer loyalty. Identifying which type of loyalty a customer is exhibiting will help you better understand his or her motivations and develop effective solutions.

BUILDING TRUST

While relationships can provide many benefits, they also come with risks. People typically are willing to accept these risks only when their trust in the other person is strong. Successful salespeople understand the importance of developing a trusting customer base. Salespeople adept at building customer relationships know that trust is a necessity; it is a prerequisite for success. Thus, in sales, the issue is how a salesperson can ensure the development of trust.

Early in this chapter, we defined *trust* as a belief that another person will act with integrity on a reliable basis. Customers willingly enter into relationships with salespeople whom they feel can serve the role of a **trusted advisor**.[13] This term, which has been used with increasing frequency in recent years, describes a salesperson who has earned the trust of a customer through displays of two components: character and competence. In order to serve as a trusted advisor, the customer must believe that the salesperson has both high character and high competence. One without the other is not enough:

- If the customer believes the salesperson is of high character but lacks competence, it will be impossible to have confidence in the solutions the salesperson proposes.
- If the customer believes the salesperson is highly competent but of questionable character, he or she will doubt whether the salesperson is well intentioned and seeking to do what is right by the customer.

The elements making up both of these trust bases are shown in Figure 3-4 and discussed in detail in the sections that follow.

The Importance of Character

What constitutes strong character? To some degree, it's contextual and depends on the situation. For example, "good character" in a potential life partner probably differs somewhat from "good character" in a politician or a teacher or a soldier. Salespeople develop character-based trust to the extent that they exhibit *likeability*, *customer-orientation*, *candor*, *dependability*, and *high integrity*. Let's look at each characteristic in the context of professional selling.

FIGURE 3-4 Elements of Character-Based and Competence-Based Trust

Character-Based Trust
- Likeability
- Customer orientation
- Candor
- Dependability
- Integrity

Competence-Based Trust
- Customer knowledge
- Company knowledge
- Product knowledge
- Competitive knowledge
- Industry knowledge
- Technological knowledge
- Service knowledge

Likeability Most customers would rather work with salespeople with whom they have a personal connection. We call that personal connection or social bond between a salesperson and a customer **likeability**. Although other characteristics are more influential than likeability in determining sales success, salespeople generally want their customers to like them. We know that salespeople are more successful when they are able to develop a social bond with their customers.[14]

However, it is also important that salespeople not confuse the importance of interpersonal friendships with what customers truly desire out of their professional relationships. Research shows that customers often struggle with the combination of interpersonal friendship and business relationship.[15] Indeed, in a qualitative study, customers talked about how these two things can be in conflict:

> The foundation of the relationship is that we have to do what's right for our firms, so there are boundaries. In a friendship, your commitment is to the other person. Business relationships should always be built around what's in it for my company.[16]

Comments such as these highlight the fact that while likeability in sales is important, building trust requires much more than likeability.

likeability
The characteristic of a social bond or personal connection between a salesperson and a customer.

fizkes/Shutterstock

Customer Orientation

customer orientation
The extent to which a salesperson places the customer's interests ahead of their own or those of their company.

Customer orientation describes the extent to which salespeople place the customer's interests ahead of their own or those of their company. Customer-oriented salespeople seek to deliver solutions that are problem-based as opposed to product-based. They recognize the customer as the starting point from which all activities originate.

Too often, salespeople become focused on objectives that pull their attention away from the customer. For instance, most salespeople operate with a quota; it's very easy to become fixated on the quota and the progress toward reaching it instead of on the customers' needs.

Sometimes salespeople lose customer orientation by falling into the trap of taking a *product orientation*. In these situations, salespeople lose track of their customers' needs. Instead, they become focused only on the products they are selling and the features associated with these products.

role conflict
A situation in which the goals a salesperson pursues are in conflict with customers' goals.

One issue that detracts from a customer orientation is **role conflict**, a situation in which the goals a salesperson pursues are in conflict with customers' goals. For example, your goal as salesperson is to sell more product, enabling you to hit your quota. This goal can be in conflict with an important customer goal, which is to keep inventory levels as low as possible while still meeting their own needs. Similarly, salespeople generally seek to sell their products and services at as high a price possible to ensure company profits. Customers want to buy these same products and services at as low a price as possible to ensure their own profitability.

Many salespeople talk about the challenges associated with managing role conflicts. Customer-oriented salespeople instead note that there is no real conflict—they will always do what is best for their customers. Although this may create short-term challenges for the salesperson (e.g., the salesperson may not get an immediate sale), customer-oriented salespeople are much more likely to be successful in building trust in the long run.[17]

Candor

candor
The characteristics of openness, honesty, and sincerity displayed by salespeople in their communications.

Candor refers to the characteristics of openness, honesty, and sincerity displayed by salespeople in their communications. Candid salespeople say only what they know to be true, and never overpromise. They are factual with their customers about what they can and cannot do for them. Candid salespeople may even go so far as to recommend a competitor when they know that their offering is not what is best for the customer. This type of communication drives a tremendous level of trust on the part of the customer; the customer knows that the salesperson is focused on their success as opposed to just getting a sale.

Candid communication contrasts with the negative stereotype salespeople have developed over the years.[18] Historically, "door-to-door" salespeople were thought to be quick to overpromise; the customer would never know whether what was promised was actually going to be delivered. As a result, many people developed a negative perception of salespeople and questioned salespeople's truthfulness. It has taken considerable time to overcome this stereotype. Modern-day sales have transitioned to the point where honest and open communications are the expectation as opposed to the exception. Customers simply will not tolerate salespeople who make promises they cannot fulfill.

Dependability

dependability
A salesperson's reliability in consistently meeting customers' expectations.

Similarly, customers will not work with salespeople whom they do not perceive to be dependable. **Dependability** refers to a salesperson's reliability in consistently meeting customers' expectations. For the customer, there is no guesswork in trying to determine what the salesperson will do.

While this may seem like a minimal expectation, it is incredibly important to the customer. For the customer, having to work with salespeople who are not dependable is frustrating; it leads to anxiety about not being able to predict whether the salesperson will do what was promised. If they feel that the dependability of the salesperson is questionable, customers will always seek to find other salespeople and/or supplier firms to purchase from.

Integrity Salespeople who are of high integrity have a strong core set of values they adhere to regardless of the situation. For these salespeople, differentiating right from wrong is not contextual; the situation has little influence over how they interact with others.

For example, imagine the challenge of ensuring your customer's best interest when your own management team is pushing you to attain organizational sales goals. Mike Fuller, vice-president of sales for Pernod-Ricard USA, noted:

> For us, meeting investor's sales expectations are absolutely critically. We cannot miss.... I feel this pressure. We all do. It is common for us to be pushing at the end of a quarter. But make no mistake, I will never take advantage of my customers to help us get there. I just won't do it. And our management team knows this and respects me for it.[19]

Such thinking is indicative of a salesperson who acts with high integrity. Importantly, Fuller has been a strong performer for the company, due in part to his uncompromising belief that there is a right way to do things. However, he noted:

> I don't act this way simply because I want to be a successful salesperson. I act this way because it's the right thing to do. I treat others as I would want to be treated. I follow the Golden Rule. Doing so has helped me tremendously in my career. My customers know who I am; they know what I stand for. And most importantly, they know that I will not compromise.[20]

Acting with integrity is a prerequisite for sales success and for building trust and long-term customer relationships.

The Importance of Competence

In order to act as a consultative salesperson, you must demonstrate a high level of competence. Competence depends on different knowledge bases: *customer* knowledge, *company* knowledge, *product* knowledge, *competitive* knowledge, *industry* knowledge, *technological* knowledge, and *service* knowledge. When you possess knowledge across these areas, you are able to provide solutions your customers value. Salesperson knowledge provides a point of differentiation that is necessary for long-term sales success.

Customer Knowledge A salesperson high in customer knowledge has a deep understanding of a customer's business and the functions and processes that support the business. Customers have noted that salespeople must understand how the solutions they propose will be applied within the customer's organization and will affect it.[21] Customer knowledge also requires an understanding of the customer as a person—what motivates the customer and what personal goals the customer is seeking to achieve within the organization. Personal needs and goals can be challenging to understand yet are vitally important in terms of driving customers' purchasing decisions.

For example, a salesperson for a Fortune 500 customer-packaged-goods firm described an instance in which the individuals involved in the purchase decisions were at odds with each other:

> It was a very delicate situation. There was significant conflict between the buyer I dealt with and the store managers for each individual (retail) location. You go into these situations thinking that your buyer will be motivated by things such as top-line sales and profit margins, but in this case, he told me that he simply wanted to win! He wanted to show his store managers that his way of thinking was indeed right. This was critically important for me to know, as it shaped my interactions with him. As much as anything, it taught me the importance of understanding and adapting to the politics that may be present on the other side of the table.[22]

---

integrity
A strong core set of values that a salesperson adheres to regardless of the situation.

customer knowledge
A deep understanding of a customer's business and the functions and processes that support the business.

As this example shows, a deep understanding of the customer as a person requires knowledge that goes well beyond what an organization chart can provide.

Company Knowledge

Company knowledge refers to a strong understanding of the resources the salesperson's own company possesses and the means of attaining these resources. Salespeople high in company knowledge understand how the different departments within their own company must work together to ensure superior customer service. In fact, research has even shown that, in certain situations, strong internal relationships are more influential in determining sales success than are strong external (customer) relationships.[23]

In many cases, customer satisfaction requires a company effort. Understanding that fact, salespeople have come to recognize the importance of networking within their own company. As discussed in Chapter 2, networking refers to activities through which individuals communicate in an attempt to strengthen their professional and/or social relationships. Salespeople who are adept at networking have established relationships across their company that help ensure success with their customers.

> **company knowledge**
> An understanding of the resources the salesperson's own company possesses and the means of attaining these resources.

Product Knowledge

Product knowledge requires a strong understanding of product features and attributes. Such knowledge has long been considered a prerequisite for sales success. In years past, the salesperson served as the primary conveyor of product information; there was value in the ability to clearly articulate product features and corresponding benefits. This has changed: Customers can now gather product information through the internet. Because of this, customers have come to rely less on salesperson product knowledge. Unfortunately, some salespeople have been slow to adapt to this change and remain overly focused on the products they sell; in such cases, they may neglect the true problems their customers are looking to solve.

Yet strong product knowledge is still vitally important in order for the salesperson to provide solutions that solve their customer's most pressing problems. Customers today demand a deep understanding of how products will be integrated into solutions that will be applied across the buying organization. Product knowledge has become an expected but nondifferentiating characteristic upon which customers evaluate the salespeople from whom they purchase.

> **product knowledge**
> An understanding of product features and attributes.

Competitive Knowledge

Often, salespeople have to demonstrate an understanding of the competition when interacting with customers. A salesperson high in **competitive knowledge** possesses an understanding of direct as well as indirect competitors. They know not only what their competitors' products and services can do but also the service capabilities competitors possess in their attempts to deliver total solutions. Differences in actual products may be difficult to discern, whereas service discrepancies across competing companies are often quite pronounced. A service discrepancy may even take the form of a salesperson who is (or perhaps is not) willing to do what is required to deliver high service levels.

Competitive knowledge also includes an understanding of price differences. This type of competitive knowledge enables the salesperson to calculate differences in the overall value propositions being offered. Customers in the business-to-business context frequently choose between multiple options when seeking ways to address their needs or problems. Not surprisingly, research has shown that the collection and use of competitive intelligence has a positive effect on salesperson performance.[24]

> **competitive knowledge**
> An understanding of both direct and indirect competitors.

Industry Knowledge

To act as consultants for their customers, salespeople must have **industry knowledge**—a firm understanding of the industry in which the salesperson operates and the trends that will affect the industry moving forward. Customers expect industry knowledge and will routinely ask questions such as, "Where

> **industry knowledge**
> An understanding of the industry in which the salesperson operates and the trends that will affect the industry moving forward.

do you see our industry going?" and "What can we do to stay ahead of any changes that may be on the horizon?" Salespeople should set aside time to enhance their industry knowledge. Salespeople who possess a high level of such knowledge have a competitive advantage.

Technological Knowledge Given the rapid infusion of technology into selling, it is also important for salespeople to have **technological knowledge** of how to use the latest technologies for gathering information and communicating with customers. Being able to use new technologies enables a salesperson to improve effectiveness and efficiency. Technological changes will continue to enable salespeople to accomplish their tasks more quickly and ensure enhanced customer interactions.

Andriy Popov/123RF

technological knowledge
An understanding how to use the latest technologies for gathering information and communicating with customers.

As an example, many salespeople now use virtual-meeting technologies such as GoTo-Meeting or Zoom to conduct customer meetings over the internet. Reliance on technologies such as these has increased dramatically with travel restrictions due to the onset of the global Coronavirus pandemic. In addition to dramatically reducing travel costs, such technologies allow for a level of interaction that is not significantly different from what can be attained in face-to-face meetings. They can additionally be used to support the heightened focus many firms are placing on their inside sales efforts. Perhaps most important, research suggests that salespeople who are proficient in using technology perform at higher levels because they are more effective in their customer interactions.[25]

The importance of being technologically proficient cannot be overstated. Embracing this change, many salespeople are now using social media platforms such as LinkedIn and Facebook as virtual-networking tools.[26] In an attempt to align their selling processes with customers' buying preferences, many salespeople now interact with potential customers electronically for extended periods of time before an initial face-to-face meeting. Although this is an uncomfortable (and perhaps unwelcome) change for some salespeople, those on the forefront of this change have an advantage that will grow only more pronounced in the years to come.

service knowledge
An understanding of the additional layer of benefits that accompanies the core offering.

Service Knowledge In the vast majority of situations, differentiation through the core offering alone has become increasingly difficult. As a result, successful salespeople have come to recognize the greater level of emphasis customers now place on the service offering they receive from selling firms. Thus it is important that salespeople possess high levels of **service knowledge**, which is an understanding of the additional layer of benefits that accompanies the core offering—whether that core offering is a tangible product or an intangible service. As shown in Figure 3-5, the *service surround* envelopes the *core offering* and enhances the overall *customer value proposition*. Service variability remains high and therefore provides salespeople with a means through which they can differentiate and ensure long-term customer-relationship success.

Salesperson service is a broad term that can encompass many different things. Salespeople who are proficient at serving their customers are responsive to the customers' needs; they act quickly on issues related to delivery, installation, warranties, and maintenance. Often their availability extends beyond traditional business hours. As an example, Zach King, a district

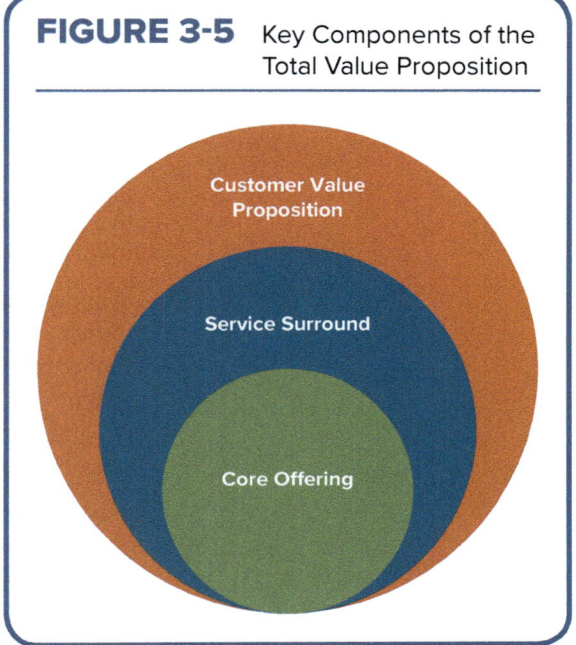
FIGURE 3-5 Key Components of the Total Value Proposition

sales manager with Fastenal, featured in the Executive Perspective, tells the story of once having to go above and beyond for a customer to ensure that a project stayed on its timeline:

> It was a Saturday, and the customer desperately needed a particular part to keep the project moving. Although this is not something we have to do on a regular basis, I literally put the part in the back of my truck and drove it down to the customer. I had to; I really did not even put much thought into it. That's what we do at Fastenal, because that's the type service our customers need. But I'll promise you this—the customer has never forgotten that. Never. It changed everything in our relationship. He became, and still is, one of our most loyal customers. When we talk service at Fastenal, that's what we mean. We are a service-driven organization; that's how we compete.[27]

connect Assignment 3-3

Trust

Please complete the Connect exercise for Chapter 3 that focuses on developing trust. Understanding how character and competence build trust will help you develop positive relationships with current and potential customers.

SALESPERSON ETHICS

LO 3-6 — Summarize the importance of ethics and the challenges associated with salesperson ethics.

As discussed in previous chapters, *ethics* deals with moral judgments, standards, and rules of conduct. These make up the standards of right or wrong behavior expected by a society. Your personal ethics provide a foundation from which you make personal judgments regarding ethical versus unethical behavior.

When we talk of being ethical, we are talking about doing the right thing. We are referring to the idea of treating others as you would want to be treated. Because of this, ethical behavior is a critical ingredient necessary for any successful relationship. Without it, you cannot trust the other person. And if you cannot trust the other person, it is unlikely you will choose to remain in the relationship. This holds true in our personal relationships and in our business relationships.

Ethical salesperson behavior is a critical component required for relational exchange. Ethical salespeople:

- Are factual in their communications with customers.
- Sell only those products and services they believe will benefit the customer.
- Promise only what can be delivered.
- Treat customer information in a confidential manner.

Similarly, ethical salespeople avoid behaviors such as:

- Lying about product availability (telling the customer a product is available simply to get the sale but knowing that it will be placed on backorder).
- Selling products or services that cannot be resold or used in a reasonable period of time.
- Providing misleading information to customers.
- Falsifying expense reports.

Through these examples, we see that truly ethical salespeople do right not only by their customers but also by the companies they work for. They understand that ethical behavior is not something you can "turn on" or "turn off" based on the situation you are in. These salespeople know that ethical behavior is a constant that must exist across all of their interactions.

Research on Salesperson Ethics

We naturally assume that it is important for salespeople to act ethically in their customer relationships. Those who examine sales relationships have verified this. Studies have found that salespeople who act ethically are more effective at building strong customer relationships—their customers are more satisfied, trusting of, and committed to them.[28] This finding suggests that ethical salesperson behavior helps ensure the development of affective loyalty in customers.

Other research questions have been raised about the relationship between ethical sales behavior and actual performance: Do ethical salespeople actually sell more? Are they more effective? Over the long term, do they outperform salespeople who act unethically in the hope of attaining short-term success?

In some instances, troubling answers have emerged through research into these questions. For instance, past research has found that some executives believe that when confronting ethical dilemmas, they have to choose the profitable option over the ethical one.[29] Similarly, some middle managers have reported that senior managers will advise them against being overly ethical so as not to deter from short-term performance.[30] In the sales context, sales researchers have even reported a belief amongst some salespeople that, "... in the short run, questionable conduct may engender selling success."[31] When examining the overall evolution of the sales function throughout the twentieth century, results such as these might not be that surprising when you consider the fact that relational selling is a new phenomenon. Salespeople face numerous ethical complexities and challenges.

Although it is easy to say that you should always do the right thing, salespeople *do* confront situations in which the right thing can be difficult to know. Salespeople have to manage the competing interests of the companies they work for and of the customers they sell to. However, conversations with top salespeople seem to reveal a consistent theme: "Do right by your customers." That is their purpose, and that is what they strive to do.

Further, top salespeople expect their companies to help them do right by customers. If their company does not do so, they will find one that will. These salespeople are able to stand firm in their ethics because they are mobile given their success. Indeed, more recent research has reported a strong and positive relationship between ethical salesperson behavior and actual sales performance.[32]

Specific Ethics Challenges

Given that ethical behavior is so important in sales, why do we see situations like the one described in the Pilot Flying J example? Researchers have found that salespeople confront more ethical dilemmas than do most other employee groups.[33] Five factors contribute to this fact:

1. As we have noted, ethical conflicts can arise as salespeople attempt to balance the interests of the buying and selling organizations.
2. Salespeople often work alone. Isolation can reduce normative group influences and lessen ethical conformance. In other words, when we work in close proximity to others, we are more likely to conform to accepted behaviors; our behaviors are visible and judged in relation to what the group expects.
3. Perhaps most important, given the objective nature of the job (for example, sales performance reports can be easily obtained), salespeople are under intense pressure to perform. Ethical issues might emerge due to this pressure.
4. Research has shown that sales managers may be willing to overlook ethical questions, particularly when the manager is facing aggressive sales goals. In these situations, the manager adopts a "don't ask, don't tell" approach. Such an approach has a profound effect on other team members who clearly understand what the manager is saying through his or her lack of action.

Today's Professional Perspective ...because everyone is a salesperson

Noah Napier
Sales-Development Program
Atlas Copco

Noah Napier

Describe your job. I am currently in a sales-development program at Atlas Copco, a world leader in industrial air-compressor sales. It is a year-long immersive program that exposes me to every aspect of business within the company. I have shadowed many people in different positions within the organization to learn about the sales process and the service that follows the sale. After training, I will move into a full-time outside sales position and will be given a territory.

How did you get your job? My college had companies coming on campus to interview students before graduation. Five companies were coming, and I signed up for four of them because I knew I needed practice interviewing. Each time I interviewed I felt more and more confident in myself and my answers. I did a ton of research into each company to formulate good-quality questions to ask the interviewer. By the end of the process, I had three offers to choose from. I used resources such as a decision-making matrix to choose which company would set me up for long-term success in my future sales career.

What has been most important in making you successful at your job? I am still in training, but I believe work ethic is pivotal to success in a sales career. In many sales positions, the sales representative has control over what they do in their day-to-day work activities. Some people choose to do the bare minimum because they can get away with it, but the best salespeople go the extra mile every day. People, whether it be coworkers or your customers, notice your effort, even when it does not seem like it. I believe that going to work every day with the attitude of being the best you can be will pay dividends in your future career.

What advice would you give future graduates about a career in sales? Wake up every day and do something to better yourself. Whether it is using a planner to become more organized or something as small as reading a few pages of a sales book every day, it will make a huge difference in your future career.

What is the most important characteristic of a great salesperson? I think the single most important characteristic a salesperson can have is being a good listener. There is a notion that the best salespeople are the most talkative people, but this is false. It is much more important to ask the right questions and actively listen to the customer, to understand what they need and to show them that you care.

5. Even though many effective negotiators are highly ethical, salespeople are often involved in negotiations that can promote dishonesty or exaggeration.

In no way, though, do these specific challenges suggest that unethical behavior is to be expected in sales. To the contrary, today's most effective salespeople are highly ethical, in large part because their buyers demand and reward such behavior. This will continue to be the case as the relationship selling approach becomes even more common in the future.

CHAPTER SUMMARY

LO 3-1 Explain the importance of trust in a relationship selling approach.

Many organizations have adopted *relationship selling* as their strategy of choice. Customers must trust salespeople, based on a belief that they will act in an ethical fashion. Without trust, there can be no relationship. It provides the foundation for our personal and business relationships.

LO 3-2 Explain what customer engagement is and how technology is affecting the way salespeople and customers interact.

Customer engagement refers to the connection that exists between the salesperson, selling firm, and customer. Technology is changing the way in which salespeople and customer interact. Many customers engage salespeople and selling firms much later in their purchasing process. Many salespeople initially engage their customers via technology. Salespeople who are adept at doing this have a tremendous advantage over those who are not.

LO 3-3 Describe how different purchase types affect the buying team and decision-making process.

Salespeople must understand that purchase type will affect who is involved in the decision-making process and what this process will look like. There are three primary types of customer purchases: *new-task, straight-rebuy,* and *modified-rebuy.*

Purchase type will dictate the composition of the *buying team,* which is a group comprising *users, initiators, deciders, purchasers,* and *influencers.* Purchase type will also affect the extensiveness of the decision-making process, which can consist of *problem recognition, information search, evaluation of alternatives, supplier-solution decision,* and *post-purchase evaluation.*

LO 3-4 Summarize differences in customer relationships based on relationship level, relationship type, and customer-relationship life cycle phase.

From the customer's perspective, the relationship with the selling firm exists at two different levels—the salesperson level and the selling-firm level. Sometimes the customer feels similarly about the salesperson and the selling firm. When this is not the case, *salesperson-owned loyalty* is usually more important than selling-firm-owned loyalty in determining whether the relationship will continue if the salesperson leaves.

Second, relationships differ based on customers' reasons for remaining loyal. *Constrained loyalty* exists when the customer purchases only because of contractual obligations. *Affective loyalty* exists when the customer purchases based on having a strong attitudinal connection with the salesperson and/or selling firm. *Spurious loyalty* exists when the customer purchases merely out of habit.

The *customer-relationship life cycle* provides a mechanism through which salespeople can examine their relationships based on phases through which customer relationships evolve as they develop: *awareness, exploration, expansion, commitment,* and *dissolution.*

LO 3-5 Explain the importance of trust and the role character and competence play in establishing trust.

Trust is the most critical element necessary for relationship-selling success. Without trust, there can be no relationship, as the customer cannot assume that the salesperson will reliably act with integrity. When this is the case, the risks associated with the level of commitment a relationship requires can become too great. Salespeople develop character-based trust to the extent that they exhibit *likeability, customer-orientation, candor, dependability,* and *high integrity.* Salespeople must be aware of potential *role conflict* and seek to reduce it.

In addition to building character-based trust, salespeople must also exhibit competence-based trust. Both are necessary for the salesperson to act as a trusted advisor. Competence-based trust requires *customer knowledge, company knowledge, product knowledge competitive knowledge, industry knowledge, technological knowledge,* and *service knowledge.*

LO 3-6 Summarize the importance of ethics and the challenges associated with salesperson ethics.

Salesperson ethics is a requirement for success in selling today. Without it, the customer cannot trust the salesperson and therefore cannot enter into a relationship with the selling firm. Thus, salespeople who do not act in an ethical fashion will not be able to maintain their customer relationships. That said, several factors make the sales job unique and perhaps more challenging from an ethical perspective. Foremost among these is the fact that salespeople must manage what can be competing interests across selling and buying firms. Other factors include salesperson isolation, pressure to meet sales goals, sales managers' failure to support ethical behavior, and the dangers of negotiation.

KEY TERMS

relationship selling (p. 48)
trust (p. 48)
customer engagement (p. 49)
new-task purchases (p. 50)
straight-rebuy purchases (p. 51)
electronic data interchange (EDI) (p. 51)
modified-rebuy purchases (p. 51)
buying teams (p. 52)
initiator (p. 52)
product users (p. 53)
influencers (p. 53)
deciders (p. 53)
purchasers (p. 53)
gatekeepers (p. 53)
problem recognition (p. 54)

latent needs (p. 54)
information search (p. 54)
evaluation of alternatives (p. 54)
supplier-solution decision (p. 54)
post-purchase evaluation (p. 55)
salesperson-owned loyalty (p. 55)
constrained loyalty (p. 56)
affective loyalty (p. 56)
spurious loyalty (p. 56)
customer-relationship life cycle (p. 57)
awareness phase (p. 57)
exploration phase (p. 57)
expansion phase (p. 58)
commitment phase (p. 58)
dissolution phase (p. 58)

trusted advisor (p. 58)
likeability (p. 59)
customer-orientation (p. 60)
role conflict (p. 60)
candor (p. 60)
dependability (p. 60)
integrity (p. 61)
customer knowledge (p. 61)
company knowledge (p. 62)
product knowledge (p. 62)
competitive knowledge (p. 62)
industry knowledge (p. 62)
technological knowledge (p. 63)
service knowledge (p. 63)

DISCUSSION QUESTIONS

1. Think of the relationships you maintain in your personal life. Discuss the similarities and potential differences that exist between these personal relationships and sales relationships.
2. Customer engagement refers to the connection that exists between the salesperson, the selling firm, and the customer. As a customer, how do you engage with companies in your personal life? To what extent do you use technology? How might this knowledge affect the strategies these companies employ when engaging with you?
3. Think about your last major purchase decision. Who helped you with this decision—that is, who was on your buying team? What role did each of these people play? How did your decision-making process unfold? How did purchase importance affect this process?
4. Think of and describe three different company relationships you are currently in, in which you exhibit spurious loyalty, affective loyalty, and constrained loyalty.
5. Describe a previous interaction you have had with a salesperson whom you considered to be questionable from an ethical perspective. How did your concerns affect how you interacted with this person? Would you be comfortable entering into a long-term relationship with this person? Why or why not?

ETHICAL CHALLENGE

Returning to the Pilot Flying J example provided at the beginning of the chapter, think about ethical issues you would face as a salesperson and as a future executive.

Questions

1. How would you have responded as a salesperson if you were asked to withhold your customers' rebates and discounts? What factors may have led to so many employees being involved in a scheme such as this?
2. In one of the more talked-about aspects of this case, top leadership at Pilot Flying J was exonerated in the probe because they claimed to be unaware of the scheme. In your opinion, is this a reasonable excuse for a leadership team? Why or why not?
3. How might you go about trying to salvage the customer relationships negatively affected by the scheme? How could you reestablish trust after an event such as this?

ROLE PLAY

This role play will give you experience in developing trust and solutions for different purchasing types. For this role play, half of your class should be salespeople for your favorite streaming service. Each salesperson should pick the streaming service he or she is working for (e.g., Netflix, Hulu, Disney+) and develop a presentation to win over customers in *new-task purchases* (never subscribed to the streaming service), *straight-rebuy* (customer wants to renew for the same monthly price), and *modified-rebuy* (customer wants to continue the service but with some changes).

The other half of class will be the current or prospective customers of the streaming service; each gets to decide which type of purchase (new-task, straight-rebuy, or modified-rebuy) he or she wants to make. Buyers will hear the sales presentations and can raise issues that are important to them (pricing, better content on the streaming service, etc.). At the end of the role play, the buyers will decide if they want to purchase new or rebuy the streaming service being sold and will provide feedback about why they made that decision.

At the end of the role play, both the salesperson and the buyer should reflect on what made the biggest positive or negative impact relative to trust and which knowledge bases might be most effective in this type of sales role.

SALES PRESENTATION

For the Connect assignment in Chapter 3, students will practice developing trust through competence. Assume you are a finalist for a sales position with a company you would like to work for after you graduate. Provide a three- to five-minute sales presentation that demonstrates your competence to that organization. Be sure to include at least two of the knowledge bases you learned about in this chapter.

Shane Hunt
Dean and Marketing Professor
Idaho State University

Building a Personal Brand

Shane Hunt

As you develop trust with new and prospective customers, one key component of a successful career in sales is having a strong personal brand. As you build your personal brand, focus on the following two key elements:

1. **What do you want your brand to be?** This personal question focuses on who you are and what you want from your life. If you want your brand image to be that of a hardworking, responsible person, you have to make the decision not to miss class, not to be late for work, and not to forget to do things when others are counting on you. Just *wanting* your brand to be characterized by descriptors like *hardworking* and *responsible* is not enough if your day-to-day actions do not support them. Similarly, if you want to be considered a problem solver, find problems to solve. Simply sitting in your office doing the bare minimum will not convince anyone. I would encourage each of you to think about your own personal strengths and weaknesses, and decide while you are in college what you want your personal brand to be as you embark on your career.

2. **How do you build your brand image?** Your brand image involves how others see you. It is being shaped every second of every day. Your brand does not take a day off. If people on your sales team or potential clients see you on the weekend acting markedly different from the way you act in the office, they will see you in a different light and your brand will be forever changed in their eyes. How you treat a stranger at a grocery store can affect your brand image just as much as how you treat someone in a college class. Every assignment you turn in, every project you work on, every sales call you make builds your brand. However, each also can be an opportunity to damage your brand if handled improperly. Remember to build and protect your brand image in everything you do.

CHAPTER ENDNOTES

1. A. Grant, "Pilot Flying J raid surprises, angers truckers who bought fuel from nationwide company owned by Cleveland Browns owner Jimmy Haslam," *The Plain Dealer,* April 29, 2013.
2. D. Heifetz, "The Pilot Flying J fraud scandal hasn't touched Browns owner Jimmy Haslam*,*" *The Ringer*, April 2, 2018.
3. A. Rogers, "The MRAP: Brilliant buy, or billions wasted?" *Time,* October 2, 2012.
4. "More attacks, mounting casualties," *Washington Post,* 2007.
5. A. Rogers, op cit.
6. Ibid.
7. Ibid.
8. H. Stevens and T. Kinni, *Achieve sales excellence: The 7 customer rules for becoming the new sales professional* (Avon, MA: Platinum Press, 2007).
9. Ibid.
10. Palmatier, R., L. Scheer, and J.-B. Steenkamp, "Customer loyalty to whom? Managing the benefits and risks of salesperson-owned loyalty." Journal of Marketing Research, 2007. 44(2): p. 185-199.
11. Ibid.
12. F. R. Dwyer, P. H. Schurr, and S. Oh, "Developing buyer-seller relationships," *Journal of Marketing*, 51, no. 2 (1987.): 11–28.
13. ThinkTV, *The new selling of America,* March 8, 2010.
14. M. Paulssen and R. Roulet, "Social bonding as a determinant of share of wallet and cross-buying behaviour in B2B relationships," *European Journal of Marketing*, 51, no. 5/6 (2017): 1011–1028.
15. L. A. Bettencourt, et al., "Rethinking customer relationships*.*" *Business Horizons*, 58, no. 1 (2015): 99–108.
16. Ibid.
17. B. D. Keillor, R. S. Parker, and C. E. Pettijohn, "Relationship-oriented characteristics and individual salesperson performance," *Journal of Business & Industrial Marketing*, 15, no. 1 (2000): 7–22.
18. ThinkTV, *op. cit.*
19. M. Fuller, personal conversation, 2019.
20. Ibid.
21. H. Stevens and T. Kinni, Op. cit.
22. G. Hayes, personal communication, 2019.
23. C. R. Plouffe, et al., "Does the customer matter most? Exploring strategic frontline employees' influence of customers, the internal business team, and external business partners," *Journal of Marketing*, 80, no. 1 (2016): 106–123.
24. A. Rapp, et al., "Competitive intelligence collection and use by sales and service representatives: How managers' recognition and autonomy moderate individual performance," *Journal of the Academy of Marketing Science*, 43, no. 3 (2015): 357–374.
25. S. Román, and R. Rodrıguez, "The influence of sales force technology use on outcome performance," *Journal of Business & Industrial Marketing*, 30, no. 6 (2015): 771–783.
26. W. C. Moncrief, "Are sales as we know it dying... or merely transforming?" *Journal of Personal Selling & Sales Management,* 37, no. 4 (2017): 271–279.
27. Zach King, personal communication, 2019.
28. R. R. Lagace, R. Dahlstrom, and J. B. Gassenheimer, "The relevance of ethical salesperson behavior on relationship quality: The pharmaceutical industry," *Journal of Personal Selling & Sales Management*, 11, no. 4 (1991): 39–47; and S. Román and S. Ruiz, "Relationship outcomes of perceived ethical sales behavior: The customer's perspective," *Journal of Business Research*, 58, no. 4 (2005): 439–445.
29. S. J. Vitell and T. A. Festervand, "Business ethics: Conflicts, practices and beliefs of industrial executives," *Journal of Business Ethics*, 6, no. 2 (1987): 111–122.
30. A. P. Webb and J. L. Badaracco, Jr., "Business ethics: A view from the trenches," *California Management Review*, 37, no. 2 (1995): 8–28.
31. A. J. Dubinsky, et al., "Ethical perceptions of field sales personnel: An empirical assessment," *Journal of Personal Selling & Sales Management*, 12, no. 4 (1992): 9–21.
32. S. Román and S. Ruiz, "Relationship outcomes of perceived ethical sales behavior: The customer's perspective," *Journal of Business Research*, 58, no. 4 (2005): 439–445.
33. J. D. Hansen and R. J. Riggle, "Ethical salesperson behavior in sales relationships," *Journal of Personal Selling & Sales Management*, 29, no. 2 (2009): 151–166.

Design elements: Marketing Insights Podcast: vandame/Shutterstock

Part TWO
Using Strategies and Tools to Meet Client Needs

Creativa Images/Shutterstock

Chapter 4
Social Selling

Chapter 5
Sales-Presentation Strategies

Chapter 4

Social Selling

Learning Objectives

After reading this chapter, you should be able to:

LO 4-1 Explain the significance of social selling in modern sales settings.

LO 4-2 Describe how social media tools can be used to enhance buyer perceptions of salesperson credibility.

LO 4-3 Describe how salespeople can use social media to grow their social networks.

LO 4-4 Explain how sharing relevant content is central to social-selling success.

LO 4-5 Describe key performance indicators for assessing social-selling performance.

Executive Perspective ... because everyone is a salesperson

MaKinzie Foos
Director of Business Operations
Memphis Hustle

MaKinzie Foos

Marketing Insights Podcast

Executive Perspective: Interview with MaKenzie Foos, Director of Business Operations, Memphis Hustle

Describe your job.

I work for the Memphis Grizzlies' NBA G-League franchise, the Memphis Hustle. The NBA G-League is the developmental league for the NBA. As the director of business operations, I am largely responsible for the overall business strategy. I'm tasked with launching and overseeing the day-to-day business operations of the team, including all of the sales functions, from ticket sales and corporate partnerships to marketing and the fan experience. I'm pretty much responsible for everything except the basketball.

How did you get your job?

I had worked my way up to senior ticket sales manager for the Memphis Grizzlies when they acquired the expansion franchise. When the Hustle launched, I took on the additional responsibility of building and managing the ticket-sales staff for the new team. After completing two seasons in that role, I was given the opportunity to take on greater responsibilities for the entire business operation and expand my skill set beyond just ticket sales. Being open to new opportunities and stepping out of my comfort zone is what ultimately helped me to get the job I have now.

What has been most important in making you successful at your job?

Although many factors go into being successful, one of the most important things for me has been being open to learning. I know I still have so much more to learn, but my desire to gain as much knowledge about every aspect of the business is really why I'm in this position. Knowing more than I may need to about a department—even if it's an area that doesn't directly apply to my job—helps me to put the best processes in place and to make more informed decisions. Always be curious and ask questions.

What advice would you give future graduates about a career in sales?

Get comfortable being uncomfortable and don't be afraid to fail. When you get your first sales job after college, you are going to find yourself in situations that are new to you. Embrace those moments and don't be afraid to step up to the challenge, even if it's your first time to do it. Be confident in yourself. Regardless of the outcome, there is always something to be learned, and ultimately those are the moments when growth happens. Having a career in sales is both challenging and rewarding. Be yourself and build good relationships with people. Focus on controlling the things that you can control such as attitude, effort, and being open to learning.

What is the most important characteristic of a great salesperson?

In my career, I've had the pleasure of working with many great salespeople, and there is one thing that I have seen that sets the best ones apart from the rest: attitude. Your attitude is one of the few things you have complete control over, and it's crucial, because sales is tough. You are going to deal with rejection more often than not, and although you can't control the outcome, you can control how you react to every situation. Salespeople who don't let losing a sale negatively affect their mindset, or even how they interact with the next potential customer, put themselves in the best position to be successful.

UNDERSTANDING SOCIAL SELLING

LO 4-1 Explain the significance of social selling in modern sales settings.

social selling A sales approach that develops, nurtures, and leverages relationships online to sell products or services.

As defined in earlier chapters, **social selling** is a sales approach that develops, nurtures, and leverages relationships online to sell products or services.[1] It is the modern way for sales professionals to initiate and develop meaningful relationships with potential customers. From the selling company's perspective, the goal is to have its salesperson and company be the first person or brand prospects think of when they're ready to buy.

The traditional selling process was often a one-way "conversation" between the sales representative and buyer. Salespeople were responsible for getting the prospect's attention and convincing him or her of a need for the product or service they were selling. Under the traditional model, sales was very much a "numbers" game, much like a funnel. If a salesperson made a 100 cold-calls, he or she could use past experience to project the resulting proportion of qualified leads, sales demos, and, ultimately, closed deals. Essentially, improved sales performance was based on either *working harder* (increasing the number of prospects at the top of the funnel via more cold-calls) or *working smarter* (improving the ratio of customers that pass through each of the phases lower in the funnel). So what has changed with social selling?

To be sure, working hard and working smart are still just as important to sales success. However, buyers today enjoy much greater control over the sales process than they did in times past. They no longer need to speak with a salesperson to begin learning about a company's solution. In fact, much of the information they are looking for is but a few mouse clicks away.

Imagine that you have just decided to purchase a used car. What would you do next? Would your first step be to contact a sales rep at a local dealership? For most individuals, that is unlikely. In most cases, buyers today will spend considerable time researching autos and other major purchases online before reaching out to a seller. In the auto-sales context, expert opinion sites likes Consumer Reports and Edmunds.com offer extensive information: vehicle ratings, pricing based on features and vehicle age, product recalls, average annual maintenance costs. You also could probably find dozens of user reviews from people just like you who have purchased the same car in the past.

Once you've narrowed down your search to a specific make and model of car, it is quite possible that the same or similar vehicle would be available for sale at multiple dealerships. At this stage, many people will consult directly with family and friends about their car-buying experiences at local dealerships. It is also quite likely you would look online for information about local dealerships through review sites like Yelp and Google Reviews. Keep in mind: All of this activity is occurring before you as a buyer have made even the first contact with a sales representative.

This same phenomenon is true for B2B buyers. In fact, one commonly cited industry report suggests that B2B customers are, on average, 57 percent of the way through the purchase process before they ever engage with a sales professional.[2] In addition, the rise of various digital-networking platforms has increased the ability of customers to gather information from each other prior to making a purchase decision. In fact, research firm IDC found that 75 percent of B2B buyers and

Roman Samokhin/michaeljung/123RF

84 percent of executives use contacts and information from social networks as part of their purchase process. Conversely, research shows that consumers as well as B2B buyers are increasingly averse to responding to cold-calls. One recent survey found that more than 90 percent of decision makers said they "never" respond to cold-calls![3]

Social Selling Versus Traditional Sales

In a relatively short time, social selling has transformed selling practices for many large companies and important industries. It has demonstrated considerable promise as a tool for helping salespeople develop customer relationships and businesses keep their brands at the forefront of customers' minds.

To be very clear, social selling is not the same as *social media marketing*. Social selling is a purposeful activity; it is not made up of random acts of social sharing, broadcasting promotional material across multiple networks, or cold-mailing content to prospects without any context or value. Effective social selling involves two-way conversations; it is not a series of broadcasts or spam messages.

Social selling augments existing sales approaches by reaching and engaging customers online, using their preferred social channels. Social selling also helps salespeople build personal relationships with buyers. Building a strong network through social media channels allows sellers to seek out introductions to new sales prospects through existing mutual connections. This enables the salesperson to more quickly create a sense of trust and personal rapport. Trust is an incredibly important resource for clients and salespeople—87 percent of B2B buyers say they would have a favorable impression of someone introduced to them through their professional network.[4] Figure 4-1 provides a graphical comparison between traditional sales approaches and social selling.

FIGURE 4-1 Comparing Traditional Selling to Social Selling

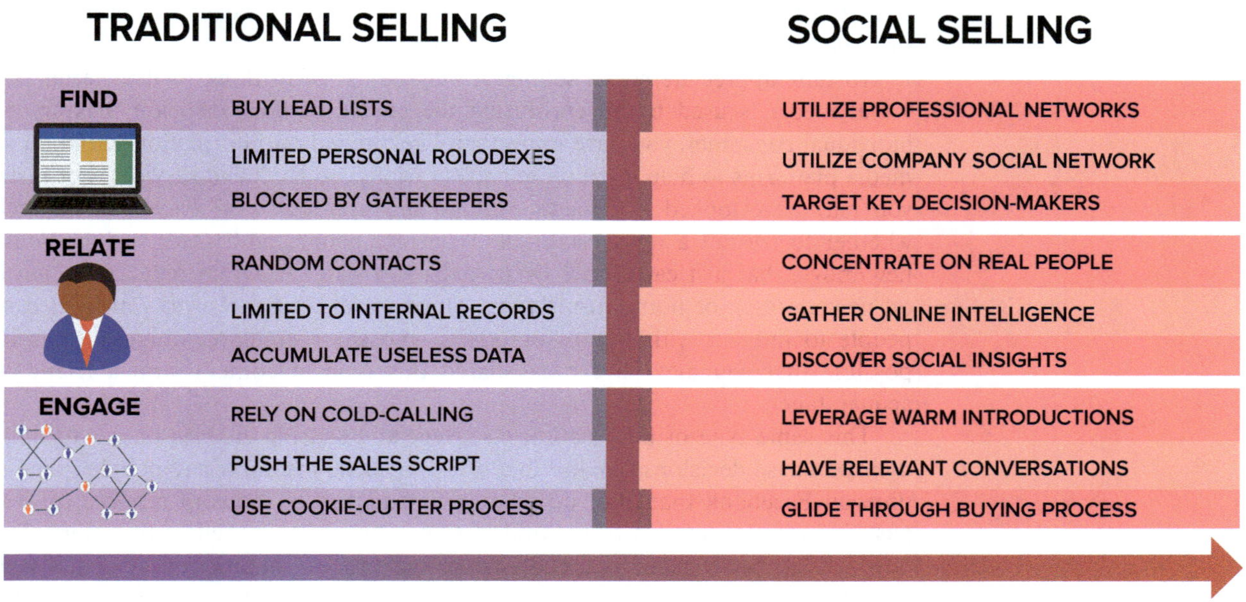

	TRADITIONAL SELLING	SOCIAL SELLING
FIND	BUY LEAD LISTS	UTILIZE PROFESSIONAL NETWORKS
	LIMITED PERSONAL ROLODEXES	UTILIZE COMPANY SOCIAL NETWORK
	BLOCKED BY GATEKEEPERS	TARGET KEY DECISION-MAKERS
RELATE	RANDOM CONTACTS	CONCENTRATE ON REAL PEOPLE
	LIMITED TO INTERNAL RECORDS	GATHER ONLINE INTELLIGENCE
	ACCUMULATE USELESS DATA	DISCOVER SOCIAL INSIGHTS
ENGAGE	RELY ON COLD-CALLING	LEVERAGE WARM INTRODUCTIONS
	PUSH THE SALES SCRIPT	HAVE RELEVANT CONVERSATIONS
	USE COOKIE-CUTTER PROCESS	GLIDE THROUGH BUYING PROCESS

Source: http://www.coldsalesprospecting.com/social-media-sales-prospecting.

Sharing insightful, helpful content with your audience is a key part of the social selling and marketing process. The benefits include:

- Building your brand, reputation, and authority.
- Generating trust by sharing and curating from a range of sources, not simply broadcasting your own content.
- Providing value to your customers and potential customers.
- Converting fans and followers into leads and customers.[5]

Most sales professionals sense that individual reps should use social-selling best practices in their day-to-day activities. But success or failure at the business level requires more: the buy-in of senior sales-team leaders and other key managers. To succeed at the business level, social selling must become an organizational strategy. Simply holding a one- or two-day workshop to teach salespeople about social media platforms is not a social-selling strategy.

What does it take to scale social selling to the organizational level? First, it often requires a fundamental shift in the firm's approach to customer relationships. In addition, implementation depends on close alignment and coordination of the sales and marketing functions. Improving social-selling efforts also requires a culture of accountability across the firm. Finally, measuring the effectiveness of such efforts requires a thoughtful approach to measurement. (After all, as the old saying goes, "If you can't measure it, you can't improve it.")

Social Buyers, Social Sellers

Why should sales professionals adopt social media? Because that is where they will find their current customers and prospects—many of whom are actively researching solutions to the very problems that salespeople can help solve. In short, social selling helps sellers meet buyers where they live, digitally speaking. Sales reps who excel at social selling help their organizations drive significantly higher revenues. One recent study suggests social sellers realize a 66 percent higher likelihood of quota attainment compared to those using traditional prospecting techniques.[6] Internet companies such as SAP, IBM, Oracle, and many others have reported significant improvements in key sales performance metrics from social selling.

To fully appreciate social selling, it may be useful to think of it in terms of how social media is used by buyers during the course of their decision making. As an individual consumer, you have more than likely relied on information found on social media platforms to help learn more about various products and services. For instance, you may have looked at reviews, videos, and user posts on Facebook in deciding whether to try out a new restaurant. What are people on Twitter saying about that new movie that just came out? Or perhaps you visit Instagram regularly to get ideas on new clothing or home furnishings? Since social media networks make it easy for people to interact with friends or others who share common interests, it is highly possible that you may have even shared this type of content with a friend or an acquaintance.

This same type of information discovery and sharing enables buyers to optimize their purchase decisions. We live in a world of social media, where people spend more time on Facebook than they do reading newspapers or industry reports. In decades past, information tended to be unidirectional, "pushed" by sellers to buyers. Today's buyers are more engaged in a customer-driven process empowered by digital technology. Buyers have more power—more tools, more information, more at stake, and more control over the sales process than they have at any time in history. What once gave salespeople a competitive edge—things like controlling the sales process, product information, and a great pitch—are no longer guarantees of success. And just to make things more difficult for salespeople, a growing array of technologies (caller ID, email spam filters, digital ad blockers, satellite radio, DVRs, and so on) enable customers to avoid marketing messages. Thus the ability to get the attention of prospects is rapidly deteriorating.

Because buyers today have become desensitized to generic messaging, social channels offer a vibrant alternative. If your buyer is a social buyer, then you need to be a social seller. When used well, social channels can foster authentic connections and personalized interactions.

Creating Value for B2B Buyers

Recent research suggests B2B buyers have started to rely extensively on social media sources during their decision making. For instance, one study shows that 83 percent of B2B executives use social media in their information searches, and 92 percent report that it influences their decisions.[7] Some estimates suggest that today's buyers complete around 70 percent of their purchase-decision journey before even initiating contact with a salesperson. As workplace demographics shift toward more millennials in decision-making roles, the trend toward greater reliance on social media as a source of information for B2B buying is likely to strengthen. A study by Google and Millward Brown Digital found that 46 percent of B2B decision makers are now between 18 and 34 years old (up from 27 percent in 2012), which, coincidentally, is the largest social media user demographic.[8] To repeat: If your buyer is a social buyer, then you need to be a social seller.

Why is social media valuable for B2B buyers? First, it enables them to conduct much of their pre-purchase information search activity independent of the seller. Accenture's State of B2B Procurement Study finds that 94 percent of B2B buyers conduct some degree of research online before making a business purchase; 55 percent conduct online research for half or more of their purchases.[9] The vast majority of these B2B buyers are now active and involved in social media. Further, while studies have shown the length of the overall purchase cycle for business buyers is unchanged, the amount of time members of buying units spend researching their problem and identifying potential solutions is increasing.[10] As a result, buyers today are much more knowledgeable about products and services prior to their initial contact with a company representative than they were in the past.

Second, compared with other digital sources, social media can speed up a buyer's information-search activity. Searching for specific information outside social media by using search engines or visiting company websites can be time-consuming. Social media searches typically provide more timely and relevant information, leading to greater buyer confidence.[11] Buyers are able to reach an understanding of their own needs and product requirements more quickly. Because they are receiving input from multiple sellers simultaneously, they are also better able to compare solutions.

Third, social media makes it easier for buyers to validate purchase-related information. Buyers can see what peers from similar organizations have experienced. Forms of such social proof are very important to B2C as well as B2B buyers. **Social proof** is independent, third-party verification that a salesperson or an organization can be counted on to deliver what they have promised. It doesn't matter if that social proof comes from friends or strangers. What matters is seeing evidence from peers—in this context, other buyers with similar needs. That evidence helps confirm for the buyer that the decision being considered is a good one.

Buyer testimonials and customer success stories are very powerful. Those that detail what is so great about a seller's product or service and how the solution benefited the customer provide valuable social proof. Increasingly, firms are investing in video-based testimonials and hosting them on branded YouTube channels. In addition

social proof
Independent, third-party verification that a salesperson or an organization can be counted on to deliver what they have promised.

to testimonials, having a strong online presence on social platforms is important. Choosing those that your buyers most often turn to enables buyers to research reviews of your product or service. There, they may even interact with other prospects and existing customers before deciding whether they want to buy.

Finally, an organization's social media content provides a convenient source of information for B2B buyers. The buyers can easily collect and share information about seller solutions with other members of the buying unit and across the organization. Individuals within the buying unit are better able to merge their own personal interpretations of the information to build a common understanding and knowledge base. Therefore, social selling organizations can quickly get their information in front of key decision makers and shape the contours of the buying conversation at an early stage. As a result, these firms are able to increase the percentage of sales "wins" and accelerate their customers' buying cycles.

USING SOCIAL MEDIA TO ENHANCE SALESPERSON CREDIBILITY

LO 4-2 Describe how social media tools can be used to enhance buyer perceptions of salesperson credibility.

If you are like most people, you put at least a little bit of thought each day into your personal appearance. In addition, certain social contexts deeply influence how we present ourselves in public. For instance, it is unlikely that you would wear the same clothes to a cocktail party reception at a fancy restaurant as you would if you were going to see a concert featuring your favorite rapper or rock band. Similarly, you and some other students reading this text probably have some experience interviewing for an internship or a job. Before your important meeting, did you take the time to think about your professional appearance? What clothes you were going to wear? Did you feel the need to get a fresh haircut or styling?

Positive feelings about one's looks and external appearance boost feelings of self-confidence and assurance. Research shows that whether you are a physician, an auto mechanic, or a salesperson, how you present yourself can likewise boost others' trust and confidence in your knowledge and abilities.[12] It is important for salespeople to "look" as good online as they do offline. After all, every salesperson is just one Google search away from being reviewed by a buyer. Positioning yourself as a capable professional who is passionate about helping customers begins with carefully "grooming" your social media profiles.

Developing a Buyer-Centric Social Profile

First impressions go a long way. There is a lot of competition for a decision maker's attention and time. Sales reps are often the first and biggest impression a target buyer has of a company, so it's important that sales reps build and maintain a professional brand. Go to LinkedIn right now and conduct a search of sales professionals in your community. Visit a few of their LinkedIn profile pages. Analyze the page as if you were a prospective customer: Does the seller's profile clearly communicate how he or she can add value to the customers or their business? What cues or signals are presented that indicate the seller is knowledgeable about the buyer's industry? Judging by the profile image, does the seller appear professional and trustworthy?

Success in social selling begins with establishing your credibility as an industry sales professional. The first question salespeople should ask in creating or revising their social media profiles is: "Who is my buyer?" Many salespeople mistakenly create social media profiles on LinkedIn and elsewhere with an eye toward attracting interest from talent recruiters: "Quota crusher." "President's Club Winner three years running." "Sales negotiation expert." None of these statements say anything about how the sales professional can help prospective customers solve *their* problems.

For salespeople just starting their social-selling journey, one way to make a social profile more buyer-centric is to take a close look at the social media profiles of several of their buyers. What are some of the keywords, business trends, and benchmarks the buyers use to describe themselves? By examining what LinkedIn groups B2B buyers belong to, salespeople may be able to gain a better idea of their interests as well as hot-button issues driving their decision making. Likewise, customer-posted comments, pictures and video, likes and dislikes posted by prospective customers on Twitter, Facebook, and Instagram can all offer similar clues for B2C as well as B2B sellers. Equipped with this information, salespeople can adapt their own profiles to more closely reflect those of their customers.

Choose a Photo, Headline, and Summary for Your Professional Profile
What's in a face? Quite a lot, apparently. From modern-day artists to ancient scholars, philosophers and poets have commented on the telling nature of the human face. Evidence from neuroscience and evolutionary biology suggests that we humans are hard-wired to pay close attention to the faces of others in order to help enhance our own chances of survival and successful reproduction. Facial expressions are among the most universal forms of body language. In fact, expressions used to convey emotions such as joy, anger, sadness, and fear are nearly identical across cultures.[13]

Prostock-studio/Shutterstock

Think for a moment about how much a person is able to convey with just a facial expression. A smile can indicate approval or happiness. While you might tell someone that you are "feeling fine," the look on your face might tell people otherwise. In the absence of other information, the expression on a person's face can help determine whether we trust or believe what that individual is saying. One study found that the most trustworthy facial expression involved a slight raise of the eyebrows and a slight smile. This expression, the researchers suggested, conveys both friendliness and confidence.[14] Research even suggests that we make judgments about people's intelligence based on their faces and expressions.[15]

So it should not surprise you to know that one of the first things anyone will notice about your LinkedIn profile is the photo. It is important to put some thought into your choice of image. It should be professional—don't use a selfie or a picture from your vacation last summer waving from the beach with a group of friends. Remember, this is a form of personal promotion not unlike an advertisement. You are the product! Whether you choose a conservative, plain-vanilla headshot or something that is a bit more edgy and creative, the photo should be consistent with how you are positioning yourself as a salesperson.

It's smart to take a similarly thoughtful approach to the professional headline, which in LinkedIn falls right below your name. You have 120 characters to differentiate yourself and establish personal credibility. This is valuable real estate, reinforcing the value you bring to a prospective client. Make it count!

Profile headlines remain useful tools in improving a company or salesperson's search page results and attracting clicks. The language you use should be precise. Include important keywords that customers might use in their searches. Don't squander the opportunity with corny messages ("Let's connect") or references to *Game of Thrones*. Most customers (not to mention prospective hiring managers) will not care about your passion for craft beer or your urban gardening hobby.

Finally, just below the headline, LinkedIn provides space for a summary section that can contain up to 2,000 characters. The first 200 characters are always visible, along with a "View More" button for the rest of the text. This huge block of text offers room for three to five short paragraphs as well as a few bullet points. Remember, this summary is not simply your résumé. Write your summary in a style that promotes your most important skills and achievements. It doesn't hurt to sprinkle in a few well-chosen keywords to enhance your profile's position on a search-engine results page.

If you are unsure what keywords to use in your headline or summary, try this tip: Copy five to ten headlines and summaries from industry professionals whom you admire—sellers as well as customers. Then paste them into a word-cloud tool or website (e.g., Wordle). Several keyword candidates should emerge prominently in the resulting cloud image.

Use Recommendations to Validate Trustworthiness
Referrals, testimonials, reviews, and recommendations have long been important sales tools. They help salespeople and selling organizations demonstrate the reliability and integrity underlying their products, processes, and people. For prospective buyers, this information serves as a form of social proof. It is particularly important under conditions of high uncertainty, in which people are unable to determine the appropriate behavior or response. Implicitly, this type of herding behavior is driven by the assumption that the other people—in this case, previous buyers—collectively possess knowledge about the current situation.

Personal recommendations are a powerful form of social proof, which can be leveraged to create new sales opportunities. However, many people are hesitant to ask others for their endorsement. So what is the key to gathering more and better recommendations from customers? It is simple—something most of us learned as children—*Do unto others as you would have them do unto you.* A staple of social psychology theory, the **law of reciprocity** suggests that when you do something thoughtful for others, that kindness is often returned to you in kind. So don't ask for a recommendation first; give one instead. Immediately following (not six months later) a great encounter, project, or experience with a customer, a socially savvy salesperson should give a recommendation to the customer. It makes sense to let the buyer know during the encounter that you will be sending him or her a recommendation, so they will be looking for it. In particular, the LinkedIn recommendation system is especially conducive to offering a recipient of such recommendations to return the favor.

law of reciprocity
Social psychology theory that when you do something thoughtful for others, that kindness is often returned to you in kind.

Connect Assignment 4-1

Salesperson Credibility

Please complete the Connect exercise for Chapter 4 that focuses on how social media can be used to improve salesperson credibility. Understanding how to develop a buyer-centric social media profile can help salespeople make a better first impression and improve the chances for sales success.

CREATING A PROSPECT-RICH SOCIAL NETWORK

Every day across virtually every industry, customers and prospects share incredibly valuable information on their social channels. They're basically telling sellers who are paying close attention exactly what they want and need! Using social tools to monitor public online conversations relevant to your industry allows members of the sales team to identify new leads who are already talking about your business, your competitors, or your industry. Smart salespeople will engage in *social listening* to hear what these customers and prospects have to say.

Social listening is the continuous scanning of social media channels for customer feedback. It might include direct mentions of your brand or discussions relating to specific keywords, topics, competitors, or industries. This information helps social sellers to improve their industry knowledge and develop professional relationships with prospects, so that they can reach out to them with useful information when the time is right. The goal of social listening is to gain insight and then act on any emerging opportunities.[16]

It's common for people to publicly share their opinions—whether about political issues or their favorite sports team. It's no surprise that people do the same about the brands and companies with whom they interact. It's far better to hear exactly what customers are saying in real time than to make assumptions about they want or need. With information prospects have shared on their public profiles about their needs, wants, and pain points, even a first point of contact can be personalized, relevant, and helpful. By tracking what people within a social network are saying, social listening helps sellers strengthen customer relationships and engage prospects with relevant and timely insights.

LO 4-3
Describe how salespeople can use social media to grow their social networks.

social listening
The monitoring of a brand's social media channels for customer feedback or discussion regarding specific keyword, topics, competitors, or industries, followed by analysis to gain insights and act on opportunities.

Tracking New Activity

As we'll discuss later in the chapter, it is useful to measure your social-selling performance. Doing so will enable you to make the most of the time and energy you spend social selling. (It also will help your manager measure *your* social-selling performance, which should help you stand out as an employee.) In terms of social listening, you will benefit from being able to track (and measure) new activity.

First, use Google Alerts and other social-monitoring tools to notify you of mentions of your customers or issues pertinent to them. Use Google search social lists and Hootsuite Streams to monitor what people are saying about you, your company, your industry, and your competitors. Watch for pain points and requests for recommendations, both of which provide natural opportunities for you to provide the solution to a problem.

Before reaching out to any of the leads you identify, check their following and follower lists to see if you have any mutual connections. If you do, ask your shared contact for an introduction. Make sure to customize your messaging based on the wealth of information people share on their professional social media profiles—mention a shared interest, for example, or that you particularly enjoyed a blog post they shared.

Then, stay in touch with your new social contacts over time. Pay attention to the content they're posting. Jump in from time to time with a "like" or a comment to let them know you've read and appreciated what they have to say. If a contact moves to a new position or company, send a quick note of congratulations. If you notice a contact asking for help or advice, jump in with a meaningful answer, even if it doesn't directly promote your product. Focus on how you can help your contacts or make their lives easier. If you can establish yourself as their go-to person in your industry, guess who they will call when they're ready to make a purchase?

By using social listening to keep up with emerging issues and concerns with key accounts, social sellers are positioned to strengthen relationships by offering timely, relevant information and support.

Building a Revenue-Generating Social Network

social CRM
The fusion of social media and customer relationship management, combining social networks, communication technology, communities, strategy, customer value, and relationships.

There is an old saying in sales that your "net-worth" is all about your "net-work." When a new salesperson is trying to make inroads with a promising account, it's important to quickly find the right decision makers and influencers. After all, competitors are trying their best to connect with these same individuals. Before salespeople can begin to leverage the power of their social connections in driving more opportunities, they must carefully build up and maintain their online social networks.

In the modern era of selling, most salespeople interact nearly daily with customer information contained in a CRM system. Modern CRM systems, such as those from Salesforce.com and Marketo, typically contain extensive details about clients and leads. In many instances today, this information is being augmented in real time with users' social media activities such as posts, comments, likes and dislikes, and white paper requests. This concept, referred to as **social CRM**, represents the fusion of social media and customer relationship management. It combines the conceptual elements of social media and CRM: social networks, communication technology, communities, strategy, customer value, and relationships. A key benefit of social CRM is the ability for companies to interact with customers across multiple channels; it enables selling

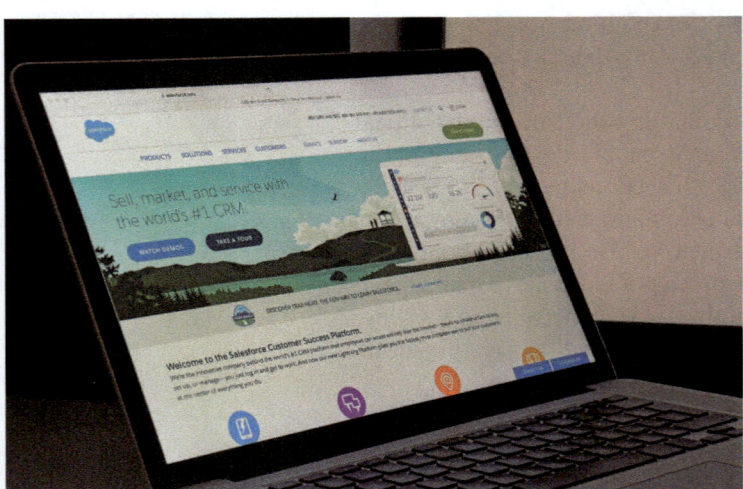
Casimiro PT/Shutterstock

companies to converse with customers in a style, manner, and online platform that are familiar and routine.

Even with the integration of these technologies, however, a CRM system should not be confused with a social network. A CRM system is simply a collection of contacts. A social network is a collection of *relationships*. In social selling, the salesperson's job is to merge these worlds together so they mirror each other. For example, a B2B salesperson for a manufacturer of industrial equipment may have 50 named accounts in her territory. If she knows that there are around five people on average involved in the typical purchase decision, then there are approximately 250 decision influencers who the sales rep needs to find for social relationships.

Socially Surrounding Your Buyer

Social-selling expert Jamie Shanks suggests it makes little sense to fastidiously keep a collection of data points within a CRM if a salesperson is not going to actively monitor and interact with that same buyer in a social environment. Shanks refers to efforts directed toward augmenting CRM data with social context as "socially surrounding the buyer." Socially surrounding a buyer is the activity of *finding* the buyer, *organizing* relevant information about the buyer, and then taking a sales *action*.[17] At its core, it is about understanding the micro- and macrostructure of the organizational buying unit. To do so, try to uncover answers to the following questions:

- Who else in the business will be part of the buying committee?
- Are there other divisions or related corporate entities and people within those organizations that I need to know?
- Who influences all those people? Stockholders? Industry experts? Competitors?

Tactics for Socially Surrounding Buyers

How do salespeople go about socially surrounding buyers? Experts suggest a number of tactics for mapping your company's CRM system to the buyer's social network. Creating a virtual organizational chart of the buyer's universe may sound complex. But it is worth a few minutes of your time to avoid finding out months later that you missed key people in the decision-making process.

The first step in socially surrounding a buyer begins by finding your buyer's information. Look on each of the major online and social platforms that are relevant for your industry and your buyer's interests:

- LinkedIn's people search criteria enable users to home in on specific geographic areas, industries, and job titles.
- Google Alerts provide a periodic (daily, weekly, monthly) digest of information from around the world on any company, person, or subject matter you need. Try this out yourself: Go to Google and set up a Google Alert about a company or a set of companies within an industry where you might be interested in working one day. You might use industry keywords to set up another Google Alert featuring news about trends in that industry.
- The Twitter Lists functions offer salespeople similar access to thought leaders and information you can use to better understand the totality of your customers' environment.

Using Trigger Events as Social-Selling Cues

Once you've socially surrounded the buyer or buying committee, what's next? In order to convert this information into leads and selling opportunities, social sellers need to search for cues that might trigger buying action. For instance, real estate professionals may wish to keep a close eye on news of executive promotions and transitions to new organizations; such information often precedes the purchase of a new home. LinkedIn offers advanced features that can notify a salesperson whenever a new hire or job change occurs within a specific account.

A similar technique would be to set up a search that identifies potential buyers who have recently left a key account that has been successfully serviced by your organization. These decision makers are going to want to make an impact quickly with their new organization. Very likely they will want to work with the same people, processes, and technology that made them successful at their previous company! LinkedIn has advanced people-search features that enable the user to specify a company name and whether the individual works there currently or has in the past.

Profiling a Buyer's Sphere of Influence

Keep in mind that your customers are inundated with information from a wide variety of sources each and every day. They care the most about information that has a direct, first-degree proximity to their own lives. To provide such information, you will want to identify your target customer's **sphere of influence**—that is, individuals or groups within one degree of separation from the sales prospect. Social sellers can use that information to selectively share content and insights that are perceived as relevant.

For instance, if you hope to create new sales opportunities based on sharing a particular client success story, it may be useful first to identify: (1) past and current employees of the featured company, (2) competitors of the company selected for the case study, and (3) vendors, partners, or customers who interact with the featured client on a regular basis. By taking the time to connect with prospects whose sphere of influence includes the firm or individuals featured in the client success story, you will likely gain a stronger response once you share and comment on the content.

You might also think about the hidden potential of your personal sphere of influence in support of your future job searches. LinkedIn's alumni search feature is a tool that allows you to highlight all previous attendees or graduates of your college or university. You may further segment the data by graduation date, cities, job function, employer, and so on. Depending on the size and reach of your school's alumni network, it is quite possible that you have an important shared life experience with someone at a business or industry in which you are interested. Even if a contact is not part of a prospective-buyer firm, by connecting and developing relationships with fellow alums, you may find that they have a first-degree connection with someone who *is* part of an organization that you are targeting in your job search. An introduction from this mutual acquaintance may help to unlock new professional opportunities.

sphere of influence
Individuals or groups within one degree of separation from the sales prospect.

CURATING AND SHARING RELEVANT CONTENT

LO 4-4 Explain how sharing relevant content is central to social-selling success.

In our digital world, access to information on nearly any topic you can think of is but a few keystrokes away. In this context, being viewed as a subject matter expert is an incredibly powerful resource. By establishing and building a strong relationship with a champion within a target account, sales reps greatly boost their chances of ultimately winning over the right people—and closing the deal.

Sales is all about influence without authority. A salesperson can build reputation and generate leads by being the first to share industry news, surveys, reports, case studies, and ideas. But first, social sellers must create or find quality content and then decide what's worth sharing and with whom. This is where content curation comes in. **Content curation** is the process of continually finding, grouping, and sharing across social networks the most relevant content on a specific issue.[18] The most important

content curation
The process of continually finding, grouping, and sharing across social networks the most relevant content on a specific issue.

component of this definition is the word "continually." Effective content curation requires a commitment: you need to stay on top of emerging ideas in areas of concern for customers and share useful information in a timely and accessible way. You add your voice—and value—to handpicked content, gathered from a variety of sources around specific topics.

Please note: Content curation is *not* the same as content creation. Writing blog posts, making YouTube videos, and Snapchatting—all examples of content creation—take considerable time and energy. Most sales managers want their sales people selling as much of the time as possible. For certain salespeople who are established authorities in a particular area, it may make sense to spend time, effort, and money to create original content. For those just starting out as social sellers, however, sharing something excellent created by someone else is usually sufficient to get and keep the conversation rolling.

Content curation involves a multi-step process by which a salesperson diligently works at:

1. Finding the best content from multiple sources in your sector or niche.
2. Filtering the content so only the most relevant and highest quality content remains.
3. Adding value to that content with commentary, context, questions.
4. Sharing the content with the right audiences, at the right time, in the right places.
5. Continuously repeating this process to build ongoing engagement and credibility.

Benefits of Content Curation

Nearly three-quarters of Americans say they suffer from information overload every day. Author Clay Shirky has a more accurate term for this experience: *filter failure*. In his view, "It's not about too much information—it's too much of the wrong information. We're letting too much of the wrong stuff in."[19] This situation creates an opportunity for social-savvy sales professionals. Customers are awash with data and information but short on insight. Content curation enables salespeople to insulate customers from information overload. By finding the best content and sharing it with the right people, salespeople can add value and save prospective customers time and effort. That's the best way to begin any relationship.

Continually curating and sharing content also helps to keep business people on their toes. For salespeople in particular, spending time finding, sifting, and reading pieces across the web, for your industry, helps you learn more about your customers and the business challenges they are facing.

Why is this important? The rise of ride-sharing apps like Uber and Lyft have transformed the way many people think about mobility. Think about the impact the ride-sharing phenomenon has likely had on automotive and car rental sales and marketing practices. In the same way, the knowledge and skills of a sales professional have a shelf life. Newly emerging technologies such as artificial intelligence, 5G networks, and virtual and augmented reality will continue to reshape the way individuals shop for products and interact with brands. Given such a rapid pace of change, how can you stay on top of your field? Continual learning is the best hope for survival. Buyers trust sales professionals who are knowledgeable about their industry and on top of news and trends. To build authority with your networks and prospects, you need to stay relevant and keep learning.

Sharing Curated Content

Social selling has been fueled in part by the sales-enablement movement that is rapidly gathering traction across many large and medium-sized sales organizations.

sales enablement
The process of providing salespeople with the information, content, and tools that help them sell more effectively.

Sales enablement is the process of providing salespeople with the information, content, and tools that help them sell more effectively.[20] Sales enablement provides salespeople with information they can use to successfully engage buyers at various stages in the sales cycle. Often this information takes the form of customer-facing content that is easy for prospects to consume and is reusable across the sales organization.

A common step in enacting a sales-enablement program is making a full audit of all sales-related content, which is hosted in a readily accessible digital library for salespeople to access. Much of the content for the library typically is developed by marketing personnel. In addition, some salespeople take the time to create their own personalized content that more closely fits their selling style or target customers.

Successful social-sales teams also share a broad range of content—not just the material they have created. Customers might not react positively if all a salesperson does on a social platform is repeatedly broadcast their own blog posts and company content. Such behavior can actually make it more difficult to build customer relationships. An expert content curator for a given sector will seek to provide a more rounded view of developments within their industry. A widely circulated guideline in digital marketing circles is the **5:3:2 rule** for social media sharing. It suggests the following breakdown for the content you share:

5:3:2 rule
Guideline for social media sharing that suggests content should be 50% curated from relevant third-party sources, 30% content you've created relevant to the brand and audience, and 20% fun, inspirational, or human-interest content.

- 50 percent should be curated from third-party sources relevant to your audience.
- 30 percent should be content you've created that is relevant to your brand and your audience.
- 20 percent should be content that's more personal: fun, inspirational, or human interest

Broadly following that guideline, at least half of social-selling content should be curated content produced from sources outside of the organization. A social seller might start by sharing a few curated posts to generate engagement and build a relationship with other content producers. That could include popular industry blogs, influencers, and even competitors. Next, the salesperson might show off his or her own expertise with an entertaining, educational piece of in-house content. Finally, mixing in some entertaining, human-interest content can help improve how relatable or likeable the salesperson appears to prospects and others within the industry.

Variations on the 5:3:2 rule include the 70:20:10 and 4:1:1 rules. These use the same categories as the 5:3:2 rule, just in different ratios. Regardless of the exact ratio that is ideal for a given industry, company, or salesperson, there is broad agreement that the majority of the content shared as part of a firm or salesperson's social selling efforts should come from external sources.

What Content Do Buyers Want?

Curated content can take a few different forms. The choice of content you use in support of social-selling efforts will partly depend on which social media channels you use. For example, audiences on LinkedIn, Twitter, Facebook, Instagram, and YouTube will have different tastes and expectations. Generally, wherever you post, it's a good idea to mix things up. Blog posts are quick and easy to read; there are literally millions of them from which to choose. Breaking news stories may be timely and offer insights that are highly relevant to your customer's interests. User-generated comments, reviews, and customer success stories may also serve to illustrate key points and bolster the credibility of the social seller and the firm they represent.

Sellers must strike a balance between the amount of self-promotion they do and the amount of engagement and conversation they participate in. When interacting with prospects and customers through social networks, it's important not to get too "pitchy." It's certainly okay to mention your product or service in some of your social posts, but don't make *all* of your posts sales pitches or presentations. Rather than simply praising the value of your product or service, your goal should be to contribute valuable information that can help establish you as an expert in your field. Write posts that share important knowledge but don't be afraid to share relevant posts from others as well. When sharing content from others, add a short comment of your own about how the knowledge can be applied in your specific field. Your goal in social selling is to establish relationships that will eventually lead to a sale, not to make a sale on first contact.

Figure 4-2 shows the most commonly shared types of curated content in B2B settings, which are discussed next.

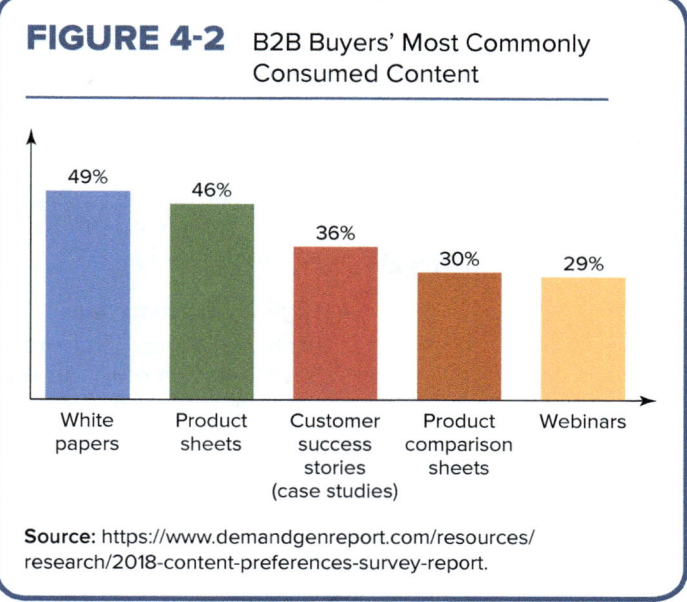

FIGURE 4-2 B2B Buyers' Most Commonly Consumed Content

Source: https://www.demandgenreport.com/resources/research/2018-content-preferences-survey-report.

White Papers
A **white paper** is an authoritative document intended to fully inform the reader on a particular topic. It combines expert knowledge and research into a document that argues for a specific solution or recommendation. The white paper allows the reader to understand an issue, solve a problem, or make a decision. White papers are data-centric, text-heavy business documents. Due to the large amount of data and research, white papers are deep reads and tend to have a formal tone. Businesses write white papers both to record expertise and to market themselves.

> **white paper**
> An authoritative document intended to fully inform the reader on a particular topic.

White papers are generally written for an audience outside of the business. Therefore they are a tool to attract readers to the company by offering top-quality industry knowledge. However, a white paper is a not a sales pitch. It sells the company by highlighting the internal expertise and valuable recommendations, not by bidding for business.

Product Specification and Comparison Sheets
A **product specification (spec) sheet** is a set of information and precisely organized data about a product. That information and data may contain:

- Description—What the product is about. Who made the product.
- Components/ingredients—What the product is made of.
- Usability—What the function of the product is. How to use it.
- Handling—How to take care of the product.
- Disposal—How to safely dispose of or recycle the product.

> **product specification (spec) sheet**
> A set of information and precisely organized data about a product.

These data are precisely organized to help the users of the sheet to a better understanding of the product. By issuing spec sheets, companies can easily tell customers a lot about the products they are selling. In addition, companies can also implement product spec sheets for internal communication between employees. Therefore, unsurprisingly, product spec sheets are useful for enterprises from various fields. Figure 4-3 shows a typical product spec sheet.

FIGURE 4-3 Example of Product Spec Sheet

Harald Biebel/123RF

Product benefits

Ergonomic footbed
The ergonomically designed foot shape provides room for your feet to spread naturally

High-grade materials
High-grade microfiber materials have been carefully selected to give you an enhanced level of breathability and comfort. Very durable and resistant to chemicals and scuffing.

Large toe box
Wider safety toe-cap prevents toes from being pinched

Safety toe cap
Lightweight composite safety toe cap giving the full 200 joule protection

CE Marked
EN ISO 20345 Certification
Anti-static

Technical information

Product code
03155 - Clog
04165 - Slip-on Shoe
04195 - Lace-up Shoe

Ordering details
Product Code + Color + Size
eg 03155BK08

Average weight (per shoe of size 6)
420g

Upper
Action-Breathe S2 microfibre

Insole
Antistatic fabric

Outsole
Antistatic direct moulded single density polyurethane SRC rated slip-resistance

Washability
Wipe-clean

Box measurements
Sizes 3-12
340×230×115mm

---

product comparison sheet
A product specification sheet that offers a side-by-side evaluation of the features or performance of alternative products.

Product comparison sheets are product specification sheets that offer a side-by-side evaluation of the features or performance of alternative products. By providing information that enables buyers to easily compare different options, social sellers are providing value to prospective clients. Product comparison sheets typically detail key performance features and advantages of different solutions in a fair and honest way. Often, this content will also include information such as prices and reviews.

One downside to using a product comparison sheet: It risks exposing buyers to rival solutions they may not have previously considered. On the other hand, this type of content can also serve to enhance perceptions of seller credibility and professionalism. Further, some buyers may be more likely to do their analysis on criteria presented by the seller's product comparison sheets.

customer success stories (case studies or testimonials)
Content that showcases one customer's experience as an example of the firm's products or services.

Customer Success Stories
Customer success stories (sometimes referred to as *case studies* or *testimonials*) are content that showcases the positive experiences of customers as the result of using a firm's products or services. This content may come in various forms—text, audio podcast, or video.

Clearly communicating how your product or service helped solve a problem for a customer makes your offerings more relatable and tangible to others. This type of content is ideal for building interest in the social-seller's solution. It helps makes clear that the salesperson and his or her firm have a clear understanding of the challenges faced by the prospect. By featuring the experiences of a real client, the depiction of product features and benefits appears more authentic. In addition, by using a story-like format, customer success stories attract stronger interest and better engage prospective buyers.

What is the trick to scripting a great customer success story? First, it is important to find the right customer. Experts suggest firms and sellers looking to create new success stories should identify customers who meet one or more of the following characteristics:

1. *Knowledgeable customers:* Social sellers should identify customers who have a great grasp of their product or service. Someone who can speak knowledgeably will better be able to describe the value of working with you.
2. *Quantifiable results*: Success stories that validate a great return on investment from working with your organization are influential. A customer who has experienced remarkable results will convey enthusiasm and be a champion for your business.
3. *Recognizable company*: A well-known client can lend credibility to the success story. In particular, smaller companies will benefit more from success stories featuring a customer with great name recognition.

Second, your success story should not be just a list of facts and stats. Great customer success stories are, first and foremost, *great stories*. As such, customer success stories typically follow a classic storytelling style. They introduce the main character (i.e., the "hero") and detail the situation, identify a problem (the "villain" in the story), introduce a solution to the problem (the hero's "ally"), and, finally, they present the outcome (the story's "happy ending"). By using a storytelling style, the customer success story will resonate more with potential customers.

Third, text-based content should be easy for time-stressed readers to skim. They should be able to review the easily digestible elements quickly and get a general sense of the story right away. This may prompt them to read the story in greater depth later. Even if they do not read the story in detail, they are more likely to recognize the key points. Careful formatting can help:

- Use bullet points and catchy-yet-informative headlines to help readers quickly determine whether the content will be useful for their decision-making process.
- Use bold or italic fonts to highlight important details (such as product name), statistics, and facts.
- In most cases, headlines should include the customer's brand or name, the selling firm's brand or product name, a compelling benefit, and if possible, a data point. For example: "How [Company] Used [Solution] to Build an Award-Winning App in Record Time" or "[Company] Saves [Amount] a Year After Switching to [Product]."
- Write the headline last, after the story comes together. This will make it easier to recognize the best elements of the story to feature in the headline.

Figure 4-4 shows some examples of attention-grabbing customer success story headlines.

Webinars Short for *web-based seminar*, a **webinar** is a presentation, lecture, workshop, or seminar that is transmitted over the Web using video-conferencing software. A key feature of a *webinar* is the ability to give, receive, and discuss information in real time. Webinars allow large groups of participants to engage in online discussions or training events. Technology enables participants to share audio, documents, or slides—even when they're not in the same place as the meeting host or in the same room where the event or presentation is taking place.

> **webinar *(web-based seminar)***
> A presentation, lecture, workshop, or seminar that is transmitted over the Web using video-conferencing software.

FIGURE 4-4 Attention-Grabbing Customer Success Story Headlines

By putting shoppers at the center of its business, adidas keeps winning.

adidas
ENTERPRISE, MARKETING CLOUD, CUSTOMER 360 PLATFORM, SERVICE CLOUD

See how KONE lifts its business to new heights with Salesforce Einstein and IBM Watson.

KONE
ENTERPRISE, MANUFACTURING, SALES CLOUD, SERVICE CLOUD

AWS grows from a startup to a powerhouse with millions of customers.

aws
SALES CLOUD, HIGH TECH, ENTERPRISE, COMMUNITY CLOUD

Salesforce.com

McGraw Hill connect | Connect Assignment 4-2

Developing Content

Please complete the Connect exercise for Chapter 4 that focuses on developing content to support social-selling efforts. Deciding which type of content is best suited for different types of potential buyers will help you strike a balance between the amount of self-promotion and the amount of engagement and conversation that is most beneficial.

MEASURING SOCIAL-SELLING PERFORMANCE

LO 4-5 Describe key performance indicators for assessing social-selling performance.

key performance indicators (KPIs)
Measurable, reliable metrics and milestones that demonstrate how effectively a company is achieving key business objectives.

How can a salesperson or organization know whether their social-selling efforts are effective? How can sales and marketing managers assess the quality of tactics and content used in social selling? A critical component to successful social selling is to develop social-selling **key performance indicators (KPIs)**. KPIs are measurable, reliable metrics and milestones that demonstrate how effectively a company is achieving key business objectives—in this case, social selling.

Of course, sales results are the ultimate metric. But the path to purchase for most buyers is often circuitous. It may take several weeks or even months for socially driven sales to emerge. Understanding the customer purchase journey for the organization's most common customer profiles is a first step to identifying social-selling KPIs. Then, sharing these metrics across the organization helps to ensure that sales and marketing management efforts are in alignment.

Experts in business-performance management often describe metrics in terms of lagging and leading indicators. **Lagging indicators** are performance measures that are *outcome* oriented. They are often easy to measure but tend to be difficult to quickly or directly improve or influence. **Leading indicators** are performance measures that are typically *process* oriented. They are hard to measure but relatively easy to influence.

A simple example illustrates the distinction between lagging and leading indicators. For many individuals, weight loss or being physically fit are important personal goals. A person's weight is a clear lagging indicator: It is easy to measure; you simply step on a scale and have your answer. But knowing how much you weigh does not necessarily help you track whether you are taking the steps you need to actually reach your goal. For that information, we need leading indicators. In this case, people seeking to lose weight will want to keep track of the number of calories they consume and the number of calories they burn each day.

lagging indicators
Performance measures that are "outcome"-oriented; often easy to measure, but tend to be difficult to quickly or directly improve or influence.

leading indicators
Performance measures that are typically "process"-oriented; hard to measure but relatively easy to influence.

Measure What Matters!

While tracking every social-selling action can seem complex and time-consuming, KPIs can help to reveal the strengths and weaknesses of any plan. With that information, sales management can fill the gaps with new tools, training, and solutions. This is particularly important for social selling—a concept still new enough to need constant monitoring. Using the available tools to record and measure metrics allows sales staff to monitor where their resources can be used most effectively.

For sellers to use social networks properly, they need to ensure that all activity is recorded. Fortunately, most modern sales teams regularly use CRM systems, many of which today include a "social network" field. Updating this information on a regular basis will help social sellers and managers demonstrate where leads are coming from and the impact of social media on lead generation and sales conversion.

Using a CRM puts customers at the heart of social-selling activity. It helps track leads and where leads that convert to customers come from. CRM systems also help to provide insight into where and how customers want to be contacted. For example, by monitoring and tracking leads on the CRM, a seller can establish that a prospect is active on Twitter and responds well to video assets on YouTube. This level of insight makes it easy to track and benchmark social media communications using tools that are standardized across the company. A monthly or quarterly report from a CRM can help identify what networks are proving successful. With that insight, salespeople can capitalize on the activities that work and revise or stop those that don't.

Establishing Social-Selling KPIs

It's important to track the success of social-selling efforts throughout the sales funnel. At the earliest stages, the focus is on *leading indicators*. Some examples of leading indicators at this stage:

- Number of posts and/or shared content.
- Engagement with shared content (for example, views, likes, comments, shares, and so on).
- Visits to your website that come from social media sites.
- Growth in community size (that is, connections, followers, and so on).
- LinkedIn Social Selling Index (SSI) score.

Social Selling Index (SSI)
A score that measures, based on four social-selling criteria, how a personal brand ranks in people's minds.

LinkedIn's Social Selling Index (SSI) is particularly noteworthy for B2B sales. It is a score that measures, based on four social-selling criteria (see below), how a personal brand ranks in people's minds. SSI has become one of the most popular social-selling metrics; it helps encourage engagement and establish goals for performance. Some studies show that sales reps with a high SSI can achieve 45 percent more sales opportunities.[21] The four different elements that help SSI to track selling efforts are:

1. Establishing a personal brand.
2. Engaging with social-selling insights.
3. Finding the right people.
4. Building relationships with decision makers.

Next, in the middle of the funnel, the focus is on *conversions*. Social networks are wonderful door openers. Most often, though, for larger and more complex sales, some sort of personal contact is required to convert that social lead into an actual sale. Some level of interpersonal interaction or collaboration is necessary for the sales professional to gain a better understanding of the customer's issue and provide the best solution at the right price. At this point, you need to measure social-to-real-life conversions—the extent to which online customer interactions with sales personnel or content lead to a phone conversation or face-to-face meeting.

social-to-real-life conversions
The extent to which online customer interactions with sales personnel or content lead to a phone conversation or face-to-face meeting.

Of course, at the end of the funnel, social sellers will be most interested in tracking socially driven sales. There's a wide range of lagging social-selling metrics that might be tracked at this stage:

- Number of leads or referrals from social selling.
- Number of phone calls or in-person meetings generated.
- Value of sales pipeline from social selling.
- Contract value of deals generated from social selling.
- Revenue generated from social-selling activities.

Given the network nature of social media platforms, referrals from social selling are of particular interest to many social sellers. According to a recent Nielsen study, "warm" referrals are four times more likely than cold-calls to result in a sale; 92 percent of people trust referrals from people they know.[22] Not only that, but new-referral business may actually be more profitable over the long run. A Wharton School of Business study found the lifetime value of a new-referral customer to be 16 percent higher than that of a non-referred new customer.[23]

Of course, sales managers are typically coaches for the sales reps they lead. At most firms today, they are interested in tracking metrics that measure use of social selling either at the granular salesperson-by-salesperson level or for a sales team as a whole. In addition, sales managers may be interested in the effectiveness of various types or pieces of content.

McGraw Hill connect | Connect Assignment 4-3

Measuring Social-Selling Performance

Please complete the Connect exercise for Chapter 4 that focuses on measuring social-selling performance. Developing measurable and reliable social-selling key performance indicator (KPI) metrics and milestones will help you be more successful with social-selling initiatives across industries.

Today's Professional Perspective... because everyone is a salesperson

Jason White
Acquisition Territory Manager
AT&T

Jason White

Describe your job. I am an acquisition territory manager. I oversee and sell to small businesses in a module of 31 Zip Codes that have combined annual revenues in excess of $16 million. I am tasked with developing strategic plans and using various execution methods to grow revenue in AT&T's wireline, wireless, and strategic portfolio, especially targeting customers not currently with AT&T.

How did you get your job? When I was a sophomore in college, I met an AT&T college recruiter at a job fair during a summer internship. He sold me on AT&T as a company and the AT&T Business Sales Leadership Development Program (now AT&T B2B Sales Program). We stayed in contact until my senior year. I accepted a position before entering my last semester in undergrad. After graduation I spent six months at the AT&T sales center in Atlanta, GA (now based in Dallas, TX). There I was taught a combination of business acumen and consultative sales skills, as well as in-depth industry and product knowledge. After completion I was moved into my current role.

What has been most important in making you successful at your job? Great people! I have been blessed to be surrounded by so many great individuals. Transitioning to a Fortune 10 company straight out of college can be a tremendous adjustment. I'm continuously surrounded by people with decades of sales and industry experience. They are invested in my personal and career growth. This is especially important in the technology industry, which is ever-changing. Having a plethora of resources is invaluable.

What advice would you give future graduates about a career in sales? First, sales is a very lucrative and rewarding career. The harder you work, the more money you make. Second, you will learn about not only your own company and industry but those of your clients as well, which will teach you something new daily. Last, don't expect to know everything at first. Give yourself time to learn and get comfortable. The most successful people are typically those who know how to best utilize their resources. When in doubt don't freak out—reach out.

What is the most important characteristic of a great salesperson? There are really three: being a great listener, likeability, and trust. As a consultative seller, you're kind of like a business therapist. Your job is to listen to understand how the customer's company works and their pain points, in order to help them solve business problems. People buy from people they genuinely like. People repeat buy from people they like AND trust. I'm a firm believer that if you can build rapport well and discover the challenges of a business while conveying that you truly have the customer's best interest at heart, you can sell almost anything.

CHAPTER SUMMARY

LO 4-1 Explain the significance of social selling in modern sales settings.

Social selling has transformed selling practices in today's business world. *Social selling* is the art of developing, nurturing, and leveraging relationships online to sell products or services. Social selling augments existing sales approaches by reaching and engaging customers online, using their preferred social channels. More and more selling organizations today are recognizing the potential of social selling to improve how their sales reps find, connect with, and engage with prospective buyers along their path to purchase. For prospective buyers, social media can serve as a form of *social proof*, independent third-party verification that a salesperson or organization can be counted on to deliver as promised. If your buyer is a social buyer, then you need to be a social seller.

LO 4-2 Describe how social media tools can be used to enhance buyer perceptions of salesperson credibility.

Success in social selling begins with establishing your credibility as an industry sales professional. One way to make a buyer-centric more buyer centric is to look at the social media profiles of several of your buyers. Notice the keywords, business trends, and benchmarks they use. Carefully develop your social media profile based on such information. Consider using referrals, testimonials, reviews, and recommendations in your social media profile to demonstrate the reliability and integrity underlying your company and your products.

LO 4-3 Describe how salespeople can use social media to grow their social networks.

Social listening is the continual scanning of social media channels for customer feedback. This information helps social sellers to improve their industry knowledge and develop professional relationships with prospects. These days, most salespeople interact nearly daily with extensive details about clients and leads in a CRM system. In many instances, such information is being augmented in real time with users' social media activities such as posts, comments, likes and dislikes, and white paper requests. This concept, referred to as *social CRM*, represents the fusion of social media and customer relationship management.

A key benefit of social CRM is the ability to *socially surround* customers across multiple channels and converse with them in a style, manner, and online platform that they use to talk with other customers. One tactic for socially surrounding target customers is to profile their *sphere of influence*—the individuals or groups within one degree of separation from the prospect. Social sellers can use that information to selectively share relevant content and insights.

LO 4-4 Explain how sharing relevant content is central to social-selling success.

Sales is all about influence without authority. Being the first to share industry news, surveys, reports, case studies, and ideas helps to build a salesperson's reputation, engage with their audience, and generate leads. But first, social sellers must find or create quality content and decide what's worth sharing and with whom. *Content curation* is the process of continually finding, grouping, and sharing across social networks the most relevant content on a specific issue.

The rise of social selling has been fueled in part by the sales-enablement movement. *Sales enablement* is the process of providing salespeople with the information, content, and tools that help them sell more effectively. A big part of sales enablement involves equipping salespeople with the tools and information they can use with customers at various stages in the sales cycle. Successful social sales teams share a broad range of content—not just the material they have created. Guidelines such as the *5:3:2 rule* suggest best practices for content sharing. Types of content to be shared in social selling include white papers, product specification and comparison sheets, customer success stories, and webinars. Sellers must strike a balance between the amount of self-promotion and the amount of engagement and conversation they participate in.

LO 4-5 Describe key performance indicators for assessing social-selling performance.

A critical component to successful social selling is to develop social-selling *key performance indicators (KPIs)*—measurable, reliable metrics and milestones that demonstrate how effectively a company is achieving key business objectives. *Lagging indicators* are performance measures that are *outcome* oriented. They often are easy to measure but tend to be difficult to quickly or directly improve or influence. *Leading indicators* are typically *process* oriented. They are hard to measure but relatively easier to influence. Using a CRM helps to keep track of leads and measure where leads that convert to customers come from (*social-to-real-life conversions*). A CRM also helps to provide insight into where and how customers want to be contacted.

KEY TERMS

social selling (p. 74)
social proof (p. 77)
law of reciprocity (p. 81)
social listening (p. 81)
social CRM (p. 82)
sphere of influence (p. 84)
content curation (p. 84)
sales enablement (p. 86)

5:3:2 rule (p. 86)
white paper (p. 87)
product specification (spec) sheet (p. 87)
product comparison sheet (p. 88)
customer success stories (*case studies* or *testimonials*) (p. 88)
webinar (p. 89)

key performance indicators (KPIs) (p. 90)
lagging indicators (p. 91)
leading indicators (p. 91)
Social Selling Index (SSI) (p. 92)
social-to-real-life conversions (p. 92)

DISCUSSION QUESTIONS

1. Identify an organization or specific salesperson who you think does a good job with social selling. What does that salesperson do that you think is most helpful to potential customers and effective in influencing buyer decisions?
2. Assume you were hired today for a sales position with an organization you would love to work for. What would you do to develop a buyer-centric social media profile for yourself? What could you do on social media to increase potential clients' level of trust in you?
2. If you were trying to sell a new computer system to your college or university, who would be in your school's sphere of influence? How do the people and organizations in that sphere of influence affect what content you share and which insights you think will be perceived as most relevant in helping you win the computer business at your school?
4. Share a customer success story for something you have bought in the past two years that has had a positive impact on you or someone you know. How has that specific product helped you or someone you know? Why do you think this story could be powerful in helping an organization sell more of the product that benefited you?
5. Establish some social-selling KPIs for yourself. As you get closer to graduating, how do the metrics on the social media content you share compare with those from one year ago? You can examine any platforms you want (Facebook, Instagram, Twitter, etc.) and you can use any of the leading indicators discussed in this chapter.

ETHICAL CHALLENGE

In 2017, TD Bank, which has its U.S. headquarters in Cherry Hill, N.J., and is one of the larger banks in North America, faced criticism that ambitious revenue goals pressured employees to aggressively up-sell and sign up customers for services they did not need. Employees alleged that they were pressured to meet high sales-revenue goals. Some employees admitted they have broken the law at their customers' expense in a desperate bid to meet sales targets and keep their jobs. These employees, who have worked more than 50 years combined at the bank, said that the sales goals incentivized them to put their own sales goals ahead of customer needs.

Hundreds of current and former TD Bank Group employees described a pressure-cooker environment, using terms like "poisoned," "stress-inducing," "insane," and "zero focus on ethics." Some employees admitted they broke the law, claiming they were desperate to earn points toward sales goals they had to reach every three months or risk being fired.

TD insisted that all of its employees are to follow the company's code of ethics. But many employees said that's impossible to do given the sales expectations. "I've increased people's lines of credit by a couple thousand dollars, just to get sales revenue points," said a teller who worked for several years at a TD branch in Windsor, Ontario. He admits he didn't tell the customers, which is a violation of the federal Bank Act.

Up-selling—selling add-on products or services to existing customers—has received a bad reputation lately. However, if done ethically, up-selling can be a positive thing. It increases the likelihood of repeat business and referrals. What is the difference between ethical and unethical up-selling? Fulfilling identified customer needs, clearly outlining fees, and mentioning any restrictions build customer trust and are ethical. On the other hand, giving misleading information, failing to mention fees, and being pushy represent unethical up-selling.

Questions

1. Can you think of a time when someone tried to up-sell products to you? Do you feel it was ethical or unethical? Describe your example and explain your answer.
2. Assume you are the CEO of a large bank. How would you set incentives for your tellers and other salespeople to balance the need for additional revenue for your bank with the requirement that they not be unethical when dealing with customers?

3. Do you think certain industries, such as finance, healthcare, sports, or higher education, have particularly unethical sales practices? If so, what would you recommend those industries do to make sure they have better ethical sales practices in the years ahead?

Source: Erica Johnson, "We do it because our jobs are at stake: TD bank employees admit to breaking the law for fear of being fired," March 10, 2017, https://www.cbc.ca/news/business/td-bank-employees-admit-to-breaking-law-1.4016569.

ROLE PLAY

This role play will give you experience in presenting social-selling strategies to a potential client. For this role play, half of your class will be salespeople for a social media marketing firm engaging small- and medium-sized businesses in the community where your college is located. The salespeople develop solutions as to which social media platform and which two types of content each client should use. The salespeople should highlight reasons why they are recommending this specific solution to the small-business owned by their role-play partner.

The other half of the class will be the owners of a small- or medium-sized business of your choice that currently exists in the community where your college is located. The business needs to improve its social-selling capability to be more successful. Each business owner will share the name of their company in advance with their role-play partner and then listen to the sales solution that is presented. The small business owners can question why the recommended solution offered by the salesperson is the best fit for their specific business and whether social media and curated content are even important to their company. At the end of the role play, the buyers will decide whether they want to purchase the recommended solution by the social media marketing firm.

At the end of the role play, both the salesperson and the business-owner student should reflect on what parts of the social-selling presentation were most effective in leading the buyer to purchase the recommended solution or what part of the presentation kept the business owner from making the deal.

SALES PRESENTATION

For the Connect assignment in Chapter 4, students will get practice presenting how their social media profiles would be effective in their social-selling efforts. Give a three- to five-minute presentation on why your social media profile would help develop trust and enhance credibility for a prospective employer whom you are trying to sell on the idea of hiring you. Be sure to discuss at least one social media tool you learned about in this chapter.

CAREER TIPS

George D. Deitz

George Deitz
Marketing Professor
University of Memphis

Managing Your Social Media Profile

Ask yourself: "What are people seeing about me online? Am I being perceived as a professional? Is there something that is being seen that might negatively affect someone's desire to work with me?" If you don't like the answers to those questions, it's time to fix your social media profile.

With so many popular social media platforms available worldwide and new ones emerging on a regular basis, it's important to know three things:

1. What platforms do your target prospects—either customers or employers—use in their businesses?
2. What platforms do employers and potential clients use to search for information about your personal credibility and expertise?
3. What techniques should be used to properly and effectively use the platforms favored by clients or prospective employers?

The simplest way to find out where your customers and prospective employers go online is to ask a few of them. The answers you receive will probably depend on your audience. If you offer products or services to consumers, you're more likely to find them on Facebook, Instagram, and Twitter. If you sell in a B2B context, the key contacts you are looking for are more likely to cultivate their professional relationships on LinkedIn.

CHAPTER ENDNOTES

1. https://business.linkedin.com/sales-solutions/social-selling/what-is-social-selling.
2. Corporate Executive Board. (2019). "The Digital Evolution of B2B Marketing," accessed at https://www.cebglobal.com/content/dam/cebglobal/us/EN/best-practices-decision-support/marketing-communications/pdfs/CEB-Mktg-B2B-Digital-Evolution.pdf.
3. InsideView. (2011). "The Death of Cold Calling—Ending the Debate," accessed at https://blog.insideview.com/2011/03/18/the-death-of-cold-calling-ending-the-debate/.
4. Newberry, Christina. (2019). "Social Selling: What is it, Why you Should Care, and How to Do it Right," accessed at https://blog.hootsuite.com/what-is-social-selling/.
5. AndersPink. (2019). "Selling is Sharing: How Content Curation Makes you a Better Social Seller," accessed at https://static.anderspink.com/AndersPink_SocialSellingAndContentCurationBook.pdf.
6. Campbell, Oleg (2020), "101 Social Selling Stats you Need to Know," accessed at https://reply.io/101-social-selling-stats.
7. E. Schimel, "Strategic social media is essential for driving B2B sales," *Forbes*, 2018, https://www.forbes.com/sites/forbesagencycouncil/2018/03/22/strategic-social-media-is-essential-for-driving-b2b-sales/#52cf25001db0.
8. Kantrovitz, Alex. (2015). "Google Says Millenial Influence on the Rise in B2B Buying," accessed at https://adage.com/article/btob/google-millennial-influence-rise-b2b-buying/297552.
9. Accenture. (2014). "2014 State of B2B Procurement: Uncovering the Shifting Landscape in B2B Commerce," accessed at https://www.accenture.com/t20150624t211502__w__/us-en/_acnmedia/accenture/conversion-assets/dotcom/documents/global/pdf/industries_15/accenture-b2b-procurement-study.pdf.
10. Mertes, Nicole. (2018). " 7 of the Best Findings from the 2018 B2b Buyers Survey Report," accessed at https://www.weidert.com/whole_brain_marketing_blog/b2b-buyers-survey-takeaways.
11. M. R. Morris and J. Teevan, "Exploring the complementary roles of social networks and search engines," in *Human-Computer Interaction Consortium Workshop (HCIC)*, 2012.
12. S. U. Rehman, P. J. Nietert, D.W. Cope, and A. O. Kilpatrick, "What to wear today? Effect of doctor's attire on the trust and confidence of patients," *The American Journal of Medicine* 118, no. 11 (2005): 1279–1286.
13. P. Ekman, "Facial expression and emotion," *American Psychologist* 48, no. 4 (1993): 384.
14. A. Todorov, S. G. Baron, and N. N. Oosterhof, "Evaluating face trustworthiness: A model based approach," *Social Cognitive and Affective Neuroscience* 3, no. 2 (2008):119–127.
15. K. Kleisner, V. Chvátalová, and J. Flegr, "Perceived intelligence is associated with measured intelligence in men but not women, *PLOS ONE* 9, no. 3 (2014): e81237.
16. Ameresan, Swetha. (2018). "What is Social Listening and Why is it Important?" Accessed at https://blog.hubspot.com/service/social-listening on 5/30/2020.
17. Jamie Shanks, *Social Selling Mastery* (Hoboken, NJ: Wiley, 2016).
18. Good, Robin. (2010). "Content Curation: Why is the Content Curator the Key Emerging Online Editorial Role of the Future," accessed at https://www.masternewmedia.org/content-curation-why-is-the-content-curator-the-key-emerging-online-editorial-role-of-the-future/#ixzz4Hax8fLtN.
19. Asay, Matt. (2009). "Shirky: Problem is Filter Failure, Not Info Overload," accessed at https://www.cnet.com/news/shirky-problem-is-filter-failure-not-info-overload/.
20. Albro, Scott. (2019). "Sales Enablement: The Who, What, When, How, and Why of Sales Enablement," accessed at https://blog.topohq.com/sales-enablement-who-what-how-when-why/.
21. LinkedIn. (2020). "Measuring your sales success with the Social Selling Index," accessed at https://business.linkedin.com/sales-solutions/social-selling/the-social-selling-index-ssi.
22. Zasso, Julia. (2015). "Referral Selling: The Easiest, Most Effective Sales Method," accessed at https://www.lessannoyingcrm.com/resources/referral_selling_2.
23. Schmitt, Philipp; Skiera, Bernd; Van den Bulte, Christophe (2011), "Referral Programs and Customer Value," *Journal of Marketing*, 75(1): 46–59.

Chapter 5

Sales-Presentation Strategies

Learning Objectives

After reading this chapter, you should be able to:

LO 5-1 Describe the three main types of sales presentations.

LO 5-2 List activities that are useful in preparing effective sales presentations.

LO 5-3 List reasons for sales-presentation failure and strategies to prevent such failures.

LO 5-4 Describe the importance of nonverbal behaviors in sales presentations.

LO 5-5 Name elements of effective virtual and team-sales presentations.

LO 5-6 Describe the impact of storytelling on sales presentations.

Executive Perspective ... because everyone is a salesperson

Lance Gooch
Contractor Sales Representative
84 Lumber

Lance Gooch

Describe your job.

I am a contractor salesman for 84 Lumber Company, a building-materials supply company that owns and operates over 250 stores throughout 30 states. In most types of sales jobs, there are two types of positions—specialists and generalists. Specialists focus primarily on limited products or markets. For example, a specialist in my industry might sell one specific building product to residential builders only. Generalists sell a wide array of products to a wide array of markets. I'm a generalist: I sell framing materials, windows, doors, and interior trim materials to residential, multi-family, and commercial contractors. I sell multiple brands within each of those categories and products.

With such a wide variety of products, it is vital that I have product knowledge on each one, to stay ahead of my competition. Though I sell to all types of contractors, the bulk of my business is framing materials for residential home builders. Using their sets of house plans, I determine the type and quantity of lumber and materials needed to build the house.

How did you get your job?

In my previous job I worked as a manufacturer's representative (a specialist) for a weatherization company. In that job, I was selling to the largest residential home builder in my market. The key decision makers for this builder told me that their lumber salesman was looking to retire, and they asked if I wanted to make a change to supplying their framing materials. They said the traits they want in their lumber salesmen were the traits they saw in me. The rewards and opportunity of this new job were more than I could dream of. While I truly hated the thought of leaving the manufacturer that was so good to me, it was a no-brainer to switch to this job in lumber.

What has been most important in making you successful at your job?

As a generalist, I have to do multiple things: provide excellent service, know my products thoroughly, understand and analyze prices to maximize revenue for my company while also being the most competitive to the builder, and keep strong relationships. Overall, to do those things, I wake up each day with the mindset of "how can I earn your business?" for each existing customer. Everyone knows the Golden Rule: "Treat others as you would want to be treated." For me to be successful in sales, I believe in a salesperson's Golden Rule: "Treat customers as *they* would want to be treated."

What advice would you give future graduates about a career in sales?

As a salesperson, always remember that "perception is reality" to your customers. To get that customer, stay persistent, professional, and be a solution to the current obstacles they're facing. There is always going to be a "buy time" for your customer. Just because the customer said "no" doesn't mean there isn't a future moment when he or she will say "yes." Once you have that customer, if you show you are honest, hard-working, responsive, and ultimately their partner, it is going to be hard to lose that customer.

Also, no matter how successful you are in sales, be that much more successful in your personal life. Never get so caught up in work that you miss out on creating memories with your family and loved ones. Find a job that makes you happy, with a work-life balance. You will one day retire from your career, but you will never retire from being a great spouse, parent, and friend.

What is the most important characteristic of a great salesperson?

A stellar reputation in your industry is important. Salespeople who display drive and professionalism, who do what they say they're going to do, who help their customers grow their business, and who show no complacency will eventually get talked about in the industry. The most rewarding sales I make come not from cold-calling a company, but come when a company calls *me* looking to do business because of what they've heard about me. At that point, the sky is the limit.

What advice do you have about making sales presentations and visiting with individual customers?

I would encourage everyone to really understand each customer individually. One customer might like a good price and to be taken out to dinner from time to time. Another customer might expect great service and your ability to answer any question about the products you are selling. I take pride in understanding my customer and in understanding what I need to do, specific to them, in order to fit into their success.

TYPES OF SALES PRESENTATIONS

LO 5-1 Describe the three main types of sales presentations.

sales presentation
The delivery of product information relevant to solving the customer's needs.

The **sales presentation** is the delivery of product information relevant to solving the customer's needs. As the "main body" of the sales call,[1] it can be the most challenging, rewarding, and enjoyable aspect of the buyer-seller interaction. The sales presentation with a prospective buyer is a crucial stage of the selling process.

Sales presentations can be formal or informal, in front of a single buyer or an entire company. They can take place in a board room, a lumber yard, or just about any place you can imagine. Regardless of the setting, salespeople who are prepared and who select the most appropriate type of sales presentation can increase their likelihood of closing the sale.

persuasion
A communication process by which you motivate someone else to voluntarily do something you would like them to do.

memorized sales presentation
Sales presentation in which the salesperson presents the same selling points in the same order to all customers; typically involves the salesperson talking 90 percent of the time and listening around 10 percent.

Developing a sales-presentation strategy begins with choosing one of the three main types of sales presentations: *memorized, formula,* and *need-satisfaction* presentations. It is important for salespeople to consider which type of presentation will be most persuasive to their customers. **Persuasion** is a communication process by which you motivate someone else to voluntarily do something you would like them to do. Each of the three types of presentations provides different advantages and disadvantages and can be appropriate for different products, industries, and salespeople with different levels of experience. The biggest difference among the three methods is the percentage of conversation controlled by the salesperson.

Memorized Sales Presentations

In a **memorized sales presentation**, the salesperson presents the same selling points in the same order to all customers. This type of presentation ensures that salespeople will provide complete and accurate information about their product or service. A memorized sales presentation typically involves the salesperson talking 90 percent of the time and listening only around 10 percent.

simonkr/Getty Images

A memorized sales presentation is often beneficial for new salespeople. It helps them speak intelligently about different products and gives them confidence. Pharmaceutical salespeople often use this technique because they can deliver accurate technical information to doctors in a short period of time. This type of presentation is also used in telemarketing and direct sales.

However, the effectiveness of the standard memorized presentation is limited. It offers no opportunity for the salesperson to tailor the presentation to the needs of specific customers. In addition, some buyers view a memorized sales presentation as amateurish, since the salesperson is not focused on providing a customized solution for the buyer's organization. Also, it is difficult to persuade customers who have complex buying needs without a greater percentage of the presentation being dedicated to listening to their specific problems.

formula sales presentation
Sales presentation in which the salesperson follows a somewhat less structured, prepared outline, allowing more flexibility and opportunity to gather customer feedback; typically involves the salesperson talking 60–70 percent of the time and listening 30–40 percent.

Formula Sales Presentations

The formula sales presentation begins to shift the focus more to the customer. In a **formula sales presentation**, the salesperson follows a somewhat less structured, prepared outline, allowing more flexibility and opportunity to gather customer feedback. It still focuses on the product, but it encourages the customer—through questions, trial closes, and objections—to become more involved in the presentation. The talk/listen ratio changes to more listening (30 to 40 percent of the time) and less talking (60 to 70 percent of the time).

Formula sales presentations are based on the simple acronym *AIDA*, which sums up the buying process: The salesperson must get the customer's *attention*, create *interest* in the product, develop a strong *desire* for the product, and move the customer to *action* (to buying the product). The salesperson controls conversation during the presentation, especially at the beginning. Formula presentations allow for the smooth handling of anticipated questions and objections from the customer, which increases customer involvement.

Formula sales presentations are ideal for a variety of organizations and brands. For example, Procter and Gamble might encourage the use of formula presentations by its salespeople. The object for consumer-products salespeople is often to persuade customers to carry more of an existing product, such as more sizes of Crest toothpaste or greater inventories of Bounty paper towels. A highly structured formula presentation, which hits specific selling points in a predetermined order while still soliciting customer feedback, can be very effective. The key to the success of the formula strategy is customer knowledge, since the presentation itself is relatively inflexible.

What are the disadvantages of the formula sales presentation? The first is that the structured outline might not be effective if the salesperson does not know the prospect's needs. Salespeople might need the customer to talk a majority of the time in order to better understand the prospective buyer's needs. In addition, the formula sales presentation is often not ideal when dealing with a complex selling situation such as selling a technical product or selling to a large group.

Need-Satisfaction Sales Presentations

In a **need-satisfaction sales presentation**, the salesperson first probes into the needs—both stated (expressed) and unstated (latent)—of the prospective buyer. The salesperson then gives a sales presentation that shows how the product will satisfy the customer's needs. Over 60 percent of a need-satisfaction presentation is dedicated to listening to the customer to learn more about their specific problems.

The need-satisfaction presentation allows a salesperson to develop a customized solution for the buyer. Think about a few positive sales experiences you have had as a customer; it is likely that one or more of those involved a salesperson asking questions and helping find the best product for your need at that time. Or, in a B2B setting, a salesperson visits a major financial company. In conversation, it emerges that the company has not changed its market segments for some time, mostly because it has been focused on short-term operational issues. In the presentation, the salesperson shows data on a competing firm that has used a new strategy to eat away at this company's customer base. When the customer starts getting worried, the salesperson talks about the need for more specific market details and rapid analysis. When the customer asks how this can be achieved, the salesperson introduces the CRM system he or she is selling.

The more interactive nature of a need-satisfaction presentation can be intimidating for a new salesperson. Less-experienced salespeople are often nervous in this type of presentation, knowing they will need to listen carefully and then quickly craft a response using what they've just learned. Training and experience can help salespeople feel more comfortable giving up control of a majority of the presentation.

Each of these sales-presentation methods can be very successful. It's also true that each can fail miserably. The decision as to which sales-presentation method to use should always be focused on (1) the strengths and weaknesses of the salesperson presenting, (2) the preferences of the potential buyer, and (3) the specifics of the

need-satisfaction sales presentation
Sales presentation in which the salesperson first probes into the needs, both stated (expressed) and unstated (latent), of the prospective buyer; typically, over 60 percent of the presentation involves listening to the customer to learn about their specific problems.

product being sold. Salespeople should think through each of these variables. Each time, you should be able to explain the decision to yourself, a colleague, or a manager as to why you chose a specific presentation method for a specific customer.

Connect Assignment 5-1

Sales Presentations

Please complete the Connect exercise for Chapter 5 that focuses on types of sales presentations. Deciding which type of presentation is best suited for different types of potential buyers will help you customize your sales strategy to maximize success.

PREPARING THE SALES PRESENTATION

LO 5-2 List activities that are useful in preparing effective sales presentations.

Regardless of sales-presentation type chosen, salespeople must actively prepare in order to achieve an effective presentation. Where do you start? A logical first step is to develop a **customer-value proposition**, which is a statement of how the sales offering will add value for the buyer and/or the buyer's organization. For example, a retail salesperson visiting with a customer about purchasing a new iPhone has to persuade the customer of the value of the product relative to other smart phones *and* the value compared to the older iPhone the customer currently uses. The salesperson is trained to present many aspects of customer value: the value proposition in the design of the new device, the ease of use that has been a cornerstone of Apple's success, the better camera (which might be especially important to a customer who has children or is active on social media), and the aspirational qualities that a new iPhone offers. For long-term success in relationship selling, it is essential to properly define the customer value of your company's products during the limited time of a sales presentation.

customer-value proposition
A statement of how the sales offering will add value for the buyer and/or the buyer's organization.

36clicks/123RF

With the customer-value proposition in mind, the salesperson can begin to prepare a sales presentation. Salespeople use a variety of activities to improve the quality of a sales presentation: identify the customer problem, plan what you want the customer to remember, consider a product demonstration, provide slick data, and practice through role play.

Identify the Customer Problem

At the heart of modern selling is the ability to come up with solutions to problems for customers that provide benefits for the customers or their organization. So, an activity essential to preparing an effective presentation is to clearly identify the problem you are seeking to solve for the customer. Being able to state the problem is almost as crucial as knowing what destination to type into digital mapping software.

features
Factual statements about the characteristics of a product.

benefits
The added value that a feature provides for the customer.

Most sales presentations, at some point, cover features and benefits. **Features** are factual statements about the characteristics of a product, such as how many pages a machine can print in a minute or the how long the battery life of a cell phone is. **Benefits** are the added value that a feature provides for the customer.

When preparing a sales presentation, it is important to think through how the product will benefit someone else's business or life. New salespeople, especially, spend so much time talking about product features that they fail to draw a connection to the benefit of solving the customer's problem. For example, imagine you are selling a local lawn care service. The sales presentation might take place in a short conversation on a homeowner's front porch. To address the benefit your service would provide, you would want to mention the homeowner's problem of needing their lawn taken care of while providing the benefit of saving a couple of hours per week for the homeowner to spend more time with family or pursue other interests.

Too often, even experienced professionals start a sales presentation by talking about the solution they are offering rather than the problem they are solving. If salespeople are presenting to outsiders, or even high-level leaders inside their own company, they might not have been closely following the development process of a specific project. If salespeople don't explain the context and why it matters upfront—that is, the problem and benefits the sale will deliver—they risk buyers tuning out early on because they are not sure if the salesperson's idea is relevant.

Plan What You Want the Customer to Remember

Great presentations are memorable. When preparing a sales presentation, spend time thinking about what you want the customer to remember. Focusing on key words, phrases, or images during the presentation can be critical to the customer remembering the information after the presentation. Customers will use these memories as they make purchase decisions.

Being memorable does not have to be saying something funny or wearing something outlandish. Presenting product information that solves a specific customer problem and helps the business be more successful is likely to be something remembered long after the meeting has ended. If you intentionally plan for a memorable takeaway message, you are more likely to make it happen.

Consider a Product Demonstration

A **product demonstration** shows the customer how the product works; it is one of your best sales tools if you have a high-quality product. A product demonstration helps get a prospect interested and excited about the proposed solution. It is also an effective way to address the prospect's specific product-related concerns. Research suggests that over 50 percent of potential buyers want to see how the product works during the first sales call.[2]

The most important thing to remember if using a demonstration is this: You must be certain the demonstration will work. Few things can ruin a sales presentation faster than a failed demonstration. For example, if you are showing how a new car feature will supposedly make life easier for a buyer only to have that demonstration fail, the customer will wonder if the salesperson is competent and if the car is best for them. If you are going to do a demonstration, be sure to practice it multiple times.

product demonstration
Sales presentation that shows the customer how the product works.

Provide "Slick" Data

A previous chapter discussed the need for salespeople to have technological knowledge. When planning your sales presentation, think about how to put that knowledge to work using "slick," cutting-edge data-visualization techniques. **Data visualization** is the presentation of data in a graphical format using visual elements like charts, graphs, timelines, and maps. Such elements add interest to a presentation; they replace data in boring tables or basic charts that a customer tunes out. Potential buyers need

data visualization
The presentation of data in a graphical format using visual elements like charts, graphs, timelines, and maps.

FIGURE 5-1 Data Visualization of Customer Complaints

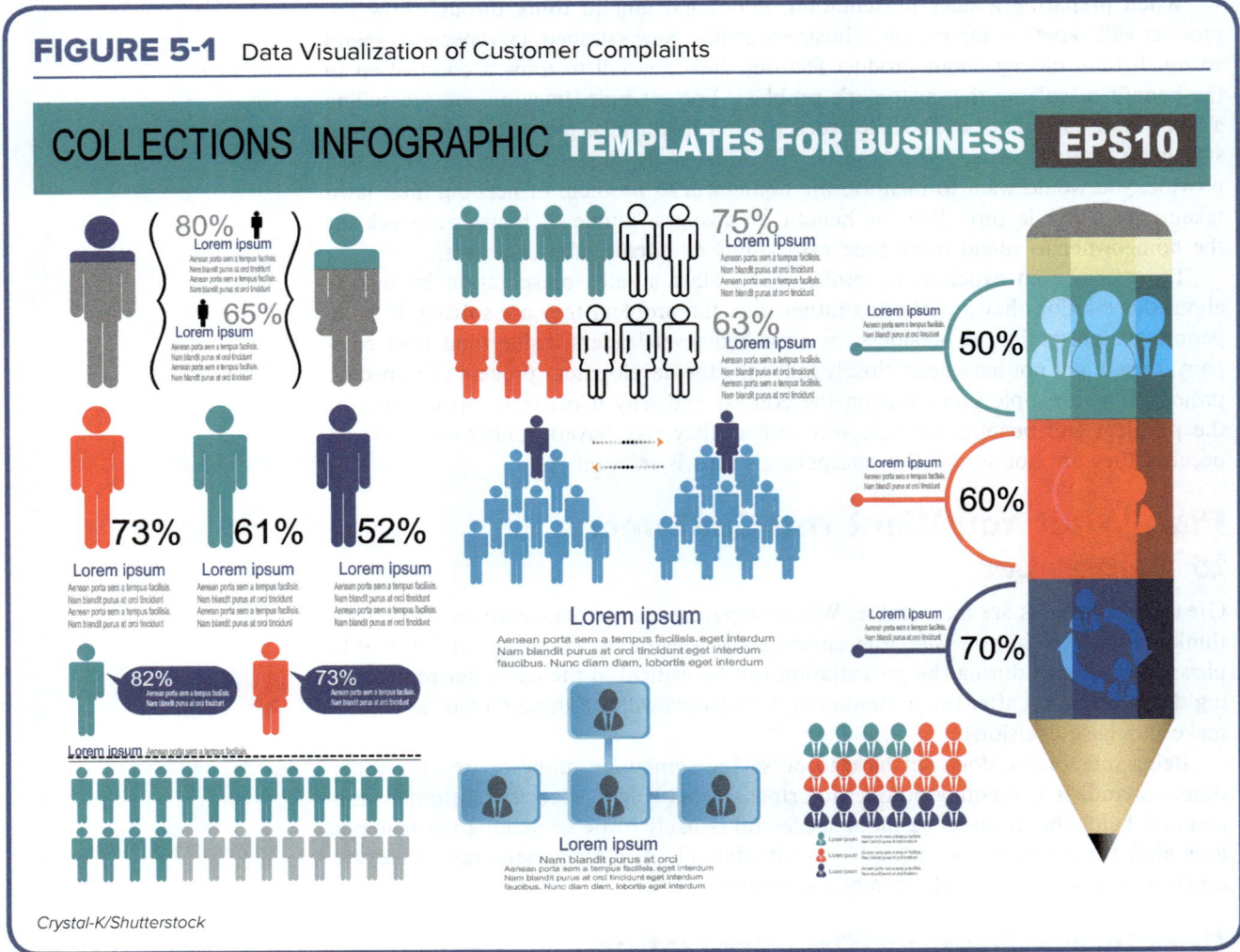

Crystal-K/Shutterstock

to have a good grasp of the data in order to make purchasing decisions. If the salesperson can transform data into a super clear picture for customers, they can quickly see how value is being added. What's needed is data presented in a form that captures the scope and urgency of the buying decision. Figure 5-1 shows an example of data visualization used during a sales presentation. Great data visualization might even be part of the memorable takeaway discussed earlier.

If your data visualization skills aren't all you want them to be, don't hesitate to consult others in your selling organization for a bit of help. You might even consider taking a course at a local community college or other school to help develop those skills.

Practice Through Role Play

As you know from earlier chapters, **role play** involves acting out conversations, attitudes, and actions, in a make-believe situation, in an effort to understand a differing point of view. Role play can be a very effective activity in preparing a sales presentation. In role play, a salesperson can:

- Practice a sales pitch with a trusted colleague and ask for feedback on ways to improve the presentation.
- Develop the best wording to use during a sales call. Top-performing salespeople are up to ten times likelier to use collaborative words and phrases than are

role play
Acting out conversations, attitudes, and actions, in a make-believe situation, in an effort to understand a differing point of view.

low-performing salespeople. Role play can help you practice using words like "we," "us," "our," and "together" (instead of "you," "I," "me," and "your") to win over prospective buyers.
- Practice a response to potential objections of the buyer.

Through role play, you can gain confidence in your sales presentation, enabling you to decrease uncomfortable or tense body language and increase a feeling of calm.

None of these activities guarantees that a sales presentation will be a success. However, salespeople who do not use activities like these to prepare their presentations greatly reduce their likelihood of closing the sale.

WHY SALES PRESENTATIONS FAIL

LO 5-3

List reasons for sales-presentation failure and strategies to prevent such failures.

A bad sales presentation can greatly reduce the likelihood of closing a sale. Sales presentations can fail for almost limitless reasons, but there are a handful of common problems that salespeople should work hard to prevent.

Technical Problems

In today's connected world technical problems sometimes happen, and that's okay. What's not okay is when the problems could have been easily prevented with the right preparation. Don't waste a prospect's time fiddling with a cable or screen-sharing tool. Salespeople should run through all the technical aspects of their presentation well before the appointed time.

A salesperson should always have a backup plan in case the wi-fi does not work or a bulb in the projector burns out. Always have a hard copy of the presentation as a backup. Also, an increasing number of salespeople carry with them their own portable projectors. If handled well, technical problems can show potential customers your thoroughness and professionalism. That demonstration might ultimately get you closer to closing the deal.

Poor Presentation Skills

Another reason for presentation failure is poor presentation skills. For example, talking with your back to people is unprofessional and often viewed by the buyer as rude. This often happens when salespeople look back to read directly from their PowerPoint slides. Buyers can easily become frustrated if they think a salesperson is wasting their time simply reading the words on the screen, which they could have read on their own.

Sometimes the setup of the room in which the presentation takes place can hurt sales reps if they're not careful. Salespeople should be very intentional in avoiding this problem. For example, a sales presentation at a table with a U-shape can put your back to half the audience if you walk too far into the center during the presentation. Use the front of the room as much as possible, and move deliberately from side to side, turning slightly to face each buyer as you speak. Also, plan to be at the center of the table when delivering the most important points of the presentation.

Dotshock/123RF

Irrelevant Information

All potential customers value their time. Too much irrelevant information about your product, service, company, or yourself during the sales presentation can reduce the likelihood of success. For example, imagine you sell a low-cost cell phone. If you go into a long-winded pitch about your company, its financial data, and other details that are not of interest to someone wanting to make a simple purchase, you may lose the sale. Often, by talking too much and sharing irrelevant information, a salesperson can bore prospects so much that they decide not to buy.

Unethical Behaviors

When making a presentation, salespeople should understand the difference between persuasion and manipulation. While persuasion will be expected, manipulation will be perceived as offensive. The difference between persuasion and manipulation is often based on intent. "Good intentions" mean "in the prospect's best interest." Conversely, if the salesperson's intention is to maximize his or her own benefit—even at the expense of the prospect's, if need be—any persuasion effort will be perceived as manipulation.

Another common unethical behavior in sales presentations is not fully disclosing information. Customers do business based on what is outlined in the contract. If salespeople omit information when agreeing to contract terms, they can catch the buyer off guard and hurt their business, not to mention damage the long-term relationship. Knowingly withholding important information included in a contract with customers is shady.

AT&T was accused in 2018 of using unethical sales tactics when presenting to potential customers about using the DirecTV Now streaming service. The salespeople told customers during their presentation that they could try out DirecTV Now for a month without paying; the salespeople said they would cancel their trials before they turned into paid subscriptions. In some cases, the cancellations never happened, and people started paying $35 a month for the service without having agreed to become subscribers. AT&T ultimately fired at least six people over the unethical tactics. Former salespeople at the company said managers had encouraged unethical tactics in order to hit sales quotas.[3]

International and Intercultural Communication Challenges

International salespeople need to be able to communicate effectively in culturally diverse sales settings.[4] To succeed in international and intercultural interactions, sales professionals need to be highly competent in communication.[5] Research suggests that in international sales presentations, the most important communication skills are related to building and maintaining relationships, personal-selling skills during the sales process, and foreign-language skills.[6] In an increasingly global business environment, salespeople should seek training, practice, and advice in developing their communication skills to be more successful in different cultures.

While language and culture can be barriers to international sales, the complexities of selling in a global market reach far beyond correct translations. First, salespeople must do their research: It may be useful to compare one's own approach with those of other companies and sales teams that have been able to sell internationally with success. Much international sales aptitude involves being able to effectively share information across the company. Having a cloud-based customer relationship management (CRM) system that updates across global boundaries is essential. Accurate information on the global supply chain, sales pipeline, accounts, and shipments will decrease overhead. The CRM data will also provide information to make sales presentations more comprehensive and effective.

Salespeople should also work to develop their **intercultural communication competence,** which is the effectiveness of skills, attitudes, and traits for building successful cross-cultural interaction. Several skills are particularly beneficial for developing intercultural communication competence:

- *Cultural awareness.* **Cultural awareness** involves the ability to stand back from ourselves and become aware of our cultural values, beliefs, and perceptions. Individuals with cultural awareness tend to be able to predict the effects of their behavior on others. They are more likely to modify their behavior after they learn something about other cultures.[7]
- *Cultural sensitivity.* **Cultural sensitivity** is the ability to understand the value of different cultures and be sensitive to the verbal and nonverbal cues of people from other cultures.[8] Individuals with high cultural sensitivity display values such as open-mindedness, high self-concept, nonjudgmental attitudes, and social relaxation. Salespeople will benefit from spending time researching and visiting with people from other cultures.
- *Cultural adroitness.* **Cultural adroitness** refers to an individual's ability to reach communication goals while interacting with people from other cultures. Individuals with high cultural adroitness quickly learn how to act effectively when in a new cultural environment. When salespeople know what to do and what not to do during a sales presentation, they will be able to communicate more effectively without offending any parties.[9]

> **intercultural communication competence**
> The effectiveness of skills, attitudes, and traits for building successful cross-cultural interaction
>
> **cultural awareness**
> The ability to stand back from ourselves and become aware of our cultural values, beliefs, and perceptions.
>
> **cultural sensitivity**
> The ability to understand the value of different cultures and be sensitive to the verbal and nonverbal cues of people from other cultures.
>
> **cultural adroitness**
> The ability to reach communication goals while interacting with people from other cultures.

Despite the care that salespeople take to prevent problems that cause presentation failures, mistakes occur. Salespeople with virtually any amount of experience can share stories about mistakes they made and problems that arose during a presentation. For example, in Hong Kong, business people typically prefer sales presentations and proposals to begin in general terms before transitioning into the narrow details. A new global salesperson could have a presentation that is customized for a specific audience with lots of details at the beginning, but it could have been more effective and well received if he or she had begun with more general terms.

Regardless of the level of preparation, it is important to maintain composure and professionalism. If you say something that is potentially offensive or ethically questionable, correct that mistake immediately. If you can tell from the customer's body language that you might be sharing irrelevant information, shift back to the focus of the presentation as quickly as you can. Salespeople have a healthy fear of making a mistake during a presentation, but they should always be prepared to try to correct that mistake as quickly as possible. Understanding verbal and nonverbal cues in international sales presentations will improve the likelihood of presentation success.

Connect Assignment 5-2

Unethical Sales-Presentation Practices

Please complete the Connect exercise for Chapter 5 that focuses on avoiding unethical practices in sales presentations. Understanding the responsibility of making a sales presentation for an organization and common ethical mistakes will help you develop an ethical framework when dealing with potential customers.

LO 5-4

Describe the importance of nonverbal behaviors in sales presentations.

nonverbal communication

Behaviors such as eye contact, posture, and facial expressions by which people communicate in ways other than words.

NONVERBAL COMMUNICATION IN SALES PRESENTATIONS

Before we get too far from the topic of why sales presentations sometimes fail, we should briefly address the topic of nonverbal communication. **Nonverbal communication** encompasses the behaviors such as eye contact, posture, and facial expressions by which people communicate in ways other than words. Such behaviors, often referred to as *body language*, are very important in effective sales presentations. Salespeople should have an understanding of their ability to communicate—both positively and negatively—through body language. Let's look at a few nonverbal behaviors to master in a sales presentation.

Eye Contact

Eye contact can be a powerful tool when used correctly. The selling process is all about making connections, and eye contact is a big part of that. If you are having a conversation with a friend, for example, you probably face him or her directly and make regular eye contact. By making eye contact in a sales presentation, you are relating to your audience and increasing engagement with them in an effort to better get your message across.

It is important, however, not to overuse eye contact. Salespeople should not make potential buyers feel they are competing in a staring contest. If you make eye contact with a prospective buyer who quickly looks away, be cautious; some people feel uncomfortable with eye contact. In some cultures, direct eye contact is considered inappropriate.

Posture

The best posture for a sales presentation is typically to keep one's head up and hands open. A posture that is professional and relaxed can help prospective buyers feel more comfortable. Keeping your head level and angling toward prospective buyers when you talk can help develop a more comfortable atmosphere for the presentation.

Posture is also important when the potential buyer is speaking or asking questions. Slouching or leaning back on a chair during a sales presentation can make it seem like the salesperson doesn't care or doesn't take the meeting seriously. Instead, sit up relatively straight and face the buyer, to show that you are highly involved in the discussion. This posture communicates confidence and also shows the prospects that you respect their time and take the meeting seriously.

Finally, be careful about crossing your arms protectively in front of your body when a potential buyer is speaking. Many people interpret crossed arms as a signal that the listener is not open to what the speaker is saying. Even if you don't mean the crossed arms in that way, it's better not to risk giving that wrong message.

Facial Expressions

In sales presentations, salespeople should also be aware of any artificial or unfriendly facial expressions they might be making. The role-play practice discussed earlier is a good way to identify any such issues and work to improve them. Salespeople should practice smiling during presentations. Don't smile as if your face is frozen (like the Joker from Batman movies), but develop a warm, friendly, pleasant smile that can make prospects feel more comfortable.

Similarly, there are several facial expressions that salespeople should avoid. Frowning projects a negative energy or moodiness that can be troubling for potential buyers.

Arching eyebrows is another common mistake that makes salespeople look surprised, questioning, or unsure of their solution.

> ### Connect Assignment 5-3
> **Nonverbal Communication**
> Please complete the Connect exercise for Chapter 5 that focuses on nonverbal communication during a sales presentation. Understanding the impact of nonverbal signals can help salespeople be more effective in building trust and developing customer relationships.

VIRTUAL AND TEAM-SALES PRESENTATIONS

Much of our discussion of sales presentations has sounded like the salesperson will be in a one-on-one discussion with a single potential buyer. If you embark on a sales career, you undoubtedly will do many such sales presentations. But it also is true that such traditional sales presentations are becoming less common in modern business. Research from Salesforce has found that 58 percent of individual consumers and 77 percent of business buyers feel that technology has changed their expectations of how companies should interact with them.[10] During the COVID-19 (coronavirus) pandemic, businesses of all sizes and and across industries were forced to quickly pivot to virtual selling (see Figure 5-2), and many were unprepared. Sales meetings that might once have been face-to-face and sealed with a handshake were now taking place over Zoom calls.

As technology plays a bigger role in the sales process, face-to-face opportunities are declining. In their place, virtual as well as team-sales presentations are increasing.

LO 5-5
Name elements of effective virtual and team-sales presentations.

The Marketing Impact of COVID-19

Virtual Presentations

Even though relationships are fundamental to long-term sales success, research shows that sales reps are spending more time in front of screens doing **virtual presentations**—online presentations in which the host and audience attend the presentation remotely. From 2016 to 2018, virtual connections with customers increased 3.2 times more than in-person meetings with customers.[11] Then during the COVID-19 pandemic in 2020, over 90 percent of B2B sales organizations transitioned to a virtual sales model during the crisis.[12] Screen-to-screen selling might be convenient and cost-effective, but the concept of building relationships might be lost if the salesperson doesn't inject some personality into the sales process. Regardless of how they interact with salespeople—whether in person or through digital media—customers continue to prize a personalized and consultative selling process.

If you use virtual presentations in your selling (or any) career, you will want to focus on increasing engagement and eliminating distractions. Mastery of those two elements will increase the likelihood of success.

virtual presentations Online presentations in which the host and audience attend the presentation remotely.

Increase Engagement In another chapter, we defined *customer engagement* as the connection that exists between the salesperson, the selling firm, and the customer. Achieving engagement is especially important to think about in virtual

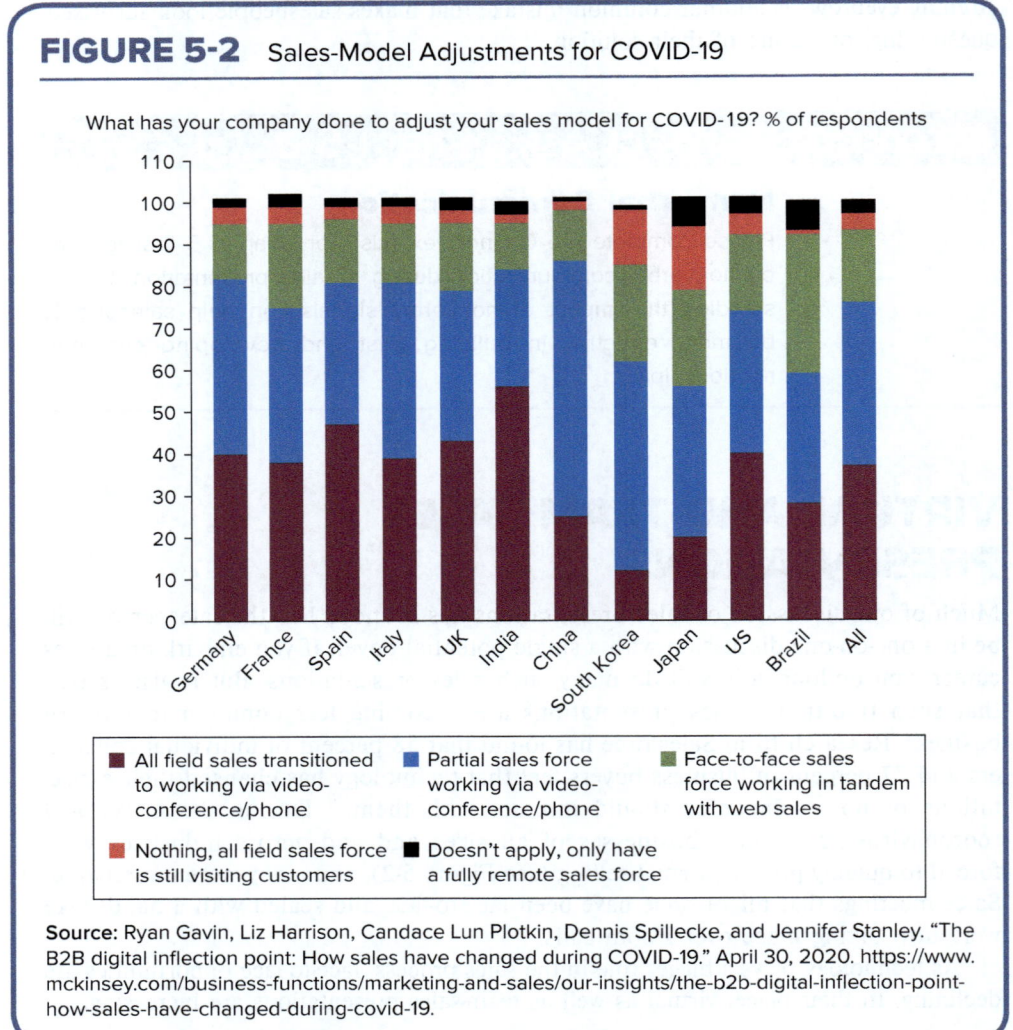

FIGURE 5-2 Sales-Model Adjustments for COVID-19

Source: Ryan Gavin, Liz Harrison, Candace Lun Plotkin, Dennis Spillecke, and Jennifer Stanley. "The B2B digital inflection point: How sales have changed during COVID-19." April 30, 2020. https://www.mckinsey.com/business-functions/marketing-and-sales/our-insights/the-b2b-digital-inflection-point-how-sales-have-changed-during-covid-19.

sales presentations. Too often, it is something many salespeople take for granted will occur.

How can you increase engagement in virtual presentations? Take advantage of your virtual-presentation tools to make the audience feel like they are sitting right next to you every time you present. Use engagement technologies like live Q&As, surveys, polling, and chats to make your audience more involved in your presentation. Be careful, though, not to use silly questions just for the sake of having people interact. Use interactivity to build engagement only when it adds value to the audience.

Eliminate Distractions Many of the people attending a virtual presentation will be listening to it through headphones, so every noise they hear will be noticeable. To ensure that such noises do not distract the audience (or yourself), use the following guidelines:

- Remove rustling papers and email pop-ups, and silence your mobile devices.
- Ask another member of the sales team to serve as a moderator to field incoming questions from your attendees.

- Make whatever arrangements are needed to prevent mid-presentation interruptions, such as a dog or cat (or child) coming into the picture.

Team Selling

Traditionally, the sales profession has not encouraged a great deal of collaboration. Many students know only the negative competitiveness displayed in movies such as *Glengarry Glen Ross* or *Boiler Room*, with salespeople striving to meet individual goals. But that culture is slowly starting to change, and for good reason. Research suggests that salespeople who collaborate with their coworkers increase overall sales performance. Sales reps who collaborate more often also win more often. This success, especially in more complex selling situations, has led to an increase in team selling. In **team selling**, a salesperson works with experts from across the firm to support new-customer acquisition and ongoing customer relationship management.

Sellwell/Shutterstock

team selling
A sales approach in which a salesperson works with experts from across the firm to support new-customer acquisition and ongoing customer relationship management.

Team selling often results in customers seeing the organization they do business with as one entity, delivering personalization across their entire experience with that company. To enable this, selling teams embrace a free and open internal flow of customer data. Indeed, 81 percent of teams say a connected view of customer data is important.[13] Top teams are more than twice as likely as underperformers to have the integrated systems that are critical to such a view.

Despite its benefits, team selling can lead to additional challenges. Think about any group presentation you have been involved in during school and the process to decide who would present which part. Now imagine if millions of dollars were at stake based on your presentation. Would that change who should do the presentation? Where would you put your best presenter—first or last? Who would be responsible for answering questions? The power of team selling is real, and the likelihood of success can be increased by making strategic decisions about the team.

Define Each Team Member's Role In most cases, one central person should lead the sales presentation. This choice is dictated by the goal of the call and the team's expectations of the prospect. For example, if it's a technical call, the sales engineer might lead.

The person who acts as a leader sets the agenda, asks the questions, and controls the call. Supporting persons can participate on certain questions when their expertise is relevant, but they should generally remain in the background. A person in the supporting role should listen, take specific notes, chat ideas directly to the lead, or just act as an extra set of ears to make sure the prospect is on track.

Carefully Assemble the Team Don't neglect thinking about group size, personality traits, and skill strengths. Design a team with a combination of people who have gravitas, technical knowledge, effective sales techniques, and management skills. Also keep in mind buyer needs, team dynamics, and group structure when forming teams. Weigh the options of a two-person versus a five-person team, for example.

Today's Professional Perspective... because everyone is a salesperson

Taylor Schneider
Sales Consultant
Tennis Australia

Taylor Schneider

Describe your job. I'm a sales consultant for Tennis Australia. Since its beginnings in 1904, Tennis Australia has developed into a multi-million-dollar business, marketing tennis as a sport and a brand, and staging international events including the Australian Open. I sell corporate hospitality for the Australian Open here in Melbourne, Australia. We reach out to clients who have been coming to the tournament for decades, and we service new business as well.

How did you get your job? Playing soccer brought me to Australia. When I first arrived, I stayed with a host family of a player who was on the under-12-year-old team sponsored by my soccer club. They were a lovely family, and I spent a lot of time with them, which naturally created a great relationship. Several years later, I was working in a job that I didn't really like; I wasn't passionate about what I was doing and I didn't believe in the business. I remembered talking with the dad of my Australian host family about what he did, so I reached out to the family and he was able to get me an interview. I ended up getting the job.

What has been most important in making you successful at your job? The most important thing about making me successful at my job is belief in myself: believing that I have what it takes to be successful, unique, and great at my job. This was my first big sales role, and I honestly had no idea what I was doing. My thoughts created my reality when I began not only thinking but really believing I could be great at this.

What advice would you give future graduates about a career in sales? When looking for a job after graduation, go for what you are passionate about and something you care about. I have grown up playing sports, so naturally sport is something I care a lot about. Even though I have never played tennis, the atmosphere in my workplace and around what we are doing is amazing.

What is the most important characteristic of a great salesperson? When you have a career in sales, the most important thing is to be organized. Organization is beneficial not only for yourself and your productivity but also in building trust between you and your clients. Staying organized enables you to track your contacts effectively and builds integrity in your brand as a salesperson.

STORYTELLING IN SALES PRESENTATIONS

Storytelling has been around for centuries. The use of storytelling for selling enables sales representatives to build relationships with customers and prospective customers, to stand out from competitors, and to sell products and services effectively.

Storytelling is on the rise in face-to-face as well as virtual-selling channels. Successful sales representatives can no longer merely talk about the features or benefits of their product (or service, event, cause). Instead, they will benefit by telling a convincing and memorable story that conveys relevant information to the customer or prospect. Stories enable salespeople to emotionally connect and engage with customers and prospects. As powerful communication tools, stories add value to the sales presentation.[14]

> **LO 5-6**
> Describe the impact of storytelling on sales presentations.

Benefits of Storytelling in Sales

Why tell stories? Storytelling in sales adds multiple benefits including capturing the attention of the audience, motivating individuals and groups to take action, and making data and facts come to life.

Good Stories Capture the Attention of the Audience
When facts and data are framed within a compelling story, the salesperson will hold the listeners' attention and help them connect bits and pieces of the story to their context. This results in better retention.

Imagine you are a fundraiser at your university making a sales presentation to a donor about potentially endowing a scholarship by giving $25,000 to the university. You are more likely to succeed if you can tell a story about how endowed scholarships have changed the lives of actual students. For example: Rebecca was a nontraditional accounting student who had exhausted all of her financial aid options; despite a high GPA, she could find no way to pay for her final semester of college. When she received the $2,500 scholarship from a donor, she became emotional as she thanked the donor for giving her the chance to finish her college education. The following year, Rebecca sent a thank-you letter to the donor saying she loved the job she found after graduation and that she was now making more money than anyone in her entire family had ever made.

Good Stories Motivate Individuals and Groups to Take Action
Stories are effective in sales presentations because they often trigger emotional responses, and emotions drive many consumer decisions. This is especially true for nonprofits in their fundraising efforts; they are often in the "business" of creating stories of perseverance, hope, and new beginnings. Nonprofits tend to have readily available the content for powerful impact stories that focus on changing the world. Such stories can lead to large donations, new scholarships, and program support that will create similar stories for future generations. Regardless of the nonprofit's focus, stories can be an incredible tool for fundraising, raising awareness, mobilizing volunteers, and building trust.

When developing a story for a sales presentation, salespeople should think about a decision maker's or potential donor's pain points and personal goals. A visceral response to a story is what often will inspire the sales prospect to take action.

Good Stories Build Trust and Rapport
One way to establish credibility is to start the sales pitch with a story that features a previous success. If you can convince a prospect to trust you, you have a chance to persuade him or her that

your product is worthwhile. Referrals from a trustworthy source can be meaningful; 84 percent of all B2B sales start with a referral.[15] A story can help prove the product is worth the investment—because it has already delivered results in another instance.

Good Stories Make Data and Facts Come to Life Stories are how we best learn and visualize information. Often, it is through stories that facts and raw data gain meaning. Stories can simplify and clarify even the most complex information and make it more interesting. Additionally, stories help people remember what they've heard. Salespeople need to become expert storytellers, or "story-sellers," by mastering the skill of telling persuasive stories.

Selling Yourself with Stories

Before we leave the topic of storytelling, let's apply it to the product you will be selling throughout your life—yourself. Whether you are planning a career in sales or not, storytelling is a powerful skill to acquire. Sooner or later, we all must sell ourselves. As you complete your college education, think about and develop stories that share something about you and your personal journey that would make future employers more likely to hire you or future employees more likely to work for you.

CHAPTER SUMMARY

LO 5-1 Describe the three main types of sales presentations.

The *sales presentation* is the delivery of information relevant to solving the customer's needs. Salespeople who are prepared and select the most appropriate type of sales presentation can increase their likelihood of closing the sale. Developing a sales-presentation strategy begins with choosing one of the three main types of sales presentations: memorized, formula, and need-satisfaction. The salesperson should consider which type of presentation will be most persuasive to their customers. *Persuasion* is a communication process by which you motivate someone else to voluntarily do something you would like them to do.

In a *memorized presentation*, the salesperson presents the same selling points in the same order to all customers. In a *formula presentation*, the salesperson follows a somewhat less structured, prepared outline in making a presentation, allowing more flexibility and enabling the salesperson to gain some customer feedback. In a *need-satisfaction presentation*, the salesperson probes into the stated as well as unstated needs of the consumer and then gives a sales presentation that shows how his or her product will satisfy the customer's needs.

LO 5-2 List activities that are useful in preparing effective sales presentations.

Regardless of the type of sales presentation they choose, salespeople must actively prepare in order to achieve an effective presentation. A logical first step is to develop a *customer-value proposition*, which is a statement of how the sales offering will add value to the buyer and/or the buyer's organization.

Salespeople can use a variety of activities to improve the quality of a sales presentation: identify the customer problem, plan what you want the customer to remember, consider a product demonstration, provide slick data, and practice through role play.

LO 5-3 List reasons for sales-presentation failure and strategies to prevent such failures.

A bad sales presentation can greatly reduce the likelihood of closing a sale. There are a handful of common presentation problems that salespeople should work hard to prevent: technical problems, poor presentation skills, sharing irrelevant information, unethical behaviors, and international and intercultural communication challenges.

LO 5-4 Describe the importance of nonverbal behaviors in sales presentations.

Nonverbal communication, often referred to as body language, encompasses the behaviors such as eye contact, posture, and facial expressions by which people communicate in ways other than words. Salespeople should have an understanding of their ability to communicate—both positively and negatively—through body language.

LO 5-5 Name elements of effective virtual and team-sales presentations.

As technology plays a bigger role in the sales process, face-to-face opportunities are declining and virtual presentations are increasing. Salespeople who use virtual presentations should focus on increasing customer engagement and eliminating distractions in order to increase the likelihood of success.

Sales reps who collaborate more often also win more often. This success, especially in more complex selling situations, has led to an increase in team selling. The power of team selling can be increased by making strategic decisions before the presentation. Two such decisions are to define the role each member will have in the presentation and to carefully assemble the team in terms of group size, personality traits, and skill strengths.

LO 5-6 Describe the impact of storytelling on sales presentations.

The use of storytelling for selling enables sales representatives to build relationships with customers and prospective customers, to stand out from competitors, and to sell products and services effectively. Storytelling is on the rise in both face-to-face and virtual selling channels. Benefits of good storytelling in sales include capturing the attention of the audience, motivating individuals and groups to take action, building trust and rapport, and making data and facts come to life. Storytelling is a powerful skill for everyone because sooner or later, we all must sell ourselves.

KEY TERMS

sales presentation (p. 100)
persuasion (p. 100)
memorized sales presentation (p. 100)
formula sales presentation (p. 100)
need-satisfaction sales presentation (p. 101)
customer-value proposition (p. 102)

features (p. 102)
benefits (p. 102)
product demonstration (p. 103)
data visualization (p. 103)
role play (p. 104)
intercultural communication competence (p. 107)

cultural awareness (p. 107)
cultural sensitivity (p. 107)
cultural adroitness (p. 107)
nonverbal communication (p. 108)
virtual presentations (p. 109)
team selling (p. 111)

DISCUSSION QUESTIONS

1. Imagine that you have been assigned by your university to sell an alumnus(a) of your school on endowing a scholarship for students. Which of the three types of sales-presentation strategies would you use? Explain why you chose that type of sales presentation and why it is better than the other two options.
2. Pretend that you have decided to sell a model of car that someone in your family drives today. If you were giving a presentation to a room of prospective car buyers, which tools would you use in your presentation? What would be your customer-value proposition?
3. In your experience, what is the most common reason that presentations fail? If you gave a sales presentation tomorrow, what steps would you take to make sure the presentation was a success?
4. What nonverbal communication signals have the most impact on you as a customer? If you started a new job as a salesperson today, which nonverbal communication signal do you think you would struggle with the most? Explain your answer.
5. Would you rather give a sales presentation in person or virtually using a web-conferencing service? Explain the reasons for your answer.
6. Tell a story about something in your life that shares with a prospective employer information that would make him or her more likely to hire you after graduation. What characteristics about you does your story highlight (intelligence, character, work-ethic, etc.)?

ETHICAL CHALLENGE

In 2016, the U.S. federal government announced its estimate that Americans lose $17 billion a year to conflicts of interest among financial advisers. Wall Street banks and salespeople dispute that math, but a wave of research over the past few years has documented serious problems with how Americans get financial advice. Financial advisers are, in part, salespeople pitching ideas in the hope that clients will trust them with their money. Many investors believe that their relationship with a financial adviser carries the same sort of solemnity as that of an attorney and client or of a doctor and patient. An attorney is bound to zealously represent you; a doctor pledges to do no harm. But the economics of the financial industry—fees, commissions, quotas—can end up standing in the way of the customer's money-accumulation goals.

The so-called *fiduciary rule*, finalized under the Obama administration, sought to fix this disconnect. All advisers would be required to put clients first when handling retirement accounts, which is where the bulk of everyday Americans' savings reside. However, the new administration ordered the Department of Labor to reconsider the rule, arguing that tying the hands of advisers would limit investor choices, raise the cost of financial advice, and trigger a wave of litigation.

Offering financial advice is enormously profitable, with U.S. investment firms achieving operating profit margins as high as 39 percent, according to the CFA Institute. And once advisers collect enough client assets, they can get huge bonuses for switching firms (and bringing their customers with them). Until recently, the going rate was a bonus of more than three times the annual fees and commissions the adviser brings in the door; an adviser with $200 million under management could expect a bonus of $6.6 million.

Meanwhile, the total cost of bad advice given to consumers—in higher fees and lower performance—is probably much higher than the $17 billion estimated by President Obama's Council of Economic Advisers (CEA). The CEA figured investors are losing an extra 1 percent annually on $1.7 trillion in individual retirement accounts controlled by conflicted advisers. But IRAs represent just an eighth of the $56 trillion in financial wealth Americans control, according to Boston Consulting Group.

Many on Wall Street argue that strict regulations on financial advice will make it less affordable for middle-class investors. The Securities Industry and Financial Markets Association wrote in a letter to the Labor Department that the fiduciary rule would "adversely affect the ability of millions of Americans to save for retirement, [and] increase the costs of retirement accounts while limiting access to advice and products." But if advice as it currently exists is riddled with conflicts and hidden costs, supporters of the rule ask, should it even be called advice?

Questions

1. If you were a financial adviser, what would be your sales pitch as to why an investor should trust you with his or her money?
2. If a potential client asked you about your stance on the fiduciary rule, how would you respond?
3. How might you go about building trust with clients who have lost money in the past?
4. How would you address mistakes you make with existing clients?

Source: Ben Steverman, Bloomberg, June 7, 2017, https://www.bloomberg.com/news/features/2017-06-07/fiduciary-rule-fight-brews-while-bad-financial-advisers-multiply.

ROLE PLAY

This role play will give you experience in presenting to prospective donors. For this role play, half of your class should be development directors for your college or university, responsible for raising money for scholarships and endowed faculty positions for your school. Each salesperson should pick the scholarship, department, or program they are raising money for and develop a presentation to win over prospective donors.

The other half of class will be the prospective donors. Each donor has up to a pretend amount of $100,000 to donate to charitable causes. Each donor will hear at least four different sales presentations and can raise issues that are important to them. At the end of the role play, each donor will decide how much money to give to each fundraising presentation and provide feedback about the choice to give to that presentation (or presentations) over the others.

At the end of the role play, both the fundraiser and the donor students should reflect on what made the biggest positive or negative impact and what they would suggest a fundraiser say and do when making a presentation to donors of your college or university.

SALES PRESENTATION

For the Connect assignment in Chapter 5, students will practice giving a presentation about their favorite sports team or theater production. Prepare a three- to five-presentation on why a person should buy season tickets to a sports team (professional or college) you like or to a theater that offers season tickets for concerts and/or Broadway-style shows. Be sure to include at least one of the tools for sales presentations you learned about in this chapter.

CAREER TIPS

Lance Gooch
Contractor Sales Representative
84 Lumber

Taking Care of the People Who Take Care of You

Before 84 Lumber, I worked in sales positions for a large retail store and then for a professional sports organization. In these roles, I've seen firsthand the importance of taking care of the people in the organization who have helped me have a successful sales career.

A career tip essential to being successful in sales is, "Take care of the people who take care of you." In my industry, the people who load the lumber, deliver it, and do many small things to make our customers happy do not get enough credit for their outstanding work. I wanted to reward that work. So, I started a few years ago to get and hand out four season tickets to a local professional basketball team, to make sure the people who help me so much can have some fun R&R away from the lumber yard.

There are so many people in the organization whom salespeople depend on. These people could easily put their time and effort into helping salespeople other than me if I do not treat them the best I can. The people I work with are a massive part of my success, and I try each day to make sure they know how much I appreciate them. Many salespeople might consider contests as rewards for sales performance, but I think that random and personal rewards are better. Listen to your co-workers and find out what they like to eat, drink, and do in their spare time. Then, collect gift cards for coffee, restaurants, movies, and other rewards they like. These cards can be valued at less than $20, but they can have a big positive impact. Have these rewards ready and find opportunities to appreciate an action for a job well done. Say thank-you to the employees who helped you, be specific about what you appreciate, and then give them the gift card. People who feel appreciated perform better, and salespeople who understand this will do a lot better throughout their careers.

CHAPTER ENDNOTES

1. W. C. Moncrief and G. W. Marshall, "The evolution of the seven steps of selling," *Industrial Marketing Management* 34, no. 1 (January 2005): 13–22.
2. Pete Caputa, "The First Call Conundrum: What Buyers Vs. Salespeople Want to Talk About" https://blog.hubspot.com/sales/the-first-sales-call-conundrum.
3. David Meyer, "AT&T Managers Reportedly Encouraged Unethical Sales Tactics to Sell More DirecTV Packages" June 25, 2018. https://fortune.com/2018/06/25/att-unethical-sales-tactics-directv-now/.
4. P. C. Earley and S. Ang, *Cultural Intelligence: Individual Interactions Across Cultures* (Redwood City, CA: Stanford University Press, 2003); J. D. Hansen, T. Singh, D. C. Weilbaker, and R. Guesalaga, "Cultural intelligence in cross-cultural selling: Propositions and directions for future research," *Journal of Personal Selling & Sales Management* 31, no. 3 (2011): 243–254.
5. B. H. Spitzberg and W. R. Cupach, "Interpersonal skills," in M. L. Knapp and J. R. Daly, eds., *Handbook of Interpersonal Communication*, 3rd ed. (Newbury Park, CA: Sage, 2002), pp. 564–611.
6. J. Kopenen, S. Julkunen, and A. Asai, "Sales communication competence in international B2B solution selling, *Industrial Marketing Management* (2019), https://doi.org/10.1016/j.indmarman.2019.01.009.
7. G. M. Chen and W. J. Starosta, "Intercultural communication competence: A synthesis," in B. R. Burleson and A. W. Kunkel, eds. *Communication Yearbook* (Thousand Oaks, CA: Sage, 1996).
8. N. Zakaria, "The effects of cross–cultural training on the acculturation process of the global workforce," *International Journal of Manpower* 21, no. 6 (2000): 492–510.
9. S. Chaisrakeo and M. Speece, "Culture, intercultural communication competence and sales negotiation: A qualitative research approach," *Journal of Business & Industrial Marketing* 19 (2004): 267–282.
10. Lynne Zaledonis. "New Research Unveils 5 Trends Shaping the Future of Sales," May 23, 2018. https://www.salesforce.com/blog/2018/05/sales-future-trends-research.html.
11. "State of Sales: The future of sales is a balancing act," June 6, 2018. https://www.salesforce.com/au/blog/2018/06/state-of-sales--the-future-of-sales-is-a-balancing-act.html.
12. Ryan Gavin, Liz Harrison, Candace Lun Plotkin, Dennis Spillecke, and Jennifer Stanley "The B2B digital inflection

point: How sales have changed during COVID-19," April 30, 2020. https://www.mckinsey.com/business-functions/marketing-and-sales/our-insights/the-b2b-digital-inflection-point-how-sales-have-changed-during-covid-19.
13. Tiffanie Bova. "26 Sales Statistics That Prove Sales Is Changing," June 25, 2019. https://www.salesforce.com/blog/2017/11/15-sales-statistics.html.
14. Lisa D. Spiller, "Story-selling: Creating and sharing authentic stories that persuade," *Journal for Advancement of Marketing Education* 26, no. 1 (2018): 11–17.
15. L. Minsky and K. A. Quesenberry, "How B2B sales can benefit from social selling," *Harvard Business Review* (November 8, 2016), https://hbr.org/2016/11/84-of-b2b-sales-start-with-a-referral-not-a-salesperson.

Design elements: Marketing Insights Podcast: vandame/Shutterstock

Part THREE

Finding and Negotiating Solutions for Customers

Creativa Images/Shutterstock

Chapter 6
Solving Problems and Overcoming Objections

Chapter 7
Negotiating Win-Win Solutions

Chapter 8
Profitology: Pricing and Analytics in Sales

Chapter 6

Solving Problems and Overcoming Objections

Learning Objectives

After reading this chapter, you should be able to:

LO 6-1 Describe the role of salespeople in solving customer problems.

LO 6-2 Describe three skills needed in solving customer problems.

LO 6-3 Summarize the process of gaining commitment and various techniques to do so.

LO 6-4 List the primary types of objections customers typically raise.

LO 6-5 Describe the process of overcoming objections and various techniques to do so.

LO 6-6 Explain the importance of ethics when overcoming objections and gaining commitment.

Executive Perspective ... because everyone is a salesperson

Mike Fuller

Mike Fuller
General Manager
Pernod Ricard USA

Describe your job.

I work in the wine and spirits industry and am currently the general manager (GM) for one of the U.S. sales divisions for Pernod Ricard, the number-two manufacturer of spirits in the world. We own many global and well-known brands such as Absolut Vodka, Jameson Irish Whiskey, Malibu Coconut Rum, and dozens of others. The 21st Amendment to the U.S. Constitution (which repealed prohibition of beverage alcohol) created a "three-tier system," which simply means that *suppliers* must sell their products to *distributors,* who then sell to *retailers* (bars, restaurants, liquor stores).

Most of my career has been on the supplier side, where our job is to ensure that our brands are distributed, promoted, merchandised, and sold in a way that grows our market share and reaches our sales targets. As the GM, my job is to oversee all functions of our field organization, including sales (distributor relations, sales execution), trade development (activating our brands by managing the local marketing mix), and finance (pricing, promotion, and budget management). I also oversee departments like human resources, operations, and analytics.

How did you get your job?

When I was coming out of graduate school, the job market was weak. I applied for an entry-level sales/merchandising job with a spirits distributor because I needed to pay the rent and it sounded like a fun industry. I worked my way into middle management, then joined the supplier side to learn new skills and because it provided more room for growth and development. Since then, I've moved three times around the country, taking increasing levels of responsibility, managing larger teams, and learning new markets. After covering 17 states as a VP of sales, I was promoted to GM and moved to Dallas to lead one of our divisions.

What has been most important in making you successful at your job?

A few things come to mind: strong work ethic, a willingness to try new things, risk-taking, and solution orientation. But if I had to select one thing, it would be communication skills. I pride myself on being able to get my message across—whether written or verbal. Performance is often judged not solely on results but also on how you communicate in a confident, succinct, insightful, and intelligent way.

What advice would you give future graduates about a career in sales?

Don't be in a hurry to climb the ladder. The entry-level experiences are what will make you a better salesperson down the road (whether you stay in sales or move into management). Be willing to pay your dues; doing so will prove invaluable later. Focus on results but make sure you are team oriented. Volunteer for special projects or ask for a mentor or job-shadowing opportunity. Be curious. Take risks. Don't be afraid to fail (forward). Overcommunicate with everyone—your customers, your boss, your company.

What is the most important characteristic of a great salesperson?

There are a ton of traits that most great salespeople possess—tenacity, charisma, and confidence are among the most common. One thing I see that really sets people apart is storytelling—the ability to communicate with others in an inspiring way.

Discuss the importance of solution-based (as opposed to product-based) selling at your company.

We encourage our sales associates to focus on uncovering problems and offering solutions to the customer. Sure, features and benefits are important. But at the end of the day, unless you have a patented or monopolistic product in high demand, your competitors can likely offer buyers something similar, and often with an advantage (better price, better quality, better terms). It's important to focus not on promoting a product, but on the customer's problems. And then address them with appropriate offerings from your company/product/service. Let's face it—nobody really likes being sold to. We encourage "consultative selling"—every buyer has challenges they are trying to overcome, and if you can be a part of a solution for them, you will stand apart from the competition.

In your opinion, what is most important in determining whether a salesperson is able to gain commitment (i.e., close the sale) when selling?

Many steps in the selling process drive the ultimate decision: aligning with existing priorities, meeting deadlines, reinforcing the value equation, and selling at the right level (to influencers and decision makers). In our business, the number-one success factor continues to be selling with confidence and "assuming the sale." Professional baseball players don't walk up to the plate expecting to strike out. Similarly, you should always assume the prospect will make the purchase when they have a need for your solution. Closing the deal is a mere formality if a salesperson has done their job correctly. Asking for the order—with confidence—is something that our highest performers do effortlessly.

What are some typical objections salespeople in your company hear, and how do they overcome these objections?

Our biggest two objections are procrastination and lack of perceived need. We do quite a bit of cold-calling and route-running, without set appointments. With that, we run into procrastinating clients who simply are too busy and don't have the time to engage with our salespeople. Continuous follow-up is key in order to catch prospects at the right time. Sometimes success is just a matter of being there at the right moment. Instead of merely asking when you can call these prospects during the next week or month, find out what they like and don't like about your product(s). Get any insight you can, and then secure an appointment and prepare a small, succinct presentation that shows you value their time.

We often hear *"we don't need that brand"* or *"that probably won't sell"* or *"I'll bring it in when people start asking for it."* This is a textbook smokescreen. When customers ask you to leave some information or say they will "think about it," they're giving you the brush off. It's the classic "don't call me, I'll call you" scenario that can stop salespeople in their tracks.

We recommend a response along the lines of, *"I wouldn't expect you to be interested yet until I tell you how it can [impact your bottom line/increase your margins/save you thousands/bring in more shoppers]. If I can have 60 seconds to explain a few high points, I'll share some initial thoughts so you can decide if you're interested in hearing more."* Another successful tactic has been the feel/felt/found method: *"I understand that you don't believe this brand will sell in your store. I had another retailer that felt the same way, but what we found is that. . . ."*

SOLVING CUSTOMER PROBLEMS

LO 6-1 Describe the role of salespeople in solving customer problems.

Perhaps nowhere is the change in professional selling more evident than in the two elements of the sales process that are the focus of this chapter—solving problems and overcoming objections. In order to effectively solve their customers' problems, salespeople must not only develop a deep understanding of these problems but also be able to craft unique and innovative solutions in response. When this is done, customers see value in the solution and are less prone to focus on price.

Inevitably, customers will voice their concerns in the form of objections. A salesperson who addresses these objections in a satisfactory manner ensures that the customer is comfortable moving forward in the sales process. As we will discuss, this cannot be done if the salesperson does not ask additional questions to develop a full understanding of the objection. In this way, selling has become much more consultative in nature. Gone are the days of the salesperson who simply brushes customer objections aside in favor of an ABC ("always be closing") approach to selling.

Today, the most effective salespeople are customer oriented rather than product oriented. They are excellent questioners and even better listeners. Having an in-depth understanding of the problems their customers face, they are able to deliver creative solutions that solve these problems. They understand the financial implications of these solutions and are able to financially quantify the solutions they provide. Through all of these skills, they create value. Value creation is important because, for most salespeople, the ability to differentiate based solely on product or price is difficult, if not impossible. Let's look in more depth at the skills salespeople need in order to effectively solve their customers' problems.

The Salesperson as Problem Solver

Along with the changes in the sales field as a whole, we have also seen significant changes in how salespeople and their customers interact. Customers have said that the salespeople they interact with are the primary determinants in their purchasing decisions. Most salespeople know that *they* have become the sale; *they* are the reason their customers choose to purchase from their firm or not. Customers have also said that salespeople must have a deep understanding of the problems they face and must provide solutions for these problems, as opposed to simply selling products.[1] The most successful salespeople understand the difference between discussing products and delivering solutions. They are successful because of their focus on the latter.

Transitioning from a product-focus to a solution-focus is no easy task. It represents a significant change for many salespeople who, through no fault of their own, have become used to simply selling products. Before the advent of the internet, a product-focus was enough; customers did not know basic product information without it being provided by the salesperson. Transitioning from products to solutions requires a different skill set. Many salespeople are finding themselves in uncharted waters, dealing with issues they have never before confronted.

In this solution-focused environment, salespeople succeed based on their knowledge of customers and solutions. Knowledge has become the most valuable resource a salesperson can possess.[2] The stakes can be high: Salespeople interact with high-ranking individuals from the customer firm, including the CEO and CFO. They spend a significant amount of time with these customers to determine their needs, regularly assessing these needs to ensure that they have not changed, and rarely relying on traditional product presentations alone.[3] Without customer knowledge, salespeople are left to compete on price, as customers see very little difference in competitors' products.

Can you blame customers for this? Think of your own personal life as a consumer. What do you typically do if you see little difference in the products you are trying to decide between? If you are like most consumers, you revert to price and choose the lowest priced option. Not surprisingly, business customers are no different. When they perceive little difference in the solutions salespeople are suggesting for them, they too make decisions based on price.

Mindful of this, salespeople who embrace the role as consultative problem solvers recognize that:

- It is very difficult to differentiate based solely on the product(s) they sell.
- The value they provide customers extends well beyond the product(s) they sell.
- The price their customers are willing to pay is largely based on the solutions they provide.
- Their sales success largely depends on an ability to deliver customized solutions for individual customers.
- The most important thing they can do as salespeople is provide and execute solutions in response to their customers' problems.
- Much of the value they provide their customers occurs after the sale is made.

Salespeople who are consultative problem solvers also understand that the customer plays an important part in helping develop solutions. Indeed, salespeople cannot develop successful solutions in a vacuum; they must seek customer input to better understand the need and the options and resources available. This type of

John Fedele/Blend Images LLC

customer co-creation

Customer input that results from the customer playing an active role in the problem-solving process.

customer input is formally referred to as **customer co-creation**. It results from the customer playing an active role in the problem-solving process.

Salespeople who embrace the customer as a solution co-creator recognize that:

- They must work hand in hand with their customers as opposed to simply selling to them.
- Most solutions are of little value without customer input and involvement.
- Customers can provide returns (e.g., knowledge) that go well beyond financial ones.
- Without customer involvement, it is very difficult to deliver customer value.

Much as the transition from products to solutions has challenged individual salespeople, it has also challenged the firms who employ these salespeople. Research has found that the transition has often required firms to replace more than 50 percent of their existing salespeople, as these salespeople were unable to adapt to the significant changes a focus on solution-based selling requires.[4] In essence, these firms must fire and rehire rather than try to teach existing salespeople new skills. This finding highlights the fact that solution-based sales requires a unique skill set. We discuss three of these skills—questioning, listening, and creativity—in the next section.

SKILLS NEEDED IN SOLVING CUSTOMER PROBLEMS

LO 6-2 Describe three skills needed in solving customer problems.

When asked to talk about salespeople, customers often say that they are seeing a difference in salespeople today, particularly in the number of questions the salespeople ask. But at the same time, many of these customers note that the solutions presented to them are very similar in nature. This would seem to indicate that salesperson questioning has outpaced salesperson creativity in recent years. In order to excel in solution-based selling, salespeople must possess three skills: questioning, listening, and creativity.

Questioning

Neil Rackham has been a pioneer in the sales field based on his development of the **SPIN selling** questioning methodology.[5] It lays out a basic, sequential questioning method for customer interactions. When developing his method in the 1980s, Rackham specifically sought to identify characteristics that differentiated highly successful salespeople from those who were less so. One primary differentiator emerged: The most successful salespeople were those who asked their customers questions to better understand their problems. Although this may sound intuitive now, it was a much more novel finding at the time. The term SPIN is an acronym that captures four types of questions contained in this questioning sequence: **S**ituational questions, **P**roblem questions, **I**mplication questions, and **N**eed-payoff questions.

SPIN selling

Methodology that lays out a basic sequence of four questions for customer interactions: Situational questions, Problem questions, Implication questions, and Need-payoff questions.

situational questions

In SPIN selling, questions designed to help the salesperson better understand the situation the customer is currently facing.

Situational Questions As the term suggests, **situational questions** are designed to help the salesperson better understand the situation the customer is facing. Although situational questions can be broad in nature, capturing the situation at the firm level, it often is useful to more narrowly focus the situational questions on those things that are specific to the problem being addressed.

For instance, if a technology firm were meeting with a university about technologies the university is currently using, the situational questions would more likely focus on these technologies and what the university is currently doing on this issue—as opposed to questions that are of a more general variety, such as questions that are not focused on technology utilization. This allows the salesperson to transition out of the situational questions more quickly. In general, it is beneficial to move quickly past the situational questions, which are of very little value to the customer. In most instances, when responding to situational questions, the customer is simply describing something that he or she is already well aware of.

Problem Questions
As the name indicates, **problem questions** are designed to help the customer and salesperson identify issues that need to be addressed. In some instances, these issues are observable, and the customer is aware of them. In other instances, the problem may be *latent;* the customer may not even know an issue exists.

GalacticDreamer/Shutterstock

problem questions
In SPIN selling, questions designed to help the customer and salesperson identify issues, sometimes latent, that need to be addressed.

For instance, a customer might believe that a particular facet of the business is performing optimally and be unaware that competitors are performing at a much higher level in that area. As a consultant, the salesperson can make the customer aware of this issue, shedding light on a latent problem.

As is the case with situational questions, problem questions are typically broader at the beginning of the questioning sequence and become narrower based on the information being provided by the customer.

Implication Questions
Implication questions are designed to help the customer and salesperson better understand the consequences arising from the uncovered problems. Focusing on implications is important—when dealing with the minutiae of daily activities, customers can easily lose focus on the negative ramifications of a problem. For instance, a customer might note that employee morale is not what it needs to be. The implications can be quite broad: Employee dissatisfaction typically shows in interactions with customers, thereby reducing customer satisfaction. When customer satisfaction dips, so do sales, as customers instead choose to buy from the competition. As sales decrease, the firm's management has fewer options, and growth becomes challenging, if not impossible. In a downward spiral like this, firms have a difficult time surviving.

implication questions
In SPIN selling, questions designed to help the customer and salesperson better understand the consequences arising from the problems uncovered in situational and problem questioning.

The connect-the-dots approach of implication questioning helps both the salesperson and customer understand the magnitude of a problem. Once this is understood, the customer becomes more likely to act.

Need-Payoff Questions
Need-payoff questions are designed to help the customer and salesperson better understand the benefits available to the firm if the customer's problem were solved. In some ways, these questions perform the opposite function of implication questions. Need-payoff questions mark a transition in the questioning process, from problems to possibilities.

need-payoff questions
In SPIN selling, questions designed to help the customer and salesperson better understand the benefits available to the firm if the customer's problem were solved.

Returning to the example introduced in the implication questions discussion, a salesperson might say: *"If you could, please take a few moments and talk about how your firm would benefit if you were able to increase employee morale and, in turn, customer satisfaction. Specifically, what opportunities would this provide both you and the firm?"* When the customer begins thinking about desirable possibilities not yet attained, as opposed to the problems currently being confronted, the motivation to address the problem increases greatly.

Thus, the SPIN selling methodology provides a sequential questioning blueprint for the salesperson. This blueprint is designed, first, to assist salespeople and their customers in understanding the most relevant problems at hand; then, to bring to the surface the implications associated with these problems; and finally, to imagine the possibilities that might exist if these problems were adequately dealt with. In this process, the salesperson and the customer are able to transition the conversation from *implied needs* to *explicit needs*:

- **Implied needs** are known to the customer but might not be important enough to merit action. For example, a customer might state that *"employee morale is not where it should be."* But this statement alone does not indicate the customer believes the need warrants attention.
- **Explicit needs**, in contrast, require immediate customer attention. Thus, if the customer were to instead state that we "must improve employee morale," he or she would be explicitly stating a desire to rectify the issue.

implied needs
Needs known to the customer but not important enough to merit action.

explicit needs
Needs that require immediate attention.

This is a critical distinction: Often, the difference between simply being aware of a problem and being motivated to act on it determines whether or not the salesperson will be able to gain commitment for a sale.

Open-Ended versus Closed Questions

Within the four categories of SPIN questions, salespeople must be conscious of *how* they structure their questions. Well-structured questions can maximize customer involvement in the selling process. Specifically, questions can be open-ended or closed. **Open-ended questions** are designed to ensure that customers respond with a great deal of information and detail. **Closed questions** are specific in nature and so require short and direct responses—often just a yes or no. For example, if a salesperson were to ask, *"Are you satisfied with your current level of customer satisfaction?"* the question would probably elicit a one-word (yes/no) response. In contrast, if the salesperson were to say, *"Talk to me about how satisfied your customers are with your company and the factors that affect this,"* the buyer would be more apt to open up and share more information.

open-ended questions
Questions designed to ensure that customers respond with a great deal of information and detail.

closed questions
Questions that are specific in nature and so require short and direct responses—often just a yes or no.

Neither question type is inherently wrong, and both serve a purpose. Salespeople typically lead with open-ended questions to encourage conversation on the part of the customer and establish a conversational flow. From there, closed questions can be used to verify and confirm the information the customer has provided.

In all, salespeople who are adept at implementing SPIN questioning have a tremendous advantage over those who are not. These salespeople have not only a sequence to follow but also a purpose to their questioning. There is a logical flow to the process, making it more conversational in nature. Customers do not want to feel that they are simply being peppered with questions. Instead, they want to engage in conversations aimed at solving their most pressing problems.

However, as we will discuss next, questioning is but one piece to the puzzle. Salespeople must also listen to the information their customers are providing.

Listening

Think of some of the great communicators you have had the pleasure of conversing with over the years. What makes these people great communicators? What do they do so well? What made you think of them? Although great communicators might do many things well, one thing typically stands out: *They talk about those things you are most interested in*. When they do this, they hold your attention—you listen to them.

This would suggest that the challenge is relatively simple: In order to communicate well, we need to talk about those things of most interest to the other person. But if getting people to listen is so simple, why do so many people struggle with it? Unfortunately, the truth is that most of us would rather talk about those things *we* care about instead of those things *the other person* is interested in.

The very same thing happens in sales: Salespeople often focus on their company and the products it sells rather than their customers' issues and problems. The fact that many professional salespeople have the "gift of gab" only exacerbates the issue. It perpetuates a belief that successful selling is more a function of talking than it is of listening.

Nothing could be further from the truth. One thing becomes immediately clear when you spend time with the salespeople who consistently outperform their counterparts: These salespeople are great listeners. They suck up every bit of information their customers provide them. They intently focus on every detail. The information they gather through listening provides the foundation for everything they do with their customers. However, listening is one of the most challenging tasks salespeople face as they first begin in the role. To increase listening effectiveness, there are several things to be mindful of:

- Stay in the moment when interacting with customers.
- Understand the difference between active and passive listening.
- Understand the valuable role that silence can play in the communication process.
- Learn to ask appropriate follow-up questions.
- Take detailed notes during customer meetings.

First, salespeople must stay in the moment when interacting with customers. As you begin participating in sales role plays, this is one of the greatest challenges you will face. As you are learning a sales process (e.g., SPIN), the process and the steps to be adhered to can overwhelm your intent to listen. That is, you are apt to think of where you are in the process and where you will go next, as opposed to being focused on the customer and what is being said.

For example, have you ever heard an interview being conducted and thought to yourself, "He (or she) is not even listening to what the person is saying"? In all likelihood, the interviewer has "scripted out" the questions to be asked. Instead of listening to what the interviewee is saying and asking questions based on this information, the interviewer is asking questions from the script. Although doing so may help the interviewer cover a range of topics, it is frustrating to the person being interviewed (and to those listening). Instead of imposing a script or a strict process onto conversations, the best salespeople listen and let their conversations emerge in a natural give and take. It is difficult for the brain to perform the two activities (questioning and listening) simultaneously, but practice will help.

Aleksandr Davydov/123RF

Second, salespeople must understand the difference between active and passive listening. **Active listening** occurs when the salesperson is fully engaged with the customer, paying careful attention to all verbal and nonverbal cues and providing appropriate responses. **Passive listening**, in contrast, is one-way communication in which the salesperson receives the information without providing feedback. Active listening makes the salesperson more engaged while selling. It also encourages the customer to provide additional information.

A third point to be mindful of when listening is the valuable role silence can play in the communication process. Silence can help eliminate one of the issues we see

active listening
Listening that occurs when the salesperson is fully engaged with the customer, paying careful attention to all verbal and nonverbal cues and providing appropriate responses.

passive listening
One-way communication in which the salesperson receives the information without providing feedback.

all too often in sales—salespeople being quick to interject their own thoughts rather than letting the customer fully explain the issue. Salespeople jump into the conversation because they *think* they know what the customer is saying. But this might not always be the case. The best listeners, instead, are comfortable with a slight pause before moving on to the next question. Often, when they do this, the customer continues to share additional information. In this way, silence can play a critical role in enhancing overall communication effectiveness.

Fourth, salespeople must also learn to ask appropriate **follow-up questions**. These are questions asked in direct response to something the customer has said. In addition to demonstrating active listening, these questions help facilitate a conversational flow. Salespeople can ask questions that elicit more information, such as *"You just mentioned [topic]. Can you tell me more about that?"* Such follow-up questions demonstrate listening and assist with an overall flow during the questioning process. They also help ensure that the salesperson gathers all relevant information.

Salespeople should also ask summary questions to ensure a joint understanding of what has been said. As the name suggests, **summary questions** are designed to review and verify information previously provided by the customer. For example, at the end of the problem-questioning sequence within SPIN, a salesperson might state, *"To summarize, you have said that your three most challenging problems are lagging sales, deteriorating margins, and operational inefficiencies. Is this correct?"*

Finally, part of active listening is to take detailed notes during customer meetings. The goal is to ensure the capture of all necessary information. In some instances, salespeople even record their customer conversations (although they should secure the customer's approval before doing this). Just as details from a meeting are lost if the minutes are not recorded, it is impossible to recall all that is discussed in a customer meeting without notes. If possible, it's useful to input the notes into a customer relationship management (CRM) system to make the information available to others within the sales organization. As a form of post-call follow-up, salespeople will often send the notes to the customer to ensure accuracy.

Creativity

As noted earlier, questioning and listening are but two elements necessary for effective problem solving. A third element is creativity in crafting solutions that are unique and of value. As you have probably observed in your own life and your observations of others, people differ when it comes to solving problems. We approach problems differently and ultimately employ different processes to arrive at a solution. Recognizing this, salespeople should first understand their own problem-solving style.

Adaption-innovation theory identifies two primary types of problem solvers: adaptors and innovators.[6] **Adaptors** prefer more-structured problem-solving methods; they are most comfortable when everyone is in agreement about the process and the solution. **Innovators**, on the other hand, are at ease with a less-structured problem-solving approach; they tend to look beyond the status quo for solutions. Adaptors tend to view ambiguity as a source of stress; innovators are more comfortable tackling highly ambiguous problems. From a customer perspective:

- Adaptors are better suited to situations in which the customer is seeking to improve existing business processes.
- Innovators are better suited to situations in which the customer is looking to change these processes

In other words, adaptors are more focused on *doing things better*, and innovators are more focused on *doing things differently*.

---

follow-up questions
Questions asked in direct response to something the customer said.

summary questions
Questions designed to review and verify information previously provided by the customer.

adaptors
Problem-solvers who prefer more-structured problem-solving methods and are most comfortable when everyone is in agreement about the process and the solution.

innovators
Problem-solvers who are at ease with a less-structured problem-solving approach and who tend to look beyond the status quo for solutions.

It is important to note that neither the adaptor nor innovator problem-solving style is inherently right or wrong. They represent different approaches and are therefore better suited for dealing with different types of customer problems. For example, an innovator might be more comfortable developing a new sales territory where little is known about potential customers and the issues they face; an adaptor might prefer an existing territory where information about customers and their issues is readily available. Further, in team-based sales situations, combining adaptors and innovators on a team can be beneficial, allowing for the merging of different problem-solving approaches.

Knowing one's problem-solving style is the first step. Salespeople can also enhance their creativity by developing an expansive problem-solving network. Creative solutions are more likely to emerge when the salesperson has contacts outside the immediate sales team. Indeed, researchers examining networks have found that individuals who operate at the intersection of multiple groups are more likely to have good ideas. In contrast, people who are insulated within strong, cohesive (i.e., more homogeneous) social networks tend to think and act the same.[7] People who interact outside their social networks not only are often the first to learn about new and useful information, but they are also able to see how different kinds of groups solve similar problems. Because of this, salespeople who have more expansive networks will be more knowledgeable and more likely to deliver creative solutions valued by the customer.

Connect Assignment 6-1

Spin Selling

Please complete the Connect exercise for Chapter 6 that focuses on SPIN-selling question methodology. By understanding these types of questions and how they can be used effectively, salespeople can better understand and solve customer problems.

GAINING COMMITMENT

We have talked extensively about the changing nature of professional sales, but make no mistake: Those who take a job in sales have to be able to sell. Salespeople are revenue generators and as such must do more than just ask questions, listen, and deliver creative solutions. At some point, they must actually get the sale. This has not changed—nor will it.

What *has* changed is the way salespeople go about getting the sale. Even the terminology associated with this portion of the sales call has changed in recent years. Most used to refer to the portion of the call where the actual sale was made as *the close*. Today, we use the term **gaining commitment**. Does this seem like a trivial difference? It's not; it captures the idea that, in a relational exchange, the initial sale is but a starting point from which the relationship can develop. It opens a relational door, as opposed to closing an isolated transaction. This thinking denotes a circular sales cycle; in this cycle, the follow-up and attention to detail provided after the sale provide the impetus for the customer to continue doing business with the salesperson and selling company.

The level of focus placed on this portion of the sales call has also changed. If you were to take a step back in time and were sitting in a sales classroom in the 1990s or earlier, your experience would be much different. In that classroom, significant

LO 6-3
Summarize the process of gaining commitment and various techniques to do so.

gaining commitment
The portion of the sales call in which the customer commits to the sale.

goodluz/123RF

attention would be given to overcoming objections and closing the sale, as opposed to questioning and listening. Role plays were quite different: Students would stand in front of the class with a flip chart and fend off objection after objection, as opposed to asking questions to better understand their customer's concerns. The ABC ("always be closing") approach to sales was in full effect. The students who turned out to be most successful were those who doggedly pursued the customer until the sale was finally closed.

Does this sound enjoyable? Would you have been motivated to pursue a career in sales if this were your experience in the classroom? (And can you see why many salespeople who began their careers in this era are struggling with the transition to a solution-based approach?) Thirty years ago, many argued that there was no need for professional selling courses in academe. They believed the skills required for sales success did not merit academic focus. Instead, they thought, the best salespeople were those who simply never took no for an answer. While unbending persistence can be beneficial in any job, this approach helped fuel the notion that salespeople were master manipulators, interested only in their own gain. It is why so many people today are still wary of salespeople.

That approach to gaining commitment is no longer the approach we embrace. Instead, we discuss a customer-oriented approach through which commitment can be obtained and the specific techniques salespeople can employ when attempting to gain commitment.

Customer-Oriented Approach to Gaining Commitment

Gaining commitment is a natural part of the overall sales process, and it should be thought of as such. Customers expect salespeople to ask them to make purchases or further engage in a process that will eventually lead to a purchase. Understanding this, salespeople should feel comfortable and confident when attempting to gain commitment. Doing so will help ensure these same feelings on the part of the customer.

As a part of the pre-call planning process, salespeople know, prior to the sales call, what type of commitment they anticipate requesting. In some instances, the objective is a sale; in many others, it is not. Moreover, call objectives should be thought of as fluid; they may change based on the information provided by the customer during the questioning process. In most instances, salespeople will have both a primary and secondary objective. The **primary objective** is what the salesperson most wants to accomplish. The **secondary objective** is what the salesperson is willing to revert to if agreement cannot be reached on the primary objective.

Throughout the sales call, salespeople should listen and look for buying signals, to know when the time is right to seek commitment. **Buying signals** are cues sent by the customer indicating a shift in thinking from *if* we should do this to *how* we should do this. For example, a customer might ask, *"Would it be possible for us to receive shipment at the end of the month instead of the beginning of the month?"* In this question, the salesperson should recognize that the customer has transitioned in thought and is now focused on how an agreement should be structured. The salesperson should confirm that the customer is willing to commit but is concerned about the specifics surrounding the commitment. The salesperson might respond, *"Based on your asking this, am I safe to assume that you would like to move forward and that we should now transition our conversation to what the specifics of any agreement will entail?"* In this way, salespeople have to adapt during the sales call; they must be agile enough to depart from their anticipated call plan in response to the verbal (and in some cases, nonverbal) buying signals provided by the customer.

Here, we focus on a **summary-benefit approach** to gaining commitment, which is most consistent with solution-based selling. Within this approach, the salesperson focuses on the benefits being provided to the customer rather than the features of the product or service itself. Salespeople employing the summary-benefit approach, in sequence:

1. Summarize what has been discussed previously, focusing on the problems being addressed and the benefits to the customer of the solution being presented.
2. Use a **trial-close question**. This question is designed to assess whether the customer has comments or concerns about the salesperson's summary.
3. Present the proposal.
4. Discuss price and the corresponding financial implications (if appropriate, depending on the call objectives).
5. Discuss the appropriate follow-up steps.

It is difficult to overemphasize how important follow-up is as a foundational cornerstone for relational exchange. The salesperson should know exactly what follow-up steps are going to be required depending on the objective achieved. Further, it is important for salespeople to understand the psychological dynamics at play during the sales call. As salespeople and customers proceed through the call, much of the burden falls on the salesperson, who feels more angst and anxiety than does the customer, not knowing whether commitment will be obtained. When a customer commits to the salesperson, particularly when making a purchase, much of this burden shifts to the customer. If it is an initial purchase, the customer might be thinking, *"Was this the right decision? Is this salesperson going to do what she said she would?"* The most forward-thinking salespeople recognize this psychological dynamic and immediately try to ease this burden. They do so by providing a thorough description of the activities that will be performed as follow-up. Even more important: They then actually do those things! The likelihood of a future sale goes up dramatically when this seemingly simple step is performed.

Techniques for Gaining Commitment

There are various techniques available when making the actual "ask" (the request for commitment). The technique that is used isn't all that important, though. More

primary objective
What the salesperson most wants to accomplish in the sales call.

secondary objective
The objective to which the salesperson is willing to revert if agreement cannot be reached on the primary objective.

buying signals
Cues sent by the customer indicating a shift in thinking from *if* we should do this to *how* we should do this.

summary-benefit approach
Approach to gaining commitment in which the salesperson focuses on the benefits being provided to the customer, rather than the features of the product or service itself.

trial-close question
Question designed to assess whether the customer has comments or concerns about the salesperson's summary.

important was what led up to the ask: the questions the salesperson asked and whether the proposed solution addresses the problems identified. There are four common commitment-gaining techniques:

1. *Alternative-choice.* In the **alternative-choice technique**, the salesperson provides two legitimate options for the customer to choose between, along with guidance about which is more appropriate.
2. *Balance-sheet.* In the **balance-sheet technique**, the salesperson lists the positives as well as the negatives associated with commitment. This technique may be most appropriate in complicated sales situations or when dealing with analytical customers (i.e., customers who are more quantitative in nature).
3. *Direct request.* In the **direct-request technique**, the salesperson simply asks for the commitment. This is the most straightforward, and perhaps common, approach.
4. *Success story.* In the **success-story technique**, the salesperson tells the story of another customer who agreed to something similar and has benefited from the decision. This technique is most appropriate when dealing with expressive customers (i.e., customers who are more emotional in nature).

An example of the overall process of gaining commitment is shown below. The customer is purchasing for a retail chain; the salesperson represents a consumer-packaged goods (CPG) firm. This is a resell situation (that is, the customer is purchasing to resell the goods rather than to use them personally). Thus, the customer's two primary needs are sales and margins—that is, how well the product will sell and how much money the company will make every time a sale is made. (The concept of *margins* is fully discussed in Chapter 8, "Profitology.") Higher sales can compensate for lower margin percentages, and vice versa. In the example, you'll notice that the salesperson employs the summary-benefit approach from an overall perspective, and the alternative-choice technique when making the ask.

---

alternative-choice technique
Commitment-gaining technique in which the salesperson provides two legitimate options for the customer to choose between, along with guidance about which is more appropriate.

balance-sheet technique
Commitment-gaining technique in which the salesperson lists the positives as well as the negatives associated with commitment.

direct-request technique
Commitment-gaining technique in which the salesperson simply asks for the commitment.

success-story technique
Commitment-gaining technique in which the salesperson tells the story of another customer who agreed to something similar and has benefited from the decision.

Salesperson: Given that we have discussed quite a bit both today and in our previous meetings, I would like to take a moment to summarize our discussions. Most important, we first discussed the problems you are currently facing—you need to increase sales and increase profits, and you need a more educated floor sales staff. Are these correct?

Customer: Yes, those are correct.

Salesperson: Good. You and I then discussed how my firm can help you overcome these problems. First, we talked about why consumers seek out our products (unique features and a good brand image) and how our products would benefit you in the form of additional sales. We then talked about the quantity discounts we offer, which would benefit you in the form of enhanced margins. Last, we talked about a plan to better educate your floor sales staff through product knowledge sessions that we will arrange at a time convenient for you and them. Does this sound correct to you?

Customer: Yes, it certainly does.

Salesperson [trial-close]: And do you have any questions, comments, or concerns about any of this?

Customer: I do not. All of this sounds correct.

Salesperson [alternative-choice]: That being the case, I have taken the liberty of drawing up two suggested orders. The first contains higher order quantities, *but with our quantity discounts you will receive additional margins through price reductions. The second has lower quantities, but with that, the anticipated margins are not as aggressive. Specifically, as you can see, the average margin for the first order is approximately 7.5 percent, while the average margin for the second order is approximately 5 percent.*

I believe you should choose the first option. Here's why: In our discussions we both agreed that your turn ratios on the order should be strong—these products will sell. Second, you talked about how important margins are to your business, and the first order provides the margins you desire.

That being said, I'll let you study both orders and will be glad to discuss any questions you may have.

Customer: *I am with you on this one. I believe that the first order is better for us. I'm comfortable moving forward with it.*

Salesperson: *Great! I'm looking forward to working with you on this. Let's now discuss our next steps. First, I'll place the order. I will pull the purchase order number and will send it to you. That way, either of us can track the order.*

Once I know when the products are to be delivered, I will set my schedule so that I will be here on site to ensure that everything is as it should be—both from a product and pricing perspective. From there, I will work with store personnel on merchandising, to ensure a proper in-store plan. I will also meet with you to find the appropriate times to hold the employee product-knowledge sessions. Finally, at a future date, we will set a time to meet and discuss how satisfied you are with the outcomes of this process. We will also discuss things that we may be able to do better in the future. Do you have any questions about this?

Customer: *I don't, and I'm looking forward to working with you.*

Salesperson: *Thank you. I feel the same.*

TYPES OF CUSTOMER OBJECTIONS

LO 6-4
List the primary types of objections customers typically raise.

Of course, not all sales situations go smoothly; customers are going to voice any concerns they may have, both prior to and during the sales call. We refer to these concerns as objections. An **objection** is an explicit expression by a buyer that a barrier exists between the current situation and what needs to be satisfied before buying. Professional sellers understand that these concerns can be raised at any point in the selling process. They represent obstacles that must be overcome prior to completing an agreement.

objection
An explicit expression by a buyer that a barrier exists that needs to be satisfied before buying.

Objections are a natural part of the sales process. They are to be expected. Just as you have concerns or may need additional information when contemplating a purchase, so too will business customers voice their concerns and questions when presented with a proposal. This is their job—what their employers pay them to do. Salespeople should expect, if not even welcome, customer objections. The ability of salespeople to deal with customer objections is one element that distinguishes personal selling from other forms of marketing communications.

We focus on the five most common objections voiced by business customers—no-need, source, time, product, and price. These objections are not specific to a particular industry or setting; they remain consistent across the different types of sales situations salespeople confront.

No-Need Objection

The *no-need objection* can be the most challenging objection salespeople face. If the customer does not perceive a need for a product, he or she will not be motivated to engage in the sales process. In some instances the need (or problem) may be latent; it exists without the customer's knowledge. There may be other instances in which the customer realizes that a particular facet of the business is not performing optimally but does not have the necessary motivation to act. It is difficult to blame customers for feeling this way, when they may already be inundated with so many issues to address. When a salesperson attempts to bring up yet another issue in need of attention, it is only natural to assume that the customer is going to resist.

Moreover, in some cases, the customer is essentially admitting to an earlier mistake by thinking about from one solution to another. Salespeople should recognize that it is sometimes difficult for customers to admit to these mistakes. Because of this, the customer may instead insist that there is no need to make a change.

Source Objection

Even when customers agree that they might have a need for the product, they may still be uncertain about your company as the best source for that solution. The *source objection* refers to the customer's concerns about the selling company, the salesperson, or perhaps both. For example, the customer may be frustrated over the fact that the selling company has shifted its manufacturing overseas, or may be bothered by the fact that a salesperson is very young. In some instances, the source objection may even exist at the industry level. For example, a car salesman may have to overcome customers' preconceived beliefs that most car salesmen are focused on their own gain, to the neglect of the customer.

Source-based objections often come in the form of direct challenges, such as *"I've never heard of your firm. How do I know your company will even be in business in two years?"* Or *"I like to know who I'm working with—that is why we typically hire local suppliers. Why should I trust my business to a large company based in another state?"* These types of objections often hide underlying issues that the buyer isn't ready to articulate. Before trying to respond to the concern, it is often useful to use open-ended "why" questions to clarify:

- Why do you think that?
- Why is that important?
- What caused you to have that concern?

Once the basis for the objection is brought to light, you are better equipped to address the root concern. You can increase confidence in the ability of your company to get the job done by providing the client with timely and relevant information, sharing testimonials and case studies, and providing references.

Time Objection

As is probably the case in your own life, time is an incredibly precious commodity in business. In many instances, customers know they have issues that need attention in their business but they are limited by time constraints and have to prioritize some issues over others. Because of this, customers will voice *time* as an objection.

One of two things is typically happening in this situation: The customer is considering the offer but needs more time to do some other things before being ready to buy. Or the customer has no intention of buying and just wants to get rid of the salesperson. If the customer is simply trying to get rid of the salesperson, there is very little you can do to save the sale, at least in the near term. But if the customer in fact does just need more time before being ready to buy, the salesperson should dig deeper into this objection. Unless you are a mind reader, it is nearly impossible for you to know which of the two scenarios you are dealing with. To uncover the truth, you need more information. As we will discuss, this information can be gained only through additional questioning.

Product Objection

With a *product objection,* the customer voices concerns about some element of the product offering. This type of concern can extend well beyond the product itself. In many instances, the customer will have concerns about warranty or installation issues. Often, product concerns are voiced in relation to competitive offerings, such as "Your competitor's products offer this feature, but yours does not."

fizkes/Shutterstock

In some instances, the customer might not be familiar with the product. As a result, the customer might see little value in the solution being presented or the need it satisfies. Although a salesperson may be excited about innovative new features of the product, customers may be concerned that the technology is unproven or will not integrate well with current systems or processes. The salesperson should present a value proposition that clearly illustrates how the product will benefit the customer.

Price Objection

Price objections are just as they sound—the customer believes the quoted price is too high. The price objection should not be confused with other, similar objections that are also of the financial variety, such as value or budget.

Most customers—even those who have every intention of eventually buying—have learned that pushing on price will get them a discount. While discounting has its place in sales negotiations, being too discount-happy can be harmful to profit margins (and sales commissions) and damage a salesperson's reputation. It also important to know that customers rarely raise a price objection unless they are seriously thinking about buying your product or service. So, a price objection can be viewed as good news.

These five objections are most common across all sales settings. There are also objections that are specific to certain industries. For example, retail buyers might frequently have concerns over in-store space for new products. Industrial buyers might be more concerned about the ability to fit a proposed solution into a preexisting manufacturing process.

Regardless of the objection, what matters most is the *process* through which the salesperson learns more about the objection and, if possible, addresses it. We present this process in the following section.

OVERCOMING OBJECTIONS

LO 6-5

Describe the process of overcoming objections and various techniques available to do so.

When confronting an objection, one of the traps to avoid is taking the objection at face value. Many salespeople attempt to answer the objection immediately, assuming that it is valid. Often, though, the voiced objection and the underlying concern are not one and the same. Salespeople who do not further question the objection may spend time addressing an issue that is not really the problem. Salespeople must therefore employ a process that both demonstrates empathy and also yields a deeper understanding of the objection.

LAER model®

Model for handling customer objections, involving four steps: Listen, Acknowledge, Explore, and Respond.

The Process of Overcoming Objections

A proven and effective method for handling customer objections is Carew International's LAER: The Bonding Process®. The **LAER model**, outlined in Figure 6-1, involves four steps—**L**isten, **A**cknowledge, **E**xplore, and **R**espond. As shown in the figure, it is vitally important to engage in all four steps, as opposed to simply responding after first hearing the objection. Even though it is natural to want to respond when first hearing an objection, salespeople have to dig deeper to ensure a true understanding of the buyer's concern. We talk more about this below, as we cover each step in the LAER model.

Listening is the most important skill you can have when understanding how to respond to an objection. It demonstrates to your customers that you respect them, are interested in their concerns, and care about what they have to say. When customers trust you enough to voice objections, you at least owe them the courtesy of listening attentively. You cannot bond with a customer, address the objection, or empathize with the situation until you have listened intently to them.

The next step is to *acknowledge* the objection. This is where you demonstrate you have been actively listening. A sincere acknowledgment can circumvent an argument and have a calming effect. Sometimes, your customers just want to know they are being heard. Your goal at this stage is to simply communicate that you heard the objection or question without immediately agreeing with or combating it.

In the *explore* phase, you want to get to the root of why your prospect thinks a certain way. It is imperative that you understand exactly what your customer meant by what was said. Now is not the time to correct them. You are simply trying to uncover the thought process that led them to a given conclusion. Without this, even your best advice might bounce off, unheeded. Asking open-ended questions that require more than a simple, one-word answer is the best way to get at the facts.

The final step is to *respond*. Once you have a complete understanding of the objection, you can offer your response in the form of a recommendation, an alternative, a solution, or a next step designed to address the customer's concern. Once you have addressed the objection with a response, it is important to affirm, through a trial-close

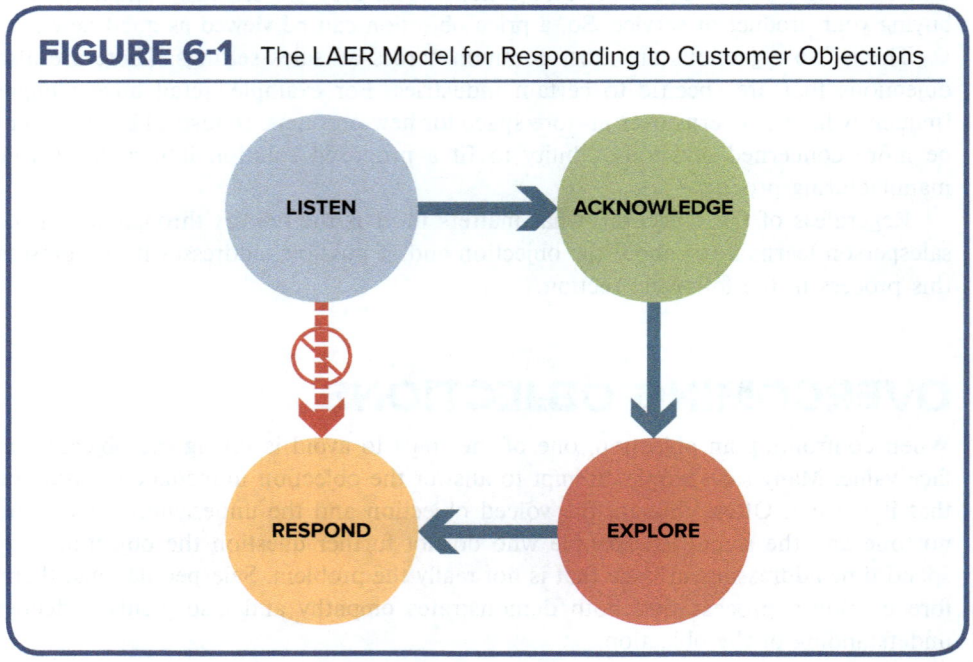

FIGURE 6-1 The LAER Model for Responding to Customer Objections

question, that the customer understood what you said and accepted your answer. This is particularly important, as objections that salespeople only superficially deal with will not go away. At some point, the customer will voice the objection again. In many instances, the objection will become even more problematic as the customer grows frustrated over the fact that the concern has not been dealt with.

To demonstrate, we focus on an objection some students may hear in their first sales role: the customer would prefer to work with an older, more experienced salesperson. Salesperson age is a type of *source objection*—one directed at the salesperson rather than the selling company. This is an interesting objection as it is one over which the salesperson has no control. For example, assume that you are a newly minted, 23-year-old salesperson. You are excited about this new role and are out meeting your customers. If a particular customer were to say that he or she is uncomfortable with your age, you cannot respond by saying that you are going to return as a 33-year-old next week. Nor should you want to!

What you *can* do, through the use of the process shown below, is transition the conversation away from something over which you have no control (salesperson age) to something that you do (salesperson performance).

Customer: Although I have enjoyed this first meeting, I have to be honest with you about a concern I have. It is your age. Unfortunately, I have worked with young salespeople in the past, and my experiences have not been good. I worry that I will have a similar type of experience with you.

Salesperson: I can certainly understand why this is a concern of yours. I would be concerned as well if I were in your shoes. Thank you for being honest and bringing this up now.

Can you tell me a bit more about why you feel this way? Specifically, can you elaborate on the experiences you have had with younger salespeople in the past?

Customer: I would be glad to. Unfortunately, I've found that younger salespeople are not as reliable. There is too much uncertainty in what they do. I never know whether they are actually going to fulfill their promises, and I cannot work with that uncertainty.

Salesperson: I can understand why that would be a problem, and I will address it. Before I do, have you had any other recurring issues with younger salespeople?

Customer: I have. Younger salespeople just do not seem to be as well connected within their own companies. They do not seem to know where their needed resources are, or where they should turn to find them. Because of this, there always seems to be a delay in accomplishing the things I need done. I do not typically encounter this problem when working with more-experienced salespeople.

Salesperson: Again, I can understand why this is a concern of yours. I know how valuable your time is and will address this point. Do you have any other issues when working with younger salespeople?

Customer: No, that's primarily it. However, those are two important issues.

Salesperson: Well, I would like to begin by again thanking you for being honest and upfront about this concern. I would like to talk more about it, specifically focusing on the two issues you discussed—reliability and networking. How does that sound?

(Continued)

> *Customer:* We can certainly discuss it further.
>
> *Salesperson:* Clearly, you have had some disappointing experiences with younger salespeople in the past, but I would like to talk with you about how I may be different from those salespeople.
>
> First, unlike many other salespeople, I focused on sales while in college. My university offered a program of study in professional selling. While you may not know exactly what that means in terms of my experience, it does show that I made a purposeful decision to pursue this career while in school. Sales is more than a job to me; it is my career. I chose it. While in the university program, I learned what it means to truly be a sales professional. I learned how important it is to be reliable and also how important it is to build a network within your organization as soon as possible. To this last point, I participated in a six-month rotational program when I first accepted this position. It enabled me to learn the organization and what I need to do to secure resources for my customers.
>
> Although I cannot change my age, I can do quite a bit to demonstrate to you that I am different from the other younger salespeople you have worked with in the past. I believe that my background is different from most and that it has prepared me for success in this role. All I ask is that you give me the opportunity to show this.
>
> *Customer:* I must admit that you do have a unique background. I was not aware of this—perhaps you are different.
>
> *Salesperson* [trial close]: Thank you. I know that to say it is one thing, but to do it is another. That said, are you comfortable with my response to your concern? Do you have any other concerns about my age or my ability to serve you as a salesperson?
>
> *Customer:* I do not. I am looking forward to working with you in this role.

This example shows the power of questioning in response to an objection. Without further questioning, one might assume the customer simply does not want to work with young salespeople. In reality, the customer is drawing a correlation between age and a perceived lack of performance. The salesperson's questioning severed this correlation and transitioned the conversation from something over which the salesperson had no control to something that can instead be addressed. In the following section, we discuss the specific techniques available to salespeople when answering objections.

Techniques for Overcoming Objections

As is the case when gaining commitment, the specific technique used when overcoming objections matters less than adherence to the overall objection-handling process. Without knowledge of the true objection, which can be identified only through questioning, you cannot attempt to answer the objection.

Once you have uncovered the true objection, you can employ several objection-handling techniques in response. These techniques are summarized below, with examples of a salesperson's response. (Names of alternate terms for techniques are provided in parentheses.)

Acknowledge Technique

acknowledge technique
Technique for overcoming an objection in which the salesperson admits that the objection is valid.

Acknowledge Technique In the acknowledge technique, the salesperson is candid in admitting that the objection is valid. As an example, a customer might voice concern that the selling company has begun manufacturing its products overseas. Assuming this is indeed the case, the salesperson will acknowledge that the firm is manufacturing overseas, and typically will provide an explanation.

> *Yes, you are correct; we have shifted our manufacturing overseas. We have done so because point-of-sale data has consistently revealed that customers are not willing to pay a premium price for products made here. What our customers tell us in surveys and focus groups (that they prefer products made in the U.S.A.), and what they actually do when making purchases, are not consistent. Hence, our decision to make this move.*

Boomerang Technique
In the **boomerang technique**, the salesperson transitions the objection from a negative to a positive by discussing how the perceived negative should actually benefit the customer.

> *That is correct, we have installed the blade-disengage feature. While this does create an additional step when the user is reengaging the mower, we have found it is a tremendous safety benefit that our customers desperately want. In fact, our customers have told us that safety is their primary concern, and this feature makes the product much safer.*

boomerang technique
Technique for overcoming an objection in which the salesperson transitions the objection from a negative to a positive by discussing how the perceived negative should actually benefit the customer.

Compensation Technique
The salesperson using the **compensation technique** is candid in admitting that the objection is valid but also discusses other benefits that offset the objection.

> *Yes, you are correct; our cordless drills are heavy. The reason is that our batteries are larger, to allow for more run-time on a single charge. Our customers have told us that run-time is their most important feature; it is a must-have. Thus, we believe that the benefit of additional run-time offsets the weight of the drills.*

compensation technique
Technique for overcoming an objection in which the salesperson admits the objection is valid but also discusses other benefits that offset the objection.

Forestall Technique
In situations in which you know that an objection will arise, you can use the **forestall technique**. Instead of waiting for the customer to bring up the objection, the salesperson intentionally brings up the issue. Forestalling is particularly effective when dealing with price objections. After all, if the solution you are presenting is of a clearly higher quality than alternatives, it would be truly surprising if the price were the same as or lower than competitors'. In such instances, you may be able to head off price objections by addressing them early in the conversation.

forestall technique
Technique for overcoming an objection in which the salesperson brings up an objection he or she knows will arise, instead of waiting for the customer to do so.

> *I know that we are just beginning, but before we go any further, I think it is important we address price, at least in general terms. We are not the lowest-priced option available, or even close to it. In fact, we charge a premium price. If you know now that you will not be willing or able to pay that, despite the additional benefits we provide, there is no sense in moving forward.*

Denial Technique
In the **indirect denial technique**, you acknowledge that you can understand why the customer would have the concern but state that the objection is not valid. A **direct denial technique** is similar but you flatly state the objection is not valid.

indirect denial technique
Technique for overcoming an objection in which the salesperson acknowledges understanding why the customer would have the concern but states that the objection is not valid.

direct denial technique
Technique for overcoming an objection in which the salesperson states that the objection is not valid.

> *I certainly understand your concern, and can see why you may feel that way, given the information you were exposed to [indirect denial]. However, that information is not accurate. We have not shifted our manufacturing overseas. We are, instead, still manufacturing domestically.*

Postpone (Coming-to-That) Technique
In the **postpone (coming-to-that) technique**, the salesperson acknowledges the objection and asks if it can instead be discussed at a later point in the sales call, as the call progresses.

> *It sounds like price is a concern of yours, which is understandable. However, if you don't mind, I would like to come back to that, so that you can develop a fuller understanding of our price in relation to the benefits we may be able to provide.*

postpone (coming-to-that) technique
Technique for overcoming an objection in which the salesperson acknowledges the objection and asks if it can instead be discussed at a later point in the sales call.

referral (feel-felt-found) technique
Technique for overcoming an objection in which the salesperson uses a third party (often a customer) to address and refute the objection.

Referral (Feel-Felt-Found) Technique
In the **referral (feel-felt-found) technique**, the salesperson uses a third party (often a customer) to address and refute the objection.

> *That is a natural concern to have. I too would be concerned if I thought I were purchasing more inventory than I could sell in a reasonable period of time. I understand that inventory is money, and that when you have too much money tied up in inventory, you are limited in other things you can do as a business. Many other customers I have sold to have had this same concern. However, they have found that they have been able to sell the product through in a reasonable period of time. In fact, with their permission, I have pulled some data of their results, which I'd like to show you.*

value technique
Technique for overcoming an objection in which the salesperson transitions the conversation away from price alone to more fully describe the value being offered through the solution.

Value Technique
With the **value technique**, the salesperson transitions the conversation away from price alone to focus on the value being offered through the solution. This technique is used primarily when confronting the price objection.

> *I understand that you have concerns about the price and that you would like us to get the price lower. However, when you study the solution in front of you, you will see that every element contained within it has some level of value attached. Now, if we must get price down, I am more than willing to discuss solution elements that you may be willing to give up.*

No technique for overcoming objections is inherently better than the others, and none of the techniques guarantee success. Instead, salespeople should choose a technique based on their knowledge of the situation and the customer.

McGraw Hill connect **Connect Assignment 6-2**

Overcoming Objections
Please complete the Connect exercise for Chapter 6 that focuses on overcoming objections. Understanding the types of objections and the process for overcoming them will help salespeople better address customer concerns and gain commitment.

ETHICS IN GAINING COMMITMENT

In all likelihood, you have dealt with a salesperson who has attempted to pressure you into a purchase, relentlessly pestering you in the hopes of making a sale. If you are like most people, all you wanted to do was get as far away from that salesperson as possible. Traditional techniques used when attempting to overcome objections and gain commitment have contributed to the fact that many people have a persistently negative view of salespeople. Typically, these high-pressure interactions occur in the consumer context, where a salesperson is attempting to sell to a final consumer. Business customers simply will not accept this type of behavior. They will quickly end the discussion and make sure that the salesperson is fully aware there will be no future discussions.

> **LO 6-6**
>
> Explain the importance of ethics when overcoming objections and gaining commitment.

Ethics and Objections

Salespeople should never attempt to deceive or manipulate the customer when confronted with an objection. The customer-oriented process of handling objections (described in the previous section) is designed to help the salesperson develop a deeper understanding of the issue in order to address it. In some instances, you will be able to resolve the issue and move forward toward a sale. In others, an issue will emerge that cannot be rectified. This is a part of sales; it is to be expected. Even the best salespeople confront this.

Unfortunately, some salespeople fall into the trap of thinking that manipulative techniques will allow them to brush past their customers' objections. Nothing could be farther from the truth. From an ethical perspective, all salespeople should understand that the primary goal in handling objections is to address the issue—whatever it may be.

Manipulative Closing Techniques

As a salesperson, using a high-pressure technique when attempting to gain commitment is unethical. *It should not be done.* The techniques described below are manipulative—and inconsistent with a customer orientation. If you ever interact with a salesperson who attempts to use one of these techniques, you should immediately walk away. Salespeople who sell this way are not focused on your interests, nor do they deserve your time. Moreover, if you are employed by a company that is teaching these techniques, you are working for the wrong company. If a company is willing to treat its customers this way, do you think it will treat its employees any better?

Assumptive Close In an **assumptive close**, the salesperson makes a statement indicating an assumption that an agreement has already been reached, when this is not the case. In essence, the salesperson never makes the ask, but instead begins talking as if an agreement is in place. For example, the salesperson may state: "I will work with our customer service department to ensure that you receive the order in no more than seven working days," even though the customer has not agreed to the purchase.

Continuous-Yes Close In the **continuous-yes close**, the salesperson asks a series of questions designed to elicit a positive (yes) response. He or she then concludes by asking for the sale, in the hope that the customer will again respond "yes." This technique is highly ineffective with business customers. Customers will immediately sense that the salesperson is being manipulative.

Emotional Close In an **emotional close**, the salesperson discusses how important the sale is for personal reasons. For example, the salesperson might state that his salary is commission-based and that he needs the sale to help provide for his family. This close is both unethical and highly unprofessional.

> **assumptive close**
>
> Manipulative closing technique in which the salesperson makes a statement indicating an assumption that an agreement has already been reached, when this is not the case.
>
> **continuous-yes close**
>
> Manipulative closing technique in which the salesperson asks a series of questions designed to elicit a positive (yes) response, and concludes by asking for the sale in the hope that the customer will again respond "yes."
>
> **emotional close**
>
> Manipulative closing technique in which the salesperson discusses how important the sale is for personal reasons.

Today's Professional Perspective... because everyone is a salesperson

Chase Schaeffer
Account Executive
Brooksource

Chase Schaeffer

Describe your job. I am an account executive at Brooksource in Birmingham, AL. We are an IT staffing and consulting firm. We specialize in assisting companies through a unique blend of service offerings. I specialize in security roles, such as government security (e.g., cyber-security defense) through contract and contract-to-hire opportunities, as well as banking information and access management, or information security.

How did you get your job? I actually got this job through a networking event that my school, the University of Alabama at Birmingham (UAB), was hosting. I was a medical distribution major. After speaking with everyone who was on my target list, I was simply waiting for the event to be over. Not too long after that, a woman walked up and tapped me on the shoulder. She described to me what Brooksource is, handed me a business card, and left. I contacted her, and two weeks later, after a phone screening and a two-hour in-person interview, I was on a flight to Indianapolis, Indiana, to the company headquarters for training.

What has been most important in making you successful at your job? "The train of opportunity comes along every five seconds. Smart people know when to hop on and when to hop off." This is something my father told me when I first started my journey through sales. It has stuck with me, and I have it written on my desk. Here's why: The most important thing in the job has been to trust the process and never stop learning. You may fall every time you start something new. It is the effort you exert to pull yourself back up that makes all the difference. I made some pretty silly mistakes—nothing big, but silly—when I first started. It is only because of those mistakes that I have grown and become better at my job. And I promise you, I will continue to make mistakes, hopefully only once for each lesson to be learned. I never stop learning. Learn from every new opportunity or encounter. It is all about how you perceive situations.

What advice would you give future graduates about a career in sales? It sounds like a cliché in any sales role, but don't be afraid of rejection. Ninety percent of the time, it really is nothing personal. Some other things I would suggest are: take your training seriously, listen to your superiors (they are incentivized to help you be successful), and don't take yourself too seriously when you move into the role. You have a lot of weight on your shoulders, and it can be stressful, but enjoy it. Respect the failures and how easy they present themselves...that makes the successes so much sweeter.

What is the most important characteristic of a great salesperson? You must remain focused. Some of the most successful salespeople in my company have an ability to get the job done no matter what. Your clients or customers are the most important factors in your career. You never want to let them down, and complete transparency is the best way to build and maintain trust. It takes a lot of work but having a "get it done at all costs" attitude goes a long way. Your clients, as well as your company internally, notice that level of commitment. It will definitely be tough to always keep that mindset, but it pays off in the end.

Standing-Room-Only Close In the standing-room-only close, the salesperson states that due to high demand for the product or service, it may not be available in the future. This technique is designed to stimulate an immediate purchase. Although there may be instances when customers need to be made aware of potential supply issues, it is unethical to state this when it is not the case. Moreover, professional customers have little tolerance for this type of approach. They tend to view it as a threat and will react accordingly: *"Well, in that case, perhaps I should instead work with a company that does not have supply issues. Thank you for making my decision much easier."*

The consistent theme across each of these techniques is that they focus on *benefiting the salesperson and the selling company*, to the neglect of the customer. Because of this, the techniques are manipulative as well as unethical. Each demonstrates a lack of respect for the customer and should be avoided. In addition, notice that each of the techniques uses the term "close" rather than "gaining commitment." This terminology indicates that each technique is highly transactional in nature, doing little to facilitate relational exchange. As we've said before, the key to successful, long-term relational selling is trust. Manipulative behavior just does not pay off in the long run, for the customers, the company, or oneself.

> **standing-room-only close**
> Manipulative closing technique in which the salesperson states that due to high demand for the product or service, it may not be available in the future.

Connect Assignment 6-3

Ethics in Gaining Commitment

Please complete the Connect exercise for Chapter 6 that focuses on ethical issues associated with gaining commitment. Understanding the ethical challenges of certain high-pressure closing techniques will help salespeople better address specific customer issues and develop positive relationships.

CHAPTER SUMMARY

LO 6-1 Describe the role of salespeople in solving customer problems.

The salesperson has become the sale. Customers make decisions largely based on the quality of the salesperson rather than on the product or price alone. The best salespeople are those who can deliver solutions that address their customers' needs.

LO 6-2 Describe three skills needed in solving customer problems.

The best salespeople are those who are able to deliver unique and innovative solutions that address their customers' needs. In order to do this, salespeople must demonstrate three skills: questioning, listening, and creativity.

The most successful salespeople ask questions to better understand customers' problems. *SPIN selling* questioning lays out a basic, sequential questioning method for customer interaction. SPIN is an acronym that captures four types of questions contained in this questioning sequence: **S**ituational questions, **P**roblem questions, **I**mplication questions, and **N**eed-payoff questions. Through this sequence of questions, the salesperson and customer are able to transition the conversation from *implied needs* to *explicit needs*. Recognition of explicit needs tends to motivate customers to action. Within the four categories of SPIN questions, questions can be *open-ended* or *closed*. Both question types serve a purpose in the SPIN sequence.

Successful salespeople also are great listeners. They fully engage with customers through *active listening*, paying careful attention to all verbal and nonverbal cues and providing appropriate responses. They know the value of silence in an interview and also ask appropriate *follow-up questions* and *summary questions*. They also take notes.

Finally, successful salespeople also demonstrate creativity in crafting solutions that are unique and of value. There are two primary types of problem solvers: adaptors and innovators. *Adaptors* prefer more structured problem-solving methods; *innovators* tend to look beyond the status quo for solutions. It's often useful to combine both styles on one sales team.

LO 6-3 Summarize the process of gaining commitment and various techniques to do so.

The summary-benefit approach to gaining commitment is most consistent with solution-based selling. Within this approach, the salesperson summarizes what has been discussed to that point, focusing on the problems being addressed and the benefit of the solution being offered. The salesperson then uses a trial close to ensure that the customer has no questions, comments, or concerns about this summary. The salesperson then makes the ask, highlighting the financial implications associated with the solution if it involves a purchase. The salesperson concludes by discussing the appropriate follow-up steps.

Four common commitment-gaining techniques are *alternative-choice, balance sheet, direct request,* and *success story.* The actual technique that is used isn't as important as the summary-benefit approach that led up to the purchase ask, though.

LO 6-4 List the primary types of objections customers typically raise.

Five objections tend to span all settings: *no need* (the customer is not aware of the issue or does not believe that it warrants immediate attention); *time* (the customer is limited by time constraints and therefore has to prioritize issues); *source* (the customer has concerns about the selling company, the salesperson, or both); *product* (the customer has concerns about some element of the product offering); and *price* (the customer believes the quoted price is too high).

LO 6-5 Describe the process of overcoming objections and various techniques to do so.

When faced with an objection, the salesperson should question the objection to ensure a true understanding of the issue. The process of overcoming objections is: acknowledge the objection to demonstrate empathy; question the customer further to ensure this understanding; answer, using an appropriate objection-handling technique; and ask a trial-close question to ensure that the objection has been adequately addressed.

The LAER model of overcoming objections involves four steps—listen, acknowledge, explore, and respond. Other specific objection-handling techniques are: *acknowledge, boomerang, compensation, forestall, denial* (either *indirect* or *direct*), *postpone, referral,* and *value.* No technique is inherently better than the others, and none guarantees success. Salespeople should choose a technique based on their knowledge of the situation and the customer.

LO 6-6 Discuss the importance of ethics when overcoming objections and gaining commitment.

A stereotype of salespeople is that they will attempt to manipulate customers in order to overcome an objection or gain commitment. Salespeople should never attempt to deceive or manipulate the customer when attempting to overcome an objection. The aim, instead, should be to learn more about an objection for the purposes of determining whether it can be dealt with.

Traditional techniques when attempting to gain commitment (assumptive close, continuous-yes close, emotional close, and standing-room-only close) are manipulative, unethical, and highly unprofessional. They focus more on making a transaction than on achieving trust and relational exchange with customers.

KEY TERMS

- customer co-creation (p. 124)
- SPIN selling (p. 124)
- situational questions (p. 124)
- problem questions (p. 125)
- implication questions (p. 125)
- need-payoff questions (p. 125)
- implied needs (p. 126)
- explicit needs (p. 126)
- open-ended questions (p. 126)
- closed questions (p. 126)
- active listening (p. 127)
- passive listening (p. 127)
- follow-up questions (p. 128)
- summary questions (p. 128)
- adaptors (p. 128)
- innovators (p. 128)
- gaining commitment (p. 129)
- primary objective (p. 131)
- secondary objective (p. 131)
- buying signals (p. 131)
- summary-benefit approach (p. 131)
- trial-close question (p. 131)
- alternative-choice technique (p. 132)
- balance-sheet technique (p. 132)
- direct-request technique (p. 132)
- success-story technique (p. 132)
- objections (p. 133)
- LAER model® (p. 136)
- acknowledge technique (p. 138)
- boomerang technique (p. 139)
- compensation technique (p. 139)
- forestall technique (p. 139)
- indirect denial technique (p. 139)
- direct denial technique (p. 139)
- postpone (coming-to-that) technique (p. 140)
- referral (feel-felt-found) technique (p. 140)
- value technique (p. 140)
- assumptive close (p. 141)
- continuous-yes close (p. 141)
- emotional close (p. 141)
- standing-room-only close (p. 143)

DISCUSSION QUESTIONS

1. Imagine that you have decided to accept a professional sales position upon graduation. When telling friends and family this news, they question your choice, bringing up many of the traditional negative sales stereotypes. How would you respond?
2. Discuss how the sales profession's thinking on gaining commitment and overcoming objections has evolved over the last 30 years. How does this change affect, if at all, your view of professional selling as a career option?
3. Based on your reading of this chapter, if a potential employer during an interview asks you to sell a pen, how would you do it?
4. Think of a situation you have been confronted with in which a salesperson attempted to hard-sell you—the salesperson kept trying to close the sale. How did this approach make you feel? Were you more or less likely to purchase? If you were to accept a sales position, how might this experience affect your thoughts on gaining commitment?
5. Assume you are taking your vehicle in to a dealership to have routine service performed. At some point, the service technician comes to you and says that additional work needs to be done. Provide examples of the five primary objections presented in this chapter that might stop you from having this service done.

ETHICAL CHALLENGE

Many of you who pursue a career in professional selling will do so for a publicly traded company. As you probably know, publicly traded companies raise capital through stock issuance, providing investors an ownership opportunity in the company, which in turn gives the company the funds to grow. Investors hope that the stock price, and corresponding value, of the company will rise. In this way, investors want to buy low and (eventually) sell high in order to generate a positive return on their investment. Thus investors seek to identify companies that they believe will grow in value over time.

One of the most influential factors in determining whether to invest in a company is whether the company is capable of hitting its revenue forecasts. Company leadership will forecast revenues for the upcoming quarter, and the assumption among those in the investment community is that these projections will be attained. In truth, they must be attained, as missing the revenue forecast causes investors to question the company as a viable investment opportunity.

Because of this pressure to meet revenue forecasts, company leadership stresses to the sales organization the importance of developing—and hitting—aggressive yet attainable revenue forecasts. As the end of a quarter looms, the pressure felt in the sales organization is real. In some instances, salespeople are told to simply "get the business," taking whatever steps necessary to ensure that they deliver on their portion of the overall forecast. (That is, they have to "hit quota.") For some salespeople, particularly those who are new to sales, working under this pressure can prove challenging.

Against this backdrop, imagine yourself in this position: One of your customers has ample inventory on the product(s) you sell, but you know that you need to get an additional sale with the customer before the end of the quarter in order to hit your own personal forecast.

Questions

What would you do in this situation? How would you balance the customer's interests against those of your company and its stockholders?

ROLE PLAY

This role play exercise will give you an opportunity to practice your questioning and listening skills. For the role play, return to the scenario presented in Chapter 5. The selling student will assume the role of a development director for your college or university, responsible for raising money to provide scholarships and endowed faculty positions for your school.

The class should be divided into teams of three. For the role play, one student will assume the role of the development director, another will assume the role of the potential donor, and the third will critique the role play. The development director should take the potential donor through the SPIN questioning sequence. The potential donor should respond to the questions. The student critiquing the role play should catalog each question asked as situational, problem, implication, or need-payoff. The student critiquing should also note whether the question is open-ended (O), closed (C), follow-up (F), or intended to summarize (S). Each question should be numbered as well.

At the end of the role play, the student critiquing should present a chart much like the one shown below and provide general thoughts regarding strengths and improvement areas. A total of three role plays should be conducted, with each student assuming each role.

Situational	Problem	Implication	Need-Payoff
O1	O4	O14	O16
O2	O5	C15	O17
O3	O9	C20	O18
C6	O10	O21	O19
O7	C11	F22	C23
F8	F12		C24
	S13		F25
			S26

Questions

1. Do the question numbers increase in value from left to right? (That is, does the selling student appear to be following the SPIN methodology in sequential fashion?) Was there a logical flow to the questioning sequence?
2. Do open-ended questions precede closed questions?
3. Are enough follow-up questions asked to demonstrate listening?
4. Are summary questions used appropriately to ensure a mutual understanding?
5. In general, did the seller seem to be listening or reading questions from a pre-determined script?

SALES PRESENTATION

For the Connect assignment in Chapter 6, you will attempt to gain commitment and overcome an objection in a job interview. First, two students will pair up and act as an interviewer and a job candidate, respectively, attempting to gain commitment at the end of the interview. The student acting as the job candidate should establish the needs and objective (e.g., a follow-up interview) and use the summary-benefit approach for gaining commitment. You should then alternate roles so that each of you can act as the interviewer and the job candidate.

Once this is complete, you will go through this same process, but the interviewer will present an objection as the job candidate is attempting to gain commitment. The student acting as the interviewer should come up with the objection. You should once again alternate roles, acting both as the job candidate and the interviewer. In all, you should complete a total of four role plays. Across all role plays, you should complete only the gaining-commitment portion of the interview. You do not need to go through an entire interview.

CAREER TIPS

John Hansen
Marketing Professor
University of
Alabama—Birmingham

Dealing with Call Reluctance

John Hansen

Most of you probably understand that in order to be successful in sales, you have to spend time with your customers. Whether it be in face-to-face meetings, over the phone, or via web-based technologies, it is important you allocate an adequate percentage of your time with current or potential customers. Unfortunately, most salespeople do not spend enough time interacting with customers in relation to the other things they are required to do (travel, paperwork, and so on).

Another contributing factor to this issue is that some salespeople can suffer from *call reluctance*—an avoidance of customer interactions—particularly when it comes to prospecting. While call reluctance may seem like an odd problem for someone in sales to confront, it is more common than you might think. In fact, 40 percent of all salespeople admit to one or more episodes of call reluctance at some point in their careers.[8] If it is something you eventually confront, you must address it.

There are certain things you should be mindful of if you are suffering from call reluctance. First, you are not the only person who has struggled with this. Many salespeople automatically assume they have made the wrong career choice. This might not be the case. It might just be that a particular customer is problematic, or that as a salesperson you are going through a temporary slump when it comes to prospecting. These things happen; they are not abnormal in sales. Thus, first and foremost, it is important to keep a positive outlook, even when suffering from call reluctance.

Second, talk with your manager about the situation. He or she may have experienced something similar in the past and can help you. If there is an issue with a particular customer or prospect, your manager should be able to help. Your manager might also be able to send in another salesperson for assistance. If you have taken over the customer from a previous salesperson who has moved into another position (within the company), your sales manager might direct you to that person for advice on how to best deal with the customer.

Last, take time to study your work patterns to ensure that you are indeed spending enough time with your current and potential customers. While planning is important in sales, you have to guard against "paralysis through analysis." That is, you cannot spend so much time planning that you compromise your customer interaction time. The plan is important, but execution is ultimately required for success.

CHAPTER ENDNOTES

1. H. Stevens and T. Kinni, *Achieve Sales Excellence: The 7 Customer Rules for Becoming the New Sales Professional* (Avon, MA: Platinum Press, 2007).
2. A. Sharma, G. R. Iyer, and H. Evanschitzky, "Personal selling of high-technology products: The solution-selling imperative," *Journal of Relationship Marketing* 7, no. 3 (2008): 287–308.
3. M. Ligos, "Editor's note: We've got the solution," *Sales and Marketing Management* 156, no. 10 (2004): 4.
4. W. Reinartz and W. Ulaga, "How to sell services more profitably," *Harvard Business Review* 86, no. 5 (2008): 90–96.
5. N. Rackham, *SPIN Selling* (New York: McGraw-Hill, 1988).
6. M. Kirton, "Adaptors and innovators: A description and measure," *Journal of Applied Psychology* 61, no. 5 (1976): 622–629.
7. R. S. Burt, "Structural holes and good ideas," *American Journal of Sociology* 110 (2004): 349–399.
8. *What Is Call Reluctance?* Behavioral Sciences Research Press, Inc. [July 29, 2019], https://salescallreluctance.com/call-reluctance-sales-training/.

Design elements: Marketing Insights Podcast: vandame/Shutterstock

Chapter 7

Negotiating Win-Win Solutions

Learning objectives

After reading this chapter, you should be able to:

LO 7-1 Describe basic negotiation concepts.

LO 7-2 Describe common negotiation styles.

LO 7-3 Explain the importance of planning for formal negotiations.

LO 7-4 List three guidelines for conducting a negotiation session.

LO 7-5 Summarize ethical considerations in sales negotiations.

Executive **Perspective** ... because everyone is a salesperson

Doug Hughes

Doug Hughes
CEO
Surgarai

Describe your job.

I am chief executive officer of a healthcare technology startup called Surgarai. At Surgarai, we are leveraging the latest in augmented reality and artificial intelligence (AI) to optimize surgery and healthcare. The single most rewarding thing about the work we do is that we are literally saving lives. That's a humbling realization.

As CEO of a startup, my job involves basically anything and everything, but my main areas of focus are:

- *Fundraising and capital strategy.* We are currently in the process of raising $5M from venture capitalists, and this takes the vast majority of my time. Rightly so, as we will go out of business if we do not have the capital we need to operate before we turn profitable.
- *Talent.* Whether you are a sales leader, a technology leader, or a general manager, there is only one way to win consistently—and that is by having the best and brightest on your team.
- *Product/technology development.* We are building a revolutionary new software platform, and this effort consumes massive amounts of my time on a daily basis.
- *Chief evangelist.* I spread the word about Surgarai far and wide, through a variety of channels.

How did you get your job?

I've been in business for quite some time, and my experience and track record unlock lots of interesting opportunities for me. My number-one criteria for any work I do is that it must have purpose. After serving in the U.S. Army, I spent 20 years advancing education. Now, I've turned my attention to healthcare. I had been advising Surgarai's founder, and when I sold my last startup, we made the decision to join forces so that I could help build Surgarai to solve the many issues facing healthcare today.

What has been most important in making you successful at your job?

The aforementioned focus on talent is the single most important thing for any leader. In addition to that, my optimism and vision for what can be done in the future are the biggest contributors to my success in this role.

What advice would you give future graduates about a career in sales?

You are what your record says you are. Sales is unique in that it's one of the only roles that can be nearly completely measured by the metrics that you produce—specifically, performance against goal and all of the reportable activity that went in to achieving (or not) that goal. The biggest mistake I see new salespeople make is to not completely own the fact that your numbers are your numbers. Excuses do not work, and they have no business in sales. Keep them out, and focus on achievement, because...you are what your record says you are.

Finally, your years in sales are not merely a stepping stone. They are a foundation to the rest of your career. Achieving great success as a salesperson will position you and your career to take off like a rocket. So, get out there and make it happen!

What is the most important characteristic of a great salesperson?

There are three, which I call the *raw materials*, because you can't teach them and the combination of them is unstoppable: drive, desire to win, and a great attitude!

BASIC NEGOTIATION CONCEPTS

LO 7-1 Describe basic negotiation concepts.

Your presentation with the client went great. It's clear that your company's product meets an important need. At each point along the way, you have successfully addressed potential concerns raised by the buyer. Finally, you quoted a price and sent over the contract. All that's left is for the prospect to sign the paperwork and the deal will be done. You're riding a high all day long. But then you get the dreaded email: *"I'd like to talk about some of the details of this contract before I sign."*

Even if a salesperson has properly qualified a prospect and correctly managed expectations throughout the sales process, the sale can still end in a negotiation. The salesperson needs to shift gears from being a consultant to a negotiator in order to engineer an agreement that will be acceptable to the client and still produce a profitable return for the company.

When most of us are asked to think about a negotiation experience from our own lives, we typically think of things like haggling with a salesman over the price of a used car or requesting a pay raise from a boss. There are many other less-obvious negotiations we enter into on a daily basis: persuading a toddler to eat, working out a disagreement with a spouse, or convincing a customer to accept a delayed delivery.

Although formal negotiations occur periodically for nearly everyone, many individuals still dread them. Because they lack extensive experience or know-how with respect to these types of encounters, many struggle to achieve their goals and are frustrated with the negotiation process, regardless of the outcome. Fortunately, research shows that people can significantly improve their negotiation ability through education, preparation, and practice. These skills can enable you to approach the inevitable negotiations in your life with less trepidation and help you to achieve more favorable results. Greater knowledge of standard negotiation processes as well as successful strategies and tactics can help us be more successful professionally and personally.

Negotiating in sales is one of the most fundamental aspects of selling. All sales professionals will spend much of their careers negotiating either with customers or with managers and associates in their own firms. Getting others to see things from your perspective, while listening to their point of view in an equally respectful manner, is a key aspect of building meaningful relationships. These skills are beneficial in both business and life.

Defined formally, **negotiation** is a dialogue between two or more people or parties, intended to reach a beneficial outcome about one or more issues over which a conflict exists. This outcome can benefit all of the parties involved or just one or some of them. Whether we realize it or not, "everyone negotiates something every day," wrote Roger Fisher, William Ury, and Bruce Patton in their seminal book, *Getting to Yes: Negotiating Agreement without Giving In*.[1] They describe negotiation as a "back-and-forth communication designed to reach an agreement when you and the other side have some interests that are shared and others that are opposed." Together, these definitions encompass the wide range of negotiations we carry out in our personal lives, at work, and with strangers or acquaintances.

In our personal lives, for instance, in purchasing a car, individuals typically conduct their own negotiations. However, it is not uncommon in larger-scale negotiations, such as in collective bargaining or organizational purchasing, for a designated agent to conduct the negotiation. In either instance, the primary decision-making authority in a negotiation is known as the **negotiation principal**. A third-party agent hired to represent the interests or objectives of a principal in a negotiation is known as a **negotiation agent**.

What leads individuals or organizations to negotiate with one another? When two or more parties need to reach a joint decision but have different preferences, they are

negotiation
A dialogue between two or more people or parties, intended to reach a beneficial outcome about one or more issues over which a conflict exists.

negotiation principal
The primary decision-making authority in a negotiation.

negotiation agent
A third-party agent hired to represent the interests or objectives of a principal in a negotiation.

motivated to negotiate.[2] In her negotiation text, *The Mind and Heart of the Negotiator*, Leigh Thompson refers to negotiation as an "interpersonal decision-making process" that is "necessary whenever we cannot achieve our objectives single-handedly."[3] At its root, negotiation is aimed at resolving points of difference between parties, to gain advantage for an individual or a group, or to craft outcomes to satisfy various interests. For salespeople, this activity basically involves resolving concerns that keep prospective customers from moving forward with a sale.

Basic Elements of Negotiation

Negotiation involves three basic elements: *substance, process*, and *communication styles*. The *substance* of a negotiation refers to what the parties are negotiating over: the agenda, issues, positions, and interests held by each side; options; and the agreement reached at the end. Negotiation *process* refers to how the parties negotiate: the context of the negotiations; the corresponding tactics used by the parties; and the sequence in which all of these play out. *Communication style* refers specifically to the negotiation styles the parties adopt. We discuss each in greater detail below, with specific attention to how each relates to sales-related negotiations.

Substance of the Negotiation
First, it may be helpful to provide an overview of the basic substance or building blocks of any negotiation. A **negotiation agenda** is an agreed-upon list of items to be discussed or goals to be achieved, in a particular order, during a negotiation.[4] Agendas can be formal and obvious or informal and subtle. Because the agenda is used to control the negotiation meeting, prior to the start of each encounter salespeople and customers will sometimes haggle over the basic items to be discussed.

Negotiation positions are the things negotiators demand you give them and also the things on which they are not willing to budge. Negotiation positions are typically communicated in meetings, emails, and proposals. Inexperienced salespeople too often take the initial positions offered by the other side at face value and don't probe with questions or challenge sufficiently. For instance, sometimes a buyer might ask for a price discount when what they really want is not a cheaper solution but more value, less risk, or simply the feeling that they've gotten "a good deal." It's helpful to have some understanding about which things can be negotiated and which cannot.

Faced with a negotiation, sales professionals must learn to ask probing questions that help uncover the negotiation interests underlying a stated position. **Negotiation interests** are considered to be the motivating factor(s) and underlying reasons behind the negotiation position adopted by a negotiation party. Negotiation interests are the desires, concerns, aims, or goals of a negotiating party in a negotiation process. They often entail some combination of economic, security, recognition, and control issues. Often hidden and unspoken, such interests nonetheless guide what negotiators do and say.

Experienced salespeople learn to dig deeper with questions that help them better understand their buyers' stated positions and underlying interests. This does not mean firing off a series of questions to pry as much information out of the prospect as possible. It is not "listening in order to respond" to every single item they raise. If the salesperson listens carefully to the response *without talking*, the buyer is more likely to reveal information about the challenges and the negotiation positions in his or her own words. A good tip for new salespeople or sales students is to ask permission to take notes and jot down key points to return to later.

negotiation agenda
An agreed-upon list of items to be discussed or goals to be achieved, in a particular order, during a negotiation.

negotiation positions
The things negotiators demand you give them and also the things on which they are not willing to budge.

negotiation interests
The motivating factor(s) and underlying reasons behind the negotiation position adopted by a negotiation party.

negotiation options
Any available choices or alternatives that parties might consider to satisfy their respective interests.

This will force you to pay genuine attention to verbal and nonverbal cues that can provide insights into what truly matters to the buyer in the course of the negotiation.

Finally, **negotiation options** are any available choices or alternatives that parties might consider to satisfy their respective interests. These might include conditions, contingencies, and trades. Options tend to capitalize on parties' similarities and differences. Therefore, gaining a better understanding of a counterpart's available options can help you create value in the negotiation and improve customer satisfaction.

Negotiation as a Process

It is important to understand negotiation as part of an ongoing interpersonal or interorganizational communication process. It is not simply a one-off conversation. Within the context of personal selling, negotiation can take place at almost any point throughout the sales process. For instance, negotiations at early stages of the sales process may involve things as simple as scheduling a time, place, and duration for an initial face-to-face meeting or phone conversation. As the sales process continues, negotiations tend to deal with more complex issues. Negotiations at later stages are typically viewed as more strategic. For example, bargaining over items such as price, guaranteed performance levels, and terms of delivery have important implications for the bottom lines of both sides.

Context is also an important component that helps shape the negotiation process. Experts most commonly distinguish between two general types: *distributive* and *integrative* negotiations. In a **distributive negotiation**, the goals of the negotiating parties are in direct opposition. In such situations, parties often engage in competitive behavior directed at maximizing their share of the outcomes.[5] In a distributive negotiation, potential outcomes of the bargaining effort are seen as a "fixed pie." Both parties wish to ensure they get as large a piece as possible. In such cases, negotiation is viewed as an adversarial process—a winner-take-all contest that pits one side against another. In the worst cases, negotiators often use aggressive strategies such as threats, bluffs, and hostility. In many cases, parties in a distributive negotiation may seek advantage by concealing information, attempting to mislead, or using manipulative actions.

distributive negotiation
A negotiation in which the goals of the negotiating parties are in direct opposition.

integrative negotiation
A negotiation in which the parties place different value on various issues, and resolutions occur through cooperative exchanges.

In an **integrative negotiation**, the parties place different value on various issues, and resolutions occur through cooperative exchanges. These types of negotiations require a more collaborative approach. Positive outcomes for integrative negotiations often depend on the development of rapport and trust among the parties. Each party ultimately gains a shared commitment to joint problem solving.

Although an integrative negotiation may seem a more attractive option, it is not always the best approach. Negotiators often fail at integrative negotiation because they fail to recognize the integrative potential of the negotiation situation. Figure 7-1 outlines fundamental preconditions for successful integrative negotiations. Without those preconditions, integrative negotiations may not be achievable.

Some buyers and sellers are turned off by the confrontational aspects of distributive bargaining. Often they would rather walk away than engage in such encounters. But for many others, the hardball argumentation and point making is the very essence of the negotiation process. Because some buyers use distributive bargaining strategies and tactics exclusively, it is important for sellers to know how to effectively counter them. Moreover, even in integrative negotiations, there may be a need to employ distributive skills at various points in the negotiation.

Understanding the differences between negotiation contexts is very important for achieving an optimal outcome. To be "fluent" in negotiations, it's also important to

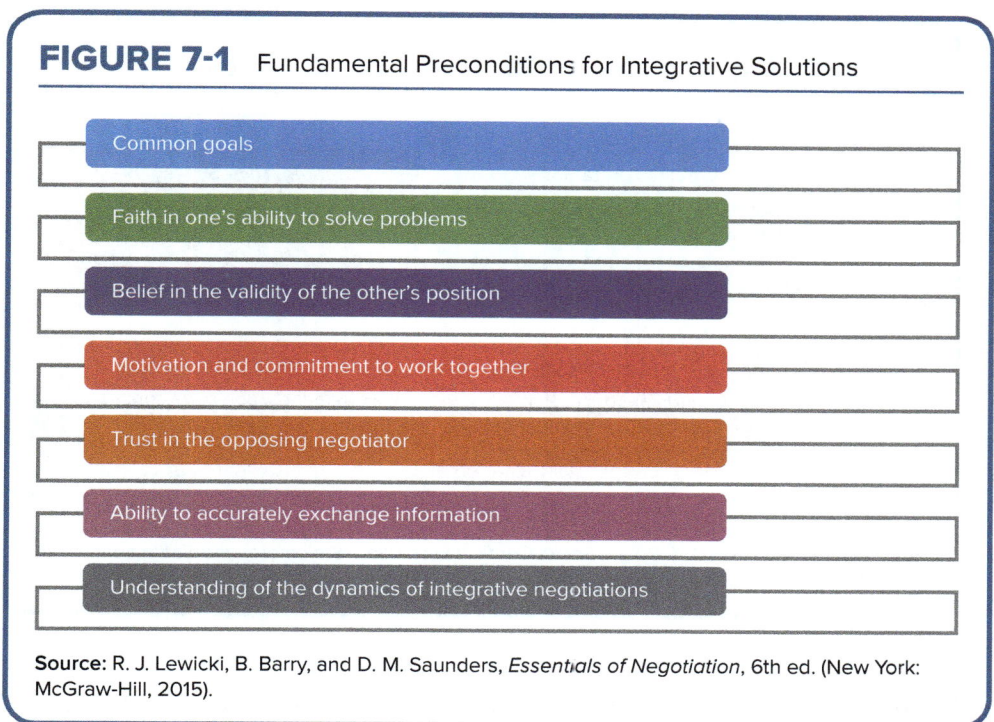

Source: R. J. Lewicki, B. Barry, and D. M. Saunders, *Essentials of Negotiation*, 6th ed. (New York: McGraw-Hill, 2015).

know the corresponding strategies and tactics. Depending on the nature of the negotiation context, certain strategies or techniques might be more or less applicable. For example, one-off encounters in which neither party is seeking to establish a lasting relationship are more likely to produce distributive negotiations. On the other hand, bargaining between parties that are seeking to build an ongoing partnership is more likely to require integrative negotiating. Some research even suggests that, depending on the situation, it may be useful to match people with different negotiation mindsets and dispositions to serve as representatives.[6]

COMMON NEGOTIATION STYLES

Each of us has a unique set of personal life experiences that, in turn, have a profound effect on how we interact with others. Our upbringing, education, personality, culture, relationships, and dozens of other factors all contribute to the manner in which we communicate with others, both at home and in the workplace. These differences in communication styles translate into how we negotiate. (see Figure 7-2)

Researchers have identified negotiation styles that are based on a theory of conflict resolution called the **dual-concern model**.[7] The model assumes people's preferred method of dealing with conflict is based on two dimensions: assertiveness and empathy. The *assertiveness dimension* focuses on the degree to which one is concerned with satisfying one's own needs and interests. The *empathy dimension* focuses on the extent to which one is concerned with satisfying the needs and interests of the other party. Figure 7-2 provides a graphical depiction of the dual-concern model.

According to this model, parties in a negotiation strive to balance the concern for personal needs and interests with the needs and interests of others. The level of emphasis a negotiator places on each dimension—that is, pro-self or pro-social—results

LO 7-2

Describe common negotiation styles.

dual-concern model

A theory of conflict resolution that assumes people's preferred method of dealing with conflict is based on two dimensions: assertiveness and empathy.

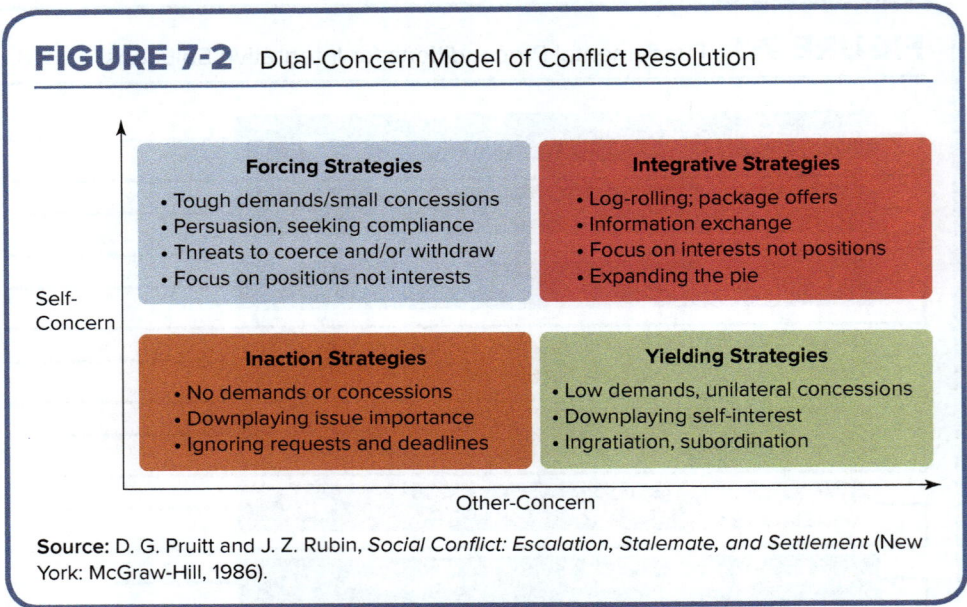

FIGURE 7-2 Dual-Concern Model of Conflict Resolution

Source: D. G. Pruitt and J. Z. Rubin, *Social Conflict: Escalation, Stalemate, and Settlement* (New York: McGraw-Hill, 1986).

in five distinct negotiation styles. As Figure 7-3 shows, they are *accommodators, avoiders, collaborators, competitors,* and *compromisers.* These styles can change over time, and individuals can have strong dispositions toward more than one style. It's always helpful to realize your own conflict style, and also to appreciate the style that your opposite number is using. As you read through the descriptions of each negotiating style, you can probably think of people in your own life who match one or more of these profiles.

Accommodators

The accommodator conflict style maximizes empathy and minimizes assertiveness. Accommodators focus on preserving relationships and building a friendly rapport by sacrificing some of their company's interests in favor of the opposite party's interests. They derive satisfaction from meeting the needs of others. They enjoy solving the other party's problems and preserving personal relationships. They are sensitive to the emotional states, body language, and verbal signals of others.

Accommodation is a passive but pro-social approach to conflict. With it, people solve large as well as small conflicts by simply giving in to the demands of others. Sometimes, people will yield because they realize that their position is in error; in other cases, they give in for the sake of group unity or in the interest of time.

Accommodating negotiation styles work best in situations in which your company has caused harm to another and needs to repair a significant relationship. These negotiators are skilled at peacemaking. They can, however, be taken advantage of in situations when the other party places little emphasis on maintaining the relationship.

Avoiders

An avoider conflict style is low in both assertiveness and empathy. Avoiders do not like to negotiate and

accommodators
Negotiators who focus on preserving relationships and building a friendly rapport by sacrificing some of their company's interests in favor of the opposite party's interests; they maximize empathy and minimize assertiveness.

avoiders
Negotiators who do not like to negotiate and don't do it unless necessary; they rate low on both assertiveness and empathy.

FIGURE 7-3 Five Types of Negotiation Styles

- Accommodators
- Avoiders
- Collaborators
- Competitors
- Compromisers

don't do it unless necessary. Inaction is a passive means of dealing with disputes. Those who avoid conflicts adopt a "wait and see" attitude, hoping that problems will solve themselves. Avoiders are adept at sidestepping pointless conflict. They are able to exercise tact and diplomacy in high-conflict situations and can artfully increase their own leverage by waiting for others to make the first concession.

At the same time, by ignoring difficult issues, avoiders can allow problems between the parties to simmer. Rather than openly discussing disagreements, people who rely on avoidance change the subject, skip meetings, or even leave the group altogether. Sometimes they simply agree to disagree. Since avoiders dislike conflict and struggle with direct communication, they come off as passive-aggressive. This can cause rifts in interpersonal business relationships.

The avoider-type negotiation style works best in situations in which the negotiation concerns a matter that is trivial to both parties. In conflict resolution, avoider-type negotiators work best in situations in which an issue being negotiated is not worth the investment of time or effort to resolve it. Avoidance is also effective as a stall tactic; if the other party is under time pressures, it may lead them to voluntarily offer concessions at the outset of the negotiation.

Collaborators

The collaborator conflict style is high in both assertiveness and empathy. **Collaborators** see conflict as a creative opportunity to satisfy both parties' goals. Collaborators are good at identifying the issues underlying the dispute; they then work together to find a solution satisfying to both sides. They do not mind investing the time and effort to dig deep to understand the concerns and interests of the other party in order to find a win-win solution. However, they are also more inclined to spend more time and resources than called for under the circumstances. Sometimes they can create problems by transforming simple situations into more complex ones.

Collaborating is an active, pro-social, and pro-self approach to conflict resolution. A collaborative negotiation style is effective in most business negotiations. Collaborating with competitive negotiators (see below) is something to be wary of, however: People with a competitive negotiation style focus on winning the most for their company; they might not be interested in developing a collaborative relationship. As a result, the more collaborative company can lose out in a negotiation between these two types.

collaborators
Negotiators who see conflict as a creative opportunity to satisfy both parties' goals; they rate high on both assertiveness and empathy.

Competitors

A competitive conflict style maximizes assertiveness and minimizes empathy. It is an active, pro-self means of dealing with conflict that forces others to accept one's view. **Competitors** see conflict as a win-lose situation. They enjoy negotiating because they view the situation as a game or sport—and they are intent on winning! Competitive negotiators tend to use power-based tactics to intimidate others and control the process. This approach to conflict resolution methods is contentious; it typically involves imposing one's solution on the other party.

Competitive negotiators have strong instincts for all aspects of negotiating, and their style often can dominate the bargaining process. However, these individuals often neglect the importance of long-term relationships. Business relationships might break, and a company's reputation may tarnish if its negotiation style is too competitive and crosses the line into bullying. A competitive negotiation style is most beneficial when you need to reach a short-term agreement quickly. This style works best in highly competitive industry settings or for one-off sales such as selling a home or a car.

competitors
Negotiators who see conflict as a win-lose situation and are intent on winning; they maximize assertiveness and minimize empathy.

Compromisers

compromisers
Negotiators who are eager to close the deal by doing what is fair and equal for all parties involved in the negotiation; they are intermediate on both assertiveness and empathy.

Many students of negotiation styles confuse the collaborative style with the compromising one. A compromising conflict style is intermediate in both the assertiveness and empathy dimensions. **Compromisers** are eager to close the deal by doing what is fair and equal for all parties involved in the negotiation. Thus, unlike the "win-win" collaborative style, the compromising negotiation style follows an "I win/lose some, you win/lose some" model. Compromisers can be useful when there is limited time to complete the deal. However, compromisers often unnecessarily rush the negotiation process and make concessions too quickly. A compromising negotiation style is most useful in situations in which the opposite party is trustworthy and the agreement is under a tight deadline. However, a competitive negotiator can easily take advantage of a compromising negotiator.

In closing, it is important to remember that negotiation style is shorthand for a broad array of mental tendencies and behaviors. Expert negotiators are not only aware of their own primary communication style; they are also able to recognize these patterns in the dominant communication styles of their counterparts. Recognizing communication style can help you to identify your own negotiation strengths and weaknesses—knowledge that can be leveraged in a strategic way. With that said, a personal negotiating style is not a straitjacket; no one is exclusively one style. Most people have the ability to call up a nondominant style should a situation call for it.

Connect Assignment 7-1

Negotiation Styles

Please complete the Connect exercise for Chapter 7 that focuses on negotiation behavior and communication styles. By understanding different negotiation styles, you will be better prepared to resolve conflicts during the negotiating process and find win-win solutions.

PLANNING FOR FORMAL NEGOTIATIONS

LO 7-3
Explain the importance of planning for formal negotiations.

Without a doubt, the biggest mistake negotiators make—and one that many young salespeople make routinely—is failing to thoroughly prepare. Negotiation expert Chris Voss suggests that good initial preparation for each negotiation yields a 7:1 rate of return with respect to time and money saved renegotiating deals or clarifying implementation.[8] For salespeople, doing extensive research on the negotiation partner and organization can pay off in larger deals that close more quickly and smoothly.

On the other hand, when you haven't done the necessary analysis and research, you are highly likely to leave value on the table and even to be taken advantage of by your counterpart. Putting together a negotiation preparation checklist, such as the example provided in **Table 7-1**, can help you avoid this scenario. Using a checklist will help you to more thoroughly think through your position, the other party's position, and what might happen when you get together.

The following sections present more detailed guidelines about planning for formal negotiations.

TABLE 7-1 Negotiation Preparation Checklist

1. What do I want from this negotiation? What are my short-term and long-term goals?
2. What are my strengths—values, skills, and assets—in this negotiation? What are my weaknesses and vulnerabilities in this negotiation?
3. Why is the other party negotiating with me? What do I have that they need?
4. Where and when should the negotiation take place? To what degree will we be negotiating electronically?
5. How long should talks last? Is either party facing a deadline?
6. What are my interests in the negotiation? What are the other party's interests in the negotiation? How do these interests rank in importance?
7. What is my relationship history with my negotiation counterpart? How might our past interactions influence the negotiation process?
8. Are there cultural differences that we should prepare for in this negotiation?
9. What is my *reservation point*—my indifference point between a deal and no deal in this negotiation? What is my *aspiration point* in the negotiation—the ambitious, but not outrageous, goal that I'd like to reach?

Source: https://www.pon.harvard.edu/daily/negotiation-skills-daily/negotiation-preparation-checklist/.

Gathering Information

The first step in planning for formal negotiations is to gather information. It is worthwhile to get a sense of your target buyer's probable limitations—whether in terms of time, money, resources, or authority—prior to the start of negotiations. In many cases, a diligent salesperson can find useful information by searching online for relevant news articles, visiting the company's websites, speaking with sales colleagues at other firms, or checking government records. It is also not uncommon for buyers to respond directly to information requests. Even sophisticated buyers will freely disclose information about their circumstances, sometimes simply as a signal of good faith.

The information quest should also include whether the negotiation counterpart has the power to make a deal. This is true regardless of the title of the buyer—whether business owner, manager, buying agent, or customer. Armed with an understanding of a negotiation agent's deal-making limits, salespeople can help to move deals forward more quickly. They can better focus the discussion on key points and bargain in a way that meaningfully addresses buyer interests.

Profiling Your Negotiating Partner

Another step in planning is to develop a profile of your negotiating partner. When you talk with long-time friends, you possess detailed knowledge about each other's personal backgrounds and life experiences, so the conversation tends to flow naturally. When entering into an important conversation with people you don't know very well, wouldn't it make sense to spend time exploring their backgrounds and experiences? Doing this type of up-front work not only can help you to avoid conversational faux pas but also will make it easier to build rapport and trust with your prospective clients and other negotiation counterparts.

Putting together such biographical information has never been easier. Most business professionals freely offer up information on sites like LinkedIn, Facebook, and their employers' websites. In many cases, details relating to notable business and personal achievements are available by searching paid databases such as Hoover's and LexisNexis or public search engines such as Google. Many individuals participate in organizations or on message boards that reflect their passions or professional interests. Through such a search, you might discover that you share common backgrounds such as attending the same university or majoring in the same subject. Or you might have similar hobbies such as coaching youth soccer or volunteering for the same cause. So, just as it is important to know as much as you can about the prospect's organization, you should also research your negotiating counterpart as a person.

Formalizing Goals and Objectives

Before the negotiation, you also will want to formalize clear goals and financial objectives. Nearly all successfully completed formal negotiations require some concession by one or both parties. It is important to have a sense of the alternatives that are available to both parties. In that way, you can help ensure that you don't give away too much or concede only the items that are important to your counterpart. In some instances, of course, there are only two fundamental choices: (1) reach a deal with the other party or (2) reach no settlement at all. In sales negotiations (and many other negotiation contexts), one or both parties may have the possibility of an alternative deal with another party.

Alternatives are important: They give negotiators the power to walk away from a negotiation when the emerging deal is not favorable. This factor has significant implications for most sales negotiations. For instance, in negotiations in which buyers have other attractive alternatives, they can set their goals higher and demand greater concessions.

Having a number of alternatives can be useful. But it is really one's *best* alternative that determines whether the other party will walk away. Thus, seasoned negotiators know the value of evaluating the other party's **BATNA**, or **B**est **A**lternative **t**o a **N**egotiated **A**greement.[9] For example, a job candidate might determine that she will apply to grad school if a job negotiation falls apart. BATNA should always be considered before a negotiation takes place. The value of knowing your best alternative to reaching a negotiated settlement is that it:

1. Provides an alternative if negotiations fall through.
2. Strengthens your negotiating power.
3. Forces the negotiator to determine the reservation point (the worst price you are willing to accept) before the bargaining begins.[10]

BATNA
Acronym for "best alternative to a negotiated agreement"; often determines whether the other party will walk away.

ZOPA
Acronym for "zone of possible agreement"; it is the gap between the seller's walk-away point and the buyer's highest willingness to pay.

Another useful tool for setting financial objectives is known as **ZOPA**, or **Z**one of **P**ossible **A**greement. The ZOPA is the gap between the seller's walk-away point and the buyer's highest willingness to pay. For the seller, the walk-away point is the lowest offer a seller will be willing to accept in the negotiation. For the buyer, the walk-away point is the highest offer he will be willing to accept in the negotiation.

Consider the following example: Tom needs a car and is negotiating with Celia to purchase her car. Celia offers to sell her car to Tom for $10,000. Tom scours through Craigslist and finds a similar car, to which he assigns a dollar value of $7,500. Tom's

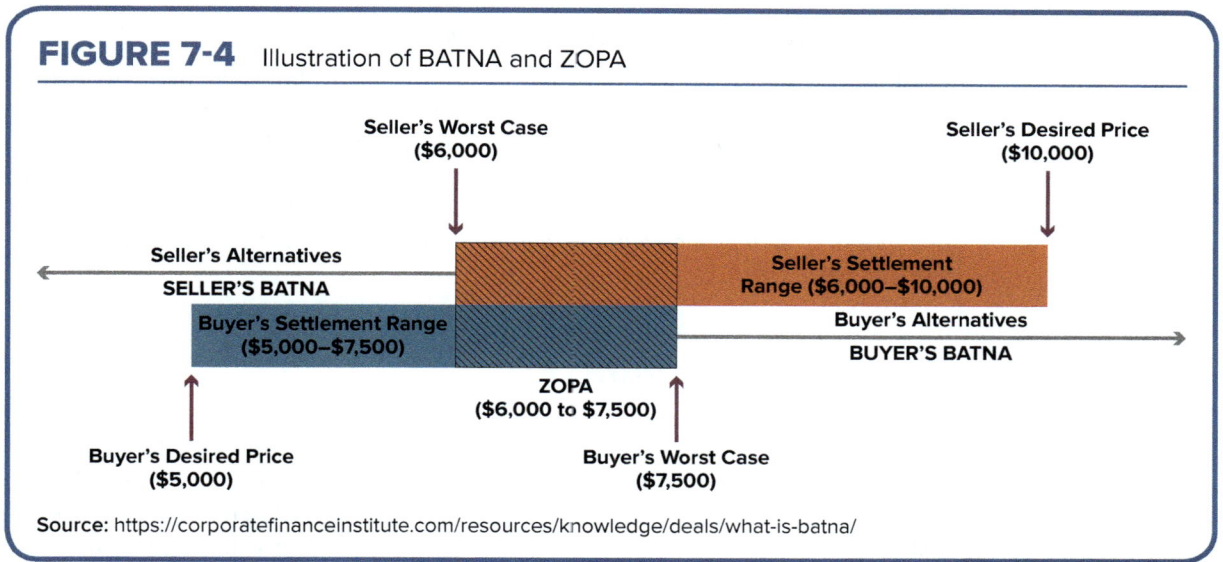

FIGURE 7-4 Illustration of BATNA and ZOPA

Source: https://corporatefinanceinstitute.com/resources/knowledge/deals/what-is-batna/

BATNA is $7,500. If Celia does not offer a price lower than $7,500, Tom will consider his best alternative to a negotiated agreement. Tom is willing to pay up to $7,500 for the car but would ideally want to pay only $5,000. The relevant information is illustrated in Figure 7-4.

If Celia demands a price higher than $7,500, Tom will take his business elsewhere. If we assume that Celia can sell her car to someone else for $8,000, then $8,000 is Celia's BATNA. In such a scenario, an agreement will not be made, as Celia is willing to sell only for a minimum of $8,000, while Tom is willing to purchase only at a maximum of $7,500.

If Celia's best alternative to the deal is selling the car to a dealership which would offer her $6,000, then both parties can come to an agreement, because Celia's reservation point would be $6,000. In this case, there is a zone of potential agreement: $6,000 to $7,500. Somewhere within this range, the two parties should be able to come to an agreement.

Limitations to BATNA and ZOPA Although widely applied in practice, use of tools like BATNA and ZOPA is not without criticism. For example, it may be difficult for someone to objectively determine a best alternative. In a sales negotiation, it is unlikely the other party will flat out tell you precisely the financial point at which he or she will walk away. Also, the use of these frameworks often fails to account for the role of emotions and cognitive biases in negotiation processes. As a result, some suggest that BATNA "tricks" negotiators into "aiming low" with respect to outcomes. Though it is easier to claim victory when you aim low, decades of goal-setting research suggest that people who expect more and articulate those expectations end up receiving more. Further, it is quite possible that until the salesperson or negotiator begins gathering information from the other side, the best case may be even better than you know at the outset.

Expert negotiator Chris Voss advises clients to think about outcome extremes. He offers the following four steps for setting negotiation goals:

1. Set an optimistic but reasonable goal and clearly define it.
2. Write down the goal.
3. Discuss your goal with a colleague. (This makes it harder to back out.)
4. Carry the written goal with you into the negotiation.[11]

Agreement on Broad Principles

Prior to the outset of any negotiation, it is sensible for each party to agree to some broad, basic principles to govern the negotiation. Criteria may emerge from earlier discussions, prior deal terms, or current prices. There are two benefits to agreeing to basic principles. First, you may be able to influence the governing framework by being the first to advocate it. Second, by reaching agreement on one point, you have moved the negotiation forward, setting the stage for later agreements.

Setting an Agenda

Similarly, it makes sense for the parties to agree to an agenda prior to the start of any meeting. The agenda helps move the negotiation forward by outlining what will be discussed during the meeting and in what order. As a result, the customer's expectations for the meeting will tend to be in line with the salesperson's objectives and goals. Further, by finalizing a meeting agenda, the customer is likely to become more psychologically invested in a productive exchange of information and achieving a mutually successful negotiation outcome.

Choosing a Location

It is often said that the first three rules of real estate are *location, location, location*. A meeting location also plays an important role in negotiations. A noteworthy meeting location can help clear minds, impress clients, speed up negotiation pace, and increase the likelihood of a deal closing. To be sure, carefully choosing an appropriate spot for a negotiation can certainly hold practical significance. For instance, offsite locations such as restaurants may be too noisy or for various reasons not conducive to effective information exchange. On the other hand, holding a meeting in a client's office can result in frequent interruptions due to other business issues and phone calls; also, it may not provide sufficient privacy.

While location is a key piece of the negotiation process, it isn't simply a matter of "my place, their place, or a neutral place." These options are good starting points, but it could be that you can find other venues that are more conducive to satisfying meeting objectives and, ultimately, achieving agreement on a deal. For instance, you might consider the viability of alternate locations, such as an upscale restaurant with private rooms that permit confidential discussion, a hotel conference room or business suite, a location or building with historic significance, or a sporting event where private skyboxes or other meeting spaces are available. Catering is typically available in these types of venues so, with proper planning, meetings need not be interrupted due to lunch or dinner breaks.

Team Negotiation

Pauline, the business-development director of a biotech start-up, is about to enter a major negotiation with a company that is seeking to license one of her firm's technologies. Her success in establishing a long-term distribution relationship with the bigger and more established partner could make or break her firm. Pauline could go into the negotiation alone—after all, she is the one who has nurtured the relationship with her counterpart. But given the stakes, she's tempted to bring along the entire executive team—marketing, sales, finance, new-product development, and legal. Is a team approach wise, or is she better off going solo?

We have all heard that "there is strength in numbers." There are quite a few negotiation contexts, like international trade and unionized collective bargaining, where team negotiations are actually the norm. In sales, though, adding team members to either or both sides of the negotiation table can be a double-edged sword: Group dynamics and relationships can be more difficult to ascertain and negotiate. On the other hand, inclusion of all interested parties and the help of technical and legal experts at the outset of the negotiation can help both parties more quickly reach a superior outcome.

When is it most appropriate to use negotiation teams? Negotiation expert Elizabeth Mannix suggests that working as a team can be particularly beneficial in the following situations[12]:

- The negotiation is complex, requiring a diverse set of knowledge, abilities, or expertise.
- The negotiation has great potential for creative, integrative solutions.
- Diverse constituencies and interests must be represented at the table, as in union negotiations.
- You want to display your strength to the other side–for example, in international contexts where teams are expected.
- You want to signal to the other side that you take the negotiation very seriously, as in a merger or acquisition.
- You trust and respect available team members.
- You have sufficient time to organize and coordinate a team effort.

The key to success in team negotiations is understanding the psychology of how teams work.

Online Negotiation

Another negotiation context is online negotiation, which has become ubiquitous. It allows negotiating parties to negotiate across the miles cheaply and quickly. Yet online negotiation creates special challenges. With email, instant messaging, and text messages, negotiators typically lack visual, verbal, and other sensory cues to interpret how their counterpart is feeling. Videoconferencing—via Zoom, Skype, Google Hangouts, and so on—adds many of these cues to the picture. Yet it's still an imperfect form of online negotiation. Fortunately, recent writing has provided some guidance on how to master the art of negotiating online.

Email and Text Messaging
Research on how emotions affect negotiation shows that people are less adept at conveying their emotions via email than they think they are. In a study published in the journal *Group Decision and Negotiation*, researchers studied how effective negotiators are at detecting specific emotions conveyed via email, such as empathy, embarrassment, anger, and interest. In one experiment, two trained data coders who independently studied the same transcripts of email negotiations agreed only about 22 percent of the time on which emotions study participants expressed.[13]

How can we improve our ability to read one another's emotions in email and other forms of online negotiation? First, don't assume a counterpart will read between the lines (*"Is this the best you can do?"*). Instead, strive to state your emotions explicitly (*"I'm feeling impatient about our progress"*). Second, check in with counterparts regularly to see how they're feeling (*"I got a sense that my last proposal upset you. Is that right?"*) Third, if possible, meet in person or pick up the phone occasionally for an emotional check-in.

Video Conferencing Compared to email and phone negotiations, videoconferencing is perceived as a "rich" medium for online negotiation. It does allow people to learn from each other's visual and verbal cues. However, there are also some limitations:

1. *Limited visibility.* When videoconferencing, we see less of the other person and their environment than we do when negotiating in person. We also can't see what's going on outside the narrow frame. To compensate for such visual deficits, keep your hand gestures within the frame so that your counterpart can see them. In addition, it helps to minimize sound and visual distractions on your end as much as possible. Make sure the area behind you is neutral and professional, and be sure to dress for business. Finally, resist the urge to check your email or attend to matters off-screen.
2. *Technical difficulties.* Anyone who regularly videoconferences knows that technical difficulties are par for the course. It's not unusual to have trouble linking up or to suddenly lose audio and/or video during a meeting. Such glitches may interrupt the flow of a negotiation or leave people feeling irritated, which could keep them from negotiating at their best. Practice using new videoconferencing apps before important meetings, but keep in mind that technical difficulties may still crop up.
3. *Privacy and security challenges.* When the privacy of a negotiation is paramount, videoconferencing may pose special concerns. Although the possibility of being secretly recorded is a risk in any type of negotiation, video negotiations may be especially easy for your counterpart—or perhaps some other interested party—to record. In addition, there could be others quietly listening in and perhaps even advising your counterpart off-screen. For this reason, when security is critical but trust is low, it is sensible to make an extra effort to negotiate in person.

Connect Assignment 7-2

Planning for Negotiations

Please complete the Connect exercise for Chapter 7 that focuses on planning for formal negotiations. By understanding the guidelines and best practices for formal negotiations, you will be better prepared and more confident as you begin the negotiating process.

CONDUCTING THE NEGOTIATION SESSION

LO 7-4 List three guidelines for conducting a negotiation session.

No two negotiations are exactly the same. Experienced sellers understand that formal negotiations with buyers tend to be as varied as the participants involved. To guide the negotiation process toward a successful conclusion, sales professionals understand the importance of three things: clearly defining the problem, generating viable alternative solutions to the problem, and making wise and timely concessions.

Defining the Problem

Negotiations often get off to a rocky start or reach an impasse because parties did not begin with full agreement as to the exact nature of the problem(s) separating the sides. This could be due to the problem being complex and multifaceted. Or it could be due to one side or the other seeking to gain an edge.

For instance, in distributive bargaining situations, it is not uncommon for parties to seek to enhance their positions by bringing a large number of secondary issues and concerns to the table at the outset, with the intent of trading them off later during the hard-bargaining phase. Achieving a successful outcome in this context is gained through correctly defining the problem during the negotiation process and making correct inferences about the buyer's true positions, interests, and walk-away points, while concealing your own.

In contrast, in an integrative bargaining context, negotiators typically work together to define a problem statement. The joint statement reflects the needs and priorities of each party. It is important to note that the problem definition in integrative negotiations should be separate from any efforts to generate or choose alternative solutions. Thus, the resulting problem statement should be worded in neutral terms and not favor one side or the other.

If nothing else, achieving agreement on defining problems provides an initial structure upon which the two sides can simply "agree to disagree" on a common, distinctly defined issue.

Generating Alternatives

What happens when negotiations hit a sticking point? In many instances, offering an alternative solution is often a viable strategy. First, the salesperson should *establish with absolute clarity his or her own desired outcomes* for the specific negotiation. Then, and only then, they can begin to generate alternative ways to meet those interests. For instance, if a prospect raises a price concern, the salesperson can still generate a win-win outcome by introducing alternative solutions such as:

- Starting with a smaller initial commitment in order to build trust.
- Taking something away from the package to lower the price.
- Providing more favorable payment terms.

Many times, sales reps will find the prospect concedes after alternative solutions have been made, as they feel it's their job to at least try to get the best price possible.

The sales rep should engage in alternative generation prior to the negotiation session. However, in an integrative negotiation, there may also be value to co-developing alternatives with the prospect. This co-generation of alternative solutions has been described as the "creative phase" of integrative negotiations. In many cases, such efforts take the focus off price and can create more value for the customer and sales opportunities for the seller. Studies have shown that joint development of a range of alternatives may provide the parties with a foundation to create even more innovative and valuable future deals.[14]

What are some strategies for generating alternative solutions? One strategy, known as **logrolling**, involves the parties identifying two or more issues in conflict and then trading off among those issues. Thus, one party achieves a highly preferred outcome on the first issue, and the other achieves a highly preferred outcome on the second issue. If the parties do in fact have different preferences on different issues, then each side should receive more, and the joint outcomes should be higher.

Another strategy involves **expanding the pie** as a means of generating a viable alternative. This strategy involves adding elements to a negotiation so that more items are negotiable. Doing so helps redefine issues from a win-lose perspective to a win-win perspective. This technique can work well when the reason bringing the two sides together involves a shortage of resources. If it is not possible to obtain their objectives

logrolling
Negotiation strategy that involves the parties identifying two or more issues in conflict and then trading off among those issues.

expanding the pie
Negotiation strategy that involves adding elements to a negotiation so that more items are negotiable; helps redefine issues from a win-lose perspective to a win-win perspective.

under the current conditions, a potential solution would be to expand the scope of the deal in such a way that both sides can achieve desired outcomes.

Making Timely Concessions That Matter

A **concession** is the act of yielding a position in a negotiation. Skilled negotiators know that a *strategic concession*—a concession made at the right time—can be an effective tactic in a negotiation. Healthy salesperson-customer relationships are born out of mutual respect and trust. But there are dangers: In the heat of the moment, a 30 percent discount or additional six months of support might seem perfectly acceptable. It's only when you get back to your desk and start drafting up the contract that you realize you agreed to terms you can't or shouldn't accept. Clearly defining the limits on price discounts, freebies, or other add-ons *before* you meet with your prospect will ensure you come to a mutually beneficial agreement. With this in mind, salespeople shouldn't accept all of a prospect's demands without making some requests of their own. Concessions should be offered methodically, with an eye toward obtaining something valuable in return.

When trust is low or when the salesperson is engaged in a one-shot negotiation, a salesperson might consider making a **contingent concession**. A concession is contingent when you make it *only if* the other party agrees to make a specified concession in return.[15]

The timing of concessions should also be considered. It can be a major mistake for salespeople to give up their original positions too quickly. If a concession is offered too easily, the buyer may interpret that as a signal that the seller is negotiating from a position of weakness. Moreover, if the buyer considers a first offer to be frivolous, willingness to move away from it hastily may not be seen as a concession at all! By contrast, seller concessions are more powerful when a customer views the opening offer as serious and reasonable.

A final word of advice regarding negotiation sessions: *Don't put anything in writing until the conversation is over.* Negotiations can swing back and forth and around again. Many ideas will be proposed. While some will be accepted, others will be shot down. A salesperson would be wise not to revise the contract until the meeting has ended and all parties have verbally agreed to the terms.

concession
The act of yielding a position in a negotiation.

contingent concession
A concession made *only if* the other party agrees to make a specified concession in return.

ETHICAL CONSIDERATIONS IN SALES NEGOTIATIONS

LO 7-5 Summarize ethical considerations in sales negotiations.

Ethics plays a part in sales negotiations, just as it does in all other aspects of our business and personal lives. However, when it comes to discussions of ethics in business negotiations, people frequently confuse the following:

- what is *ethical* (what society defines as right or wrong)
- what is *prudent* (what is wise in terms of achieving a desired outcome)
- what is *practical* (what a negotiator can make happen in a given situation)
- what is *legal* (what the law defines as acceptable practice).

According to business ethics expert Larue Hosmer, finding the path to a convincing solution requires that a negotiator consider:

1. The economic outcomes of a potential course of action.
2. The legal requirements that bear on the situation.
3. Ethical obligations to other parties in terms of what is right and fair.[16]

Questions of Ethical Conduct

Why do some sellers and buyers engage in unethical conduct when engaged in sales negotiations? It would be overly simplistic to say that they do so because they are corrupt or bad. People tend to view *other people's* unsavory behavior as caused by disposition or personality traits, while attributing the causes of their *own* behavior to outside factors.[17] Thus it is possible that a salesperson may view an ethically questionable tactic by a rival as unprincipled and profit-driven, yet justify his or her own use of the very same tactic in a separate negotiation as ethically justified by the circumstances.

Most ethics issues in negotiations concern standards of truth telling—that is, how candid, honest, and forthcoming a negotiator should be. While most people profess to place a high value on maintaining a reputation for truthfulness, achieving that plateau is not straightforward. Think about an ethical dilemma you've experienced in your own life. The extent to which you feel good about your ethical conduct likely depends on your answers to the following questions:

- *How does one define truth?* Do you have a clear and objective set of personal or organizational guidelines, or do you simply follow your conscience?
- *How do you classify deviations from the truth?* Are all such deviations *lies*, no matter how big or small?
- *Should a person tell the truth all the time, no matter what?* Are there situations in which not sharing the truth with someone is acceptable?

Ethically Ambiguous Tactics

In negotiations, achieving successful outcomes is rooted in *information dependence*—that is, the exchange of information about the true preferences and priorities of the other party. All parties are interested in maximizing their self-interest. This can lead them to think they can do better in the negotiation by manipulating or not disclosing information relating to their preferences and priorities. This attitude results in fundamental dilemmas involving trust and honesty:

- The **dilemma of trust** is that a negotiator who believes everything the other party says can be manipulated by dishonesty.
- The **dilemma of honesty** is that negotiators who shares all of their exact requirements and limits will never achieve an outcome better than their walk-away point.

As a result of these dilemmas, negotiators might be motivated to engage in ethically ambiguous tactics. Research on deceptions and subterfuge in negotiations identifies six categories of ethically ambiguous tactics, listed in Table 7-2.

Experienced negotiators understand that there are tacit rules and guidelines that are relevant in most negotiation settings:

- The first two categories—traditional competitive bargaining and emotional manipulations—are generally viewed as appropriate and expected.
- Even minor forms of bluffing and misrepresentation, the next two categories of tactics, are often viewed as ethically acceptable and within the rules. For instance, studies show that people in many negotiations make a distinction between passive and active forms of deception.
- **Misrepresentation by omission**, which is the failure to disclose all information that would benefit the other party, is typically seen as sometimes acceptable.
- In contrast, **misrepresentation by commission**, which involves outright falsification of information, is nearly always viewed as unethical.

dilemma of trust
Situation in which a negotiator who believes everything the other party says can be manipulated by dishonesty.

dilemma of honesty
Situation in which a negotiator who shares all of their exact requirements and limits will never achieve an outcome better than their walk-away point.

misrepresentation by omission
Failure to disclose all information that would benefit the other party; seen as sometimes acceptable.

misrepresentation by commission
Outright falsification of information; nearly always viewed as unethical.

TABLE 7-2 Categories of Ethically Ambiguous Tactics

Category	Examples
Traditional competitive bargaining	Not disclosing your walk-away position; low-balling or making an inflated opening offer.
Emotional manipulation	Faking negative emotions (anger, fear, disappointment) or positive emotions (joy, satisfaction) with the intent of influencing behaviors of the other party.
Bluffing	Making insincere threats or promises.
Misrepresentation	Distorting information in describing an event to others.
Misrepresentation to opponent's networks	Corrupting an opponent's reputation with their peers.
Inappropriate information gathering	Bribery, infiltration, spying, and so on.

Source: R. J. Lewicki, B. Barry, and D. M. Saunders, *Essentials of Negotiation,* 6th ed. (New York: McGraw-Hill, 2015).

Due to cultural and individual differences, individuals may differ in their attitudes toward various negotiation tactics. By asking yourself the following five questions, you can help illuminate the boundaries between right and wrong at the negotiation table and in the process discover your own ethical standards:[18]

1. *Reciprocity:* Would I want others to treat me or someone close to me this way?
2. *Publicity:* Would I be comfortable if my actions were fully and fairly described in the newspaper?
3. *Trusted friend:* Would I be comfortable telling my best friend, spouse, or children what I am doing?
4. *Universality:* Would I advise anyone else in my position to act this way?
5. *Legacy:* Does this action reflect how I want to be known and remembered?

How to Deal with Deception

Those who choose to engage in unethical negotiations increase the likelihood of reputational risk for themselves and their organization.[19] But what should salespeople do if they think the buyer they are negotiating with is engaging in tactics that are outside the bounds of ethical standards? This is a tough question.

Many companies have adopted formal, written guidelines to help their employees maintain their integrity and the professional standards of the organization in dealing with such situations. In some instances, it may make sense to consult with a sales manager or even to bring the manager into the negotiation. In addition, experts suggest several potential response tactics, discussed below.

Force the Other Party to Lie or Back Off
What if the other party seems to be cagey on an issue and seems reluctant to make a clear statement using plain language? It may be useful to pose a question that forces him or her to tell a direct lie or else abandon or qualify the assertion. Some people are comfortable with being misleading by omission of information, but they face

Today's **Professional Perspective** . . . because everyone is a salesperson

Savannah Rawlston
Inbound SMB Account Executive
Fleetio

Savannah Rawlston

Describe your job. I'm an inbound SMB account executive for Fleetio, a SaaS (software as a service) company that helps organizations track, analyze, and improve their fleet operations. My job title means three things: (1) "Inbound" means my leads are generated from marketing. (2) "SMB" means I work with leads of small and medium sizes, as determined by the market. (3) In the SaaS world, there is a defined role for each phase of a customer life cycle; as an "account executive," I support the evaluation phase through the closing of the deal.

How did you get your job? Networking, networking, and more networking! I started my career in a channel-marketing role. When I decided to branch into sales, I reached out to any and every connection for support, potential job openings, and recommendations.

I found my current role posted online, and I immediately applied and emailed the recruiter. Upon talking to a mentor about the company and asking his advice, we realized he had a senior-level connection within the company. On his own terms, he reached out to his contact and vouched for my skills and experience. I had an interview within a week and was hired within three.

Furthermore, during a follow-up interview, I realized that the nonprofit organization I work with in my free time is a customer of the company! Do not underestimate the power of your network.

What has been most important in making you successful at your job? Several people, practices, and experiences have been key in the early successes of my career. Above all else, I've learned to leverage my innate skills. There is no mold you must fit to succeed in sales. Rather, every person has traits that will lend success in the role. Personally, I've found that I have a knack for making people feel comfortable enough to open up. My conversations are not always as aggressive as they could be, and some deals may progress more slowly, but people I work with feel comfortable telling me not only about their day but also about their broken business processes. Sharing such information is where you win, both as the buyer and the seller. Being a genuine listener will take you farther in all conversations, whether personal or professional.

In addition to doing some introspection, remember the basics. Whether you're trained in SPIN or some other sales methodology, the practices will ring true over and over again. Having studied SPIN, for example, I felt confident guiding customers through their buying journey.

What advice would you give future graduates about a career in sales? Take advantage of every interaction and bit of experience you can find in the professional world! From every company, job, manager, and co-worker, keep a mental list of things you want to carry with you (and those you don't!). Research the differences in sales organizations: Do you want to work in transactional or relational sales? Inbound or outbound? Construction or software? Find something you're passionate about, and your customers will feel that.

What is the most important characteristic of a great salesperson? Respect. Great salespeople have mutual respect for themselves, their product(s), their customers, and their teammates. While you might be the one guiding the conversation, there are teams of people behind the scenes supporting it. Remember the same for your customer: Bring those teams into the conversation, and create a groundswell of value that you represent through your product.

a crisis of conscience when they are forced to flatly lie while looking someone in the eye.

"Call" the Tactic What if you know for certain that your negotiation counterparts are being untruthful? You might tactfully, but firmly, make them aware that *you* know they are bluffing or misrepresenting information. You can let them know that in the long run, telling the truth is more likely than bluffing or deception to result in the outcome they are looking for.

Silence When the other party makes a deceptive comment or claim, simply maintain direct eye contact and don't respond at all. You may create a "verbal vacuum" that makes them uncomfortable and gets them to talk and disclose information.

McGraw Hill connect Connect Assignment 7-3

Ethics in Sales Negotiations

Please complete the Connect exercise for Chapter 7 that focuses on ethical considerations in sales negotiations. By understanding ethically ambiguous tactics, you will be better prepared to avoid mistakes that could be costly for your organization and your career.

CHAPTER SUMMARY

LO 7-1 Describe basic negotiation concepts.

Negotiating in sales is one of the most fundamental aspects of selling. All sales professionals will spend much of their careers negotiating either with customers or with managers and associates in their own firms. Getting others to see things from your perspective, while listening to their point of view in an equally respectful manner, is a key aspect of building meaningful relationships—in business and in life. Formally, *negotiation* is a dialogue between two or more people or parties, intended to reach a beneficial outcome about one or more issues over which a conflict exists. The primary decision-making authority in a negotiation is the *negotiation principal*. A third-party agent hired to represent the interests or objectives of a principal is a *negotiation agent*. Negotiation involves three basic elements: substance, process, and communication styles.

The *substance* of a negotiation refers to what the parties are negotiating over. In the negotiation process, the *negotiation agenda* is the agreed-upon list of items to be discussed, in a particular order. *Negotiation positions* are the things negotiators demand you give them and also the things on which they are not willing to budge. *Negotiation interests* are the motivating factor(s) and underlying reasons behind a negotiating party's negotiation position. *Negotiation options* are any available choices parties might consider to satisfy their interests.

Negotiation process refers to how the parties negotiate: the context of the negotiations, the corresponding tactics used by the parties, and the sequence in which all of these play out. In a *distributive negotiation*, the goals of the negotiating parties are in direct opposition. In an *integrative negotiation*, the parties place different value on various issues, and resolutions occur through cooperative exchanges.

LO 7-2 Describe common negotiation styles.

Communication style refers to communication between the parties, specifically the negotiation styles they adopt. Researchers have identified distinct negotiation styles based on a theory of conflict resolution called the *dual-concern model.* It assumes people's preferred method of dealing with conflict is based on two dimensions: assertiveness and empathy. The five negotiation styles are accommodators, avoiders, collaborators, competitors, and compromisers. *Accommodators* rank high in empathy and low in assertiveness. *Avoiders* rank low in both assertiveness and empathy. *Collaborators* rank high in both assertiveness and empathy. *Competitors* rank high in assertiveness and low in empathy. *Compromisers* rank intermediate in both the assertiveness and empathy.

LO 7-3 Explain the importance of planning for formal negotiations.

In negotiating, preparation is everything. Doing extensive research on the negotiation partner and the organization they represent can pay off in larger deals that close more quickly and smoothly. First, gather information, especially about the target buyer's probable limitations. Profile the negotiating partner by searching online for relevant news articles, visiting the company's websites, speaking with sales colleagues at other firms, or checking government records.

Because nearly all formal negotiations require some concession, formalize clear goals and financial objectives. To ensure that you don't give away too much, have a sense of alternatives available to both parties. Seasoned negotiators know the value of evaluating the other party's *BATNA* (best alternative to a negotiated agreement) and the *ZOPA* (zone of possible agreement), which is the gap between the seller's walk-away point and the buyer's highest willingness to pay.

Prior to the negotiations, seek agreement on broad principles, set the agenda, and choose a strategic meeting location. Deciding whether and when to use *negotiation teams* depends on contextual elements of the negotiation such as its complexity and the constituencies involved. Finally, master the art of online negotiation via email, text messaging, and videoconferencing.

LO 7-4 List three guidelines for conducting a negotiation session.

To guide the negotiation process toward a successful conclusion, sales professionals understand the importance of clearly defining the problem, generating viable alternative solutions to the problem, and making wise and timely concessions. One strategy for generating alternative solutions is *logrolling*, in which the parties identify the issues in conflict and then trade off among those issues. Another strategy, *expanding the pie,* involves adding elements to a negotiation so that more material is negotiable. Making strategic *concessions*—yielding positions in a negotiation—at the right time can be an effective tactic in a negotiation. A *contingent concession* is one made *only if* the other party agrees to make a specified concession in return.

LO 7-5 Summarize ethical considerations in sales negotiations.

As in all aspects of our business and personal lives, ethics play a part in sales negotiations. In negotiations, achieving successful outcomes is rooted in information dependence—the exchange of information about the true preferences and priorities of the other party. Each party is interested in maximizing their self-interest, which results in fundamental dilemmas involving trust and honesty. The *dilemma of trust* is that a negotiator who believes everything the other party says can be manipulated by dishonesty. The *dilemma of honesty* is that a negotiator who shares all of their exact requirements and limits will never achieve an outcome better than their walk-away point.

A few rules are tacitly understood in most negotiations: Competitive bargaining and emotional manipulations are generally viewed as appropriate. Even minor forms of bluffing are often viewed as within the rules. *Misrepresentation by omission*—failing to disclose all information that would benefit the other party—is typically seen as sometimes acceptable. *Misrepresentation by commission*—outright falsification of information—is nearly always seen as unacceptable.

A few strategies can be used if you think a negotiating party is engaging in unethical tactics. You might pose a question that forces him or her to tell a direct lie or else abandon or qualify the assertion. You might tactfully but firmly "call the tactic" by indicating that *you* know they are misrepresenting information. Or create a "verbal vacuum" by simply maintaining direct eye contact but not responding at all.

KEY TERMS

negotiation (p. 150)
negotiation principal (p. 150)
negotiation agent (p. 150)
negotiation agenda (p. 151)
negotiation positions (p. 151)
negotiation interests (p. 151)

negotiation options (p. 152)
distributive negotiation (p. 152)
integrative negotiation (p. 152)
dual-concern model (p. 153)
accommodators (p. 154)
avoiders (p. 154)

collaborators (p. 155)
competitors (p. 155)
compromisers (p. 156)
BATNA (p. 158)
ZOPA (p. 158)
logrolling (p. 163)

expanding-the-pie (p. 163)
concession (p. 164)
contingent concession (p. 164)
dilemma of trust (p. 165)
dilemma of honesty (p. 165)
misrepresentation by omission (p. 165)
misrepresentation by commission (p. 165)

DISCUSSION QUESTIONS

1. What preconditions should be in place in order to successfully pursue an integrative negotiation solution?
2. Based on the dual-concern negotiation model, researchers have outlined five basic communication styles. What are they? Which one do you believe is closest to your primary communication style? Why?
3. With respect to negotiation ethics, what is the dilemma of honesty? What is the dilemma of trust?
4. In your view, do ethically ambiguous tactics like emotional manipulation, bluffing, and misrepresentation by omission have a place in relationship-based selling?

ETHICAL CHALLENGE

In 2011 a pharmaceutical named Nuedexta hit the market, approved by the federal government only for a rare condition (pseudobulbar affect, or PBA), characterized by uncontrollable laughing and crying. In 2015, whistleblowers alleged that Avanir Pharmaceuticals paid kickbacks to doctors to prescribe its main drug Nuedexta to control dementia patients in nursing homes. The drug's use for dementia patients had not been approved by the FDA.

The whistleblowers alleged in lawsuits that from the drug's early years, Avanir illegally directed salespeople to market Nuedexta in nursing homes as an alternative to antipsychotic drugs. This came as the government was attempting to crack down on the use of antipsychotics in controlling outbursts of elderly dementia patients. They also claimed that salespeople had engaged in other unethical behavior: They coached doctors on how to fill out prescriptions to ensure approval. They forged physicians' signatures on paperwork for insurers. They asked nursing home employees for names of patients so they could create lists of people physicians should target with Nuedexta. At least one Avanir salesperson went so far as to dress in scrubs, review patients' files at the nurses' station in nursing homes, and write the diagnosis for PBA in the medical files of patients, one lawsuit stated. These tactics were allegedly praised by an executive on a national sales call.

Federal laws restrict the tactics pharmaceutical sales representatives can use to sell a medication. They can't give favors or payments in exchange for a doctor prescribing the drug. They can't have any contact with private patient records without the patient's consent. And they can't promote use of a drug off-label in a way that hasn't been approved by the FDA.

Pharmaceutical companies *are* allowed to pay a doctor to promote a drug to colleagues and other medical professionals. It is illegal, however, for doctors to prescribe the drug in exchange for kickback payments from a manufacturer.

In 2019, the Department of Justice announced a settlement that required Avanir to pay more than $116 million to settle fraud allegations. In addition to the settlement with Avanir, Justice Department officials indicted two doctors and two of the drugmaker's salespeople for their alleged involvement in a "kickback conspiracy." Avanir admitted it paid one of the doctors "to induce him to not only maintain, but increase his prescription volume."

Questions

1. What could the leadership at Avanir have done differently to make sure this type of unethical sales behavior did not happen?
2. If you were a salesperson responsible for a potentially lucrative drug like Nuedexta, how would you have responded to pressure from your employer to engage in the behaviors that led to the settlement? Why do you think the Avanir salespeople responded the way they did?
3. Do you think pharmaceutical salespeople have any different ethic responsibilities than do salespeople who sell other products, such as insurance or telecommunications solutions? Explain your answer.

Source: Blake Ellis and Melanie Hicken, "Cashing in on dementia patients: Drugmaker to pay $116 million in fraud settlement," CNN, September 26, 2019, https://www.cnn.com/2019/09/26/health/nuedexta-avanir-doj-settlement-invs/index.html.

ROLE PLAY

This role play will give you experience in dealing with and finding solutions for an unhappy customer. For this role play, half of your class will be retail salespeople who sell a specific type of smartphone. Each retail salesperson will have a customer walk in complaining that the smartphone they were sold is terrible. The salespeople should do their research on the specific type of smartphone they are selling so they can be prepared to handle customer complaints. The salespeople should ask questions to find out exactly what the problem is and ultimately highlight potential solutions for the customer. The salespeople should show empathy and make sure the customer knows they want to help.

The other half of class will be customers who are very unhappy with the smartphone device they have been sold. Each buyer will develop a list of two or three specific problems with the smartphone. The salespeople can provide solutions to help satisfy the customers, but the customers will decide if they are satisfied with the solution and with the customer service provided by the salespeople.

At the end of the role play, both the salesperson and the buyer should reflect on what parts of the complaint were handled best by the salesperson and how the salesperson's responses, body language, and attitude made the customer feel about the purchase and the likelihood they would buy from them again.

SALES PRESENTATION

For the Connect assignment in Chapter 7, students will get practice planning for a formal negotiation. Assume you are being recruited to work in sales in an industry that you would love to work in. The company has offered a salary and commission plan that you like but has not offered any type of benefits. Before you accept the position, you want to negotiate a benefits package (vacation days, medical insurance, company car, retirement benefits, etc.) that meets your needs.

Provide a three- to five-minute sales presentation in which you propose to your potential employer some broad principles for the upcoming negotiation, a suggested agenda, and location for the negotiation.

George D. Deitz

George Deitz
Marketing Professor
University of Memphis

Ten Useful Negotiation Skills

Here are ten important sales negotiation skills to develop:

1. *Define in advance the concessions you're willing to accept.* During a negotiation, you might be tempted to make concessions you can't or shouldn't accept. You will be better off if you clearly define the limits on price discounts or other add-ons before you meet with your prospect. Doing so will help ensure you don't "give away the store" as you seek to come to a mutually beneficial agreement.

2. *Let the prospect speak first.* You've presented the terms of the deal and the prospect would like to negotiate them, so let the prospect start the conversation. In the spirit of being accommodating, salespeople are often tempted to offer a discount or an adjustment *before* the prospects even opens their mouths. Just as in other areas of sales, it pays to listen first and then speak.

(Continued)

3. *Steer clear of ranges.* If the customer would like money knocked off your product's price tag, don't say, "*Well, I could probably reduce the cost by 15 or 20 percent.*" Who would accept 15 percent when 20 percent has been mentioned? Always quote *one* specific number or figure, and then go higher or lower as necessary. Avoid the word "between" at all costs.
4. *Avoid "splitting the difference."* According to sales expert Art Sobczak, offering to split the difference can do more harm than good. For example, if the product or service costs $100 and the prospect wants a 50 percent discount, the salesperson should not counter with $75 even though it seems logical to do so. If the salesperson offers a slight discount but still keeps the number in the neighborhood of the original price, the prospect will likely accept, and the margin takes less of a hit.
5. *Write terms at the right time.* Don't put anything in writing until the conversation is over. Negotiations often swing back and forth and around again. Some proposed ideas will be accepted, but others will be shot down. You would be wise not to write the contract until the meeting has ended and all parties have verbally agreed to the terms.
6. *Negotiate with the decision maker.* This tip might seem obvious, but according to John Holland, many salespeople make the mistake of negotiating with the wrong person. Doing so means that when talks begin with the *true* decision maker, they'll likely start at the already-discounted price quoted at the end of the first meeting. That's a great outcome for the prospect but a poor outcome for the salesperson.
7. *Get something in return for concessions.* Healthy salesperson-customer relationships are born out of mutual respect and trust. With this in mind, you should not accept every one of a prospect's demands without making some requests of your own. By keeping the negotiation a win-win for both sides, salesperson and client remain on equal footing, which lays the groundwork for a mutually beneficial relationship.
8. *Talk about more than money.* The most commonly negotiated aspect of a sales deal is price, so salespeople should be prepared to talk discounts. However, price is tied to value, and value is tied to a customer's perception of and satisfaction with a product. So, you might consider offering other add-ons or freebies in lieu of a smaller price tag. But this is not a hard-and-fast rule—the specific concessions a salesperson can offer depend on the situation.
9. *Be human.* Although prospect and salesperson sit on opposite sides of the table during a negotiation, they will be partners if the deal is signed. Keep the talk light and jovial to avoid creating bad blood.
10. *Walk away if necessary.* You shouldn't be willing to accept any curveball a prospect throws at you. If demands become unreasonable or unprofitable for the company, don't be afraid to walk away from the deal. Customers who agree to sign only if the contract is radically amended or the price is drastically dropped are bound to cause problems down the road. And since they clearly don't see much value in the offering, it's only a matter of time before they become dissatisfied. Get out for your own and your prospect's sake.

CHAPTER ENDNOTES

1. R. Fisher, W. L. Ury, and B. Patton, *Getting to Yes: Negotiating Agreement without Giving In* (New York: Penguin Books, 2011).
2. M. H. Bazerman and D. A. Moore, *Judgment in Managerial Decision Making* (New York: Wiley, 1994).
3. L. L. Thompson, *The Mind and Heart of the Negotiator* (Upper Saddle River, NJ: Pearson/Prentice Hall, 2009).
4. Malhotra, D. (2015). Control the negotiation before it begins. *Harvard Business Review,* 93(12), 67–72.
5. R. J. Lewicki, B. Barry, and D. M. Saunders, *Negotiation,* 6th ed. (New York: McGraw-Hill, 2010).
6. N. Dimotakis, D.E. Conlon, and R. Ilies, "The mind and heart (literally) of the negotiator: Personality and contextual determinants of experiential reactions and economic outcomes in negotiation," *Journal of Applied Psychology* 97, no. 1 (2012): 183.
7. Kenneth W. Thomas, "Conflict and conflict management: Reflections and update," *Journal of Organizational Behavior* 13, no. 3 (2006)): 265–274.

8. C. Voss and T. Raz, *Never Split the Difference: Negctiating As If Your Life Depended on It* (New York: Random House, 2016).
9. R. Fisher, W. L. Ury, and B. Patton, *Getting to Yes: Negotiating Agreement Without Giving In* (New York: Penguin, 2011).
10. https://corporatefinanceinstitute.com/resources/knowledge/deals/what-is-batna/
11. C. Voss and T. Raz, *Never Split the Difference: Negotiating As If Your Life Depended on It* (New York: Random House, 2016).
12. Mannix, Elizabeth A. (2005), "Strength in Numbers: Negotiating as a Team," **Negotiation,** 8(5): 3–5.
13. C. Laubert and J. Parlamis, "Are you angry (happy, sad) or aren't you? Emotion detection difficulty in email negotiation," *Group Decision and Negotiation*, 2019.
14. R. J. Lewicki, B. Barry, and D. M. Saunders, *Negotiation*, 6th ed. (New York: McGraw-Hill, 2010).
15. Harvard Law School Program on Negotiation. (2020). Four strategies on Making Concessions in Negotiations," accessed at https://www.pon.harvard.edu/daily/negotiation-skills-daily/four-strategies-for-making-concessions/.
16. L. T. Hosmer, *The Ethics of Management*, 4th ed. (Boston: McGraw-Hill/Irwin, 2003).
17. D. T. Millerand M. Ross, "Self-serving bias in the attribution of causality: Fact or fiction?," *Psychological Bulletin* 82 (1975): 213–225.
18. Harvard Law School Program on Negotiations. (2020). "Ethics and Negotiations: Five Principles of Negotiations to Boost Your Bargaining Skills in Business Situations," accessed at https://www.pon.harvard.edu/daily/negotiation-training-daily/ questions-of-ethics-in-negotiation/.
19. L. Ma and J. Parks, "Your good name: The relationship between perceived reputational risk and acceptability of negotiation tactics," *Journal of Business Ethics* 106, no. 2 (2012): 161–175.

Design elements: Marketing Insights Podcast: vandame/Shutterstock

Chapter 8

Profitology: Pricing and Analytics in Sales

Learning Objectives

After reading this chapter, you should be able to:

LO 8-1 Summarize the role of pricing in professional selling.

LO 8-2 Compare markup pricing to a research-based profitology pricing strategy.

LO 8-3 Explain how salespeople can contribute to strategic pricing.

LO 8-4 Describe the impact of predictive analytics on modern sales.

LO 8-5 Explain the major legal and ethical issues in pricing and how they relate to salespeople.

LO 8-6 Describe how CRM systems can help salespeople with strategic pricing.

Executive **Perspective** ... because everyone is a salesperson

Jeremy Andrews
District Sales Manager
Zayo Group Holdings

Jeremy Andrews

Describe your job.

I manage part of the wholesale sales team for Zayo Group. Zayo is a wholesale communications-infrastructure provider, a niche within the telecom industry. Our solutions are leveraged by virtually every large consumer of bandwidth in the world. We offer a variety of "lit" services (ethernet, wavelengths, sonet) and dark fiber. If you were to draw a line from Chicago to Dallas, my team manages everything west of that line, which equates to roughly 100 accounts and $200 million in annual revenue. We are responsible for keeping the existing base of revenue while also selling new services and increasing the overall revenue from each account.

How did you get your job?

During my last year of undergraduate school, the professor of my sales management class brought in a guest speaker who was vice president of sales for a telecommunications company. The speaker had a no-nonsense style and pulled no punches with the class. I loved his honesty and knew immediately I needed to learn from him. I spent the next several months calling and emailing him to try, at least, to get an interview.

I had no B2B sales experience and no telecom experience, but the vice president, Tom, gave me a chance anyway. There have been a lot of twists and turns since then, but that was the beginning of my sales and telecom career.

What has been most important in making you successful at your job?

The most important thing for me is grit. Grit is the ability to get up and push through the tough times. When a barrier pops up (which it inevitably will), you have to be able to persevere and push through. My greatest learning experiences have come from the greatest obstacles. Without grit, I might have rolled over and given up.

What advice would you give future graduates about a career in sales?

In my opinion, sales can be one of the most rewarding careers in any industry or profession. A good sales professional will be highly compensated not just financially but also with flexibility, travel, and executive exposure. Find a good company: You don't necessarily go to work for the biggest company or the highest salary; smaller companies often offer better training, better support, and the opportunity to move up faster. Additionally, find a mentor boss—someone who will teach you and take you under their wing.

What is the most important characteristic of a great salesperson?

There are different types of sales and salespeople:

- *Technical expert,* whose customers call for advice and guidance.
- *Customer service expert,* whose customers know they can count on you to be their advocate.
- *The friend*, who becomes more than just the sales guy/gal but also gets to know the customers personally.

Regardless of what type of salesperson you want to be, you need to be willing to work hard and to learn from the people who have come before you.

THE ROLE OF PRICING IN SALES

LO 8-1 Summarize the role of pricing in professional selling.

Pricing affects your life each day; it is part of almost every consumer decision you make. Whether you are buying a new car or scouting out a new shirt online, the prices of the products you are considering typically factor into your decision about what to purchase. If the price for a lunch special is too high, you might buy something else to eat. But consider that if the restaurant charges less than you would have been willing to pay, it has reduced its revenue.

As you know, price is one of the four elements of the marketing mix. The other three elements—product, promotion, and place—come together to determine how marketers capture value through pricing. **Price** is the amount of something—money, time, or effort—that a buyer exchanges with a seller to obtain a product. Pricing is one of the most important strategic decisions a firm and its salespeople deal with. It directly reflects the value the product delivers to consumers as well as the value the product captures for the firm.

Pricing is the essential element for capturing *revenue* and *profit*. **Revenue** is the result of the number of units sold multiplied by the price charged to customers:

$$Revenue = Units\ sold \times Price$$

Profit is the firm's "bottom line"; that is, revenue minus total costs:

$$Profit = Revenue - Total\ costs$$

The calculations of revenue and profit underlie the firm's entire marketing strategy.

From a sales perspective, the objective of pricing is **profitability**—the ability to use resources to generate revenue in excess of expense. The majority of salespeople and firms throughout the world seek to increase revenue, which can ultimately lead to increased profit. There are only two ways to increase revenue: sell more products or sell them at a higher price. As a result of this reality, in order to maximize profit, salespeople must understand strategic trade-offs between volume and price. When used correctly, pricing strategies can maximize profit, increase salesperson commissions, and help the firm take a commanding market position. When used incorrectly, pricing strategies can limit revenue and profit and prevent salespeople from having the professional success they desire.

price
The amount of something—money, time, or effort—that a buyer exchanges with a seller to obtain a product.

revenue
The result of the number of units sold multiplied by the price charged to customers.

profit
Revenue minus total costs; the firm's "bottom line."

profitability
The ability to use resources to generate revenue in excess of expense.

There's one more point to make here, which is related to the point made earlier about the price of the lunch special: When you are selling yourself to potential employers, keep the importance of pricing in mind when you negotiate the price an organization is willing to pay you as an employee (your salary). If the price to hire you is too high, the company you are interviewing with might hire someone else. However, if you ask for a lower salary than what the company is willing to pay, you have sacrificed initial earnings potential. If your raises are based on percentage increases in your initial salary, a low starting salary could, in turn, affect your earnings for years to come. Thus, it is critical that you understand the strategy and tactics of pricing and how they affect both your future and the future of the organizations you work for.

Blend Images/123RF

WHAT IS PROFITOLOGY?

We've just seen that most for-profit firms seek to increase revenue, which ultimately leads to increased profit. **Profitology** is the study of increasing profit through sales. As the formulas for revenue and profit indicate, price, costs, and sales volume are important considerations in profitology.

Setting and negotiating prices involves two steps: (1) working out all of the costs associated with a product and then (2) adding an amount to ensure you make a profit that is valuable relative to the *seller's opportunity cost*. The **seller's opportunity cost** is the value of what a seller gives up in time and money in pursuing a particular sale. Essentially it is the investment a salesperson and company must make to achieve a sale.[1]

Knowing how much to price something is part of the science of profitology. It involves researching data, using experience, being aware of industry standards, and then tailoring those numbers to a customer's specific circumstances. An organization's pricing will probably differ from the pricing of its competitors. Why? Because each organization's costs will be slightly different. If the price doesn't reflect all the cost differences, the organization's profit may be eroded. Profitology involves understanding all of the costs involved in a sale in order to maximize profitability.

Whether the product is a good, service, idea, or some combination of these, a salesperson should understand all of the costs associated with the product offering. Accurately determining the costs sets a lower price limit for salespeople; as they negotiate with customers, salespeople will know that if they go below that floor, the company will lose money on the sale. Maximizing the profit of each transaction begins by knowing the major types of costs—*fixed* and *variable*—that go into producing a good or service.

Calculating the total cost of a product begins with an understanding of these two major types of costs:

- Costs that remain constant and do not vary based on the number of units produced or sold are **fixed costs**. Examples of fixed costs include salaries, rent, insurance, and advertising costs. Since these costs will be incurred regardless of the level of production or sales activity, they must be recovered during the course of doing business. Salespeople must secure a final price that allows the firm to cover fixed costs over the long term.
- Costs that vary depending on the number of units produced or sold are **variable costs**. Variable costs include things such as raw material, sales commissions, and delivery costs.

To illustrate the difference between the two types of costs, let's use an example of a salesperson at a car dealership: Fixed costs for a car dealership include rent for the offices and showroom and employee base salaries and benefits. These costs exist each month. They do not change even if, for example, an additional 10 cars are sold in one month. Variable costs for a car dealership would include things like commissions on cars sold by the dealership's salespeople.

Salespeople must ensure that the prices they negotiate generate profit after accounting for *both* fixed and variable costs. A $20,000 car might generate an $800 per-car profit for the dealership after all of the fixed costs are accounted for. However, if the dealership offers its salespeople a 5 percent commission (a $1,000 variable cost) on each new car sold, the dealership would actually lose money on each sale of a car. Firms, including their salespeople, must watch costs closely and set prices accordingly to avoid such scenarios.

The variable costs of a product or specific transaction are usually fairly easy to allocate on a piece-by-piece basis. But fully understanding, and then accurately

---

LO 8-2

Compare markup pricing to a research-based profitology pricing strategy.

profitology
The study of increasing profit through sales.

seller's opportunity cost
The value of what a seller gives up (in time and money) in pursuing a particular sale; essentially, the investment a salesperson must make to achieve a sale.

fixed costs
Costs that remain constant and do not vary based on the number of units produced or sold.

variable costs
Costs that vary depending on the number of units produced or sold.

allocating, the value of fixed costs across the products being sold can prove difficult. This is especially difficult for salespeople who are selling a service instead of goods. Many salespeople and organizations have historically used *mark-up pricing* because of its ease of use. It is important for salespeople to understand the benefits and potential problems of mark-up pricing as they attempt to maximize profits.

Challenges of Traditional Markup Pricing

As mentioned, markup pricing is one of the most commonly used pricing tactics, largely because it is easy. In **markup pricing** (also known as *cost-plus pricing*), marketers add a certain amount, usually a percentage, to the cost of the product, to set the final price. The general formula for calculating markup price is:

Markup price = Unit cost of product + (Desired % return × Unit cost)

The company's management typically determines the desired percentage return.

For example, a salesperson can easily implement markup pricing by reviewing a spreadsheet and adding 20 percent to the cost of each item, such as a lawn chair, as illustrated here:

Markup price = $10 unit cost of lawn chair + (0.2 × $10) = $12

Though markup pricing has the advantage of being easy, it's not very effective at maximizing profits, which is the ultimate objective of profitology. To understand why, let's look at an example of how markup pricing does *not* capture value for our lawn chair. As we have discussed, different customers place different values on the products they purchase. Imagine we have four target customers who personally value the lawn chair at $10, $14, $15, and $20, respectively. That is, one customer is willing to pay $10, but no more, for the lawn chair. Another will pay $14, and so on. The information about the value that each customer places on the lawn chair comes from the firm's marketing research and salespeople.

Table 8-1 shows how much profit margin the firm would earn on each lawn chair if it uses a 20 percent markup. **Profit margin** is the amount a product sells for above the total cost of the product itself. Notice that if the firm uses the 20 percent markup, the profit margin for each customer who purchases a lawn chair will always be $2 ($12 selling price − $10 unit cost) due to the 20 percent markup. Customer 1 would not purchase the chair because its perceived value is less than the $12 price. Customers 2, 3, and 4 would purchase the chair, giving the firm a total profit of $6 ($2 profit margin × 3). But you probably see the problem: If the firm uses markup pricing, it would lose the difference between the amount of each customer's perceived value and the $12 price ($2 + $3 + $10), a total difference of $15.

markup pricing (*cost-plus pricing*)
Pricing tactic in which marketers add a certain amount, usually a percentage, to the cost of the product, to set the final price; generally calculated as Unit cost of product + (Desired % return × Unit cost).

profit margin
The amount a product sells for above the total cost of the product itself.

TABLE 8-1 The Profit Implications of a Markup Pricing Strategy

	Perceived Value of the Lawn Chair to the Customer	Does the Customer Purchase at the 20% Markup Price ($12)?	Profit Margin for the Firm ($12 price − $10 cost)	
Customer 1	$10	No	$0	
Customer 2	$14	Yes	$2	Total profit = $6
Customer 3	$15	Yes	$2	
Customer 4	$20	Yes	$2	

TABLE 8-2 The Profit Implications of a Research-Based Pricing Strategy

	Perceived Value of the Lawn Chair to the Customer	Does the Customer Purchase at the Research-Based Price ($15)?	Profit Margin for the Firm ($15 price − $10 cost)
Customer 1	$10	No	$0
Customer 2	$14	No	$0
Customer 3	$15	Yes	$5
Customer 4	$20	Yes	$5

Total profit = $10

Now compare the markup pricing scenario to a research-based approach. This second—profitology—approach considers the salesperson's knowledge of the individual customers and the competitive price environment. The cost of producing the product is still $10 per lawn chair. The salesperson knows that competitors charge $16 or more per chair and that many customers value their lawn chairs at $15 or more. As a result, the firm sets its price at $15. **Table 8-2** shows the firm's improved profit margin outcomes using this alternate pricing strategy. The firm ends up with one fewer sale: Customer 2 perceives the price to be too high. But the firm has a total profit of $10 ($5 + $5), which is close to 50 percent higher than the $6 total profit the firm earned using a simple markup strategy.

Marketing departments typically set initial prices in most organizations; most reps don't have a lot of leeway in pricing. Yet it is critical that salespeople understand the costs and pricing structure involved in setting prices. This is especially true in organizations and industries where salespeople *can* negotiate final prices. Salespeople are essential parts of profitable deal-making and must be prepared to effectively communicate value and price to existing and potential clients. For example, as will be discussed in the next section, salespeople have the ability to affect *gross margin* (which is the net sales revenue minus the cost of goods sold) when they can influence price and/or when they sell multiple products with varied margins. Increasingly, organizations are paying salespeople commissions only for the profitability they generate.[2]

Connect Assignment 8-1

Markup Pricing

Please complete the Connect exercise for Chapter 8 that focuses on profitology. By understanding the dynamics of pricing tactics such as markup pricing and being able to perform the necessary pricing calculations, you should gain insight into how organizations choose specific prices and when salespeople using those in negotiations will be most effective.

The Power of Pricing

STRATEGIC PRICING

LO 8-3

Explain how salespeople can contribute to strategic pricing.

Pricing builds or destroys value faster than almost any other business action does. If your organization is not setting the right prices, it may be losing sales if prices are too high or missing out on hidden profit if prices are too low. Small changes in price can lead to big profits. Research by McKinsey & Company found that if organizations raised prices by just 1 percent—and if demand remains constant—profits would go up on average by 8 percent.[3] Effective pricing requires understanding the value to the customer versus the firm's cost to serve customers—and how both vary across segments. Strategic pricing involves proactively creating the conditions under which better and more-profitable pricing outcomes are the result.

strategic pricing
Proactively creating conditions under which better and more-profitable pricing outcomes are the result.

How Salespeople Can Contribute to Strategic Pricing

In most firms, the best understanding of customer value is held by a combination of people in product, sales, and service departments. Meanwhile, costs are managed in procurement, operations, and finance departments. Salespeople can help break down these silos and enhance the strategic use of pricing in several ways throughout the organization. Here's how.

Provide Market Research on Pricing

Marketing departments are constantly looking for more and better research about customers and the competitive environment. Salespeople conduct qualitative research all the time as they interact with current and potential customers. Talking to salespeople is perhaps the lowest-cost qualitative research project an organization can do. It's also often an organization's best chance to achieve a strong sales strategy in sync with the profit goals of the organization.

For example, a B2B sales cycle can last months or even years. Salespeople engage with a buying team of people through what might amount to tens or even hundreds of online, phone, and in-person interactions. During those conversations, buying teams might share competitive price information about where the salesperson's organization is, relative to competitors. Or they might share their thoughts about how they prioritize pricing as they assess the value of a product offering. Salespeople provide an extensive and often untapped amount of data on customers and potential customers that can help organizations set and manage prices.

Discuss Pricing in the Negotiation Process

Too often, salespeople don't sell in a manner that yields the maximum potential profit. The salesperson's goal should be to achieve the highest price for which the customer still perceives value. To accomplish that, salespeople need to be able to confidently articulate during the sales presentation and negotiation process why their product offers the highest value compared to rivals.

Rawpixel.com/Shutterstock

Salespeople should be trained to discuss openly with prospects that "value" doesn't mean the lowest price. Instead, it is the offering that provides the best set of benefits at a specific price point for clients. If you are selling a product that is better than what competitors are offering, let customers know how it is better. Many salespeople fail at this most basic task, and organizations can increase their likelihood of closing more profitable deals by addressing this situation in sales training.

Lower prices can also provide salespeople a great opportunity to discuss value in a potentially profitable way. Salespeople also have opportunities if their product *isn't* as good as the competition. After all, if customers purchased only the best, we'd all be driving luxury cars and eating every meal at only the most expensive restaurants. Price can often compensate for product shortcomings. It is okay for salespeople to acknowledge that their product has fewer features compared to its competitors and then use price to seal the deal by asking, "Are all of the competitor's extra features worth the 30 percent premium they are charging?"

Salespeople who understand costs and the potential profits at different price points can also save time in the negotiating process by not having to always go back to the marketing team to ask questions. If salespeople know what prices meet their organization's profitability goals, they can provide answers more quickly to customers during negotiations, saving them time and expediting the process of closing the sale.

Align Compensation with Profit Traditionally, most sales forces have been compensated on the revenue they bring in. While this metric is often the easiest and most straightforward (like mark-up pricing), it provides little incentive for salespeople to fight for the highest prices at which customers still perceive value. Historically, salespeople have had very little authority to change pricing. Some organizations today still offer salespeople no authority on pricing; the management team sets the price on every deal. However, an increasing number of organizations give salespeople pricing tiers that they must stay within when negotiating deals. Others offer their salespeople tremendous latitude for client pricing.

Tying compensation to salespeople's contribution to profit is another way to enhance strategic pricing. As mentioned earlier, **gross margin** is the net sales revenue minus the cost of goods sold. Not all salespeople will have the ability to affect gross margin through pricing. But when they do, it encourages sales reps to pursue higher-margin business as a way of maximizing profit. For example, setting a $45 price for a product that costs $40 to manufacture may be an easy sale that leads to a $5 profit. But if pushing harder leads to a $50 negotiated price, profit increases by 100 percent ($10 instead of $5). Compensating on gross margins also discourages discounting; even a small drop in price might have a big impact on overall margin and therefore on salespeople's commissions. Using profitability is increasingly a key component of sales-force compensation.

gross margin
Net sales revenue minus the cost of goods sold.

Connect Assignment 8-2

Strategic Pricing

Please complete the Connect exercise for Chapter 8 that focuses on how salespeople can help their organization with strategic pricing. By understanding specific ways that sales can help with the pricing process, salespeople can help ensure they are maximizing profit throughout the organization.

PREDICTIVE ANALYTICS AND THE SCIENCE OF SALES PRODUCTIVITY

LO 8-4
Describe the impact of predictive analytics on modern sales.

Major league baseball and sales organizations have several things in common—the competitiveness of sales professionals and professional athletes, and the use of data to drive better performance. Michael Lewis wrote the bestselling book *Moneyball,* which tells the fascinating story of how major league baseball evolved from an old-fashioned, stodgy business to one driven by data and analytics. Today, many baseball

Stephen Brashear/Getty Images

predictive analysis
The use of data, statistical algorithms, and machine-learning techniques to identify the likelihood of future outcomes based on historical data.

lead scoring
Analytics-based application in which a company numerically rates its best prospective customers.

teams, such as the Seattle Mariners, use analytics to drive draft-pick and player signings, trades, lineups, and even pitch selections.

For a long time, many sales organizations operated like the stodgy baseball scouts and GMs depicted in *Moneyball;* they relied only on the "art of the sell," using gut feel and intuition. Today, salespeople across a variety of industries are increasingly using tools like predictive analytics to improve sales productivity. **Predictive analytics** is the use of data, statistical algorithms, and machine-learning techniques to identify the likelihood of future outcomes based on historical data. This technology not only gathers information about past outcomes but also uses the data to understand things that have yet to happen.

One significant analytics-based application for sales is **lead scoring**. In this approach, a company numerically rates its best prospective customers. The company runs various internal and external data through statistical models; the end result is a rating that identifies traits that make the customer more likely to purchase. Figure 8-1 shows the result of a lead-scoring software application. Using lead scoring, companies can optimize the selling situation: They can make sure that prospects are matched to the right sales reps, at the most appropriate time, based on prospect behaviors, buying stage, interests, or demographic factors.

Table 8-3 provides an example of lead scoring. Here, prospects are watching promotional videos for a firm's telecom equipment. The potential customers are likely to be purchasing managers and engineers at companies that provide phone, cable, and high-speed internet to consumers. Using lead scoring, the company can have the most appropriate salesperson reach out to the customer to provide more information. For example, a lead score of 74 might indicate that, based on the interest a client shows in the product, their current place in the buying cycle, and their fit with your business, this is an ideal time to dedicate more sales resources to close the sale. The lead score of 22 in Table 8.3 suggests that the organization should consider a different approach to nurture that account or reallocate resources to other prospects with a higher lead score.

Using lead scoring, GE's Commercial Finance division determined that the top 30 percent of prospects were three times more likely to do a deal than were the bottom 70 percent.[4] Sales managers had previously categorized only about half of this top group as high-priority prospects. Using lead scoring, GE substantially increased overall revenue and profitability for the division. For GE, the approach contributed to:

- Identification of new prospects.
- Better matching of sales approaches and channels to customer needs.
- Acceleration of the time to get new and inexperienced representatives up to speed.
- More effective territory design.

Use of AI in Sales

Many believe *artificial intelligence*, or *AI*, can help firms better leverage the investments they've made in CRM. Some have even gone so far as to suggest AI applications, such as chatbots, may one day eliminate the need for human salespeople. However, this perspective understates the complexity of many buying situations as well as the role salespeople play in building trust and driving the sales process.

Chapter Eight **Profitology: Pricing and Analytics in Sales**

FIGURE 8-1 Lead-Scoring Application

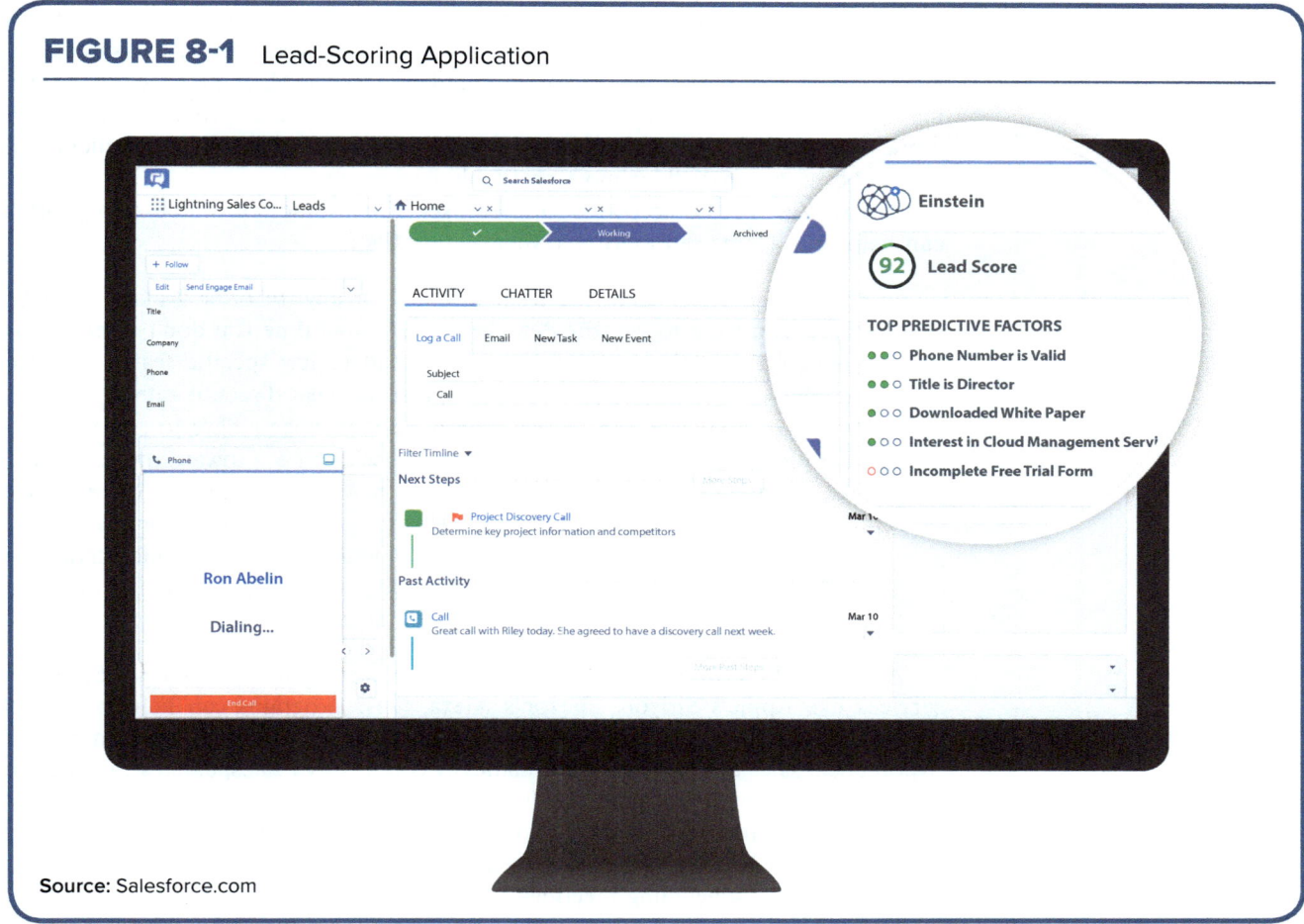

Source: Salesforce.com

TABLE 8-3 Lead-Scoring Example

Criteria	Reporting Data	Points
Completed registration	Registration record created	1
Viewer of program	View time greater than 15 seconds	1
Job function/level	User demographics	3
Purchase influence	User demographics	2
Responded to link in confirmation e-mail	Click-through analysis	2
Dynamic branching/menu selection	Dynamic branching click-through analysis	1
Highly engaged viewer	Watched more than 50% of program	2
Clicked on Resources in player	Click-through analysis	2
Provided additional demographics during program	Polling responses	2
Number of views	Repeat view reporting	2
Q&A participation	Question stored in record	1
Referred program to a friend	Referral address	1
Responded to incremental e-mail resource offer	Click-through analysis	2
Total lead score		**22**

While it is unlikely that a machine can replace the human aspect of sales, the use of AI can help take a lot of the guesswork out of the sales process. It also can help eliminate many of a salesperson's more mundane tasks, such as prospecting, processing transactions, and administrative chores. As a result, sales professionals can put more time, energy, and resources into building relationships with key clients and winning business from their most profitable customers.

Author Victor Antonio points to several specific instances in which AI algorithms can help sales teams sell more and increase profits[5]:

- *Price optimization:* Knowing what discount, if any, to offer a client is always tricky. You want to win the deal, but at the same time you don't want to leave money on the table. An AI algorithm could review specific features of each past deal that was won or lost and suggest an ideal discount rate.
- *Performance management:* Every month, sales managers have to assess the revenue pipelines of each of their salespeople, with an eye toward nurturing deals that might stall or, worse, fall through. With AI, sales managers can use dashboards to see which salespeople are likely to hit their quotas along with which outstanding deals stand a good chance of being closed. This information will allow managers to focus attention on helping salespeople close the deals that will enable the company to meet its sales targets.

Another promising area is the use of AI-enabled "sales assistants." Similar to services like Apple's Siri or Amazon's Alexa, these programs can help salespeople perform a wide range of routine tasks. For instance, AI assistant "Amy Ingram" (a hypothetical sales assistant) can automatically connect to a salesperson's calendar and e-mail contacts on his or her behalf. Amy proposes free times to the prospect or customer and sends out calendar invites once an agreement on time and place has been met. As a bonus, Amy can even learn favorite places for coffee or lunch and will add those in scheduling meetings.

LEGAL AND ETHICAL ISSUES IN PRICING

LO 8-5 Explain the major legal and ethical issues in pricing and how they relate to salespeople.

Pricing is one of the most watched and regulated marketing activities because it directly affects the financial viability of organizations as well as individuals. Many legal and ethical issues affect salespeople and pricing decisions. In this section, we'll discuss some of the issues salespeople must be aware of as they negotiate prices for their products. These issues include price discrimination, price fixing, predatory pricing, deceptive pricing, and nonprofit fundraising.

Price Discrimination

It is likely that you have benefited from discriminatory pricing in various ways. Does that surprise you? If you've paid student prices at a movie theater or have been given an introductory price to switch cell phone or cable providers, you've taken advantage of price discrimination. **Price discrimination** is the practice of charging different customers different prices for the same product. Price discrimination sounds negative, but it is illegal *only if it injures competition*. It is perfectly legal for organizations to charge customers different amounts for legitimate reasons. This is especially common in B2B settings, in which different customers might be charged different rates due to the quantities they buy, the strategic value of the company, or simply because one firm did a better job negotiating the contract.

price discrimination
The practice of charging different customers different prices for the same product. It is legal for organizations to charge customers different amounts for legitimate reasons, and illegal *only if price discrimination injures competition.*

Salespeople, who are on the front line in negotiating prices with customers, should be aware of the Robinson–Patman Act (also called the *Anti-Price Discrimination Act*). This federal law, passed in 1936, requires sellers to charge customers the same price for the same product. It grew out of concerns that large companies could leverage their buying power to purchase goods at lower prices than smaller companies could. Although the purpose of the act was to reduce injurious price discrimination, it did provide for three scenarios in which price discrimination may be allowed:

- A firm can charge different prices if the price differences are part of a quantity or manufacturing discount program. For example, a company selling 5,000 laptops to a multibillion-dollar company can charge less per unit than if it sells the same laptop to an individual consumer buying just one.
- A firm can lower prices for certain customers if a competitor undercuts the originally quoted price. This rule affects retail salespeople who promise to match any competitor's price if the consumer produces proof of the lower price. These retailers are not legally required to extend this same discount to customers who do not present proof of the lower price, effectively resulting in different prices for different customers.
- Market conditions such as going-out-of-business sales or situations in which the quality of products has changed give firms the opportunity to charge different prices for the same product. For example, a furniture store salesperson might sell new recliners at a certain price based on the costs associated and the profit goals of that firm. However, it would be allowed to sell the same recliners the next month at a steep discount if the store were going out of business or discontinuing recliners from the product line that it sells.

Robinson–Patman Act (*Anti-Price Discrimination Act*)
A federal law, passed in 1936, that requires sellers to charge customers the same price for the same product.

Price Fixing

When two or more companies collude to set a product's price, they are engaging in price fixing. Price fixing is illegal under the Sherman Antitrust Act of 1890 and the Federal Trade Commission Act. Salespeople who sell products that are very similar to products sold by other companies often are particularly at risk for price-fixing behavior. For example, in 2018 federal prosecutors investigated some of the world's biggest tuna companies for colluding to stifle competition in the canned-fish market. Products like tuna, for which salespeople don't have a unique product to sell to grocery stores or consumers, can lead salespeople to think that the only way to get a buyer is to sell at a lower price. Governments watch closely to ensure that competitors do not get together and fix prices, which is illegal.[6]

Another example of price fixing occurred when British Airways and its rival Virgin Atlantic agreed to simultaneously increase their fuel surcharges. Over the next two years, fuel surcharges increased from an average of 5 British pounds (£) a ticket to over £60.[7] When the price-fixing scheme was reported by Virgin, British Airways was punished with record fines: The British Office of Fair Trading fined the airline £121.5 million, and the U.S. Department of Justice levied an additional $300 million fine. Virgin was given immunity for reporting the collusion and was not fined.

price fixing
Collusion of two or more companies to set a product's price; illegal under the Sherman Antitrust Act of 1890 and the Federal Trade Commission Act.

Predatory Pricing

Consider a situation in which a large building-supply chain opens across the street from a locally owned hardware and lumber store. Theoretically, the prices at both stores should be similar because the costs and customer demand will be similar. However, because the large building-supply store can rely on corporate backing for support, its salespeople decide to radically lower prices, attracting more customers to its facility and eventually driving the smaller competitor out of business. It then can raise its prices to normal levels. This example illustrates a strategy called *predatory pricing*. **Predatory pricing** is the practice of first setting prices low with the intention of reducing competition and then raising prices to normal levels. The reduction in competition could involve either pushing competitors out of the market or keeping new competitors from entering the market.

predatory pricing
The practice of first setting prices low with the intention of reducing competition and then raising prices to normal levels.

This type of long-term aggressive pricing strategy could be considered an attempt to create a monopoly. It is therefore illegal under U.S. law. However, predatory pricing is difficult to prove. The Supreme Court has ruled that the victim must prove that the company being accused of predatory pricing (the building-supply chain, in our example) would be able to recoup its initial losses by charging higher prices later on, once it has driven others out of business.

Deceptive Pricing

deceptive pricing
Illegal practice that involves intentionally misleading customers with price promotions.

Probably the most frequent ethical issue in pricing involves deception. **Deceptive pricing** is an illegal practice that involves intentionally misleading customers with price promotions. Deceptive pricing practices can lead to price confusion, with consumers finding it difficult to discern what they are actually paying. The most common examples of deceptive pricing involve firms that falsely advertise wholesale pricing or salespeople who promise a significant price reduction on an artificially high retail price. Deceptive pricing practices have come under fire in recent years in industries ranging from credit cards to home loans. In these cases, important information was often buried deep within little-noticed and hard-to-read disclaimers and information.

There are many examples of deceptive pricing over the past decade. One that involved two retail giants occurred when China accused Walmart and its French competitor Carrefour of deceptive pricing. The Chinese cited instances in which Carrefour and Walmart overcharged their consumers or quoted a higher original price to make the discounts they offered on products seem more substantial. For example, a Walmart store in the city of Nanning, China, priced Nescafé coffee at $5.44, discounted from an advertised price of $6.67; in fact, the original price was $5.66. Similarly, a Carrefour store in Changchun, China, allegedly discounted men's cotton undershirts to around $7 from an advertised original price of just over $25. The original price was verified by regulators to be $18.07.[8]

In the United States, deceptive pricing is regulated by the Federal Trade Commission (FTC). Cases may be prosecuted by a state attorney general or by a district attorney at the state or local level.

Pricing Issues for Nonprofit Fundraising

Laws can also affect salespeople responsible for fundraising and other activities for nonprofits, such as universities selling season tickets to athletic events. The federal tax law passed in 2017 removed tax deductions for alumni contributions related to season tickets. It was a common practice for fundraisers in athletic departments to require donations before alumni and fans were able to purchase season tickets. The pricing of those tickets and/or contribution levels had been a major source of income for athletic departments nationwide. In the past, contributions linked to the right to purchase season tickets were considered charitable donations, which alumni could write off against their tax liabilities. The new tax law essentially takes away that charitable deduction. The House Ways and Means Committee projected the change in the law will net the government $200 million per year.[9] University athletic departments are scrambling to find ways (such as adjusting season-ticket prices) to make up the lost revenue. Potentially higher ticket prices could make the job of both the fundraiser and the season-ticket salesperson much more challenging in the years ahead. The tax law's reduction of the allowability of charitable deductions have also hit other nonprofit fundraisers and left them looking for ways to maintain fundraising levels.

Connect Assignment 8-3

Pricing Laws

Please complete the Connect exercise for Chapter 8 that focuses on important laws that affect pricing. By recognizing the specific requirements of each law and how they relate to salespeople, you will understand the legal requirements of pricing decisions and be able to avoid violating pricing rules and regulations when dealing with customers.

CRM AND STRATEGIC PRICING

LO 8-6 Describe how CRM systems can help salespeople with strategic pricing.

When many businesspeople think of customer relationship management (CRM), they think of a place simply to store customer information. A key value of CRM, though, is in its actionable data—and pricing presents a valuable use of such data. For example, developing a history of which price quotes and margin levels have been successful with a specific customer can help salespeople ensure they are not underpricing new and additional services and leaving profits on the table. CRM systems give salespeople virtually instant access to this type of historical pricing data. They also provide a variety of tools that can help salespeople prioritize their most profitable customers and reduce customer acquisition costs.

Profitability analysis measures how much profit the firm generates. It can be broken down to measure the profit contribution of regions, products, channels, or customer segments. For example, a national advertising rep might see that sales in the northwestern United States are far more profitable than in other areas of the country because of increased television viewership and a strong economy in that area. Salespeople often use CRM to evaluate two other important metrics for profitability: customer acquisition and customer profitability.

Customer-acquisition analysis measures how much a firm spends to gain new customers. Customer-acquisition costs typically include spending on marketing, advertising, public relations, and sales. Why measure customer-acquisition costs? Because sometimes additional customers don't equal additional profit. The firm's goal should be to allocate sales resources to obtain additional customers at a low cost. Selling to existing customers as opposed to new customers is less focused on price. And since existing customers are more likely to already

profitability analysis
Analysis that measures how much profit the firm generates; can be broken down to measure the profit contribution of regions, products, channels, or customer segments.

customer-acquisition analysis
Analysis that measures how much a firm spends to gain new customers.

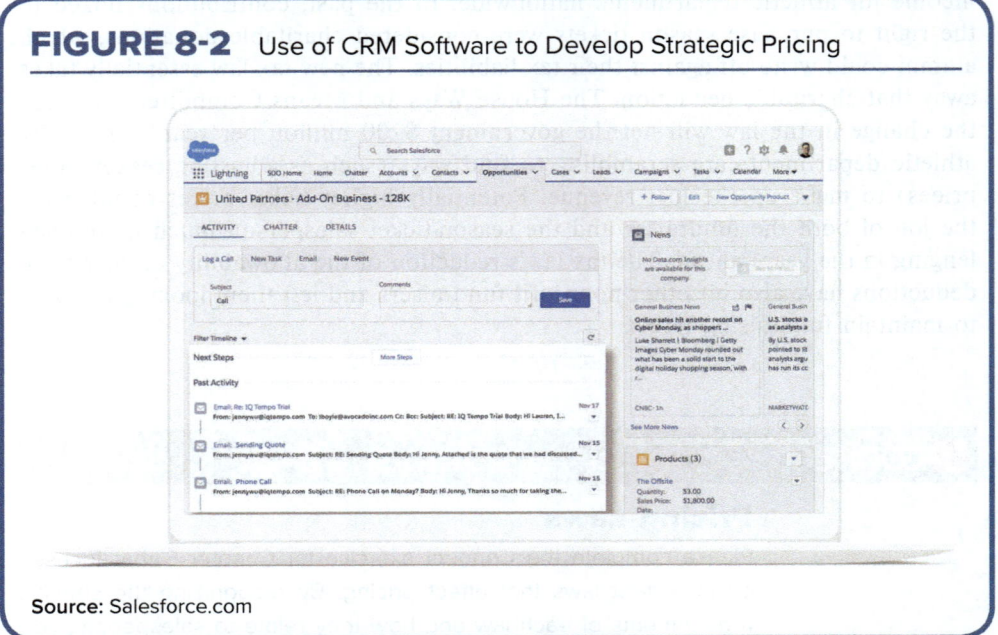

FIGURE 8-2 Use of CRM Software to Develop Strategic Pricing

Source: Salesforce.com

trust their salesperson, it gets easier to persuade them to become interested in additional products or services through up-selling and cross-selling. The fastest and most economical way to grow revenue is to sell more to an existing client base.

But the million-dollar question is, "*Who* is more likely to buy more?" CRM systems can help identify which existing clients are more likely to buy a better version of what they currently own (through up-selling) and which are most likely to want a new product offering altogether (through cross-selling). The net effect is an increase in revenue and a drop in acquisition costs. CRM software also gives salespeople the opportunity to collect customers' details. The salesperson can then use these details to maintain the customer relationship and deliver helpful and relevant information that increases the frequency of purchase. See Figure 8-2 for an example of CRM software that includes details on products, product pricing, client emails, and news affecting that client. Using the tools in a CRM system like this helps salespeople and marketers better develop strategic pricing for specific clients.

Salespeople also find value using CRM systems to measure **individual customer profitability**, which is the profit a firm makes from a customer over a specified period of time. Salespeople have only so many hours available in a day. By measuring individual customer profitability, you can prioritize where you can increase customer retention and generate the greatest profits. For example, via such an analysis, a telecommunications company might discover that its two most-profitable customer groups are healthcare and education. How might the company use this data? For one thing, it could increase the number of salespeople in those areas. The data could help guide the most effective way to deploy the necessary resources, budgets, and requirements to sell to hospitals and universities so as to grow those customer segments. Research suggests that increasing customer retention rates by 5 percent increases profits by 25 percent to 95 percent.[10] With the help of a CRM system, salespeople can gather and manage profitability information on their customers and also manage activities around customer engagement.

individual customer profitability
The profit a firm makes from a customer over a specified period of time.

Today's **Professional Perspective**...because everyone is a salesperson

Will Hudson
Director of Sales
Hydro-Temp

Describe your job. I work for a small, family-owned, niche HVAC manufacturer that produces geothermal heat and air equipment. Our company operates in the rapidly growing renewable and green-energy sector, and we often compete against companies that are much larger in scale than we are. As with many small businesses, my job requires me to wear many hats throughout the course of a typical day, week, or year.

How did you get your job? I grew up in the business and have worked in virtually every division of the company, from sweeping factory floors to managing operations. I was always a hands-on learner as a kid, and I was incredibly interested in how mechanical things worked; it wasn't unusual to see me taking apart my toys and rebuilding them again. To say my interests lent themselves well to working in a manufacturing setting would be an understatement.

Will Hudson

While I did not always know this is a field I wanted to work in, I was always sure that I wanted to be a leader of something larger than myself. As I neared the end of college, I decided to complete an internship to help myself make a decision about whether I would enjoy working in this industry for the long term. That internship is ultimately what led to the job I have today.

I jumped right in and soon found that I was able to make a positive impact. Working in this capacity allows me to support families that work with me, actively contribute to the success of our company, and empower customers to save money on their energy bills while also reducing their carbon footprints. Now I am eight years down the road, in an entirely different role than the one I started in, and haven't looked back since.

What has been most important in making you successful at your job? I believe that not waiting for a diploma to get work experience has contributed immensely to my success. By working part-time jobs in both high school and college and taking vocational classes in high school, I was able to receive invaluable experience and develop vital skill sets; I feel that these skills all contribute to making me a better salesperson, someone who can respond to whatever is thrown my way. These experiences, combined with my degree in Marketing, helped me learn how to not only see the big picture but also get down in the trenches to get things done.

What advice would you give future graduates about a career in sales? Always pay attention to your customer and make a habit of envisioning yourself in the customer's shoes. If you are tuned in to what makes your customers tick and have a clear understanding of the challenges they face on a daily basis, you are going to be better suited to provide solutions that fit your customers' needs.

I also think it is important not to take yourself too seriously either, because there will always be something on which you can improve. For me, the day that I decide I know everything would be the day I stop being good at or enjoying my job.

What is the most important characteristic of a great salesperson? Easy: You have to have great listening skills and a positive attitude. To me, listening is about way more than just hearing words coming out of someone's mouth; it's about truly understanding your customer's situation and adapting to help them solve problems and reach goals with your product or service. The better you understand what drives your customer's decision-making process, the more successful you will be in sales. In business, you won't always have a second chance to close a deal. I always try to remind myself to keep an open mind and pay attention to the details; sometimes the smallest things make all the difference in the world. I have made mistakes in my approach more times than I care to admit, but at the end of the day, I try to maintain a positive outlook and learn something from the missed opportunities so that I never make the same mistake twice.

CHAPTER SUMMARY

LO 8-1 Summarize the role of pricing in professional selling.

Pricing is part of almost every consumer decision. *Price* is the amount of something—money, time, or effort—that a buyer exchanges with a seller to obtain a product. Price is the essential element for capturing revenue and profit. *Revenue* is the result of the number of units sold multiplied by the price charged to customers. *Profit* is the firm's "bottom line": revenue minus total costs.

From a sales perspective, the objective of pricing is *profitability*—the ability to use resources to generate revenue in excess of expense. Most salespeople and firms seek to increase revenue, which can ultimately lead to increased profit. There are only two ways to increase revenue: sell more products or sell them at a higher price. In order to maximize profit, salespeople must understand strategic trade-offs between volume and price.

LO 8-2 Compare markup pricing to a research-based profitology pricing strategy.

Profitology is the study of increasing profits through sales. Price, costs, and sales volume are important considerations in profitology. Setting and negotiating prices involves working out the costs associated with a product and then adding an amount to ensure you make a profit that is valuable relative to the seller's opportunity cost. The seller's opportunity cost is the value of what the seller gives up in time and money in pursuing a particular sale. Essentially it is the investment a salesperson and company must make to achieve a sale.

Many organizations employ *markup pricing* because of its ease of use. Markup price is generally calculated as the unit cost of a product plus the desired percentage return times the unit cost. Though markup pricing is easy to calculate, it may not maximize profit, which is the ultimate objective of profitology. A profitology strategy, based on knowledge of individual customers and the competitive price environment, can improve profit. It is critical that salespeople understand the costs and pricing structure involved in setting prices.

LO 8-3 Explain how salespeople can contribute to strategic pricing.

Pricing builds or destroys value faster than almost any other business action. If your organization is not setting the right prices, it may be losing sales or missing out on hidden profit. Effective pricing requires understanding the value to the customer versus the firm's costs. Salespeople can help break down the silos in which organizations keep cost data and enhance the strategic use of pricing in several ways. First, salespeople do qualitative research all the time in their interactions with customers. Talking to salespeople is perhaps the lowest-cost qualitative research project an organization can do. Second, to achieve the highest price where the customer still perceives value, salespeople need to be able to confidently articulate during the sales presentation and negotiation process why their product offers the highest value compared to rivals. Salespeople should be trained to discuss openly with prospects that "value" doesn't mean lowest price. Finally, sales compensation should be aligned with profit rather than revenue. Compensation tied to contribution to the bottom line encourages sales reps to pursue higher-margin business and to maximize profits.

LO 8-4 Describe the impact of predictive analytics on modern sales.

Predictive analytics is the use of data, statistical algorithms, and machine learning techniques to identify the likelihood of future outcomes based on historical data. You can think of predictive analytics as a technology that not only gathers information about past outcomes but also uses the data to understand things that have yet to happen. One significant analytics-based application for sales is *lead scoring*, in which a company numerically rates its best prospective customers.

Many believe artificial intelligence (AI) can help firms better leverage the investments they've made to CRM. The use of AI can help take a lot of the guesswork out of the sales process and eliminate many of the more mundane tasks such as prospecting, processing transactions, and administrative chores. Sales professionals can then put more time, energy, and resources into building relationships with key clients and winning business from their most profitable customers.

LO 8-5 Explain the major legal and ethical issues in pricing and how they relate to salespeople.

Pricing is one of the most watched and regulated marketing activities because it directly affects the financial viability of organizations as well as individuals. As a result, many legal and ethical issues affect salespeople and pricing decisions.

Price discrimination is the practice of charging different customers different prices for the same product. Price discrimination is illegal *only if* it injures competition. It is perfectly legal for organizations to charge customers different amounts for legitimate reasons, as outlined by the *Robinson–Patman Act* (also called the *Anti-Price Discrimination Act*), passed in 1936.

When two or more companies collude to set a product's price, they are engaging in *price fixing*. Price fixing is illegal under the Sherman Antitrust Act of 1890. Salespeople who sell products that are very similar to products sold by other companies often are particularly at risk for price-fixing behavior.

Predatory pricing is the practice of first setting prices low, with the intention of pushing competitors out of the market or keeping new competitors from entering the market, and then raising prices to normal levels. This type of long-term aggressive pricing strategy can be an attempt to create a monopoly and is therefore illegal under U.S. law.

Deceptive pricing is an illegal practice that involves intentionally misleading customers with price promotions. Deceptive pricing practices can lead to price confusion, with consumers finding it difficult to discern what they are actually paying.

The tax law's reduction of the allowability of charitable deductions has hit nonprofit fundraisers and left them looking for ways to maintain fundraising levels.

LO 8-6 Describe how CRM systems can help salespeople with strategic pricing.

CRM is not just a place to store customer information. A key value of CRM is in its actionable data, and pricing is a good use of such data. CRM systems give salespeople virtually instant access to historical pricing data and provide a variety of tools that can help salespeople.

Profitability analysis measures how much profit the firm generates. Salespeople often use CRM to evaluate two important metrics for profitability: customer acquisition and customer profitability. *Customer-acquisition* measures how much the firm spent to gain new customers. *Individual customer profitability* measures the profit a firm makes from a customer over a specified period of time. With a CRM system, salespeople can manage profitability information on customers and activities around customer engagement.

KEY TERMS

price (p. 176)
revenue (p. 176)
profit (p. 176)
profitability (p. 176)
profitology (p. 177)
seller's opportunity cost (p. 177)
fixed costs (p. 177)
variable costs (p. 177)
markup pricing (cost-plus pricing) (p. 178)

profit margin (p. 178)
strategic pricing (p. 180)
gross margin (p. 181)
predictive analysis (p. 182)
lead scoring (p. 182)
price discrimination (p. 184)
Robinson–Patman Act (Anti-Price Discrimination Act) (p. 185)

price fixing (p. 185)
predatory pricing (p. 186)
deceptive pricing (p. 186)
profitability analysis (p. 187)
customer-acquisition analysis (p. 187)
individual customer profitability (p. 188)

DISCUSSION QUESTIONS

1. What is the problem with standard markup pricing? How do salespeople lose from this type of pricing strategy?
2. Assume you are selling season tickets for a team in the National Football League. What are the fixed and variable costs associated with pricing these season tickets? When you look at the existing season ticket prices for the team, how would you sell those same season tickets at a 10 percent higher price?
3. Think about your previous experiences with a salesperson, for any reason from buying a new car to buying a house to donating to a charity. What feedback did you provide any salesperson that you think could be used as valuable market research to that salesperson's organization? Explain your answer.
4. Which of the legal issues discussed in this chapter do you think salespeople are most likely to violate? What advice would you give new salespeople to make sure they do not have ethical or legal problems due to violating this specific issue?
5. Pick an industry you want to work in after you graduate. As a salesperson in that industry, which CRM benefit do you think would be most helpful to you? Explain your answer.

ETHICAL CHALLENGE

In 2019 the National Association of Realtors (NAR) and four of the largest realty companies were accused of a conspiracy to systematically overcharge home sellers by forcing them to pay commissions to the agents who represent the buyers of their homes. The class-action suit, filed in federal district court in Chicago, focuses on a rule it says has been imposed by the NAR. The rule requires brokers who list sellers' properties on local multiple listing services (MLSs) to include a "non-negotiable offer" of compensation to buyer agents. That is, once a home seller agrees in a listing to a specific split of the commission, buyers cannot later negotiate their agents' split to a lower rate. That requirement, the suit alleges, "saddle(s) home sellers with a cost that would be borne by the buyer in a competitive market," where buyers pay directly for the services rendered by their agents.

In overseas markets there is no such mandatory compensation rule for buyer agents. As a result, total commission costs tend to be lower—averaging 1 percent to 3 percent in the United Kingdom, for example, versus 5 percent to 6 percent that is commonplace in the United States. The suit alleges that if buyers in the United States could negotiate fees directly with the agents they choose to represent them, fees would be more competitive and lower. Today many American buyers are unaware of their agent's commission split.

Questions

Since most of you will at some point in your life be involved in buying or selling a home, please consider the following questions from your perspective as a future home owner:

1. What commission percentage should a real estate salesperson receive for showing and selling a home? Explain your answer.
2. Should home buyers have the ability to negotiate the commission rate paid to the real estate agent who represents the buyer of the home?
4. Why is it important for real estate agents to be as transparent as possible as to how much they will receive for a home sale transaction?

ROLE PLAY

This role play will give you experience in using strategic pricing to maximize profits selling a house. For this role play, half of your class should be real estate salespeople. Each salesperson should pick an actual home he or she is familiar with and develop a price at which to sell the house. The salespeople should look at what price similar houses have sold for in that community and do additional market research online to make sure they are providing value to the customer. The salespeople should also highlight reasons why the potential buyer should purchase this specific house.

The other half of class will be the current or prospective home buyers looking to move to the community where the salesperson's house is located. Each buyer will hear the sales presentations and can make an offer to buy the house based on the market and what they are willing to pay. The salesperson can present a counter-offer from the home's (hypothetical) current owner. The buyer will decide if he or she wants to purchase the house, and if so at what price.

At the end of the role play, both the salesperson and the buyer should reflect on what parts of the sales presentation were most effective in leading the buyer to pay more or less for the home.

SALES PRESENTATION

For the Connect assignment in Chapter 8, students will get practice generating profits for their organization by emphasizing value in their sales presentation. Assume you are a salesperson for laptop computers of the brand you like best. Research to find the current retail price of the product you want to sell as well as the prices of competing, less-expensive products. Prepare a three- to five-minute sales presentation in which you sell a customer on why he or she should pay full price for your product. Be sure to include why your product is worth the higher price and how it will provide increased value to the consumer to whom you are selling.

CAREER TIPS

Shane Hunt
Marketing Professor and Dean
Idaho State University

Shane Hunt

The Value of Understanding Pricing

My first job after graduating from college was as a pricing analyst. In that role, I worked with telecommunications salespeople from across the world to develop pricing for products and services for businesses of all sizes, ranging from *Fortune 500* telecom companies like AT&T and Verizon, to the U.S. federal government, to small businesses. These activities helped me tremendously when I became part of a sales organization. Based on this experience, here are three things to remember if you are a salesperson who enjoys pricing and the analytical nature of the sales profession:

1. *The law of supply and demand works in your favor.* Some jobs in sales are highly sought after because they are glamorous or sound cool to new graduates. Everyone wants to be the salesperson who accompanies clients to the Super Bowl or the U.S. Open. Account executive and district manager jobs have impressive-sounding titles. In my years as a professor, I have taught thousands of sales students who had all kinds of career goals, and not one has come to me on the first day of class and said, "Dr. Hunt, I am passionate about pricing."

   This is a good thing if you are one of the few who *do* enjoy thinking about pricing. Here's why: Pricing is an essential element for profitable sales in virtually every organization on the planet, yet most new graduates don't consider developing their pricing and analytics skills as they relate to a career in professional selling. When demand for a job is high and the supply is low, the salary and incentives for that job increase. I encourage you to learn as much as possible about pricing to help in your sales career in the years ahead.

2. Pricing is a great way to combine sales with other disciplines. Perhaps you are pursuing a major other than marketing but think sales might make for a great career. I want to especially encourage you to consider professional selling, which requires a combination of skills such as knowledge of finance and psychology. Pricing knowledge and how it relates to sales and profitology can also lead to career paths in marketing or finance, which will give you increased flexibility as your career develops.

3. Develop your skills using Excel. One important piece of career advice I would give you, regardless of your major, is to become proficient at using Excel. While PowerPoint, Word, and other products may be most common in your college courses, Excel is by far the most frequently used tool in day-to-day sales jobs (and many other jobs as well). I would encourage you to take courses that use Excel and to develop skills that will help your career in sales and many other areas.

CHAPTER ENDNOTES

1. Note that the economics discipline typically defines *opportunity cost* from the buyer's point of view. Because we're concerned with pricing from the seller's side, we've introduced the term *seller's opportunity cost*.
2. Andres A. Zoltners, PK Sinha, and Sally E. Lorimer (2015) "When Sales Incentives Should Be Based on Profit, Not Revenue" Harvard Business Review. June 10, 2015. https://hbr.org/2015/06/when-sales-incentives-should-be-based-on-profit-not-revenue.
3. Michael V. Marn, Eric V. Roegner, and Craig C. Zawada (2003) "The Power of Pricing," February 1, 2003. http://www.mckinsey.com/business-functions/marketing-and-sales/our-insights/the-power-of-pricing.
4. D. Ledingham, M. Kovac, and H. L. Simon, "The new science of sales force productivity," *Harvard Business Review,* September 2016.
5. V. Antonio, "How AI is changing sales," *Harvard Business Review,* July 2018.

6. Chase Purdy (2018) " Here's why US prosecutors are hungry to catch canned tuna," May 21, 2018. https://qz.com/1283470/why-us-prosecutors-are-charging-tuna-fish-company-executives-with-price-fixing/.
7. BBC News, "BA's Price-fix fine reaches $270m," August 1, 2007, http://news.bbc.co.uk/2/hi/business/6925397.stm.
8. P. Kavilanz, "China accuses Wal-Mart of deceptive prices," CNNMoney, January 26, 2011, https://money.cnn.com/2011/01/26/news/international/walmart_china_fines/index.htm.
9. C. Smith, "New tax law could cost top college athletic departments millions," *Forbes*, December 22, 2017.
10. A. Gallo, "The value of keeping the right customers," *Harvard Business Review*, October 29, 2014, https://hbr.org/2014/10/the-value-of-keeping-the-right-customers.

Design elements: Marketing Insights Podcast: vandame/Shutterstock

Part FOUR

Achieving Success in a Sales Career

WHYFRAME/Shutterstock

Chapter 9
Sales Compensation and Career Development

Chapter 10
The Psychology of Selling: Knowing Yourself and Relating to Customers

Chapter 9

Sales Compensation and Career Development

Learning objectives
After reading this chapter, you should be able to:

LO 9-1 Describe the elements of a sales compensation plan.

LO 9-2 Summarize the different types of sales compensation plans.

LO 9-3 Analyze the potential challenges in designing sales compensation plans.

LO 9-4 Describe important factors in selecting a career path in sales and sales management.

Executive Perspective ... because everyone is a salesperson

David McClain
Executive Director of University Advancement
Arkansas State University

David McClain

Describe your job.
My job is to connect alumni with the university. The goal for the connection is to match alumni's time, talent, and treasure with the university's mission and goals.

How did you get your job?
I got the job by accident. I was not looking to work in higher education fundraising. I wanted to work with the FBI. When the congressman I worked for retired, I had a conversation with the VP of advancement at the university at that time about working in development. That was nine years ago.

What has been most important in making you successful at your job?
The most important thing is my ability to connect with people and have really personal conversations with them. My goal is always to build a relationship. I've been able to build relationships and gain trust from donors by always delivering on what I said I would do. Another piece is taking responsibility when you mess up. Donors, customers, and clients know you are human and will mess up. Accept it as your fault when you do and correct it. Don't become the constant "I'm sorry" person who never resolves the problem.

What advice would you give future graduates about a career in sales?
I would tell future graduates to be open to career changes. Do your best to build meaningful relationships, and deliver on what you say you will do. Sales is hard, but we're all selling something—whether it's ourselves, a product, or a service. Be willing to hear "no" and when you do, move on and don't take it personally. You will hear "no" more than you will hear "yes" in a sales career. Read a lot or listen to podcasts of successful sales people and leaders in order to learn what success is to you. Is success working 80 to 100 hours a week and earning $100k? Or is it working 20 hours and earning $10 an hour while spending time with family? Knowing what success is for you will help you set appropriate goals.

What is the most important characteristic of a great salesperson?
The most important characteristic of a great salesperson is the willingness to continue to work hard. You have to learn to prioritize and execute.

What advice would you give students about career advancement?
I would advise students to push their own boundaries and take on challenges that stretch their limits. Overcoming such challenges will make you a stronger leader and also will provide you opportunities to grow and take on new positions with more responsibility in any organization for which you work.

ELEMENTS OF A SALES COMPENSATION PLAN

LO 9-1 Describe the elements of a sales compensation plan.

Compensation is an important factor in attracting and retaining employees, especially in sales. Sales compensation plans stem from a basic behavioral principle: If you want a particular behavior to occur or to continue, reward it; if you want a behavior to cease, ignore it or punish it. This principle applies to organizations as well as to individuals in their personal lives.

Thus organizations set up sales compensation plans that enable them to produce targeted results by rewarding salespeople who are responsible for those results. The main purpose of a sales compensation plan is to motivate sales professionals to achieve specific objectives that directly translate to the organization's bottom line. Research makes obvious the importance of such plans: 43 percent of workers would be willing to leave their jobs for a 10 percent salary increase.[1] It is difficult to imagine how an organization would survive if almost half of its sales team left the company because of a poorly designed compensation plan.

Sales compensation plans are broadly distinguished by *fixed* and *incentive* components:

- The *fixed* amount, referred to as a *base salary*, gives the salesperson some stable income.
- *Incentive* pay is typically based on achievement of sales goals. Often referred to as a *sales quota*, these goals represent the minimum desired sales level for an individual or team for a specified period of time (e.g., a month, a quarter, a year). Quota-based *commissions* and *bonuses* are the two most common incentive compensation plans.

Compensation plans vary greatly across industries, but almost all include these three core elements: base salary, commissions, and bonuses, described below.

Base Salary

base salary
A fixed amount of money paid to an employee by an employer in return for work performed; does not include benefits, bonuses, or any other potential compensation.

Base salary is a fixed amount of money paid to an employee by an employer in return for work performed. Base salary does not include benefits, bonuses, or any other potential compensation.

Organizations that pay sales reps a base salary often try to achieve a balance between base salary and incentives. That is, they want the base salary low enough to allow room for sufficient incentives and motivation but high enough to give reps some breathing room in meeting ongoing financial obligations. Typically, the base salary should range between 25 and 50 percent of anticipated total compensation. This general range is usually a sliding scale; as the salesperson gains more incentive pay, the ratio of salary to total compensation will fall.

Commissions

commissions
A per-unit payout on sales beyond the salesperson's quota.

Commissions are a per-unit payout on sales beyond the salesperson's quota. For example, a salesperson who is selling a $20,000 boat to a customer might receive an 8 percent commission ($20,000 × 0.08 = $1,600) from the boat manufacturer when the sale is finalized. Employers pay employees a sales commission to incentivize the employees to produce more sales and to reward and recognize people who perform most productively.

One option for a sales compensation plan is to forgo salary altogether and instead pay the salesperson a straight commission. Certainly it can be tempting for a business owner to base compensation on the results of the salesperson's efforts.

However, some sales executives suggest that straight-commission compensation could be a disincentive that might keep potentially outstanding sales reps from joining the organization. Whatever portion of the total compensation package is made up of commissions, organizations can structure those commissions based on sales or gross profit.

A commission could also be arranged in the form of a recoverable draw. A **recoverable draw** is a set amount of money paid to the sales representative by the company at regular intervals. For example, an Ethan Allen furniture salesperson might receive a $750 draw against commissions that would be paid on the 15th of each month. On the last day of the month, the salesperson is paid his or her total commission for that month's sales minus the $750 received on the 15th of the month. This payment method provides the salesperson with funds with which to plan and pay for basic living expenses. When a salesperson's compensation is derived largely from commissions, a recoverable draw can pay the salesperson a substantial sum of money even before the commissions are earned. When the commissions are earned, the salesperson pays back the draw. This is most often applicable in the early stages of sales reps' careers while they are building their sales pipeline. The decision to make the draw recoverable revolves around an organization's desire to collect commissions paid if they are not earned within a particular time frame.

recoverable draw
A set amount of money paid to the sales representative by the company at regular intervals.

Bonuses

A sales **bonus** is a lump sum paid out to salespeople for the achievement of their respective sales quotas. Sales bonuses might be expressed as a percentage of a cumulative revenue milestone, such as a dollar amount awarded once a sales rep brings in a certain amount of revenue for a particular period. Normally, bonuses are paid after the end of the year for meeting or exceeding sales goals. Adding a bonus structure to a sales compensation plan can incentivize the salesperson to aim even higher and reach new levels of success. For the organization, the key benefit to an annual bonus is that it is paying this additional sum *after* the desired performance is attained.

bonus
A lump sum paid out to salespeople for the achievement of their respective sales quotas.

In response to the evolution of personal selling from transactional to relational approaches, many firms have reevaluated the financial incentive plans for their sales forces. A long-term customer relationship management approach places greater emphasis on customer-retention efforts. As a result, sales personnel often must regularly engage in activities that do not result in immediate sales. One study found that a change from a bonus-based system to a commission-based system at a large pharmaceutical firm resulted in a 24 percent increase in overall sales force productivity. The larger increases came from lower-performing reps. At the same time, bonus-based reps were more likely to spend time on the types of nonincentivized tasks that are crucial to relationship management.[2]

Non-Core Elements of Sales Compensation Plans

In addition to these core elements, sales compensation plans also have several important decisions related to choice of the structure for individual salespeople (salesperson compensation choice) and how long before salespeople are paid (incentive pay horizon), discussed below.

Salesperson Compensation Plan Choice
The issue of salesperson compensation plan choice has emerged in a variety of industries over the past decade. **Salesperson compensation plan choice** is the selection of a compensation plan alternative from a set of choices. In the past, the employee was simply assigned a given compensation plan by an external agent (the organization or employer).[3] Today,

salesperson compensation plan choice
The selection of a compensation plan alternative from a set of choices.

employees are more often being given a choice of compensation plan from among a set of approved alternatives. Trade journals are encouraging this trend by asking employers questions such as, "How often do your salespeople like to receive their commissions—monthly or quarterly?" and "What puts sales people into productivity overdrive—lots of small rewards for small-step gains or a big payout for a big kill?"[4] Trade magazines have also recently noted that choices are becoming the hallmark of an evolved and effective compensation system.

The salesperson's freedom to choose from among compensation alternatives rather than being assigned a compensation plan has been found to be positively associated with individual well-being in studies in both psychology and consumer behavior. Research also suggests that the mere perception of a person having a choice can have a positive impact on his or her satisfaction with the outcomes.[5]

Despite the attention in the sales trade press to sales compensation plan choice, executives still struggle with how the idea fits into their typical model of sales management control. As the number of companies, large and small, that offer some type of compensation plan choice increases, organizations must continue to examine the role this choice has on salesperson success.

Incentive Pay Horizon

incentive pay horizon
The time between incentive payments.

The **incentive pay horizon** is the time between incentive payments.[6] It differs from the *sales performance horizon,* which is the time from initial sales contact to close. In many industries, including telecommunications and manufacturing, the sales performance horizon can be quite long. When a salesperson believes that current-period prospecting efforts are likely to result in future sales, it can be difficult for the salesperson to wait for those sales efforts to pan out. However, if the company makes incentive payments over a shorter horizon than that over which sales are made, the salesperson has an incentive to misrepresent the probability of closing future sales.[7]

Past research examined incentive pay horizons by looking at four categories: monthly, quarterly, semiannually, and annually. It suggested that companies should closely align the incentive pay horizon with the sales performance horizon. By doing so, the firm can make salespeople more responsible for the sales outcome of their sales efforts even when it may take several months to see the outcome.[8]

More recent research suggests the desirability of measuring and compensating performance over a longer time frame. Stretching the compensation period may signal to the salesperson that the organization is protecting him or her from temporary setbacks in sales performance—and thus amplifying the motivational power of bonuses over a longer period of time.[9] In addition, research found that salespeople in organizations who receive incentive compensation annually have significantly lower turnover rates than do those in organizations with a shorter incentive pay horizon.[10]

Sales executives and entrepreneurs should be thoughtful about how emerging trends in sales compensation can help their organizations increase sales and reduce turnover.

McGraw Hill connect Connect Assignment 9-1

Elements of Sales Compensation

Please complete the Connect exercise for Chapter 9 that focuses on the elements of sales compensation. By understanding the ways that salespeople are compensated, you should gain insight into how those methods can motivate salespeople and benefit the organization.

TYPES OF SALES COMPENSATION PLANS

LO 9-2
Summarize the different types of sales compensation plans.

Salespeople are usually compensated with a mix of fixed earnings and incentive pay. The *compensation mix*—that is, how much is fixed vs. incentive—hinges on a variety of factors depending on industry and the salesperson's level of control. For example, base salary should make up a greater percentage of the total compensation mix when sales representatives do not exert much control over customer buying decisions. When sales representatives have a greater level of influence over the buying decisions of customers, commissions should provide a greater portion of the total compensation mix.

Most businesses selling high-value services opt for a ratio of fixed-to-variable compensation somewhere between 60 percent fixed/40 percent variable and 80 percent fixed/20 percent variable. The compensation plan stands a greater chance of success when participants believe that the plan is competitive and that it provides appropriate levels of compensation for extra effort.

The examples we will now discuss include the most common types of sales compensation plans: salary-only compensation, commission-only compensation, base salary plus commission, and base salary plus bonus. Each example has a different structure that organization executives can apply to their specific sales team and industry based on their needs, resources, and goals.

Salary-Only Compensation

With a **salary-only compensation** structure, organizations decide ahead of time how much they will pay their salespeople. Take-home earnings each month are set regardless of how much a rep sells. Salary-only compensation plans can work well when the sales team is tightly involved in delivery and overall company performance. It's also good for organizations that have a very collaborative culture.

Salary-only compensation plans are fairly uncommon for sales teams, though. Without incentive compensation, reps are usually less motivated to go above and beyond. After hitting the sales quota, the salesperson may relax instead of pushing for the next deal. Plus, many salespeople love the thrill of the high-stakes, competitive nature of earning a commission; this thrill is often part of the reason reps go into sales in the first place. In addition, very high-performing salespeople often leave organizations that use these plans so they can make higher commissions elsewhere.

There are, however, several positives about salary-only compensation plans. First, they make it simple for organizations to calculate sales expenses and budget projections. Additionally, because salespeople don't have to worry about the financial consequences of missing their target or the weight of the competition, they may be less anxious. Salary-only compensation plans are often more attractive for salespeople who have more significant personal financial commitments (bills) to cover each month. Finally, a salary-only compensation plan is ideal for industries whose regulatory structure prohibits direct sales.

salary-only compensation
Payment structure in which organizations decide ahead of time how much they will pay their salespeople; take-home earnings each month are set, regardless of how much a rep sells.

Commission-Only Compensation

In a **commission-only compensation** structure, organizations pay salespeople based purely on their performance. For example, assume your organization offers a commission-only plan in which you make 5 percent commission on everything you sell. If you don't sell anything during a month, your total compensation is $0. If you sell $20,000 worth of products in a month, your compensation would be $1,000 ($20,000 × 0.05). If you sell $100,000 in the month, your compensation would be $5,000 ($100,000 × 0.05).

commission-only compensation
Payment structure in which organizations pay salespeople based purely on their performance.

There are several positive aspects of a commission-only compensation plan. Due to the simplicity of such a plan, organizations reduce their risk: As their salespeople succeed, revenue increases; when they fail, the organization is out nothing. Commission-only plans tend to attract fewer candidates in the hiring process, but they do tend to attract the most eager and top-performing salespeople who know they can make a good income from their selling skills. Salespeople also tend to be able to make their own schedules with commission-only sales compensation plans, which can improve morale and satisfaction.

Commission percentages vary widely; organizations may decide to pay anywhere between 3 percent and 50 percent, depending on a host of factors. For example, the more support the organization expects salespeople to give customers, such as implementation help or account management, the higher the commission should be. Organizations should also factor in the salesperson's level of involvement in the sale; if the salesperson is only producing leads (rather than closing them), he or she should likely receive a smaller commission percentage.

Organizations should consider several potential negatives when implementing a commission-only compensation plan. These plans can create aggression and high competition within your sales team, which can sometimes lead to ethical challenges. In addition, commission-only plans can create income insecurity for salespeople with no guaranteed income, which can lead to high turnover. Finally, salespeople who worry about the risk of no income guarantee might burn out quickly from the stress.

Base Salary Plus Commission

base salary plus commission
Payment structure in which organizations pay a fixed base salary as well as a commission.

The most common sales compensation plan is a **base salary plus commission** structure. In this structure, organizations pay reps a fixed base salary as well as a commission. Salespeople get the security of a steady income along with the economic incentive to sell. This plan is ideal for most businesses; the organization benefits from greater clarity into its expenses and the opportunity to hire highly motivated, competitive salespeople. In addition, since salespeople are provided a base salary, they fulfill some nonselling tasks such as sharing marketing research they learn from customers or training new team members.

In a base salary plus commission plan, the commission percentage is lower than in a commission-only plan. To determine the *base salary portion* of the compensation split, organizations think about the following factors:

- How difficult is the sale?
- How much autonomy is needed?
- How much experience is necessary?

To determine the *variable compensation portion* of the split, organizations think about the following factors:

- How complex is the sales cycle?
- How much influence does the rep have over the purchasing decision?
- How many leads do reps work at a given time?

A general guideline is this: The shorter and simpler a sale is and the less impact a rep has over the customer's behavior, the smaller the percentage of variable compensation should be. The industry standard today is a 60 percent base salary to 40 percent variable split. These percentages can be adjusted depending on the answers to the earlier questions. For example, if the sale is more difficult, the base salary percentage would likely be higher, perhaps 70 or 80 percent.

Base Salary Plus Bonus

In a **base salary plus bonus** plan, organizations augment a base salary with a bonus when the salesperson meets preset sales targets. This pay structure can be an ideal combination of predictability and motivation for salespeople. By agreeing on bonus amounts ahead of time and forecasting the number of bonuses, an organization can calculate an accurate idea of sales expenses. For a sales compensation plan that lights a fire under a sales team while still keeping expense planning manageable, base salary plus bonus is effective.

> **base salary plus bonus**
> Payment structure in which organizations augment a base salary with a bonus when the salesperson meets preset sales targets.

Absolute and Relative Commission Plans

You've seen the basic types of sales compensation plans. Let's now dig a little deeper into the details within commission plans. The first thing to consider is whether the commission will be *absolute* or *relative*.

An **absolute commission plan** is one in which organizations pay reps when they reach specific targets or milestones. The specific targets or milestones might be an amount of commission per new customer or per upsell on an existing customer. For example, salespeople might be paid $1,000 for every new customer they obtain or they might be paid 15 percent of the revenue. Absolute commission plans are easy for reps to understand, which often fosters more trust and drives better results.

> **absolute commission plan**
> Sales compensation plan in which organizations pay reps when they reach specific targets or milestones.

A **relative commission plan** is one that bases pay on performance against a preset target, called a *quota*. The quota or predetermined target typically is based on earnings revenue or sales volume. It is almost always the case that exactly meeting the quota results in exactly making the on-target commission amount. This type of compensation plan is often ideal for sales territories with different levels of opportunity but similar required effort. The major potential disadvantage of a relative commission plan is that setting quotas isn't easy for sales managers, and sales reps will often try to negotiate the most favorable possible terms.

> **relative commission plan**
> Sales compensation plan that bases pay on performance against a preset target, called a *quota*.

An organization needs to carefully consider what's best for the overall company when determining the commission. If the organization is trying to drive customer growth or aiming for an exponential increase in upsells, then absolute commission can effectively help reps target their selling. If the organization is trying to shift focus to higher-margin products to create net higher overall earnings, relative commission will be more effective.

Straight-Line Commission

One form of commission plan is the **straight-line commission**, which is based on how close sales people get to their quota. A rep who sells 50 percent of his quota will be paid 50 percent of his commission; a rep who sells 200 percent of her quota will be paid 200 percent of her commission. Like absolute and relative commissions, this is paid *in addition* to a salary.

> **straight-line commission**
> Commission based on how close salespeople get to their quota.

Straight-line commission is good when the company is compensating a sales team formed of different personalities or professional profiles. It motivates salespeople by giving them the freedom to manage their time and accounts as they see fit. High-flying members of the team will be able to reap all the rewards for a month in which they outperformed expectations.

There are several potential issues with this type of plan. For example, an organization may want to encourage overperformance as much as possible. If an organization is already paying a base salary, getting a salesperson to hit 140 percent of quota from 110 percent has a greater financial impact than does getting an underperformer from 70 to 100 percent quota. Plus, some salespeople may feel just fine making 70 percent of quota; this plan disincentivizes salespeople who are content with a lower salary.

Gross Margin Commission

gross margin commission
Commission based on profit rather than sales amount.

A **gross margin commission** is based on profit rather than sales amount. In other words, a rep would be compensated more for selling a $20,000 product with a $2,500 gross margin than for a $40,000 product with a $1,000 gross margin. Such gross margin commission plans are increasingly popular because they discourage discounting on price. Reliance on discounts to close deals isn't good for your business: It erodes margins, lowers the perceived value of your product, and often leads to future price reductions. Instead, tying commission to the product's final cost encourages reps to give fewer and smaller discounts. Additionally, this type of plan is ideal for startups that do not have liquidity in the early stages of the business. Finally, gross margin commission plans promote the sales of more-profitable product lines.

However, there are three main things to keep in mind when it comes to gross margin commission plans.

1. *Revenue must not be your priority.* Perhaps an organization is trying to build market share or attract the large clients in their industry. They will want salespeople to focus on those goals; compensating reps on profit may distract them and cause them to pursue the wrong customers.
2. *Salespeople must have control over pricing.* Salespeople have to either be selling multiple products at different price points or have discounting power.
3. *The organization must be able to track gross margins.* Shifting product and/or distribution costs, rebates, and territory changes can make it extremely hard to calculate gross margins. There can also be accounting challenges identifying the exact gross margin on each sale. These problems are typically the most common reason this type of sales compensation plan is not used.

Comparison of Sales Compensation Plans

Sales compensation plans can differ substantially across industries and include a wide range of benefits. Table 9-1 shows some actual examples of compensation plans. (These data came from various businesses and industries, so you'll see different, sometimes conflicting, information about salary and commission offers on different lines.) Studying these examples will help you familiarize yourself with the elements of an actual offer as you consider a career in sales.

connect Connect Assignment 9-2

Types of Sales Compensation Plans

Please complete the Connect exercise for Chapter 9 that focuses on different types of sales compensation plans. By understanding the different types of sales compensation plans, you should gain insight into which type of plan would be best for you if you pursue a career in sales and which plan is better for a specific type of organization.

TABLE 9-1 Examples of Sales Compensation Plans in Different Industries

MERCHANT SERVICES, OUTSIDE SALES

- Starting base salary of $32,000 plus 3% commission on total sale.
- Lease commissions ranging from $125 to $450.
- Up to $200 up-front bonus for each account plus up to 75% residual.
- For each activation, agents are paid a one-time $200 bonus plus a monthly residual of 30%.
- Starting commission rate of 40% with an opportunity for 60% with enough accounts.
- 20% commissions on gross revenue for a period of 2 years, even if not employed, with a cap of $20,000 per client. Register 50+ businesses and commission rate grows to 25%.
- Lifetime residuals: 25% to 40% residuals for lifecycle of customer. 30x buyout options twice yearly.
- 401k after 90 days. Medical, dental, vision after 90 days. Life and AD&D insurance. Includes iPad.

Jacob Lund/Shutterstock

CABLE INTERNET, DOOR-TO-DOOR

- 100% commission and $130 to $140 per contract.
- $180 commission per contract; average reps sell about 25 per month.
- Two options: (1) $1,000/base plus 15% residuals, or (2) 100% commission, 50% first month up front and 15% residuals.
- 100% commission and 4 tiers: Up to 22 sales/month, $137; up to 32 sales, $148; up to 42 sales, $160; up to 52 sales, $171 per contract.
- $500 sign-on bonus after 15 sales in the first 30 days.
- Health benefits after 90 days.

radist/123RF

ROOFING AND STORM RESTORATION

- Generally, 10% of total contract. Incentives and bonuses after $250,000 in sales.
- Pay based on sales invoice minus costs for office and materials. Sales rep receives 50% of profit after costs. If invoice is $20,000 and material and office cost is $14,000, remaining profit is $6,000, and rep makes $3,000.
- Average commission is $800 to $2,000 per job and paid 50% upon turn-in.
- Paid training ranges from 4 to 7 weeks at $375/week.
- Paid housing, $10,000 per year on average. Gas allowance, $75/week. Paid cell hot spot, $140/month.
- Health insurance, including 50% of HSA deductible.
- Profit sharing. 401(k). Vacations.
- Canvassing reps make $20 per inspection.

sculpies/Shutterstock

(Continued)

TABLE 9-1 *(Continued)*

HOME IMPROVEMENT: WINDOWS, DOORS, BATH, KITCHENS

- 100% commission. The average sale is $14,000 and with 10% commission, reps make between $100k and 200k.
- $400 a week for 4 weeks training.
- *Basement solutions:* 7% commission on provided leads; 9% commission on self-generated leads.
- Health insurance and simple IRA.
- *Bath remodeling:* Base salary of $35,000 to $54,000 per year plus 2% commission after break-even is met.
- *Shower door installations:* $25,000 base salary + commissions ranging from 6% to 12% based on a par selling scale. Benefits after 90 days.
- *Windows, siding, gutters:* 50% commission for experienced reps, 35% commission for nonexperienced reps, with $300 weekly training pay.
- *Windows, roofing, siding, doors:* Base salary of $300/week plus commission at 5% of all good sales generated.
- *Patios:* 8% commission of total of contract sold. Estimator must pay for own gas and provide own transportation. Two options: (1) $400 per week base pay plus 7% commission or (2) 100% commission and 10% commission on job total.
- *Iron fencing:* $450 per week for up to 60 days, then 10% to 12% of the total sale. Average sale is $7,000.
- *Large window company:* $10 to $14/hour plus 3% commission on total job.

sturti/Getty Images

SOLAR SALES, IN-HOME + DOOR-TO-DOOR

- $40,000 base plus 3% commission. Team commission is also paid at 0.05% on sales above $4 per watt (energy produced).
- $1,000 draw against commission for first 90 days and 100% commission thereafter.
- $600 gas bonus per month if 1+ deal sold.
- $100 per lead plus 1% entire gross of sold project. *(This is for canvassers only, not the in-home sales rep.)*
- Solar canvassing sales manager earns $50,000 base plus $250/sale override on managed rep. Solar sales rep earns $1,000 per sale (expected to close 2 sales per week).

elenathewise/123RF

- True base salary of $30,000 plus 3% commission on gross system cost. 3% of system costs will be paid 25% on Friday after signed and rest (75%) after install is complete. Promotion targets include opportunity to earn 4% to 5% commission rates as well as higher salaries. $20,000 per month in compensation is possible for the highly motivated rep.
- We pay $12 to $15 per hour and $25 to $50 per appointment depending on weekly productivity.
- We pay $50 for setting an appointment, with bonuses for a higher number of appointments, plus $200 for each appointment that becomes a sale.
- $300 commission per kW sold on self-generated deals. Average deal is 5 kW or $1,500. 70% of commission paid the following Friday and then remaining 30% when deal is closed.
- $500 per kW minimum commission.

TABLE 9-1 (Continued)

PEST CONTROL, DOOR-TO-DOOR

- 25% commission on all sales.
- 20% commission until 100 sales closed, then goes up to 25%.
- One company mentioned paid training at $9/hour for two weeks and a $100/month gas reimbursement.

BraunS/Getty Images

ALARM AND SECURITY, DOOR-TO-DOOR

- Training salary of $2,000 for month 1; $1,500 for month 2; $1,000 for month 3; and $500 for month 4. Rep also receives $500/mo auto allowance. Commissions range from 10% to 18%.
- We pay $500 minimum commission per sale.
- 5x monthly contracted revenue paid out in 2 installments at signing and at 6-month anniversary. Once successful, converts to 3-month draw against commission of $2,000/month.
- We pay 10% commission on profit of each sale.
- Commission plus $2,000 guarantee against commissions per month.
- iPad, iPhone, and full benefits after 90 days, plus bonuses.
- Sell 1 new account per day for a year and make $100,000.
- Earn $200 to $500 per sale.
- Experienced reps are guaranteed $650 per sale.

Andriy Popov/Alamy Stock Photo

DESIGNING SALES COMPENSATION PLANS

LO 9-3
Analyze the potential challenges in designing sales compensation plans.

"You get what you pay for" is accepted as a truism by sales compensation professionals. A poorly designed sales compensation plan can wreak havoc on an organization. It can drain profits, encourage the wrong behavior, and drive away top-level talent. Compensation plan risk has existed ever since variable pay was introduced. At best, poorly designed incentives can result in counter-productive or dysfunctional behavior. At worst, these incentive programs can encourage poor customer outcomes and fraud.

Two of the biggest potential issues with sales compensation plans are the complexity of the plan and whether to have sales compensation caps.

The Dangers of Complex Compensation Plans

Researchers studying sales-force compensation have long been guided by the *principal-agent theory*. This theory, drawn from the field of economics, describes the problem that results from conflicting interests between a *principal* (a company, for instance) and an *agent* hired by that principal (an employee). For example, a company wants an employee's maximum output, but a salaried employee may be able to slack off if the company can't observe how hard the employee is working. Most incentive or variable-pay plans are attempts to align the interests of principals and agents. Commission-based plans described earlier in this chapter are one example.

To be successful, sales reps must understand what's expected of them and what they can gain from their compensation plan. Sales leaders (managers) must ensure clear plan communication, emphasize the benefits, and make sure reps fully understand the plan. The best way to ensure that a plan is easy to understand and effective is to aim for simplicity. Making incentives simple and clear helps align sales behaviors with company goals. The plan doesn't need to encompass every potential sale; it needs to address only the most common scenarios, with a bit of flexibility for special circumstances.

Most companies review their sales compensation plans at the end of the year and make adjustments for the upcoming year. However, a once-a-year review of the plan may not be enough; such timing makes it difficult to proactively make changes before problems derail sales performance. Instead, analyzing plans on a quarterly basis can identify potential issues early and help keep an organization on track.

It's also important to track the right sales performance metrics. The wrong performance measures can have significant unintended consequences. For example, compensation plans that focus only on top-line revenue might lead salespeople to sell less-profitable products to generate more commissions for themselves, rather than drive company profit.

The Problem with Capping Sales Compensation

When organizations refuse to pay salespeople more than a certain amount, regardless of exceptional performance, they are capping sales compensation. Organizations cap commissions for a variety of reasons. One common reason is the belief that having salespeople achieve higher earnings than other employees are able to could cause internal conflicts. However, capping sales compensation is more likely to result in outcomes that can *hurt* an organization: employees who are less motivated and fewer high-performing sales reps.

Employees Who Are Less Motivated
A salesperson who knows that he or she can't receive compensation above a given number likely won't push too hard for deals above that range. Compensation caps also establish a culture in which sales teams feel unrewarded for giving their best performance. The unspoken message to many salespeople is that an ambitious effort won't be appreciated. It sets the expectation at the outset that your team can't achieve beyond a certain point—a belief that makes it all the more likely that they won't.

Fewer High-Performing Sales Reps
Capping commissions actively discourages top performers from considering a career with your sales organization. Fantastic salespeople will be attracted to environments in which there is no ceiling to what they can achieve. These super-high-performing salespeople will instead be attracted elsewhere, to positions where they can push their abilities to the limit without feeling their efforts are going to waste.

Today's **Professional Perspective**...because everyone is a salesperson

Stephanie Ziller
Inside Sales Representative
Optus

Stephanie Ziller

Describe your job. Optus is a telecommunication-services company that helps business clients meet their communications needs. We help design, deploy, and support new platforms with the latest technology in numerous industries, including education, retail, and healthcare. My job is to bring on new businesses for the company to sell to and also to grow existing accounts that are under my deck. I call on many customers and prospects during the day and occasionally go on customer visits. I sell solutions for my customers that often include nationwide technology rollouts, cabling installations, refurbished and new telephone hardware, telephone repair services, nationwide technician field/remote support, telephone help-desk services, and surveillance solutions such as cameras and software.

How did you get your job? I met my employer at a "Meet and Mingle" event through the sales center at my university. He left me his card after doing a "speed-interviewing" exercise at the event. He was impressed with the fact that I had doubled my quota attainment on a sales project in one of my courses. This was around $2,800 in attainment when the quota was set at $1,300 for fundraising through sponsorships. I wrote a thank you note to every employer at the Meet and Mingle. My soon-to-be boss was so appreciative of the thank you note that he posted it on his LinkedIn account. Next I was interviewed at my university's Career Services Center. Then I did an on-site interview at Optus and gave a presentation over the VOIP solution Optus offers.

I would definitely say that networking and hard work got me this job. Some recommendation letters helped as well. I've asked my boss what I did to get this job over others who were applying, because sometimes it's good to get some positive reassurance. He said, "You always follow up, follow up, and follow up."

What has been most important in making you successful at your job? I think the most important thing in making me successful at my job is being myself and having a great work/life balance. I have a lot of energy and I'm a pursuer. I also care a lot about people; my mission every day is to "make" at least one person's day. Also, relationships in sales aren't just about the money that customers spend with your company; they're also about the people you talk to and get to know. Building a relationship is the cornerstone of sales.

What advice would you give future graduates about a career in sales? I'd tell soon-to-be graduates that sales is hard. It is an upward grind for an average of six months to two years to get a healthy sales pipeline and for your productivity to be solid.

The hardest thing about sales is getting up every morning and getting back at it. You have to be able to cope with anxiety, stress, a sales quota, economic changes, work/life balance, and the constant lack of control from your customers' variables that affect your sales outcomes. You have to love sales to make it in the industry for the long-haul.

Also, I highly recommend getting a mentor. Pursuing a good mentor is key because they don't just grow on trees. Finally, don't forget that thank-you notes are a must. Do whatever you can to stand out, because you can't fly with the eagles if you're surrounded by a flock of turkeys. So, be an eagle.

What is the most important characteristic of a great salesperson? I think the most important characteristic of a great salesperson is being genuine. If you can't be yourself, then you can't be in sales. People want someone they can trust and talk to easily to handle their business. In order to gain that foundation of trust and credibility you have to be yourself and confident in what you believe. That starts with knowing who you are. I think it's important for people to grow, and that starts with working on yourself every day.

CAREER PATHS IN SALES AND SALES MANAGEMENT

LO 9-4 Describe important factors in selecting a career path in sales and sales management.

If you are interested in a career in sales, you should know there are more career paths open to you than ever before. Thanks to the advent of CRM and the increased importance of sales across industries, there are now countless sales roles and potential career paths. Regardless of which path you choose, it is very possible to advance from an entry-level position into a high-earning role in an organization. Your choice of sales role will depend on your skills and preferences.

What to Look For

Before you can analyze a sales job, you need to know what to look for. As you begin to look at sales jobs, consider the following: industry and career path, long-term job outlook, type of compensation offered, and personality fit.

Elnur/Shutterstock

Industry and Career Path The industry you work in will determine the type of sales roles open to you, and vice versa. Before you commit to a certain career path or industry, make sure the positions and focus are compatible with your goals and preferences. For example, are you interested in working for software-as-a-service (SaaS) companies? If so, the chances are that you'll need to start as a business-development rep and work your way to an account-executive position. On the other hand, if you go into manufacturing sales, you'll probably be responsible for handling deals from start to finish.

Long-Term Job Outlook The overall job outlook for sales is very positive, but not all sales jobs are created equal. Certain jobs, like those for account managers, are steadily growing more popular. Others, like outside sales, are on the decline. Before you commit to a career path, be sure to consider if that role will likely still be relevant in a decade. You can seek help by talking with your professors and professionals who are currently working in fields you are considering and by researching employment trends through sources like the U.S. Bureau of Labor Statistics.

Type of Compensation How do you like to make money? As discussed in this chapter, sales compensation ranges from only base salary to pure commission, with a variety of hybrid compensation models. As you start a sales career, be honest with yourself about what level of risk tolerance and security you would be comfortable with in your new job.

Personality Fit Most sales professionals will be miserable if they dislike the main activities of their role. Try to assess how well those activities fit your personality: How much time will your new sales role put you with customers or traveling away from your family or in the office using CRM systems? You should develop an understanding of what makes you happy and seek roles that maximize those roles. For instance, someone who loves to get to know their customers and help them achieve their goals over an extended period would likely be best in account management.

Salesperson Motivation, Training, and Performance Management

Congratulations—your sales performance has earned you a promotion to sales manager! In your new sales manager role, you are faced with new career challenges, which you should understand before you accept this type of position. Great sales managers are more than just supervisors—they are leaders who inspire their employees and help them achieve *their* (the employees') personal and career goals. Like all good coaches, top sales managers strive to place their people in positions where they can succeed.

In the past, this sales manager type of mentoring took place on a periodic, face-to-face basis. These days, much of it is digitally mediated. In fact, some sales-playbook systems enable sales managers to provide deal-specific coaching to help their reps in real time. However, technology can never replace one-to-one interpersonal bonds. In fact, research shows that a salesperson's interpersonal identification with the sales manager contributes to superior customer satisfaction ratings for the representative *and* to stronger sales performance.[11]

To remain competitive, companies must also continuously train sales employees on new products and services, technology, and sales skills. Given the importance of market and sales-related knowledge to sales success, most top sales organizations proactively seek to develop a culture of continuous learning and development within their sales force. U.S. businesses spend billions annually on sales training.

In order to obtain desired results, sales training programs should be customized to the needs of the representative(s) and changing market conditions. A large portion of that investment goes toward training new representatives. Plans for sales training need to consider the following:

- All new hires, regardless of experience level, require education about a company's products, processes, and culture.
- New hires with little or no experience will also need programs covering a wide range of customer and market knowledge, the sales process, and general sales skills.
- Major events like new-product launches, mergers, and key environmental shifts will often create a need for changes in sales strategy or new skills and knowledge. For instance, at the height of the internet boom, computer networking giant Cisco Systems acquired a new company roughly every three weeks. Cisco was constantly adding new products to the portfolio. The firm developed an online learning portal that gave its sales force access to thousands of educational videos so they could keep up with new-product offerings.

Finally, sales managers also play a central role in the sales performance management process. They work with their people to set challenging yet achievable goals for their territories. They then help their employees develop plans for meeting those goals. Good managers keep track of the results of each salesperson's efforts. They also use this market feedback as a constructive tool to benchmark successful tactics and provide reps with individualized guidance to correct perceived weaknesses.

Careers in Sales Management

As you get promoted to higher levels of sales management, your day-to-day responsibilities will continue to evolve. Following is some basic information about different sales management and executive roles.

Regional Sales Manager
Regional sales managers lead teams of sales reps and account managers. They typically set individual quotas and team goals, analyze data, coordinate sales trainings and call reviews, and manage sales territories. They are also likely to be involved in the recruiting, hiring, and firing of employees. Also, depending on your organization's hierarchy, you might need to represent your team in executive and company-wide meetings. Most regional sales managers' jobs require at least three years of sales experience.

Director of Sales A *director of sales* works with regional sales managers. As a team, they determine sales objectives, forecast and develop sales quotas, maintain sales volume, and are a crucial part of the hiring process. A director of sales will maintain a more strategic role than that of a sales manager. The director of sales typically reports to the vice president of sales and communicates executive directives to the rest of the sales organization.

Vice President of Sales A *vice president of sales* should contribute to the overall growth and strategy of the sales organization and the company as a whole. A sales VP is responsible for identifying strategic hiring opportunities that will strengthen the organization and aid in recruiting top talent. A VP of sales is also typically in charge of the organization's sales strategy, including decisions on which markets the organization will expand to and developing the tactics the sales team will need to get there. This role is often a launching place for a role as a president or chief executive officer of an organization.

Connect Assignment 9-3

Career Paths in Sales

Please complete the Connect exercise for Chapter 9 that focuses on potential career paths for salespeople. By understanding the different roles and opportunities a sales career can offer, you should gain insight into which opportunities best fit your personality and professional goals.

CHAPTER SUMMARY

LO 9-1 Describe the elements of a sales compensation plan.

If an organization wants a particular behavior to occur or continue, it should reward it. Sales compensation plans provide incentive programs that enable organizations to produce targeted results by rewarding salespeople who are responsible for those results. Sales compensation plans can broadly be distinguished by *fixed* and *incentive* components. The fixed amount, referred to as a *base salary*, gives the salesperson some stable income. Incentive pay is typically based on achievement of sales goals. Often referred to as a *sales quota*, these goals represent the minimum desired sales level for an individual or team for a specified period of time. Quota-based *commissions* and *bonuses* are the two most common incentive compensation plans. Compensation plans vary greatly across industries, but almost all include three core elements: base salary, commissions, and bonuses. Important non-core elements of sales compensation plans are *salesperson compensation choice* and the *incentive pay horizon*.

LO 9-2 Summarize the different types of sales compensation plans.

The compensation mix (how much is fixed vs. incentive) depends on a variety of factors such as the industry and the level of control a salesperson has. Plans stand a greater chance of success when participants believe the plan is competitive and provides appropriate levels of compensation for extra effort.

With a *salary-only structure,* organizations decide ahead of time how much they will pay their salespeople. A *commission-only structure* pays salespeople based solely on their performance. The most common sales compensation pay structure is *base salary plus commission*. With that plan, salespeople get the security of a steady income with the economic incentive to sell. *Absolute commission plans* use specific targets or milestones such as a commission per new customer. *Relative commission plans* use a quota or predetermined target based on earnings or sales volume to motivate sales reps. A *straight-line commission plan* rewards reps based on how close they get to their quota. With a *gross margin commission plan*, organizations pay salespeople based on profit rather than sales.

LO 9-3 Analyze the potential challenges in designing sales compensation plans.

To be successful, sales reps must understand what's expected of them and what they can gain from their compensation plan. The best way to ensure a plan is effective is to aim for simplicity, with simple and clear incentives that align with company goals.

Organizations that refuse to pay salespeople more than a certain amount, regardless of exceptional performance, are capping sales compensation. Some organizations cap commissions because they fear internal conflicts if some salespeople earn more than others. However, capping sales compensation is more likely to result in less motivated employees, fewer high-performing sales reps, and less capacity to grow as a business.

LO 9-4 Describe important factors in selecting a career path in sales and sales management.

There are more career paths open in sales than ever before. Regardless of which path you choose, it is very possible to advance from an entry-level position into a high-earning role in an organization. Your choice of sales role will depend on your skills and preferences. As you look at sales jobs, you should consider the following: industry and career path, long-term job outlook, type of compensation, and personality fit.

If promoted into a sales manager role, you should understand the career challenges you will face. Great sales managers are leaders who inspire their employees and help them achieve their personal and career goals. Sales managers also play a central role in the sales-performance management process, working with their people to set challenging yet achievable goals for their territories.

KEY TERMS

base salary (p. 198)
commissions (p. 198)
recoverable draw (p. 199)
bonus (p. 199)
salesperson compensation plan choice (p. 199)
incentive pay horizon (p. 200)
salary-only compensation (p. 201)
commission-only compensation (p. 201)
base salary plus commission (p. 202)
base salary plus bonus (p. 203)
absolute commission plan (p. 203)
relative commission plan (p. 203)
straight line commission (p. 203)
gross margin commission (p. 204)

DISCUSSION QUESTIONS

1. Based on your personal strengths and weaknesses, which type of sales compensation plan do you think would be best for you? Explain your answer.
2. How often should sales commissions be paid? Would this incentive pay horizon be a factor for you in choosing one sales job over another?
3. Based on what you have read about compensating salespeople, do you think salespeople should be compensated using only fixed salary, only commission, or a combination of the two? Please explain your answer. If you choose the combined approach, what would you consider to be the optimal ratio of fixed salary to commission?
4. What do you think would be the most difficult part about transitioning from being a salesperson to a sales manager? Would you seek to follow that career path? Explain your answer.
5. In your opinion, should sales commissions be capped? Pick a company you are familiar with and provide an example how sales caps might be positive or negative for that organization.

ETHICAL CHALLENGE

In 2016, Morgan Stanley was charged by Massachusetts's top securities regulator with "dishonest and unethical conduct" for having pushed its brokers to sell loans to their clients. Secretary of the Commonwealth William Galvin alleged that the bank ran high-pressure sales contests in Massachusetts and Rhode Island where brokers could earn thousands of dollars for selling so-called securities-based loans (SBLs). The contests, designed to boost business, were officially prohibited by Morgan Stanley but turned out to be lucrative for the bank, with the pace of loan origination tripling and adding $24 million in new loan balances. Securities-based loans let clients borrow against the value of their investment accounts but involved certain risks, including the bank's ability to sell securities to repay the loan.

The practice of cross-selling—or getting customers to buy products and services from a range of business lines—is common across the banking industry. But the scandal involving Wells Fargo (see the Ethical Challenge in Chapter 1) has raised questions about whether it is appropriate to set aggressive sales targets for employees and whether customers really need all the products they are being offered.

Thirty financial advisers working in five Morgan Stanley offices from Springfield, Massachusetts, to Providence, Rhode Island, joined in the contest that began in January 2014. The incentives were: $1,000 for 10 loans, $3,000 for 20 loans, and $5,000 for 30 loans, and performance was closely tracked by supervisors. In 2012, the bank shifted the way its advisers are paid, rewarding them for growing assets and loans.

Questions

1. Did compensation plan structure lead to unethical behavior from the Morgan Stanley sales team? Explain your answer.
2. Is cross-selling ethical? Please provide an example of how it can be ethical and an example of what you would consider to be unethical cross-selling.

Source: https://www.reuters.com/article/us-morganstanley-massachusetts/morgan-stanley-charged-with-running-unethical-sales-contests-regulator-idUSKCN1231KD.

ROLE PLAY

This role play will give you experience negotiating sales compensation plan choices. For this role play, half of the class will be regional sales managers who are offering a new salesperson a job selling insurance to companies and individuals. The sales managers will offer the salespeople three compensation mix options: 100 percent commission, 40 percent salary with 60 percent commission, or 80 percent salary with 20 percent commission.

The other half of the class will be salespeople who have to select one of the options and justify to the sales manager why that option is the best for the salesperson and the overall sales organization.

The sales manager has been told by the vice president of sales that the company would prefer salespeople be compensated using 100 percent commission plans as much as possible. The students acting as sales managers should push back on any option that is not 100 percent commission. Even if the sales rep chooses 100 percent commission, the sales manager should question why the company should be confident that the salesperson can hit his or her goals using this type of compensation plan.

At the end of the role play, both the salesperson and the sales manager students should reflect on what parts of the discussion about sales compensation plan choice were most effective in justifying a specific compensation plan and what each of them could have done differently to improve the outcome from their perspective.

SALES PRESENTATION

For the Connect assignment in Chapter 9, students will practice presenting a compensation plan they think will motivate salespeople. Assume you are a vice president of sales for a professional sports team. Prepare a three- to five-minute sales presentation in which you present what type of sales compensation plan should be used for the salespeople in that organization. Be sure to include what the mix will be between salary, commission, bonuses, and other incentives and why you think this plan will be most effective in helping the sports franchise sell tickets.

CAREER TIPS

Erin Brewer

Erin Brewer
Small-Business Owner

Corporate Social Responsibility and Sales

The term *corporate social responsibility* gets tossed around a lot these days. We live in a time when corporate "personhood" is a growing legal phenomenon, in which companies are being given greater opportunity to express themselves or protect their rights as if they were individual citizens. While I may not agree with this perspective shift, I am hopeful that it will result in more sales organizations feeling obligated to behave as positive corporate citizens, impacting their communities for the better.

Having owned a business of about 35 employees, I have found that all businesses have the ability to behave in a way that is socially responsible. Yes, even a one-woman or one-man operation has something to offer their community! Very large corporations tend to get more attention in this regard for their employee volunteer programs or charitable sponsorships, but literally all businesses can give back something. I know CPAs who offer free tax assistance to the less fortunate and private attorneys who take on pro-bono cases through the year. My friend's home healthcare company sends a team of employees to Guatemala annually, offering free medical care to disadvantaged people. Another local business has adopted a nearby elementary school and allows employees time each week to volunteer as reading tutors. There are myriad examples of companies choosing to do good, regardless of the size of the corporation or annual revenue.

Corporate social responsibility isn't limited to external activities. It actually begins internally with an employee-focused corporate culture. In fact, I'd be willing to bet that offices that are most active in their communities probably invest the most time and effort in their work environments. Companies have an obligation to create an atmosphere of appreciation, trust, and empowerment for their staff. Recognizing the value of the human beings working for an organization is the most basic element of corporate social responsibility. A few environmental factors go a long way toward creating healthy work places for employees. These include opportunities for advancement, flexible schedules, good benefits, educational options, extra vacation time, incentives for performance, appealing dress codes, clear lines of communication, transparent leadership, and profit sharing.

No matter how well employees are treated, if the business doesn't operate with integrity, the company will struggle to be successful. Socially responsible corporations approach their customers and vendors with the same respect they show their staff. Sales and purchases are transparent, contracts are honored, negotiations are fair, and pricing is clear. Their ethics are evident in their financial accountability as well as in their advertising and marketing. Being a good corporate citizen requires earning the public trust through positive, honest interactions with individual customers and vendors.

CHAPTER ENDNOTES

1. "The 2019 Employee Engagement Report: The End of Employee Loyalty" https://www.tinypulse.com/hubfs/EE%20Report%202019.pdf.
2. S. Kishore, R. S. Rao, O. Narasimhan, and G. John, "Bonuses versus commissions: A field study,"*Journal of Marketing Research* 50, no. 3 (June 2013): 317–333.
3. S. Botti, "Freedom of choice and perceived control: An investigation of the relationship between preference for choosing and outcome satisfaction," Unpublished Doctoral Dissertation (2004), University of Chicago, Chicago, Ill.
4. E. Neuborne, "A compensation plan checkup," *Sales and Marketing Management* 155, no. 5 (2003): 38–42.
5. S. Botti and S. S. Iyengar, "The psychological pleasure and pain of choosing: When people prefer choosing at the cost of subsequent outcome satisfaction,"*Journal of Personality & Social Psychology*, 87 (2004): 312–326. See also Ellen J. Langerand J. Rodin, "The effect of choice and enhanced personal responsibility for the aged: A field experiment in an institutional setting," *Journal of Personality & Social Psychology*, 34 (1976): 191–198.
6. A. T. Coughlan and C. Narasimhan, "An empirical analysis of sales-force compensation plans,"*The Journal of Business* 65, no. 1 (1992): 93–122.
7. Ibid.
8. D. Fudenberg, B. Holstrom, and P. Milgrom, "Short-term contracts and long-term agency relationships,"*Journal of Economic Theory,* 51 (1990): 1–31.
9. C. Shane Hunt, "The emerging influence of compensation plan choice on salesperson organizational identification and perceived organizational support,"*Journal of Leadership, Accountability and Ethics* 9, no. 1 (2012): 71–80.
10. K. Joseph and M. U. Kalwani, "The role of bonus pay in salesforce compensation plans,"*Industrial Marketing Management* 27 (1998): 147–159.
11. M. Ahearne, T. Haumann, F. Kraus, and J. Wieseke, "It's a matter of congruence: How interpersonal identification between sales managers and salespersons shapes sales success,"*Journal of the Academy of Marketing Science* 41 (2013):10.

Design elements: Marketing Insights Podcast: vandame/Shutterstock

Chapter 10

The Psychology of Selling: Knowing Yourself and Relating to Customers

Learning objectives
After reading this chapter, you should be able to:

LO 10-1 Explain the characteristics of grit in salespeople and sales organizations.

LO 10-2 List strategies for overcoming fears and building self-confidence in sales.

LO 10-3 Describe how salespeople can strengthen sales emotional intelligence (sales EQ).

LO 10-4 List tools and techniques to improve time management in sales.

Executive **Perspective** ... because everyone is a salesperson

Jerry Gorman
Executive Director
Atria Senior Living

Jerry Gorman

Describe your job.

In my position as executive director, I am responsible for leading the day-to-day operations of a large senior living community and for motivating our sales team to be the best by exceeding sales goals. Those responsibilities require me to provide leadership to all departments: Sales and Marketing, Life Activities, Food Service and Culinary, Business Office, and Maintenance and Housekeeping.

How did you get your job?

I found my career opportunity on the internet and went directly to the company's website and applied for the position. After many interviews, I started my career path as the community sales director. After several successful years in Sales and Marketing, I was promoted to executive director.

What has been most important in making you successful at your job?

I believe in *servant leadership*—a leadership philosophy in which my main goal is to serve team members each day, to make everyone I touch better by listening to their needs and helping all achieve their goals. I still hold my team members accountable to achieve their goals, but I am always there to help them be the best. I believe that if you have very satisfied employees you will have very satisfied customers.

What advice would you give future graduates about a career in sales?

First, stay a student of the sales process and believe in yourself and your abilities. Always take the time to listen to your prospects' needs and look for ways to resolve their concerns before you move to your sales presentation and try to close. You must earn the right to close by becoming a trusted consultant rather than another salesperson.

What is the most important characteristic of a great salesperson?

People buy from people whom they trust. Great sales professionals—those who achieve "President's Club" status—understand this principle. If you want to be in the top 5 percent of all sales professionals and to receive the rewards accorded that status, you must remember to put your prospects' needs first.

LO 10-1

Explain the characteristics of grit in salespeople and sales organizations.

extroverts
People who are naturally outgoing and who enjoy talking to and being with other people.

introverts
People who are naturally reserved and tend to shrink from social contacts.

grit
A personality trait defined as perseverance and passion for long-term goals.

TRUE GRIT: SALESPERSON PERSISTENCE AND RESILIENCE

You've probably heard someone comment about a particularly persuasive friend or loved one that he or she was a "born salesperson." Sales researchers and managers have spent a good bit of time and money in testing whether certain types of personality traits or characteristics make someone better at sales. The results are far from conclusive. It is true that **extroverts**—people who are naturally outgoing and who enjoy talking to and being with other people—are more likely to be drawn to sales careers. Yet the science suggests that **introverts**—people who are naturally reserved and tend to shrink from social contacts—can perform just as well.

So, what are some of the most important factors that lead to *long-term* success in sales careers? In this chapter, we focus on some answers to that question. It is important to note that these factors are not fixed—each can be improved with proper training and practice. Moreover, they are all qualities that can help you attain greater success, satisfaction, and happiness in any career field you may choose.

The first characteristic we'll focus on is grit. **Grit** is a personality trait defined by psychologist Angela Duckworth as perseverance and passion for long-term goals.[1] Think of the last long-term goal you worked toward. What was the time span—a month or two? Half a year? Several years? Were there setbacks along the way that you had to push through? Ultimately, were you successful in achieving the goal?

Research suggests that in many fields, a person's grittiness may have a bigger impact on success than IQ or talent do. What does grit look like? Many people mistakenly believe "grit" is just another term for "self-control." While these personality traits are related, they are not the same. *Self-control* is about *short-term* choices, like resisting the urge to procrastinate instead of starting on a big class project.[2] Grit, meanwhile, is about staying the course over the *long-term*, no matter how difficult or what obstacles you encounter along the way.

Grit emphasizes perseverance. It is having the strength of mind to maintain realistic optimism while not letting failures slow you down. Organizational psychologist Dr. Matt Barney writes that in sales contexts,

> [G]rit is this idea of really passionately persevering in spite of the fact that your sales aren't always going to pan out or you don't get a good price point or the full size of the deal that you wanted. And it's relentlessly learning from that.[3]

In sales, long-term career success doesn't necessarily depend on someone's ability to dazzle a prospect in a first meeting. More often, it involves a commitment to detail and doing a multitude of unglamorous little things: making prospecting calls, following up with long-term unsold customers, making repeated calls for subsequent repeat and referral business, and networking. Grit is not about raw sales ability. In fact, it may be that those with the most grit aren't the most talented. Gritty salespeople often have had to work harder, be more aggressive, or become more creative than others in addressing problems when things weren't going their way.

Sales managers are beginning to recognize the importance of grit. They see grit as a trait to look for in new hires as well as one to enhance in existing sales personnel. As a result, sales recruiters in many firms and industries are seeking out sales talent from non-traditional fields and personal backgrounds. Examples include people who had to work full-time to put themselves through school, military veterans, college athletes, accomplished artists, dancers, and musicians. All are seen as individuals who are more likely than not to have set and achieved challenging goals through hard work in the face of adversity.[4]

Developing Grit in Sales Organizations

In terms of developing greater grit in sales employees and other workers, organizational psychologists point to the importance of a person's mindset. According to Carol Dweck, there are two basic mindsets[5]:

- With a **fixed mindset**, you believe your character, intelligence, and creativity are basically unchanging and that success reflects your innate talents.
- With a **growth mindset**, you believe your traits can change over time and that failure actually helps you learn and improve.

fixed mindset
The personal belief that your character, intelligence, and creativity are basically unchanging and that success reflects your innate talents.

growth mindset
The personal belief that your traits can change over time and that failure actually helps you learn and improve.

Believing that you can cultivate your abilities—that is, having a growth mindset—makes a huge impact on your long-term results. You are less afraid of making mistakes or falling short; you know that short-term pitfalls won't define you. As a result, you are much more likely to take risks and push yourself, even if it means you might fall short. Grit is epitomized by being willing to keep going rather than giving up when you fail. How can sales students and sales professionals strengthen their grit?

First, it is important to monitor how you approach failure. People who take failure as an opportunity to learn and grow do much better at sales in the long run. This can be tricky, since strengthening grit requires challenging oneself by setting ambitious goals. Whenever a sales opportunity falls through, it is important to steer clear of labeling the situation or your efforts as a complete waste. Instead, think about the long-term: What can you take away from the situation that can help you in the future? Did you get the chance to practice a new skill? Were you able to achieve anything positive, even if the ultimate outcome wasn't a success?[6] You might not be able to change your mindset overnight, but consistently trying to take a healthy attitude will definitely help over the long run.

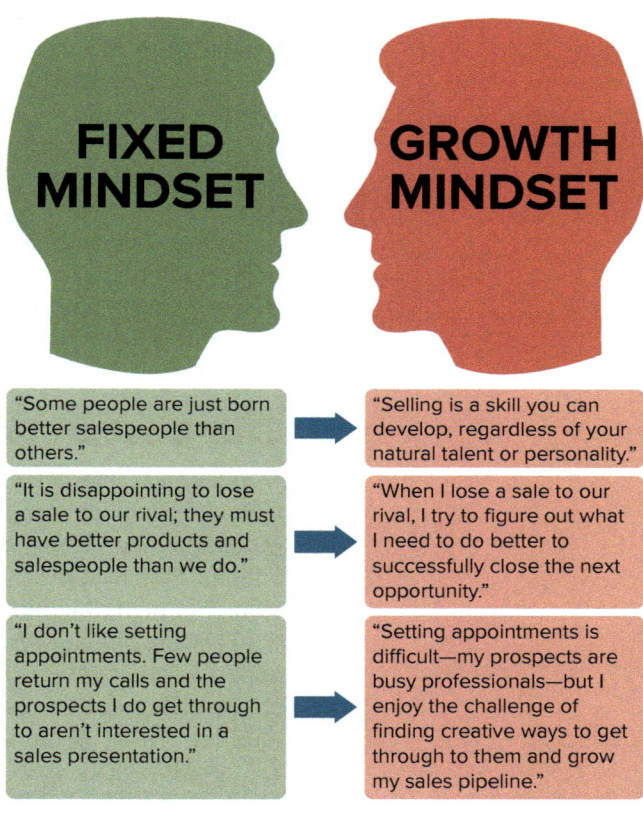

Second, improving grit requires practice, practice, and more practice. Hard work sharpens skills, and we are more likely to stick with things we are good at. Psychologist Anders Ericcson, who has spent his career studying experts from a wide variety of fields, has suggested a **10,000-hour rule**—that is, the amount of specialized practice time needed in order for someone to become a world-class performer. While the precise number of hours may differ somewhat from area to area and individual to individual, Ericcson states:

> [I]n most domains it's remarkable how much time even the most "talented" individuals need in order to reach the highest levels of performance. The 10,000 hour number just gives you a sense that we're talking years of 10 to 20 hours a week . . . to get to the highest level.[7]

But it is important to note that we are not talking about practice in terms of simple rote repetition. To develop grit, it is important that you engage in what Ericcson refers to as "deliberate practice." This entails activities that mean constantly pushing yourself beyond your comfort zone and using feedback to identify weaknesses and work on them.

Finally, the importance of passion cannot be understated. It's hard to stick with something over the long haul if it doesn't deeply interest you or you don't care. Gritty people don't merely have a "job." They have a calling in life. You must feel a passion for what you do and who you do it for if you hope to achieve your long-term

10,000-hour rule
Guideline proposed by Anders Ericsson that 10,000 hours of specialized practice time are needed in order for someone to become a world-class performer.

aspirations. The more passionate you are, the likelier you are to keep going, even when things get tough.

What if you want to be grittier but don't find tremendous meaning in your work? Experts suggest that making small tweaks to how you view your job can make a big difference. Think about what you do that helps others. Reflect on how the work you're doing makes a positive contribution to your company, to your clients, and to society. When you stop to consider it, salespeople perform a tremendously important service within society. They create value by educating customers and helping to solve other people's problems. Further, the livelihood of the vast majority of employees within most companies depends directly on the daily efforts and successes of individual salespeople.

SELF-CONFIDENCE: OVERCOMING FEARS AND BUILDING TRUST

LO 10-2 List strategies for overcoming fears and building self-confidence in sales.

imposter syndrome The feeling of self-doubt about oneself or one's abilities.

Do you ever doubt yourself or your abilities? All of us doubt our own abilities from time to time, no matter how successful we are. In fact, it is such a common issue that psychologists have given it a name: **imposter syndrome**. Regardless of your career field, avoiding and overcoming imposter syndrome can help you to improve your performance. It's crucial in sales to improve and maintain confidence in yourself. You can know everything about your product and possess significant experience in the field, but if potential buyers don't perceive you as confident, it will be difficult for you to succeed.

Selling with confidence does not mean that you feel 100 percent confident all the time. Rather, selling with confidence is immediately putting customers at ease and talking to them with conviction and sincerity. This is not a skill all people are born with. But it is one you can continuously refine and improve. A first step toward selling with confidence is recognizing the effects of fear on sales productivity.

The Cost of Fear in Sales

Fortune magazine has estimated that fantasy football costs U.S. employers approximately $17 billion per year in lost productivity.[8] Other research has estimated the economic losses associated with workplace depression in the U.S. to be around $210 billion.[9] Employee absenteeism costs companies around $225 billion per year.[10] These seem like pretty big numbers, right?

They *are* big numbers. But these costs are relatively tiny compared to the negative impact salesperson fear has on sales. Think about it for a minute: How much revenue is lost each year as a result of prospecting phone calls never made because of fear of rejection? What is the sum total of the business not asked for because of a fear of failure? How many sales opportunities are missed as a result of referrals and testimonials never asked for because the salesperson did not want to upset the customer? The sum total of these costs, if they could be accurately estimated, quite likely would run into the tens or perhaps even hundreds of trillions of dollars.[11]

fear An automatic emotional response, induced by a perceived threat, that causes a change in brain and organ function, as well as in behavior.

Looking deeper, **fear** is an automatic emotional response, induced by a perceived threat, that causes a change in brain and organ function as well as in behavior. Thinking in evolutionary terms, we actually might thank fear for our survival as a species. It is a powerful and primitive human emotion, linked to our fight-or-flight instincts. Fear alerts us to the presence of physical and social dangers. Salespeople are subject to the same types of fears as anyone else, though the sources and perceived consequences may be different. For example:

- Fear of rejection: *What if the customer says no?*
- Fear of failure: *What if I don't succeed in making this sale?*
- Fear of not being liked: *What if the prospect hates me?*

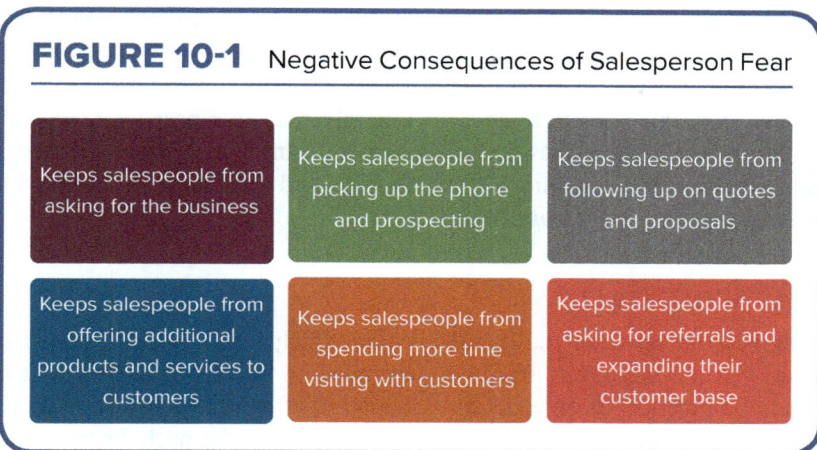

FIGURE 10-1 Negative Consequences of Salesperson Fear

- Fear of upsetting the customer: *What if they get angry? Will they start yelling at me? Will they talk badly about me to other prospects or my boss?*
- Fear of embarrassment (or shame): *What would I tell my colleagues or my family? How will others judge me?*
- Fear of the consequences associated with negative sales outcomes: *If I don't make this sale, how will it affect my income? What will happen if I don't make my quota—will I lose my job? Will I be able to provide for my family?*

In all but the fewest cases, these types of concerns are overwrought and not justified. But since they are occurring at a nonconscious level, they nonetheless can drive salesperson behaviors. Fear keeps salespeople from doing the many activities that will improve their long-term success, as detailed in Figure 10-1.

Alex Goldfayne proposes a two-step process to help salespeople overcome their fear and improve their earning potential.[12] First, identify the fear precisely. (It is nearly always one of the ones listed above.) Second, pinpoint what will happen—exactly—if the feared outcome happens:

If this customer says no, will I really lose my house? Will my wife and kids go without groceries? Will I really die?

Of course not, nothing like the imagined outcomes is very likely to happen. But unless the salesperson shines the light on both the fear and its imagined consequences, the fear will continue to drag on his or her performance:

What happens if this particular customer rejects my offer at this specific time?

Absolutely nothing. Just move on to the next prospect. And remember that the *"no"* is only temporary; you can always try again at a later date.

Improving Self-Confidence in Sales

Many research studies in the past few decades have delved into the science of confidence. Not surprisingly, evidence suggests that having confidence in oneself is positively associated with higher **task performance**—ability to perform tasks. For instance, findings from research by behavioral scientists Albert Bandura and Robert Wood reveal that higher self-confidence leads to greater overall effectiveness through enriched problem solving capabilities and improved adaptability.[13]

Confidence also enhances **social performance**—that is, how someone perceives and interacts with others. David DeSteno notes that "[C]onfidence is so alluring that we're often willing to trust anyone who expresses it, especially when money or other resources are at stake."[14] Numerous empirical studies support the idea that acting

task performance
The ability to perform tasks.

social performance
How someone perceives and interacts with others.

confidently adds more weight to what you are saying; that is, you become more believable. For instance, one study found that displaying confidence was more influential in establishing trust than was past performance.[15]

Findings from this field of research convey clear, science-based strategies that can help guide anyone who wishes to become more confident. What are some of the strategies these experts recommend for students and aspiring sales professionals to improve and maintain their confidence levels?

Self-Affirmation

A growing body of research shows *self-affirmation* helps to reduce stress and improve confidence.[16] **Self-affirmations** are verbal reminders to oneself of one's earlier achievements and competence. In order to construct a self-affirmation, you should reflect on how you have succeeded under similar circumstances in the past. Then verbally proclaim how that past success is evidence that you will perform well in an upcoming similar endeavor. By focusing the mind on personal strengths and past successes, self-affirmation produces a self-fulfilling prophecy that inspires confidence. It primes the mind to behave in a manner that is consistent with the affirmation. It's important, too, to understand what self-affirmation is not: Self-affirmation statements aren't hollow declarations that you know to be untrue. Saying nonsensical, shallow phrases like "I am full of energy" when you are tired is not a self-affirmation.

How do you come up with effective self-affirmation statements?

1. Begin by placing your name or first-person pronoun (I, me) toward the start of the phrase.
2. Phrase the goal in the present tense to bring it into reality.
3. Add a feeling to strengthen the affirmation ("I feel," "I enjoy")
4. Add a reward to reinforce what you are working toward.
5. Make sure the goal or reward is realistic, achievable, and meaningful.[17]

For example:

- *I get paid a lot of money because I'm terrific at what I love doing.*
- *I understand that life comes down to how I invest my seconds. I do the most productive things at every given moment.*
- *I have a high degree of personal integrity that leads me to put out extra effort.*
- *It's amazing how often I meet and speak with interesting new people who have an enthusiastic outlook.*
- *My well-being is in the best hands it could possibly be in: my own.*[18]

You might try out this technique the next time you are nervous about making a class presentation or have an important test!

Alter-egos

As you're approaching a task that you are dreading, such as public speaking, how do you feel? Are you nervous? Does the task make you anxious? If you are operating in a state of nervousness or uncertainty when it comes to securing sales, you'll be subconsciously alerting potential customers to your mindset, and they will go elsewhere. Now, let's flip the situation: What would happen if you felt truly confident? Would you feel more comfortable talking to people you don't know? Would that feeling lead more customers to agree to make a purchase?

Todd Herman is an expert in helping people adapt to challenging situations. His secret? He tells people to develop an **alter-ego**—an alternative or different version of oneself. Alter-egos are not just for superheroes. Creating an alter-ego allows you to

---

self-affirmations
Verbal reminders to oneself of one's earlier achievements and competence.

alter-ego
An alternative or different version of oneself.

"step into" a different persona to aid in achieving your goals. For example, imagine if you were a new salesperson suffering from a lack of confidence. What if an alternative version of you was the *best salesperson* at your company? Think about what it would feel like to be that person: How do they talk? What words do they choose? Notice their body language. What changes might you make to your own posture and language to walk like them and sound like them? Once you know how to create an alter ego that serves your mission—making sales—you can channel this person whenever you need.

Body Language and Confidence

People judge you within seconds of meeting you. It's just a fact. Your body language and facial expressions send a silent message to everyone you communicate with. In the sales context, before the salesperson has even said a word, a customer or prospect will subconsciously notice these signals and make inferences about whether that sales rep is knowledgeable and trustworthy. If a buyer doesn't sense your self-assurance and feel comfortable around you, no amount of price concession on the amazing features of your product is going to matter. This buyer is not going to make a purchase.

It is important to be aware of what your body language conveys. Stand up straight (like your mom or dad always told you). Try to curb any nervous habits you may have; fidgeting makes you appear nervous. Assess how you are approaching the prospect: Are you shuffling your feet or are you taking bold strides when you meet? During conversation, are you looking at the floor or out a window instead of making solid eye contact?

Strike a Power Pose
Though feelings influence our body movements, the opposite is also true. If you are feeling one way and you purposefully display body language that reflects a different feeling, soon you will begin to feel more like what your body is representing. Research by social psychologist Amy Cuddy suggests that our body language governs how we think and feel about ourselves. She suggests that how we hold our bodies can have an impact on our minds, changing not only how we see ourselves but others' perceptions of us as well.[19]

In nature, when animals are attempting to ward off rivals and predators they often attempt to make themselves appear larger. Likewise, according to research conducted by Cuddy and others, commanding a more expansive stance—what she calls "postural feedback"—helps people feel more powerful. **Power movements** are poses or movements that stimulate feelings of confidence. The simplest way to create power movements is to think about or observe how you naturally move when you are extremely confident. You will notice there are certain gestures or poses that you instinctively adopt. For instance, this might involve making a conscious effort to sit or stand straight, crossing your arms, or placing your hands upon your hips. Power movements are the intentional use of these movements and poses to produce greater confidence.

power movements
Poses or movements that stimulate feelings of confidence.

Dress for Success

Do the clothes make the person? Social scientists have long been fascinated with how clothing influences internal feeling states and social perceptions. Prior research suggests that wearing dressier clothes heightens feelings of confidence and authority.[20] What's more, when someone is wearing professional attire, others find him or her to be more persuasive, competent, and trustworthy.[21]

One famous social science study demonstrated how clothes shape the perceptions and behaviors of others. The researchers designed an experiment to be conducted on a busy city intersection. A trained associate of the scientists' team would repeatedly ignore a "Don't Walk" sign and cross the intersection. When the associate was dressed in casual clothing, only 4 percent of those around him would violate the "Don't Walk" sign and follow him. However, when he was dressed in formal attire, more than 20 percent of those waiting to cross followed him.[22]

Of course, the customer's environment and the nature of the sales area can dictate what constitutes appropriate attire. A rep who sells mainly to construction site managers would not dress quite the same as one who pitches C-level executives in corporate high-rises. However, regardless of setting, when salespeople dress appropriately and neatly, they exude competence. The sales rep feels more confident and prompts others to perceive them as more influential.

Belief in What You Are Selling

It doesn't matter how much you believe in yourself if you don't also believe in the products and services you are selling. You can't fake this. "What gets people to buy is a salesperson's belief in the product," said Sherrie Campbell, a psychologist who studies her field's intersection with sales. "When a salesperson genuinely believes the product will make a huge difference in the customer's life, it inspires hope. What gets people to buy is belief in the product. A good salesperson thrives on hope."[23] Genuine belief also offers another big benefit: the sales rep's genuine belief can trigger positive emotions and belief on the part of the customer.

McGraw Hill connect Connect Assignment **10-1**

Overcoming Salesperson Fear

Please complete the Connect exercise for Chapter 10 that focuses on the consequences of salesperson fear. Understanding the different types of fear typically experienced by salespeople, and strategies to help overcome fear, will help you feel more comfortable and improve your earning potential.

EMOTIONAL INTELLIGENCE IN SALES

LO 10-3 Describe how salespeople can strengthen sales emotional intelligence (sales EQ).

Here is a real-world sales scenario: Laura is a new account manager for MediFacts, Inc., a healthcare financial management software provider. She has poured her heart and soul into landing what she expects to be her most significant sale to date—to a large university-based healthcare system with headquarters in her region. She has taken the time to carefully build the business case for why the hospital should do business with her firm: She has analyzed their current situation and helped the prospect to quantify how a switch to MediFacts would result in saving the hospital money, time, and employee stress. Laura provided members of the buying unit with an impeccable list of references, each of whom glowingly lauded the quality of the software and her firm's customer service. There is even a recent trigger event—a critical service failure on the part of the hospital's current vendor. In writing up the proposal, Laura gained approval from her manager to offer special pricing incentives to help close the deal this quarter.

But, instead of signing the agreement, the hospital CFO just emailed Laura to let her know that the health system has decided to give her rival a second chance! Laura is crushed and is now second-guessing herself. Logically, it makes very little sense that the client chose to stick with the current vendor. What more could she could have possibly done to win the deal? What will she tell her sales manager?

Perspectives on Decision Making

In many businesses, top managers tend to examine business processes in *operational terms*. To squeeze out increases in efficiency, they build managerial systems that rely on strict assumptions about the rationality and motivations of suppliers, employees, and customers. From this perspective, organizational managers reason, "Customers will buy our products if our salespeople reach out to enough of them and provide decision makers with relevant facts." From this perspective, if Laura did not make the sale, it must be because she did not work hard enough or provide the client with the proper set of facts.

In reality, however, these types of approaches do not always work so well when applied to external, customer-facing processes such as sales. As in Laura's case, customers routinely make seemingly illogical choices that do not appear to be in their own or their company's best interests. They fail to deliberately weigh each bit of information they receive. As a result, the sales process often moves forward in an uneven manner and not in an organized, fact-based way.

Emotions in Decision Making

Recent advances in neuroscience, psychology, and behavioral economics suggest that people's decisions can be highly influenced by emotions and other nonconscious processes. Buyers are not robots. Even in cases in which we are convinced that our own decisions were made using rational criteria, those choices may have actually been colored by emotions and a variety of cognitive biases.

Does this mean that the various attributes of the salesperson's offering—product features, quality, delivery options and speed, customer service, new technology, convenient location, and price—do not matter? Of course not. All of these things absolutely matter. However, as access to information has grown and the pace of innovation has become more rapid, these attributes are more and more just tickets into the game. A deficiency in one of these areas might eliminate a seller from consideration. But, increasingly, product attributes are not enough to win the deal outright. These findings have important implications for those who expect to spend their careers in sales or any role that involves regular interactions with customers.

First, keep in mind that understanding how emotions contribute to decision making is critical to improving your performance, job satisfaction, income, and career advancement. People buy for *their* reasons, not *yours*. Being able to identify and influence the emotions of others as you move deals through the sales pipeline can provide you with a winning edge.

Second, the ability to regulate your own disruptive emotions is fundamental to a successful career in sales and many other managerial fields. You get a lot of "no's" in sales. It simply comes with the territory. Understanding that rejection in sales is rarely personal is what allows high-performing sales professionals to maintain optimism and confidence in the face of disappointment and adversity. The customer or prospect is not saying no to you as a person. They are saying no to your offering, and really, they are saying no to it only for the time being.

The concept of emotional intelligence is very important for high-performing sales professionals. **Emotional intelligence** (or **EQ**) is a person's ability to recognize and understand emotions in themselves and others and to use this awareness to manage their own behavior and relationships. EQ affects how we manage behavior, navigate social complexities, and make personal decisions that achieve positive results.

Emotional intelligence is distinct from **cognitive intelligence** (or **IQ**), the ability to learn. You can't predict how socially adept someone is based on how smart they are. IQ is relatively fixed from adolescence on; emotional intelligence is a skill that can be learned and improved.

emotional intelligence (EQ)
A person's ability to recognize and understand emotions in themselves and others and to use this awareness to manage their behavior and relationships.

cognitive intelligence (IQ)
The ability to learn; differs from *emotional intelligence (EQ)*.

Sales EQ

sales EQ
Emotional intelligence in sales, comprising four skill sets: self-awareness, self-management, social awareness, and relationship management.

Emotional intelligence in sales is called **sales EQ**. For our purposes, we can think of sales EQ as comprising four skill sets: self-awareness, self-management, social awareness, and relationship management. Figure 10-2 provides a graphic representation of these EQ dimensions. Self-awareness and self-management are personal competence skills. They are focused more on you individually than on your interactions with others. Your social awareness and relationship management abilities are social competence skills. They deal with your aptitude for recognizing other people's moods, emotions, and behaviors in order to enhance your relationships. More specifically:

self-awareness
The ability to perceive your own emotions and the impact they may have on your actions and on other people.

self-management
The ability to use awareness of your emotions to positively direct your behaviors.

social awareness
The ability to pick up on and understand emotions in other people.

relationship management
The ability to build rapport and maintain meaningful connections with other people.

- **Self-awareness** is the ability to perceive your own emotions and the impact they may have on your actions and on other people.
- **Self-management** is your ability to use awareness of your emotions to positively direct your behaviors. This means effectively managing your emotional reactions to situations and to people.
- **Social awareness** is your ability to pick up on and understand emotions in other people. This often means perceiving what other people are thinking and feeling, even if you do not feel the same way.
- **Relationship management** involves your ability to build rapport and maintain meaningful connections with other people.

What Can Salespeople Do to Strengthen Sales EQ?

Salespeople with high sales EQ enjoy key advantages:

- High-EQ sellers are always aware of their own emotional state. They know how to cover up emotions such as anxiety, irritation, or distraction that might turn off customers.
- High EQ also is associated with greater patience and the ability to delay gratification. This helps salespeople to emotionally manage the inherent uncertainties and frustrations often associated with buyers' decision-making processes.
- In comparison with low-EQ sellers, high-EQ sellers are more motivated to perform prospecting activities, even when they know it will take time to sign a new deal.
- They *remain positive* even in the face of repeated rejection. They do not take rejections personally, and they consistently avoid harboring negative emotions.

High-EQ sales professionals are not only better able to discern customers' emotional states, they also possess the ability to adapt and align their own emotional state in response. For instance, they can fine-tune their pitches in order to address emotion-based customer concerns. By understanding what their customers feel, need, and expect, high-EQ salespeople are superior in using relational sales approaches and *establishing strong interpersonal connections* with their clients and prospects.

Because high sales EQ pays off in the long run, we will now dive a bit deeper into each of the four skill sets of sales EQ, including ideas for improving your abilities and performance in each area.

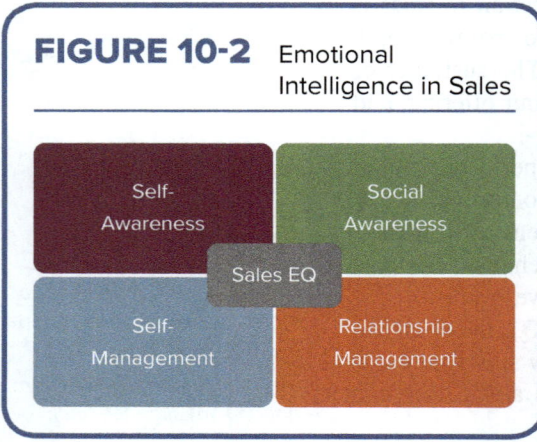

FIGURE 10-2 Emotional Intelligence in Sales

Self-Awareness *Self-awareness* is the ability to perceive one's own emotions and the impact they may have on your actions and on other people. It is a foundational skill: When you have it, self-awareness makes the other emotional intelligence skills much easier to use. Self-aware salespeople are better able to manage the time and energy around their emotional states. By being emotionally aware, they are less likely to anger or annoy a potential customer with their own negative emotions. They also bounce back from disappointment and rejection faster than sales reps who ignore or are unaware of their negative feelings.

Self-awareness is not about discovering deep, dark secrets or hidden desires. Rather, it comes from an honest assessment and understanding of who you are, what you do well, and what your motivations are. The only way to really understand your own emotions and emotional tendencies is to spend enough time in reflection so you can figure out where they come from and why they are there.

An interesting and surprising thing about self-awareness is that just thinking about being more self-aware helps you to strengthen this skill. Getting in touch with your emotions on a deeper level is hard work and can be unsettling. You begin noticing things about yourself—positive as well as negative things that you might not have been previously aware of. But remember, emotions serve an evolutionary purpose; they are designed to help us navigate and survive the physical and social worlds that surround us. Suppress the urge to label your emotions as good or bad. Don't worry about whether you should or shouldn't be feeling them. By letting the emotion run its course, you can begin to better understand its root causes.

It is also important to reflect on the ripple effects of emotions. To imagine that their effects are momentary and limited to you alone is to do yourself a grave disservice. **Emotional contagion** is a psychological phenomenon that occurs when one person's emotions and related behaviors directly trigger similar emotions and behaviors in other people. The key to understanding these contagion effects is to closely watch the immediate effects of your emotions on other people and then use that information to help guide your understanding of the long-term effects of unleashing the emotion. The more you understand how your emotions have ripple effects, the better equipped you will be in choosing the types of ripples you wish to unleash.

emotional contagion
Psychological phenomenon when one person's emotions and related behaviors directly trigger similar emotions and behaviors in other people.

Self-Management Sales professionals must be able to maintain control in the face of daily events that can trigger negative feelings. We previously touched on the devastating impact of fear on sales performance. However, to attain long-term success in the profession, sales reps must regularly face and overcome a long list of other disruptive emotions, including:

- Fear
- Anger
- Uncertainty
- Insecurity
- Impatience
- Detachment
- Arrogance
- Delusion
- Overconfidence
- Disappointment

Regulating disruptive emotions is not easy—in sales or in your personal life. Have you ever said, perhaps to a friend or loved one, something that you regretted the moment it left your lips? It has happened to all of us. Just as soon as you let down your guard—you are feeling tense, tired, or hungry—your emotions can run amok at your own expense. Gaining emotional self-control begins with emotional self-awareness. Over and above this, however, several techniques can help "tame the savage beast" that is inside each of us.

First, it helps to understand the situations, words, and types of people that always seem to set you off. These *emotional triggers*, like getting cut off in traffic or dealing with an obnoxious waiter, are mostly unavoidable. Some are self-inflicted, such as walking into a potentially stressful situation when you are already on the verge of mental exhaustion. Still others are simply a regular part of the sales routine, such as prospecting calls, making presentations, and dealing with upset customers. Knowing your triggers makes it easier to avoid, anticipate, plan for, and respond to them appropriately.

Second, if you know that you will be facing a situation that triggers disruptive emotions, advance preparation and practice can help bring a sense of calmness and control. For instance, imagine you are starting to feel anxious about an upcoming meeting with a top decision maker while your manager observes. You can help ease those nerves by spending extra time researching the client, placing yourself in the client's shoes, and drawing up a list of the questions they might ask. In addition, you might even role-play the sales conversation with a peer or sales manager, making sure to include surprises and worst-case scenarios.

L.E.MORMILE/Shutterstock

A third approach involves *positive visualization,* a technique used by many elite-level athletes, such as golfer Jason Day. This approach involves walking through each step of the upcoming sales call in your mind's eye. Imagine what you will ask and what you will say in response to the prospect's questions. Focus on how you feel when you are confident. Visualize the sales conversation reaching a successful conclusion. Doing this over and over in your head will help to cast out the dark feelings and thoughts that induce failure.

The ability to address and manage disruptive emotions minimizes self-defeating behaviors. These behaviors can derail sales conversations, cloud situational awareness, sap motivation, promote irrational decision-making and misjudgments, and rationalize procrastination. No matter what you sell, no matter how simple or complex the buying decision, no matter how short or long the buying cycle, excellence in sales requires the ability to manage your own disruptive emotions. Only when you can do so will you be able to effectively recognize and influence the emotions of others.

Social Awareness
Social awareness is the ability to pick up on and understand emotions in other people. This often means perceiving what others are thinking and feeling, even if you don't agree with them. It's easy to get caught up in your own emotions and needs and forget the perspective of the other party. Tuning in to others' emotions as you interact with them helps you to get a more accurate view of your surroundings. Thus, social awareness helps reps who have high sales EQ to stay focused on the prospect and absorb important information that leads to closing the sale.

Better listening and observational skills are critical to building greater social awareness. To listen well, we need to stop talking. We have to learn to hit "pause" on the inner monologue and stop thinking about what we are going to say next. We need to not anticipate the point the other party is about to make.

Once you consciously attempt to build your social-awareness skills, you will find yourself listening and observing people in all kinds of situations. It could be observing someone from a distance as you wait for food at a quick-service restaurant. Or it could be someone you are right in the middle of a conversation with. Not only will you gather meaning of the words they are saying but you will also start to pick up on emotional cues revealed through their tone of voice, body language, and facial expressions. A good practice technique is to intently watch a movie or TV show, paying close attention to character interactions, relationships, and conflicts. Look for clues in the body language, words, and tone of the actors that might reveal how each character is feeling. As the plot unwinds, how do these cues signal changes in the characters' emotional state of mind?

Relationship Management In sales, relationships typically matter a lot more than actual products or services do. Relationships based on emotional connections have the strongest bonds. *Relationship management* is the ability to build rapport and maintain meaningful connections in order to successfully manage interactions. This helps ensure clear communication and effective conflict resolution. Relationship management capability helps sales professionals tap into the first three emotional intelligence skills (self-awareness, self-management, and social awareness) to build strong connections with customers. People with high relationship-management skills may not see eye to eye with everybody they meet. However, they recognize the benefits of connecting with many different people and building stronger bonds with them over time.

Empathy: Stepping into Customers' Shoes

Sales reps who *can establish strong emotional connections* with customers are better at understanding what customers feel, need, and expect. Without empathy, however, building rapport and nurturing these types of authentic relationships with peers and clients is extremely difficult. **Empathy** is the ability to understand and identify with others' feelings and motivations—to step into someone else's shoes and experience emotions from his or her perspective. Even though we may not have personally experienced what another person is going through, we acknowledge the situation (good or bad) and recognize that there are feelings and emotions attached to it. This doesn't mean that we have to share those emotions with them; we just need to "get where they're coming from."[24] While similar in some respects, empathy is distinct from *sympathy*—an entering into or feeling sorry about someone else's trouble, grief, or misfortune.

empathy
The ability to understand and identify with others' feelings, motivations, and emotions from their perspective.

A rep who has high sales EQ actually strives to see things from the buyer's perspective. Doing so enables the rep to build trust and gain a deeper understanding of customers' goals, priorities, and pain points. In turn, the rep is better able to use this information to develop tailored solutions that squarely match customers' needs and meet their expectations.

How can salespeople become more empathetic with respect to their customers? Research suggests that you might find the answer, at least in part, by reading a good book—but not just any book. Reading literary fiction, specifically, has been shown to improve empathy.[25] These findings come from a fascinating series of studies led by David Kidd and Emanuele Castano, social psychologists at The New School in New York City.[26] In the studies, participants were split into different reading groups based on genre: popular fiction, literary fiction, nonfiction, or nothing. They then were given a test to infer and understand other people's emotions. When the participants read nothing, non-fiction, or popular fiction, their results were unimpressive. But reading literary fiction led to big increases in the reader's ability to empathize. Why is this? Literary fiction books tend to look into the psychological complexities of characters. As these interesting, complex characters drive the story, we as readers become emotionally involved in their desires and motivations. It turns out that when it comes to improving empathy, it's perfectly fine to practice on fictional characters.

> **Connect Assignment 10-2**
>
> **Emotional Intelligence**
>
> Please complete the Connect exercise for Chapter 10, which focuses on emotional intelligence. Strengthening your sales EQ will help you discern customers' emotional states and develop the ability to adapt and align your emotional state in response.

TIME MANAGEMENT

LO 10-4 List tools and techniques to improve time management in sales.

time management How people schedule and organize their time for different activities.

We've all heard the saying that "Time is money." This is especially true for people who make a living in sales. **Time management** refers to how people schedule and organize their time for different activities. Most managers and sale trainers would agree that it is one of the most important skills for sales professionals. Yet recent research shows that only 22 percent of sales reps use any sort of time management methodology.[27] The absence of proper time-management skills is the most common pitfall for early-career salespeople—they are more prone to mistake *looking busy* with *being productive*. When you're selling, your time is your most valuable asset. You must protect it vigilantly, even if it means learning to do business differently. In many cases, this simply means shifting time spent doing administrative work to nonselling hours and referring requests for customer service to individuals who work on the customer-service team.

Salespeople can increase their productivity in only one of two ways: by improving their sales skills, or by spending more time in front of their customers in selling situations. Improving sales knowledge and business acumen can take time—sometimes even years—to develop. Therefore, the payoff on this type of investment can be lengthy. However, by spending more time in front of more customers, salespeople can make immediate improvements to their sales pipeline and quickly improve their sales performance.

While this makes intuitive sense, it is most certainly easier said than done. Time management is one of the most challenging disciplines for most of us to master. But it is a skill that is particularly critical for sales professionals. After all, there are only so many business hours in a day and selling days in a year. In fact, sales expert Mark Hunter says that effective time management is the *one thing* that sets great salespeople apart from the average. According to Hunter, great salespeople never allow a day to end without knowing how they are going to use the next day effectively. They don't just say they're going to prospect the next day. They actually build their list, develop their questions, and get everything in place to make sure it happens. Average salespeople, on the other hand, are far too willing to wait to see how time evolves to determine whether they can get something done.[28]

There are many different tools and techniques to help you get more done in less time. What are some of the best time-management tips employed by high-performing sales professionals? Read on.

Work from a List

Nearly every high-performing sales professional works from a daily master list. Keeping a structured and thought-out list sounds simple enough. But it can be surprising how many people fail to use lists at all, never mind use them effectively. When approached with discipline, a list is one of the most powerful techniques for maximizing productivity and helping achieve your goals. A common guideline is that you will increase your efficiency by 25 percent on the very first day you start using a list. This means you will have two extra hours of productive time in an eight-hour workday if, before you start work, you make a list of everything you have to do.[29]

To create your daily list:

- Begin by writing down every single task that you intend to complete over the course of the day. If some of the tasks are large and complex, break out the first step in the task and write it down along with the larger task.
- Next, organize the activities by order of importance, assigning them into four or five categories. If you find that too many tasks have a high priority, run through the list again and demote the less important ones. Think of the items in terms of how they contribute to closing potential sales: which ones will produce the highest level of results?
- Now, rewrite the list, placing them in order of significance.

Once your daily list is organized in this manner, it serves as a blueprint that guides your day in the most effective and efficient way.[30]

Prioritize Activities and Accounts

Sales reps almost always have several important tasks simultaneously competing for their attention. How should they prioritize time with each prospect and other sales activities in order to maximize their time? After all, allotting time to one customer over another could be the difference between closing a million dollar deal and having the door closed on you. Spending a certain amount of time on one group of activities could set up a rep for a record week; concentrating on something else might launch you down the path to a slump.

For most salespeople, 80 percent of sales revenue comes from 20 percent of the leads they're working on. It logically follows that reps should focus most of their attention on the 20 percent of leads that generate 80 percent of the results. Recognizing those "golden" leads is the trick. A good time-management tip is for the sales rep to start the day by looking at the to-do list and asking two questions:

- What can I get done today that will have the biggest impact on increasing my pipeline?
- What can I get done today that will have the biggest impact on moving my best targets closer to a decision?

Once this is done, the rep should focus on those activities first.[31]

Pomodoro Technique
A time-chunking method that uses a timer to break down work into intervals, traditionally 25 minutes in length, separated by short breaks.

"Time-Chunk": Using the Pomodoro Technique

The **Pomodoro Technique** is a time-chunking method that uses a timer to break down work into intervals, traditionally 25 minutes in length, separated by short breaks. Introduced by productivity consultant Francesco Cirillo as a free e-book in 2006, the Pomodoro Technique has emerged as one of the more popular time-management "life hacks."[32] The process is simple: For every project throughout the day, you budget your time into short increments and take breaks periodically. You work for 25 minutes, then take a 5-minute break. Each 30-minute interval

aroax/Getty Images

is known as a "Pomodoro," from the Italian word for "tomato" and named after the tomato-shaped kitchen timer that Cirillo used as a university student. Every time you finish a Pomodoro, you mark your progress with an "X." After four Pomodoros have passed (100 minutes of work time with 15 minutes of break time), you take a longer 20- to 30-minute break, then begin the next task.

The Pomodoro Technique improves focus, motivation, and personal productivity by breaking down larger tasks into separate "time-boxes." A Pomodoro cannot be interrupted—it marks 25 minutes of pure work. It is indivisible; there is no such thing as half a Pomodoro. The length of one Pomodoro (25 minutes plus a 5-minute break) is just short enough for people to resist the temptation to check their email or social media accounts. If a Pomodoro is interrupted by something or someone, that Pomodoro is considered void, as if it had never been set; then you just make a fresh start with a new Pomodoro. Today, numerous Pomodoro-themed mobile apps are available. However, Cirillo encourages a low-tech approach, using a mechanical timer, paper, and pencil. The physical act of winding the timer confirms the user's determination to start the task; the ticking of the timer externalizes the desire to complete the task; the ringing announces a break.

Automate Administrative Tasks

To maximize your selling time, look for ways to automate as many of your nonselling activities as possible. Saving a few minutes here and there will quickly add up. As an added benefit, you can direct more energy toward activities that are actually challenging, such as giving demos or answering tough questions.

A few examples:

- Many CRM systems let you make your customer-contact calls from within the software, eliminating the need to log in information manually with each conversation.
- HubSpot Meetings is a valuable CRM add-in that lets buyers book open slots on your calendar instantly, putting an end to long email chains of *"What about X time?" "Sorry, I'm busy. . . . What about Y?"*
- PandaDoc is a good tool for reps who send sales collateral and quotes. It automatically pulls in data from your CRM so you don't have to tediously copy and paste key details. You can send an error-free, personalized, professional-looking proposal in a few clicks.
- Route planning software can help you figure out the most efficient way to travel between prospects' offices. With it you'll never have to manually plan your route again.
- Todoist, a to-do list app, uses artificial intelligence to learn your personal productivity habits and schedule your overdue tasks accordingly.[33]

Create Email Templates
Another way to automate administrative tasks is to create email templates. It's vastly inefficient to write a brand-new email every time you contact a prospect. Of course you should tailor each message to the individual and his or her situation. But you'll save a huge amount of time if you start with a template rather than a blank slate. Look through your "Sent" folder to find the emails you send repeatedly. That doesn't include just outreach emails. You should also make templates for following up, scheduling meetings, recapping calls, and so forth.

Stop Multitasking

The effectiveness of multitasking is a myth! You may think you're being more productive, but studies have shown that multitasking actually slows you down. When you think you're multitasking, your brain is actually darting from one task to another in rapid succession. Switching between tasks dilutes focus and slows people down because their brains have to adjust to each task. Thus, multitasking hurts your efficiency and performance.

Thinking about this from a sales perspective, different tasks engage different mental muscles. For instance, actually giving a demo requires a much different mindset and level of focus than does conducting pre-call preparation and planning. Grouping similar tasks together leads to greater productivity and efficiency. For example:

- Block off a specific amount of time to make cold calls each day.
- Return calls at the same time each day rather than continually checking your voicemail all day long.
- Designate an hour or two in the afternoon for prospecting for the following day. Once the time is up, move on to another task.

Scheduling activities this way improves your workflow. When you concentrate on one activity at a time, you become faster, better at the task, and more accurate.[34]

Minimize Distractions

Jennifer H. Tatara

Focus and attention are hot commodities these days. When you need to complete important or complex tasks, it's important to set aside time to shut yourself away physically. Getting away from ringing phones, other people, and other distractions will help you concentrate. You will experience not only a physical benefit but a mental one too, helping you to focus. Remember to turn off your phone so you're not interrupted that way either.

While you are at it, stop checking your email so much! The average professional spends 28 hours a week checking email—15 times each day—according to the *International Journal of Communications*.[35] Of course, email is an integral part of sales reps' ability to communicate with and sell to prospects, but much time is spent checking for replies. It may be beneficial to turn off email notifications, which will decrease distraction when you are prospecting and reporting.

Of course, it's okay to occasionally take a break and check Twitter or the latest headlines on the Web. However, its important to realize that smartphones and many social media apps are designed to be addictive, in much the same way as slot machines and other gambling devices. With our ever-present smartphones, it can be all too easy to jump from your work email to Instagram. The next thing you know, you've wasted 25 minutes scrolling through your feed. Don't let cute kittens kill your sales. While there is a time and place for social media in our professional and personal lives, we may not even realize that we're distracted or recognize the consequences of that distraction: anxiety, low self-esteem, lack of confidence, and loss of motivation or creative inspiration.

Connect Assignment 10-3

Time Management

Please complete the Connect exercise for Chapter 10 that focuses on time management. Using strategies to improve your time-management skills will help you be more efficient at every stage of your career and improve your sales productivity.

Today's Professional Perspective ... because everyone is a salesperson

Hope Richardson
VIP-Owner Concierge
Vistana Signature Experiences, Marriott Vacations Worldwide

Hope Richardson

Describe your job. I work for Marriott Vacations Worldwide at a resort in Orlando, Florida, in the vacation-ownership segment. As a VIP-Owner Concierge, I work directly with owners pre-arrival and during their stay at the resort. Every two weeks, I am assigned a list of owners who will be arriving to the property. I contact them pre-arrival and retrieve their villa requests, estimated arrival time, number of room keys, and need for tickets to attractions—all to ensure they have a smooth check-in at the resort. The arriving owners are considered VIPs and receive a separate check-in area on property, with complimentary refreshments, while they wait for their unit to be ready.

Upon check-in, I go over their requests and property details as well as surrounding attraction information. The goal is to make them feel "at home" when they arrive. I share information to get them excited about everything going on with the company and their ownership, and I then book them for an owner's update/timeshare sales presentation while they are on property. Although this seems easy, my job is very challenging. Customer service is key to building trust with the owners and setting up a presentation for them.

How did you get your job? Five years ago, in my marketing class, a guest speaker came to talk about her career and how college set her up for success. She worked for Wyndham Vacation Ownership. She helped me get a few interviews with Wyndham in Orlando, and I was hired for an entry-level guest-service position. Shortly after, I moved into the sales and marketing role at one of the resorts. After a few years, I decided it was time to grow in my career, and my manager told me about this amazing company and position that was about to open. The people I interviewed loved my personality and experience and thought I would be a great fit for this role. In return, I was excited to have a job in which I go above and beyond for the guests and help drive the vacation-ownership industry from the frontline.

What has been most important in making you successful at your job? What has made me successful at my job is keeping a positive mindset. In any customer-service role, you have a lot of different personalities to deal with and very challenging situations to handle. Also, my position is a performance-based job. This means that if you do not perform and meet monthly standards and capture rates, you will not keep your job long. That's a good incentive to keep working my best every day.

What advice would you give future graduates about a career in sales? My advice to future graduates is to work hard, love what you do, and do it well. Nine times out of ten, if you are passionate about what you do, then it's not a "job." Do not rush into a position because it is expected of you. Your parents, grandparents, teachers, or anyone else are not the ones who have to show up every day—it's your life and your happiness. Through hard work and desire, you will achieve success. And please . . . vacation! I say that not just because I work for a company that sells the dream. Really, you have to take time off to give your mind, body, and spirit a break. This is one of the driving factors of health and stability in any industry.

What is the most important characteristic of a great salesperson? Great salespeople have to provide great customer service but also be strong and persuasive. After every no, you will finally get that "yes," and finding the stamina to keep a positive mind is critical. I think that is the best way great salespeople keep focused on their end goal—knowing that you lose some, but you also win some.

CHAPTER SUMMARY

LO 10-1 Explain the characteristics of grit in salespeople and sales organizations.

Grit is a personality trait of perseverance and passion for long-term goals. Perseverance in sales is maintaining realistic optimism while not letting failures slow you down. Sales managers see grit as a trait to look for in new hires.

A *growth mindset*— the belief that traits can change over time—makes a huge impact on long-term results. People who take failure as an opportunity to learn and grow do much better at sales in the long run. Improving performance requires practice, practice, and more practice. The *10,000-hour rule* suggests that 10,000 hours of practice time is what is needed to become a world-class performer. Gritty people don't merely have jobs—they have a calling and a passion for what they do.

LO 10-2 List strategies for overcoming fears and building self-confidence in sales.

Psychologists call the tendency to doubt yourself or your abilities *imposter syndrome*. Salespeople are subject to the same types of fears as anyone else, though the sources and perceived consequences may be different. Fear keeps salespeople from doing many of the activities that will improve their long-term success. Confidence enhances both task performance and social performance.

The ability to sell with confidence is a skill you can continuously refine and improve. Experts recommend various strategies to improve and maintain confidence: *Self-affirmations*—verbal reminders of one's earlier achievements and competence—help to reduce stress and improve confidence. Creating an *alter-ego* allows you to "step into" a different version of yourself to aid in achieving your goals. Confident body language and *power movements* will convey signals that a sales rep is knowledgeable and trustworthy. Research suggests that *dressing for success*, as appropriate for the sales setting, heightens feelings of confidence and authority. Finally, genuinely *believing in what you are selling* can trigger positive emotions and belief on the part of the customer.

LO 10-3 Describe how salespeople can strengthen sales emotional intelligence (sales EQ).

Emotional intelligence (EQ) is one's ability to recognize and understand emotions in oneself and in others, and to use this awareness to manage one's behavior and relationships. It is distinct from *cognitive intelligence (IQ)*, one's ability to learn. Cognitive intelligence is relatively fixed from adolescence on; emotional intelligence is a skill that can be learned and improved. Emotional intelligence in sales is called *sales EQ*.

Sales EQ comprises four skills sets: (1) *Self-awareness* comes from an honest assessment and understanding of who you are, what you do well, and what your motivations are. Just thinking about being more self-aware helps strengthen this skill. Also, it is important to reflect on *emotional contagion*—the ripple effects of one's emotions. (2) *Self-management* involves regularly facing and overcoming disruptive emotions. Understanding one's *emotional triggers* is important in maintaining self-control. *Positive visualization* can also help. (3) *Social awareness* is the ability to pick up on and understand emotions in other people. Better listening and observational skills are critical to building greater social awareness. (4) *Relationship management* is the ability to build rapport and maintain meaningful connections in order to successfully manage interactions. This is difficult to do without *empathy*—the ability to step into someone else's shoes and experience emotions from their perspective.

LO 10-4 List tools and techniques to improve time management in sales.

One of the most important skills for sales professionals is *time management*—how people schedule and organize their time for different activities. By spending more time in front of more customers, salespeople can make immediate improvements to their sales pipeline and quickly improve their sales performance.

High-performing sales professionals use various time-management tools and techniques: They work from a daily master list. They prioritize activities and accounts. Some use the *Pomodoro Technique*, a time-chunking method that improves focus, motivation, and personal productivity by breaking down larger tasks into separate (typically 25-minute) "time-boxes." Others automate administrative tasks, including use of email templates. Grouping similar tasks together, instead of trying to multitask, leads to greater productivity and efficiency. Getting away from ringing phones, other people, and distractions also will help you concentrate.

KEY TERMS

extroverts (p. 218)
introverts (p. 218)
grit (p. 218)
fixed mindset (p. 219)
growth mindset (p. 219)
10,000-hour rule (p. 219)
imposter syndrome (p. 220)
fear (p. 220)
task performance (p. 221)
social performance (p. 221)
self-affirmations (p. 222)
alter-ego (p. 222)
power movements (p. 223)
emotional intelligence (EQ) (p. 225)
cognitive intelligence (IQ) (p. 225)
sales EQ (p. 226)
self-awareness (p. 226)
self-management (p. 226)
social awareness (p. 226)
relationship management (p. 226)
emotional contagion (p. 227)
empathy (p. 229)
time management (p. 230)
Pomodoro technique (p. 231)

DISCUSSION QUESTIONS

1. What is grit? Why is having grit especially important to success in a sales career?
2. List one or two of your long-term professional or personal goals. What are some ways you can strengthen your grit in order to help you achieve those outcomes?
3. List some of the implications of imposter syndrome and the emotion of fear for salesperson performance.
4. Think about an upcoming event that is causing you anxiety. For instance, perhaps you have a job or internship interview coming up or a sales role-play that you are preparing for. Based on the technique described in the chapter, create a self-affirmation statement that can help you attain greater confidence.
5. Go to the TED Talks website (https://www.ted.com/talks) and randomly select a recently released presentation, one that you have not previously seen. Watch only the first 10 seconds, taking note of the speaker's nonverbal cues such as posture, body movements, facial expression, eye contact, and vocal tone (e.g. pitch, loudness, rate of speech). Compared to other videos released at the same time or on similar topics, do you think this video is likely to attract a lot more views, shares, and positive comments? Return a few weeks later to test your prediction.
6. Use the internet to look up video footage of experts (e.g., athletes, musicians, actors) conducting a task with which you are highly familiar and at which they excel. Closely watch their body language as they complete the performance. Create a list of some of the nonverbal cues you notice.
7. Explain the difference between emotional intelligence (EQ) and cognitive intelligence (IQ).
8. In relation to the concept of emotional intelligence (EQ), what is self-awareness? Why do you think that many EQ experts believe that greater self-awareness is foundational to improving your self-management, self-awareness, and relationship management abilities?
9. Spend some time watching a rerun of one of your favorite television shows, an episode that you may have enjoyed before. This time, though, carefully monitor and write down all the nonverbal behaviors you observe in the interactions between the characters. How do nonverbal cues such as the actors' body language, expressions, choice of words, and tone of voice contribute to the successful development of the plot?
10. What is empathy? How does it differ from sympathy? Why is empathy critical in building and maintaining long-term business and personal relationships?
11. Explain why effective time management is especially important for sales professionals.

ETHICAL CHALLENGE

As noted in this chapter, customers are not robots. They are human beings, just like you and me. Although customers may attempt to be rational in their decision making, their emotions can and do play a role. It is only natural and is to be expected. Thus it is important for salespeople to both possess and display emotional intelligence in their interactions with customers.

As an example, in his previous life as a salesperson, one of the authors (John Hansen) was calling on a regional retail chain. When working with this retailer, he would regularly call on the buyer for the chain as well as the store managers who managed each of the five stores within the chain. There existed a delicate relationship between the store managers and the buyer. More bluntly, the store managers did not like the buyer, and the feeling was mutual. There was no love lost between these individuals. The store managers believed that the buyer, who was younger, was too analytical in his decision making. They felt that he was disregarding the human element in these decisions, and they did not agree with many of his decisions.

On the other hand, the buyer felt that the older store managers were stuck in their antiquated ways. With the incredible level of data available, he saw no reason to rely on a "gut-feel" when making decisions about what products to stock. The store managers vehemently disagreed, and simmering conflict would erupt on a regular basis.

In talking with the buyer one day, the rep asked what the buyer's goals for the organization were and what he, the salesperson, could do to help make the buyer more successful in his role. The buyer's response was quite direct: "I want you to help me win. I have to show that my approach to the business is right and that the store managers are wrong. Whatever that requires, that is what I need." In addition to recognizing the strong emotional response just received, the salesperson immediately felt a sense of discomfort over the fact that he now sat squarely in the middle of this dispute between the buyer and store managers.

Questions

When considering these questions, remember that, as a salesperson, you must develop and maintain strong relationships with *all* individuals who may ultimately have a say in purchase decisions within the account (i.e., the buyer and store managers alike).

1. From an ethical perspective, how would you respond to the buyer?
2. Would you consider it unethical to work with the buyer as he requested, with the sole intention of proving him right and the store managers wrong?

ROLE PLAY

As shown in the Ethical Challenge, customers' emotions not only can play an important role in their decision making but also can, on occasion, place salespeople in challenging situations. Salespeople must be able to respond appropriately in these situations. As an extension of the Ethical Challenge above, this role play will give you an opportunity to practice a response to a customer's emotions.

For the role play, the class should be divided into teams of three. Each student within each team should first develop an emotional response that he or she will use when acting as a buyer. You could use an emotional response similar to the one discussed in the Ethical Challenge *("I want you to help me win")*. Or you could come up with a different emotional response, such as:

> "I am willing to make a purchase only if I receive some sort of personal kick back (i.e., something of personal value) as an incentive for making the purchase."

For each of the role plays, one student should act as the seller, another should act as the customer, and the third should critique the selling student's response to the emotional response. Students should transition roles for each successive role play.

SALES PRESENTATION

For the Connect assignment in Chapter 10, students will practice presentation skills on the topic of why a new college student should take a professional selling course. In a three- to five-minute presentation, explain why a student should consider a career in sales and what important skills students can learn from a professional selling course. Be sure to include the things that you found most beneficial from this course and what you would most want new students to know about professional selling.

CAREER TIPS

Shane Hunt

George D. Deitz

John Hansen

Shane Hunt, George Deitz, and John Hansen, *Text Authors*

Adjusting to Life after College

And now, a final word from your authors: "Be quick. Don't hurry." This quote from legendary UCLA college basketball coach John Wooden is important for you to think about as you go through your career journey in a digital and social world. Similar to the salespeople and organizations discussed in this chapter and throughout the text, you need to *be quick* as a new graduate: You need to quickly learn that if you don't think, solve problems, and work hard, your career will show it. We have seen countless new graduates waste their first year or two after graduation, ruin their personal brand, and incur lots of debt. You must be quick in adjusting from the protective structure of school to the self-accountability of professional life, especially in sales. You are responsible for your actions. As long as you embrace that, you can have a fulfilling career and life.

But *don't try to hurry through life*, taking the shortest route you can find. Despite what anyone may have told you, your college degree does not entitle you to anything. It doesn't guarantee you a job, a career, or the life you want. Your ability to succeed in your career is *directly tied* to your ability to solve problems for organizations and customers. There are no Scantron tests or study guides as you begin your career. You will not be judged by whether you make a 91 percent or a 78 percent. Rather, your value will be measured by how much better your organization is because you are there. Be quick to engage in the incredible experience of building a career and a life. But don't be in such a hurry that you miss out on the skills, relationships, and experiences that will give you the best memories and the highest-quality career going forward.

Be quick to find something you are passionate about. We love being marketing and sales professors, and we have loved creating the materials you have read and engaged with this semester. Our lives are better in every way because we love what we do. Your career will consume over half of your life; if you are doing something you hate, we doubt that the money you make from it will ever be enough. Once you find the career you are passionate about, don't hurry, because the best, most meaningful parts of your career are ahead. Good luck to you!

CHAPTER ENDNOTES

1. A. Duckworth, *Grit: The Power of Passion and Perseverance, vol. 234* (New York: Scribner, 2016).
2. A. Duckworth and J. J. Gross, "Self-control and grit: Related but separable determinants of success," *Current Directions in Psychological Science* 23, no. 5 (2014): 319–325.
3. Dunn, Jule. (2016). Grit is the Ultimate Sales Productivity Secret, accessed at https://leveleleven.com/2016/10/grit-ultimate-sales-productivity-secret/.
4. Makela, Ray. (2015). Sales Grit: Its What to Look for in an Employee, accessed at https://www.salesreadinessgroup.com/blog/sales-grit-its-what-to-look-for-in-an-employee.
5. C. S. Dweck, *Mindset: The new psychology of success* (New York: Random House Digital, 2008).
6. Frost, Aja. (2018). Grit: The Ultimate Guide for Salespeople, accessed at https://blog.hubspot.com/sales/grit.
7. A. Ericsson and R. Pool, *Peak: Secrets from the New Science of Expertise* (New York: Houghton Mifflin Harcourt, 2016).
8. Darrow, Barb. (2016). Employers pay the Real Cost of Fantasy Football, accessed at https://fortune.com/2016/08/30/why-fantasy-football-costs-money/.
9. Kaiser Health News. (2015). Depression Costs Employers $210 Billion, accessed at https://www.psychcongress.com/news-item/depression-costs-employers-210-billion.
10. Stinson, Claire. (2015). Worker Illness and Injury Costs U.S. Employers $225.8 Billion Annually, accessed at https://www.cdcfoundation.org/pr/2015/worker-illness-and-injury-costs-us-employers-225-billion-annually.
11. Goldfayn, Alex. (2017). The Massive Cost of Fear in Sales, accessed at https://goldfayn.com/massive-cost-fear-sales/.

12. A. Goldfayn, *Selling Boldly: Applying the New Science of Positive Psychology to Dramatically Increase Your Confidence, Happiness, and Sales* (Hoboken, N. J.: John Wiley & Sons, 2015).
13. R. E. Wood and A. Bandura, "Impact of conceptions of ability on self-regulatory mechanisms and complex decision making," *Journal of Personality and Social Psychology* 56 (1989): 407–415.
14. D. DeSteno, "Who can you trust?" *Harvard Business Review* 92, no. 3 (2014): 112–115.
15. P. Aldhous, "Humans prefer cockiness to expertise," *New Scientist* 2711 (2009): 15.
16. S. K. Kang, A. D. Galinsky, L. J. Kray, and A. Shirako, "Power affects performance when the pressure is on: Evidence for low-power threat and high-power lift," *Personality and Social Psychology Bulletin* 41, no. 5 (2015): 726–735.
17. Guptha, Leena. (2017). To Affirm or Not Affirm?, accessed at https://www.psychologytoday.com/us/blog/embodied-wellness/201704/affirm-or-not-affirm.
18. Hopkins, Tom. (2015). 13 Self Instructions for Sales Success, accessed at http://www.tomhopkins.com/blog/motivation-overcoming-rejection/13-self-instructions-for-sales-success.
19. A. J. Cuddy, S. J. Schultz, and N. E. Fosse, "P-curving a more comprehensive body of research on postural feedback reveals clear evidential value for power-posing effects: Reply to Simmons and Simonsohn," *Psychological Science* 29, no. 4 (2017): 656–666.
20. M. L. Slepian, S. N. Ferber, J. M. Gold, and A. M. Rutchick, "The cognitive consequences of formal clothing," *Social Psychological and Personality Science* 6, no. 6 (2015): 661–668.
21. S. U. Rehman, P. J. Nietert, D. W. Cope, and A. O. Kilpatrick, "What to wear today? Effect of doctor's attire on the trust and confidence of patients," *The American Journal of Medicine* 118, no. 11 (2005): 1279–1286.
22. Hoffeld, David. (2016). *The Science of Selling: Proven Strategies to Make Your Pitch, Influence Decisions, and Close the Deal*. Penguin.
23. Campbell, Sherrie. (2017). The 10 Traits Every Good Salesperson Has in Common, accessed at https://www.entrepreneur.com/article/296789.
24. Mallory, Alan. (2018). Emotional Intelligence: Understanding the Role of Empathy and Social Skills, accessed at https://www.linkedin.com/pulse/emotional-intelligence-understanding-role-empathy-social-alan-mallory/.
25. Six Seconds: The Emotional Intelligence Network. (2017). How to Increase Your Empathy: 5 Practical Tips to Increase Your Empathy in any Situation, accessed at https://www.6seconds.org/2017/07/20/how-to-increase-your-empathy/
26. D. C. Kidd and E. Castano, "Reading literary fiction improves theory of mind," *Science* 1239918 (2013).
27. Krogue Ken. (2018). "Why Sales Reps Spend Less than 36% of Time Selling (and less than 18% in CRM)," accessed at https://www.forbes.com/sites/kenkrogue/2018/01/10/why-sales-reps-spend-less-than-36-of-time-selling-and-less-than-18-in-crm/.
28. Hunter, Mark. (2014). "How Lack of Time Management is Killing Your Sales," accessed at https://www.salesforce.com/blog/2014/04/sales-time-management-gp.html.
29. Tracy, Brian. (2017). "Time Management Tips thaat will make you a Prouctiity Master," accessed at https://www.briantracy.com/blog/time-management/time-management-tips/.
30. Mind Tools. (2011). "To-do Lists: The Key to Efficiency," accessed at https://www.mindtools.com/pages/article/newHTE_05.htm.
31. Quinn, Andrew. (2015). 13 Time Management Hacks for Sales Reps," accessed at https://blog.hubspot.com/sales/8-time-management-hacks-for-sales-reps.
32. F. Cirillo, *The Pomodoro Technique* (New York: Simon and Schuster, 2014).
33. Coppock, Mark. (2016). "Task Manager Todoist Gets some Machine INtelligence Smarts in Windows 10 App Update with Smart Schedule," accessed at https://www.onmsft.com/news/task-manager-todoist-gets-some-machine-intelligence-smarts-in-windows-10-app-update-with-smart-schedule.
34. Edwards, Tabitha. (2016). 11 Time Management Tips for Busy Sales Reps," accessed at https://resources.datanyze.com/blog/time-management-tips-for-sales.
35. Drury, Alyssa. (2015). "7 Productivity Tips for Crazy Busy Sales Reps from Jill Konrath," accessed at https://seismic.com/company/blog/7-productivity-tips-for-crazy-busy-sales-reps-from-jill-konrath/.

Design elements: Marketing Insights Podcast: vandame/Shutterstock

GLOSSARY

10,000-hour rule Guideline proposed by Anders Ericsson that 10,000 hours of specialized practice time are needed in order for someone to become a world-class performer.

5:3:2 rule Guideline for social media sharing that suggests content should be 50% curated from relevant third-party sources, 30% content you've created relevant to the brand and audience, and 20% fun, inspirational, or human-interest content.

absolute commission plan Sales compensation plan in which organizations pay reps when they reach specific targets or milestones.

accommodators Negotiators who focus on preserving relationships and building a friendly rapport by sacrificing some of their company's interests in favor of the opposite party's interests; they maximize empathy and minimize assertiveness.

account executives Sales position that offers increasing responsibility above the sales rep job.

acknowledge technique Technique for overcoming an objection in which the salesperson admits that the objection is valid.

active listening Listening that occurs when the salesperson is fully engaged with the customer, paying careful attention to all verbal and nonverbal cues and providing appropriate responses.

adaptors Problem-solvers who prefer more-structured problem-solving methods and are most comfortable when everyone is in agreement about the process and the solution.

affective loyalty The loyalty that exists when the customer feels a strong attitudinal connection and true attachment with the salesperson and/or selling firm.

alter-ego An alternative or different version of oneself.

alternative-choice technique Commitment-gaining technique in which the salesperson provides two legitimate options for the customer to choose between, along with guidance about which is more appropriate.

assumptive close Manipulative closing technique in which the salesperson makes a statement indicating an assumption that an agreement has already been reached, when this is not the case.

avoiders Negotiators who do not like to negotiate and don't do it unless necessary; they rate low on both assertiveness and empathy.

awareness phase Phase in the customer-relationship life cycle in which the customer recognizes a need and begins seeking out selling firms that may potentially be able to solve a problem or fulfill a need.

balance-sheet technique Commitment-gaining technique in which the salesperson lists the positives as well as the negatives associated with commitment.

base salary A fixed amount of money paid to an employee by an employer in return for work performed; does not include benefits, bonuses, or any other potential compensation.

base salary plus bonus Payment structure in which organizations augment a base salary with a bonus when the salesperson meets preset sales targets.

base salary plus commission Payment structure in which organizations pay a fixed base salary as well as a commission.

BATNA Acronym for "best alternative to a negotiated agreement"; often determines whether the other party will walk away.

benefits The added value that a feature provides for the customer.

bonus A lump sum paid out to salespeople for the achievement of their respective sales quotas.

boomerang technique Technique for overcoming an objection in which the salesperson transitions the objection from a negative to a positive by discussing how the perceived negative should actually benefit the customer.

buying signals Cues sent by the customer indicating a shift in thinking from *if* we should do this to *how* we should do this.

buying teams Groups of individuals who ultimately have a voice in the purchase decision.

call reluctance An avoidance of customer interactions.

candor The characteristics of openness, honesty, and sincerity displayed by salespeople in their communications.

center of influence Someone who is both connected to and respected by a group of prospects.

closed questions Questions that are specific in nature and so require short and direct responses—often just a yes or no.

cognitive intelligence (IQ) The ability to learn; differs from *emotional intelligence (EQ)*.

cold lead An individual or organization that has yet to demonstrate interest in the product or service being offered.

cold-call An unsolicited call or visit by a salesperson.

collaborators Negotiators who see conflict as a creative opportunity to satisfy both parties' goals; they rate high on both assertiveness and empathy.

commission-only compensation Payment structure in which organizations pay salespeople based purely on their performance.

commissions A per-unit payout on sales beyond the salesperson's quota.

commitment phase Phase in the customer-relationship life cycle in which the customer has decided to continue the relationship with the salesperson and the selling firm.

company knowledge An understanding of the resources the salesperson's own company possesses and the means of attaining these resources.

compensation technique Technique for overcoming an objection in which the salesperson admits the objection is valid but also discusses other benefits that offset the objection.

competitive knowledge An understanding of both direct and indirect competitors.

competitors Negotiators who see conflict as a win-lose situation and are intent on winning; they maximize assertiveness and minimize empathy.

compromisers Negotiators who are eager to close the deal by doing what is fair and equal for all parties involved in the negotiation; they are intermediate on both assertiveness and empathy.

concession The act of yielding a position in a negotiation.

constrained loyalty The loyalty that exists when the customer is constrained to the relationship, usually by a contractual obligation.

content curation The process of continually finding, grouping, and sharing across social networks the most relevant content on a specific issue.

contingent concession A concession made *only if* the other party agrees to make a specified concession in return.

continuous-yes close Manipulative closing technique in which the salesperson asks a series of questions designed to elicit a positive (yes) response, and concludes by asking for the sale in the hope that the customer will again respond "yes."

cultural adroitness The ability to reach communication goals while interacting with people from other cultures.

cultural awareness The ability to stand back from ourselves and become aware of our cultural values, beliefs, and perceptions.

cultural sensitivity The ability to understand the value of different cultures and be sensitive to the verbal and nonverbal cues of people from other cultures.

customer acquisition analysis Analysis that measures how much a firm spends to gain new customers.

customer co-creation Customer input that results from the customer playing an active role in the problem-solving process.

customer engagement The connection that exists between the salesperson, the selling firm, and the customer.

customer knowledge A deep understanding of a customer's business and the functions and processes that support the business.

customer lifetime value A sales approach that focuses on the net present value of a customer's business over the span of his or her relationship with an organization.

customer orientation The extent to which a salesperson places the customer's interests ahead of their own or those of their company.

customer success stories (*case studies* or *testimonials*) Content that showcases one customer's experience as an example of the firm's products or services.

customer-relationship life cycle The distinct phases through which customer relationships evolve as they develop: awareness, exploration, expansion, commitment, and dissolution.

customer-value proposition A statement of how the sales offering will add value for the buyer and/or the buyer's organization.

data visualization The presentation of data in a graphical format using visual elements like charts, graphs, timelines, and maps.

deceptive pricing Illegal practice that involves intentionally misleading customers with price promotions.

deciders Individuals on a buying team who make the *actual choice* of a product or service for purchase.

dependability A salesperson's reliability in consistently meeting customers' expectations.

dilemma of honesty Situation in which a negotiator who shares all of their exact requirements and limits will never achieve an outcome better than their walk-away point.

dilemma of trust Situation in which a negotiator who believes everything the other party says can be manipulated by dishonesty.

direct denial technique Technique for overcoming an objection in which the salesperson states that the objection is not valid.

direct-request technique Commitment-gaining technique in which the salesperson simply asks for the commitment.

dissolution phase Phase in the customer-relationship life cycle characterized by a customer's desire to end the relationship.

distributive negotiation A negotiation in which the goals of the negotiating parties are in direct opposition.

dual-concern model A theory of conflict resolution that assumes peoples' preferred method of dealing with conflict is based on two dimensions: assertiveness and empathy.

electronic data interchange (EDI) A technology designed to integrate the computer systems of supplier and buyer firms.

emotional close Manipulative closing technique in which the salesperson discusses how important the sale is for personal reasons.

emotional contagion Psychological phenomenon when one person's emotions and related behaviors directly trigger similar emotions and behaviors in other people.

emotional intelligence (EQ) A person's ability to recognize and understand emotions in themselves and in others and to use this awareness to manage their behavior and relationships.

empathy The ability to understand and identify with others' feelings, motivations, and emotions from their perspective.

ethics Moral standards expected by a society.

evaluation of alternatives Phase of the decision-making process in which the customer assesses the competing solutions, weighing their decisions based on criteria that are most important in the decision.

expanding the pie Negotiation strategy that involves adding elements to a negotiation so that more items are negotiable; helps redefine issues from a win-lose perspective to a win-win perspective.

expansion phase Phase in the customer-relationship life cycle in which the customer invests money, time, and effort to expand or strengthen the relationship with the salesperson and the selling firm.

explicit needs Needs that require immediate attention.

exploration phase Phase in the customer-relationship life cycle in which the customer engages in initial prospecting activities to determine the desirability of a long-term relationship with a particular selling firm.

extroverts People who are naturally outgoing and who enjoy talking to and being with other people.

farming orientation A focus on selling to existing customers by building long-term relationships.

fear An automatic emotional response, induced by a perceived threat, that causes a change in brain and organ function, as well as in behavior.

features Factual statements about the characteristics of a product.

field reps Sales reps who work "in the field," calling on customers at their places of business.

fixed costs Costs that remain constant and do not vary based on the number of units produced or sold.

fixed mindset The personal belief that your character, intelligence, and creativity are basically unchanging and that success reflects your innate talents.

follow-up questions Questions asked in direct response to something the customer said.

forestall technique Technique for overcoming an objection in which the salesperson brings up an objection he or she knows will arise, instead of waiting for the customer to do so.

formula sales presentation Sales presentation in which the salesperson follows a somewhat less structured, prepared outline, allowing more flexibility and opportunity to gather customer feedback; typically involves the salesperson talking 60–70 percent of the time and listening 30–40 percent.

gaining commitment The portion of the sales call in which the customer commits to the sale.

gatekeepers Individuals within the buying organization who control access to the buying-team members; typically not part of the buying team.

grit A personality trait defined as perseverance and passion for long-term goals.

gross margin Net sales revenue minus the cost of goods sold.

gross margin commission Commission based on profit rather than sales amount.

growth mindset The personal belief that your traits can change over time and that failure actually helps you learn and improve.

hot lead An individual or organization that has shown some level of interest in the product or service being offered.

hunting orientation A focus on securing new customers through lead generation, prospecting, pre-call planning, and delivering sales presentations.

ideal customer profile A profile of organizational characteristics shared by current, highly desirable customers

implication questions In SPIN selling, questions designed to help the customer and salesperson better understand the consequences arising from the problems uncovered in situational and problem questioning.

implied needs Needs known to the customer but not important enough to merit action.

imposter syndrome The feeling of self-doubt about oneself or one's abilities.

inbound leads Leads initiated by the potential buyer.

incentive pay horizon The time between incentive payments.

indirect denial technique Technique for overcoming an objection in which the salesperson acknowledges understanding why the customer would have the concern but states that the objection is not valid.

individual customer profitability The profit a firm makes from a customer over a specified period of time.

industry knowledge An understanding of the industry in which the salesperson operates and the trends that will affect the industry moving forward.

influencers Individuals on a buying team who help determine the priorities to be addressed when making the purchase decision and express their opinions regarding potential solutions.

information search Phase of the decision-making process in which the customer gathers information and identifies potential suppliers.

initiator The individual or group of individuals on a buying team who first recognizes the customer's need.

innovators Problem-solvers who are at ease with a less-structured problem-solving approach and who tend to look beyond the status quo for solutions.

inside salespeople Salespeople who perform selling activities at the employer's location, typically using email and telephone.

integrative negotiation A negotiation in which the parties place different value on various issues, and resolutions occur through cooperative exchanges.

integrity A strong core set of values that a salesperson adheres to regardless of the situation.

intercultural communication competence The effectiveness of skills, attitudes, and traits for building successful cross-cultural interaction.

introverts People who are naturally reserved and tend to shrink from social contacts.

key performance indicators (KPIs) Measureable, reliable metrics and milestones that demonstrate how effectively a company is achieving key business objectives.

LAER model® Model for handling customer objections, involving four steps: **L**isten, **A**cknowledge, **E**xplore, and **R**espond.

lagging indicators Performance measures that are "outcome"-oriented; often easy to measure, but tend to be difficult to quickly or directly improve or influence.

latent needs Needs that are undetected or of which the customer is unaware.

law of reciprocity Social psychology theory that when you do something thoughtful for others, that kindness is often returned to you in kind.

lead An individual or organization that exhibits characteristics similar in nature to those exhibited by current customers.

lead qualification A process designed to differentiate leads from prospects.

lead scoring Analytics-based application in which a company numerically rates its best prospective customers.

leading indicators Performance measures that are typically "process"-oriented; hard to measure but relatively easy to influence.

likeability The characteristic of a social bond or personal connection between a salesperson and a customer.

logrolling Negotiation strategy that involves the parties identifying two or more issues in conflict and then trading off among those issues.

markup pricing (*cost-plus pricing*) Pricing tactic in which marketers add a certain amount, usually a percentage, to the cost of the product, to set the final price; generally calculated as Unit cost of product + Desired % return × Unit cost.

memorized sales presentation Sales presentation in which the salesperson presents the same selling points in the same order to all customers; typically involves the salesperson talking 90 percent of the time and listening around 10 percent.

misrepresentation by commission Outright falsification of information; nearly always viewed as unethical.

misrepresentation by omission Failure to disclose all information that would benefit the other party; seen as sometimes acceptable.

modified-rebuy purchases Purchases that combine elements of both new-task purchases and straight-rebuy purchases, involving moderate information needs, a moderate timeline, and moderate dollar volume.

need-payoff questions In SPIN selling, questions designed to help the customer and salesperson better understand the benefits available to the firm if the customer's problem no longer existed.

need-satisfaction sales presentation Sales presentation in which the salesperson first probes into the needs, both stated (expressed) and unstated (latent), of the prospective buyer; typically, over 60 percent of the presentation involves listening to the customer to learn about their specific problems.

negotiation A dialogue between two or more people or parties, intended to reach a beneficial outcome about one or more issues over which a conflict exists.

negotiation agenda An agreed-upon list of items to be discussed or goals to be achieved, in a particular order, during a negotiation.

negotiation agent A third-party agent hired to represent the interests or objectives of a principal in a negotiation.

negotiation interests The motivating factor(s) and underlying reasons behind the negotiation position adopted by a negotiation party.

negotiation options Any available choices or alternatives that parties might consider to satisfy their respective interests.

negotiation positions The things negotiators demand you give them and also the things on which they are not willing to budge.

negotiation principal The primary decision-making authority in a negotiation.

networking Activities through which individuals communicate to strengthen their professional and/or social relationships.

new-business salespeople Salespeople responsible primarily for finding new customers and securing their business.

new-task purchases Purchases that are new to the purchasing organization, typically involving high information needs, a high number of purchasing participants, and an extended timeline.

nonprofit organizations (*not-for-profit organizations*) Organizations whose motive is something *other than* to make a profit for owners.

nonverbal communication Behaviors such as eye contact, posture, and facial expressions by which people communicate in ways other than words.

objection A customer concern, prior to and/or during the sales call.

open-ended questions Questions designed to ensure that customers respond with a great deal of information and detail.

opportunity costs For the buyer, the costs associated with doing nothing or with other alternatives.

order-taker salespeople Sales representatives who primarily process orders that a customer initiates.

outbound leads Leads in which the selling firm proactively contacts the lead (the potential buyer).

passive listening One-way communication in which the salesperson receives the information without providing feedback.

personal selling The two-way flow of communication between a buyer and a seller, paid for by the seller and seeking to influence the buyer's purchase decision.

persuasion A communication process by which you motivate someone else to voluntarily do something you would like them to do.

Pomodoro Technique A time-chunking method that uses a timer to break down work into intervals, traditionally 25 minutes in length, separated by short breaks.

post-purchase evaluation Phase of the decision-making process in which the customer assesses how well the solution-implementation process promised by the salesperson and selling firm actually unfolded.

postpone (coming-to-that) technique Technique for overcoming an objection in which the salesperson acknowledges the objection and asks if it can instead be discussed at a later point in the sales call.

power movements Poses or movements that stimulate feelings of confidence.

predatory pricing The practice of first setting prices low with the intention of reducing competition, and then raising prices to normal levels.

predictive analysis The use of data, statistical algorithms, and machine-learning techniques to identify the likelihood of future outcomes based on historical data.

price The amount of something—money, time, or effort—that a buyer exchanges with a seller to obtain a product.

price discrimination The practice of charging different customers different prices for the same product. It is legal for organizations to charge customers different amounts for legitimate reasons; illegal *only if price discrimination injures competition*.

price fixing Collusion of two or more companies to set a product's price; illegal under the Sherman Antitrust Act of 1890 and the Federal Trade Commission Act.

primary objective What the salesperson most wants to accomplish in the sales call.

problem questions In SPIN selling, questions designed to help the customer and salesperson identify issues, sometimes latent, that need to be addressed.

problem recognition Phase of the decision-making process in which the customer first recognizes a need.

product comparison sheet A product specification sheet that offers a side-by-side evaluation of the features or performance of alternative products.

product demonstration Sales presentation that shows the customer how the product works.

product knowledge An understanding of product features and attributes.

product specification (spec) sheet A set of information and precisely organized data about a product.

product users Individuals on a buying team who use the product or service in their daily activities; because of their involvement, they often focus on product functionality.

profit Revenue minus total costs; the firm's "bottom line."

profit margin The amount a product sells for above the total cost of the product itself.

profitability The ability to use resources to generate revenue in excess of expense.

profitability analysis Analysis that measures how much profit the firm generates; can be broken down to measure the profit contribution of regions, products, channels, or customer segments.

profitology The study of increasing profit through sales.

prospect An individual or organization that demonstrates a need for the product or service being offered, possesses the authority and ability to purchase, and demonstrates both organizational potential and purchasing alignment.

prospect prioritization A process through which salespeople rank-order prospects based on their desirability.

prospecting The process through which salespeople identify and engage with new customers or new areas of business with existing customers.

purchasers Individuals within the buying organization who negotiate final terms and make the actual purchase.

quota A quantifiable sales goal for a given time period.

recoverable draw A set amount of money paid to the sales representative by the company at regular intervals.

referral A lead provided by an existing customer, based on a belief that the potential buyer may benefit from the products or services provided by the selling firm.

referral (feel-felt-found) technique Technique for overcoming an objection in which the salesperson uses a third party (often a customer) to address and refute the objection.

relationship management The ability to build rapport and maintain meaningful connections with other people.

relationship selling A sales approach that involves building and maintaining customer trust over a long period of time.

relative commission plan Sales compensation plan that bases pay on performance against a preset target, called a *quota*.

revenue The result of the number of units sold multiplied by the price charged to customers.

Robinson–Patman Act (*Anti-Price Discrimination Act*) A federal law, passed in 1936, that requires sellers to charge customers the same price for the same product.

role conflict A situation in which the goals a salesperson pursues are in conflict with customers' goals.

role play Acting out conversations, attitudes, and actions, in a make-believe situation, in an effort to understand a differing point of view.

salary-only compensation Payment structure in which organizations decide ahead of time how much they will pay their salespeople; take-home earnings each month are set, regardless of how much a rep sells.

sales analysts Salespeople responsible for the collection and analysis of sales data. (Ch 1)

sales directories Lists of leads that are typically compiled by third parties.

sales enablement The process of providing salespeople with the information, content, and tools that help them sell more effectively.

sales engineers Technical specialists who sell in high-tech sectors like aerospace and enterprise software.

sales EQ Emotional intelligence in sales, comprising four skill sets: self-awareness, self-management, social awareness, and relationship management.

sales managers Sales positions with managerial oversight of selling efforts at varying levels of the organizational hierarchy.

sales presentation The delivery of product information relevant to solving the customer's needs.

sales representatives Entry-level, customer-facing or business-to-business sales positions.

sales-development representatives Inside salespeople tasked with generating leads.

salesperson compensation plan choice The selection of a compensation plan alternative from a set of choices.

salesperson-owned loyalty The loyalty directed toward an individual salesperson as opposed to the selling firm.

secondary objective The objective to which the salesperson is willing to revert if agreement cannot be reached on the primary objective.

self-affirmations Verbal reminders to oneself of one's earlier achievements and competence.

self-awareness The ability to perceive your own emotions and the impact they may have on your actions and on other people.

self-management The ability to use awareness of your emotions to positively direct your behaviors.

seller's opportunity cost The value of what a seller gives up (in time and money) in pursuing a particular sale; essentially, the investment a salesperson must make to achieve a sale.

service knowledge An understanding of the additional layer of benefits that accompanies the core offering.

situational questions In SPIN selling, questions designed to help the salesperson better understand the situation the customer is currently facing.

social awareness The ability to pick up on and understand emotions in other people.

social CRM The fusion of social media and customer relationship management, combining social networks, communication technology, communities, strategy, customer value, and relationships.

social listening The monitoring of a brand's social media channels for customer feedback or discussion regarding specific keyword, topics, competitors, or industries, followed by analysis to gain insights and act on opportunities.

social performance How someone perceives and interacts with others.

social proof Independent, third-party verification that a salesperson or an organization can be counted on to deliver what they have promised.

social selling A sales approach that develops, nurtures, and leverages relationships online to sell products or services.

Social Selling Index (SSI) A score that measures, based on four social selling criteria, how a personal brand ranks in people's minds.

social-to-real-life conversions The extent to which online customer interactions with sales personnel or content lead to a phone conversation or face-to-face meeting.

sphere of influence Individuals or groups within one degree of separation from the sales prospect.

SPIN selling Methodology that lays out a basic sequence of four questions for customer interactions: Situational questions, Problem questions, Implication questions, and Need-payoff questions.

spurious loyalty The loyalty that exists when the customer continues to purchase only out of habit.

standing-room-only close Manipulative closing technique in which the salesperson states that due to high demand for the product or service, it may not be available in the future.

straight-line commission Commission based on how close salespeople get to their quota.

straight-rebuy purchases Purchases the customer makes on a frequent basis, involving low information needs and a short timeline.

strategic pricing Proactively creating conditions under which better and more-profitable pricing outcomes are the result.

success-story technique Commitment-gaining technique in which the salesperson tells the story of another customer who agreed to something similar and has benefited from the decision.

summary questions Questions designed to review and verify information previously provided by the customer.

summary-benefit approach Approach to gaining commitment in which the salesperson focuses on the benefits being provided to the customer, rather than the features of the product or service itself.

supplier-solution decision Phase of the decision-making process in which the customer actually chooses a vendor from which to buy.

task performance The ability to perform tasks.

team selling A sales approach in which a salesperson works with experts from across the firm to support new-customer acquisition and ongoing customer relationship management.

technological knowledge An understanding how to use the latest technologies for gathering information and communicating with customers.

time management How people schedule and organize their time for different activities.

trade shows Industry-specific events designed to bring selling companies and customers to the same location.

traditional networking Face-to-face communications that are designed to strengthen an individual's professional and/or social relationships.

trial-close question Question designed to assess whether the customer has comments or concerns about the salesperson's summary.

trust The belief that another person will act with integrity on a reliable basis.

trusted advisor A salesperson who has earned the trust of a customer through displays of both character and competence.

value technique Technique for overcoming an objection in which the salesperson transitions the conversation away from price alone to more fully describe the value being offered through the solution.

variable costs Costs that vary depending on the number of units produced or sold.

virtual networking Networking activities that take place via social media.

virtual presentations Online presentations in which the host and audience attend the presentation remotely.

webinar (*web-based seminar*) A presentation, lecture, workshop, or seminar that is transmitted over the Web using video-conferencing software.

white paper An authoritative document intended to fully inform the reader on a particular topic.

ZOPA Acronym for "zone of possible agreement"; it is the gap between the seller's walk-away point and the buyer's highest willingness to pay.

NAME INDEX

A

Ahearne, M., 45, 215
Albers, S., 21
Albro, Scott, 97
Aldhous, P., 239
Ameresan, Swetha, 97
Andrews, Jeremy, 175
Andrianos, Ethan, 10
Andzulis, J. M., 45
Ang, S., 117
Antonio, Victor, 184, 193
Asai, A., 117
Asay, Matt, 97

B

Badaracco, J. L., Jr., 70
Bandura, Albert, 221, 239
Barney, Matt, 218
Baron, S. G., 97
Barrick, Murray, 21
Barry, B., 153, 166, 172, 173
Bazerman, M. H., 172
Bettencourt, L. A., 70
Botti, S., 215
Bova, Tiffanie, 117
Brewer, Erin, 214–215
Brooks, Candence, 209
Burt, R. S., 147

C

Campbell, Oleg, 97
Campbell, Sherrie, 224, 239
Caputa, Pete, 117
Castano, Emanuele, 229, 239
Chaisrakeo, S., 117
Chen, G. M., 117
Chvátalová, V., 97
Cirillo, Francesco, 231–232, 239
Conlon, D. E., 172
Cope, D. W., 97, 239
Coppock, Mark, 239
Coughlan, A. T., 215
Cuddy, Amy, 223, 239
Cupach, W. R., 117

D

Dahlstrom, R., 70
Darrow, Barb, 238
DeCarlo, T. E., 45
Deitz, George, 96, 171–172, 238
DeSteno, David, 221, 239

Dimotakis, N., 172
Drury, Alyssa, 239
Dubinsky, A. J., 70
Duckworth, Angela, 218, 238
Dudley, G. W., 21
Duffin, Darrious, 41
Dunn, Jule, 238
Dweck, Carol, 219, 238
Dwyer, F. R., 70

E

Earley, P. C., 117
Edwards, Tabitha, 239
Ekman, P., 97
Ellis, Blake, 170
Ericcson, Anders, 219, 238
Evanschitzky, H., 147

F

Ferber, S. N., 239
Festervand, T. A., 70
Fisher, Roger, 150, 172, 173
Flegr, J., 97
Foos, MaKinzie, 73
Fosse, N. E., 239
Frost, Aja, 238
Fudenberg, D., 215
Fuller, Mike, 61, 70, 121–122

G

Galinsky, A. D., 239
Gallo, A., 194
Galvin, William, 213
Gassenheimer, J. B., 70
Gates, Robert, 50
Gavin, Ryan, 110
Gold, J. M., 239
Goldfayn, Alex, 221, 238–239
Gooch, Lance, 99, 117
Good, Robin, 97
Goodson, S. L., 21
Gorman, Jerry, 217
Grant, A., 70
Greisman, L., 45
Gross, J. J., 238
Guesalaga, R., 117
Guptha, Leena, 239

H

Hansen, John D., 45, 70, 117, 146–147, 238
Hanssens, D. M., 21

Harrison, Liz, 110
Haumann, T., 215
Hayes, G., 70
Hayes, George E., 23
Heifetz, D., 70
Herman, Todd, 222
Hicken, Melanie, 170
Hoffeld, David, 239
Hoggard, Randy, 3
Holland, John, 172
Holstrom, B., 215
Hopkins, Tom, 239
Hosmer, Larue, 164, 173
Hudson, Will, 189
Hughes, Doug, 149
Hunt, Shane, 20–21, 69, 193, 215, 238
Hunter, Mark, 230, 239

I

Ilies, R., 172
Iyengar, S. S., 215
Iyer, G. R., 147

J

John, G., 215
Johnson, Erica, 96
Joseph, K., 215
Judge, Timothy, 21
Julkunen, S., 117

K

Kalwani, M. U., 215
Kang, S. K., 239
Kantrovitz, Alex, 97
Kavilanz, P., 194
Keillor, B. D., 70
Kidd, David, 229, 239
Kilpatrick, A. O., 97, 239
King, Zach, 47, 63–64, 70
Kinni, T., 70, 147
Kirton, M., 147
Kishore, S., 215
Kleisner, K., 97
Kopenen, J., 117
Kotler, P., 45
Kovac, M., 193
Kraus, F., 215
Kray, L. J., 239
Krishnaswamy, S., 45
Krogue, Ken, 239

L

Lagace, R. R., 70
Lam, S. K., 45
Langerand, Ellen J., 215

Laubert, C., 173
Ledingham, D., 193
Lewicki, R. J., 153, 166, 172–173
Lewis, Michael, 181–182
Ligos, M., 147
Lorimer, Sally E., 193

M

Ma, L., 173
MacDonald, Steven, 10
Makela, Ray, 238
Malhotra, D., 172
Mallory, Alan, 239
Mannix, Elizabeth, 161, 173
Mantrala, M. K., 21
Marn, Michael V., 193
Marshall, G. W., 117
Mayberry, M., 45
McClain, David, 197
Mertes, Nicole, 97
Meyer, David, 117
Milgrom, P., 215
Millerand, D. T., 173
Minsky, L., 117
Moncrief, W. C., 70, 117
Moore, D. A., 172
Morris, M. R., 97
Mosher, Brian, 48
Mount, Michael, 21

N

Napier, Noah, 66
Narasimhan, C., 215
Narasimhan, O., 215
Neuborne, E., 215
Newberry, Christina, 97
Nietert, P. J., 97, 239

O

Obama, Barack, 116
Oh, S., 70
Oosterhof, N. N., 97

P

Palmatier, R., 70
Panagopoulos, N. G., 45
Parker, R. S., 70
Parks, J., 173
Parlamis, J., 173
Patton, Bruce, 150, 172–173
Paulssen, M., 70
Pettijohn, C. E., 70
Pink, Daniel, 8, 21
Plotkin, Candace Lun, 110

Plouffe, C. R., 70
Pool, R., 238
Purdy, Chase, 194

Q

Quesenberry, K. A., 117
Quinn, Andrew, 239

R

Rackham, N., 45, 124, 147
Rao, R. S., 215
Rapp, A., 45, 70
Rawlston, Savannah, 167
Raz, T., 173
Rehman, S. U., 97, 239
Reinartz, W., 147
Richardson, Hope, 234
Riggle, R. J., 70
Rodin, J., 215
Rodriguez, R., 70
Roegner, Eric V., 193
Rogers, A., 70
Román, S., 70
Ross, M., 173
Roulet, R., 70
Rouziés, D., 45
Ruiz, S., 70
Rutchick, A. M., 239

S

Saunders, D. M., 153, 166, 172–173
Schaeffer, Chase, 142
Scheer, L., 70
Schimel, E., 97
Schmitt, Philipp, 97
Schneider, Taylor, 112
Schultz, S. J., 239
Schurr, P. H., 70
Shanks, Jamie, 83, 97
Sharma, A., 147
Shirako, A., 239
Shirky, Clay, 85
Simon, H. L., 193
Singh, T., 117
Sinka, PK, 193
Skiera, Bernd, 97
Slepian, M. L., 239
Smith, C., 194

Sobczak, Art, 172
Speece, M., 117
Spillecke, Dennis, 110
Spiller, Lisa D., 117
Spitzberg, B. H., 117
Sridhar, S., 217
Stanley, Jennifer, 110
Starosta, W. J., 117
Steenkamp, J.-B., 70
Stevens, H., 70, 147
Steverman, Ben, 116
Stinson, Claire, 238
Strout, E., 21

T

Teevan, J., 97
Thomas, Kenneth W., 172
Thompson, Leigh, 151, 172
Todorov, A., 97
Tracy, Brian, 239
Trainor, K. J., 45

U

Ulaga, W., 147
Ury, William, 150, 172, 173

V

Van den Bulte, Christophe, 97
Vitell, S. J., 70
Voss, Chris, 156, 159, 173

W

Webb, A. P., 70
Weick, Paul, 48
Weilbaker, D. C., 117
White, Jason, 93
Wieseke, J., 215
Wood, Robert, 221, 239
Wooden, John, 238

Z

Zakaria, N., 117
Zaledonis, Lynne, 117
Zasso, Julia, 97
Zawada, Craig C., 193
Ziller, Stephanie, 14
Zoltners, Andres A., 193

SUBJECT INDEX

A

ABC approach to sales, 130
Absolute commission plans, 203
Accenture, 77
Accommodating negotiation style, 153–154
Account executives, 12
Account managers, 27
Acknowledge technique, 139
Acquisition, customer. *See also* Prospecting
   analysis of, 187–188
   vs. retention, time allocated to, 26, 39
Active listening, 16–17, 127
Adaption-innovation theory, 128–129
Adaptors, 128–129
Administrative tasks, automation of, 232
Advertising, in promotion mix, 4
Advisors, trusted, 58–59
Affective loyalty, 56
Affirmations, self-, 222
Agendas, negotiation, 151, 160
Agents
   negotiation, 150
   in principal-agent theory, 208
   purchasing, 52
AI. *See* Artificial intelligence
AIDA (attention, interest, desire, action), 101
Airline industry, 185
Alliance Security, 43
Alter-egos, 222–223
Alternatives
   in alternative-choice technique, 132–133
   in decision-making process, 54
   in negotiations, 158–159, 163–164
Alumni searches, on LinkedIn, 84
American Association of Inside Sales Professionals, 28
Analytics
   predictive, 181–184
   sales, 7–8
Anti-Price Discrimination Act, 185
Apple, 102
Artificial intelligence (AI), 182–184, 232
Assertiveness dimension of conflict resolution, 153–156
Assessment, professional, 27
Assumptive close, 141
AT&T, 93, 106
Atlas Copco, 66
Atria Senior Living, 217
Attention, interest, desire, action (AIDA), 101
Attitude
   toward failure, 219
   positive, 40, 226

Automation, of administrative tasks, 232
Avanir Pharmaceuticals, 170
Average salaries, 11–12
Avoider negotiation style, 153–155
Awareness phase of customer-relationship life cycle, 57

B

Balance-sheet technique, 132
Baseball, 181–182
Base salaries, 198
   definition of, 198
   as percentage of compensation, 198
   plus bonus, 203
   plus commission, 202
   in salary-only compensation, 201
BATNA (best alternative to negotiated agreement), 158–159
Belief, in products, 224
Benefits, of product features, 102–103
BLS. *See* Bureau of Labor Statistics
Bluffing, 165–166
Body language
   definition of, 108
   facial expressions as form of, 79–80, 108–109
   in presentations, 108–109
   and self-confidence, 223
Bonuses, 198, 199, 203
Books, literary fiction, 229
Boomerang technique, 139
Boston Consulting Group, 116
Brands, personal, 69
British Airways, 185
Brooksource, 142
Bureau of Labor Statistics (BLS), 8
Business-to-business (B2B) sales, vs. personal selling, 6
Buyer-centric social profiles, 78–81
Buyers
   in buying teams, 52–53
   socially surrounding, 83–84
Buying signals, 131
Buying teams, 52–53

C

Call planning
   call objectives in, 130–131
   in prospecting, 28–29, 32–34
Call reluctance, 26, 146–147
Candor, 60
Caps, commission, 208

Careers, sales, 210–212
   in management, 12–13, 210–212
   types of roles in, 11–13, 210
   what to look for in, 210
Career Tips
   on call reluctance, 146–147
   on corporate social responsibility, 214–215
   on early career success, 20–21
   on life after college, 238
   on negotiations, 171–172
   on personal brands, 69
   on pricing, 193
   on social media profiles, 96
   on taking care of coworkers, 117
   for territory management, 45
Carew International, 136
Carrefour, 186
Case studies. *See* Success stories
CEA. *See* Council of Economic Advisors
Centers of influence, 37
CFA Institute, 116
CFPB. *See* Consumer Financial Protection Bureau
Character, trust based on, 59–61
Chatbots, 182
Checklists, negotiation preparation, 156–157
China, deceptive pricing in, 186
Choice, in compensation plans, 199–200
Closed questions, 126
Closing. *See also* Gaining commitment
   manipulative techniques in, 141–143
   traditional approaches to, 129–130, 140–141
Clothes, 223–224
CLV. *See* Customer lifetime value
Co-creation, customer, 124
Codes of conduct, 15–16
Cognitive intelligence, 225
Cold-calling
   customer aversion to, 43, 75
   definition of, 36
   ethics in, 43
   lead generation through, 36
Cold leads, 30
Collaboration, in team selling, 111
Collaborator negotiation style, 153, 155–156
Colleges. *See* Universities
Collusion, in price fixing, 185
Coming-to-that technique, 140
Commissions, 198–199
   caps on, 208
   in compensation mix, 201–204
   definition of, 198
Commitment, gaining. *See* Gaining commitment
Commitment phase of customer-relationship life cycle, 57–58

Communication
   intercultural, 107
   in international sales, 106–107
   in negotiation styles, 151, 153–156
   nonverbal (*See* Nonverbal communication)
   one-way, 74, 127
   by successful salespeople, 17
   two-way, 4, 75
Company knowledge, 62
Compensation mix, 201–204
Compensation plans, 196–215
   aligning profit with compensation in, 181
   average salaries in, 11–12
   base salaries in, 198, 201–203
   commissions in (*See* Commissions)
   elements of, 198–200
   examples of, 204–207
   problems with design of, 207–208
   salesperson choice in, 199–200
   types of, 201–207
Compensation technique, 139
Competence-based trust, 59, 61–64
Competition, in predatory pricing, 186
Competitive knowledge, 62
Competitor negotiation style, 153, 155
Compromiser negotiation style, 153, 156
Concessions
   definition of, 164
   in negotiations, 164, 171–172
Conduct, codes and standards of, 15–16
Confidence. *See* Self-confidence
Conflict resolution
   dual-concern model of, 153–154
   negotiation styles in, 153–156
Conflicts of interest, among financial advisors, 115–116
Constrained loyalty, 56
Consumer Financial Protection Bureau (CFPB), 19
Content creation, 85
Content curation, 84–89
   benefits of, 85
   vs. content creation, 85
   definition of, 84–85
   process of, 85–86
   types of content in, 86–90
Contingent concessions, 164
Continuous-yes close, 141
Contracts, writing, in negotiations, 164, 172
Conversions
   from referrals, 36
   social-to-real-life, 92
Core offering, 54–55, 63
Coronavirus pandemic, 109–110

Subject Index

Corporate social responsibility, 214–215
Cost(s). *See also* Pricing
   in cost-plus pricing, 178–179
   fixed vs. variable, 177–178
   opportunity, 25, 177
   of personal selling, 5
Council of Economic Advisors (CEA), 116
COVID-19 pandemic, 109, 110
Creativity
   in negotiations, 163
   in problem solving, 128–129
Credibility, on social media, 78–81
CRM. *See* Customer relationship management
Cross-selling, 188, 213
Cues
   buying signals as, 131
   social-selling, 83–84
Cultural adroitness, 107
Cultural awareness, 107
Cultural diversity, 106–107
Cultural sensitivity, 107
Customer acquisition. *See also* Prospecting
   analysis of, 187–188
   vs. retention, time allocated to, 26, 39
Customer co-creation, 124
Customer decision making. *See* Decision making
Customer engagement
   definition of, 49, 109
   in virtual presentations, 109–110
Customer knowledge, 61–62, 123
Customer lifetime value (CLV), 6
Customer objections. *See* Objections
Customer orientation, 60
Customer profiles, ideal, 32
Customer referrals. *See* Referrals
Customer relationship(s), 46–70. *See also* Relationship selling
   differences in, 55–58
   ethical behavior in, 64–67
   levels of, 55–56
   life cycle of, 57–58
   lifetime value of, 6
   loyalty types in, 55–56
   purchase types in, 50–55
   trust in, 48, 58–64
Customer relationship management (CRM)
   definition of, 8
   in emotional intelligence, 226, 229
   in international sales, 106–107
   in pricing, 187–188
   social, 82–83, 91
   in time management, 232
Customer retention, vs. acquisition, time allocated to, 26, 39
Customer-value proposition, 63, 102

D

Data visualization, 103–104
Deception
   in negotiations, 165–168
   in pricing, 186
Deciders, in buying teams, 53
Decision-making processes
   buying teams in, 52–53
   emotions in, 225
   five-step model of, 53–54
   purchase types affecting, 49, 53–55
   websites in, 36–37
Demographics, of social media users, 9–10
Demonstrations, product, 103
Denial technique, 139
Dependability, 60–61
Detail, attention to, 17
Digital era
   customer engagement in, 49
   personal selling in, 8–10
   purchasing processes in, 36–37, 49, 74–75
Dilemma of honesty, 165
Dilemma of trust, 165
Direct denial technique, 139
Directories, sales, 37
Directors of sales, 212
Direct-request technique, 132
DirecTV Now, 106
Discrimination, price, 184–185
Disruptive emotions, 225, 227–228
Dissolution phase of customer-relationship life cycle, 57, 58
Distractions
   in time management, 233
   in virtual presentations, 110–111
Distributive negotiations, 152–153, 163
DOD. *See* U.S. Department of Defense
Do Not Call Registry, 43
Dressing for success, 223–224
Dual-concern model of conflict resolution, 153–154

E

84 Lumber, 99
Electronic data interchange (EDI), 51
Email
   creating templates for, 232
   negotiation via, 161
   time spent checking, 233
Emotion(s)
   in decision making, 225
   disruptive, 225, 227–228
   empathy with, 229
   in facial expressions, 79
   in manipulative closing techniques, 141
   in negotiations, 159, 161, 165–166

Emotion(s)—(Continued)
   self-awareness of, 226–227
   self-management of, 226–227
   in storytelling, 113
Emotional close, 141
Emotional contagion, 227
Emotional intelligence (EQ), 224–230
   vs. cognitive intelligence, 225
   and decision making, 225
   definition of, 225
   ethics and, 236–237
   sales, 226–229
   strategies for improving, 226–229
Emotional triggers, 228
Empathy
   in conflict resolution, 153–156
   definition of, 229
   in emotional intelligence, 229
Engagement, customer
   definition of, 49, 109
   in virtual presentations, 109–110
Entry-level sales representatives, 11
EQ. *See* Emotional intelligence
Ethical Challenge assignments, 16
   on cold calling, 43
   on emotional intelligence, 236–237
   on financial advisors, 115–116
   on pharmaceutical sales, 170
   on publicly traded companies, 145
   on realtor commissions, 192
   on rebate withholding scheme, 68
   on securities-based loans, 213–214
   on unauthorized bank accounts, 19–20
   on up-selling, 95–96
Ethics, 64–67
   in corporate social responsibility, 214–215
   in customer relationships, 64–67
   definition of, 15, 64
   factors contributing to problems with, 65–67
   in gaining commitment, 140–143
   in negotiations, 164–168
   in presentations, 106
   in pricing, 184–187
   in prospecting, 40
   research on, 65
   in standards of conduct, 15–16
Excel, 193
Executive Perspectives
   from business operations director, 73
   from CEO, 149
   from contractor sales representative, 99
   from co-owner, 23
   from district sales managers, 47, 175
   from executive directors, 197, 217
   from general manager, 121–122
   from managing director, 3
Executives, account, 12
Expanding the pie strategy, 163–164
Expansion phase of customer-relationship life cycle, 57–58
Explicit needs, 126
Exploration phase of customer-relationship life cycle, 57
Extroverts, 218
Eyebrows, 109
Eye contact, in presentations, 108

F

Facebook, 9–10
Facial expressions
   in presentations, 108–109
   in social media profiles, 79–80
Failures
   attitudes toward, 219
   fear of, 220–221
   filter, 85
   of presentations, reasons for, 105–107
   technological, 105, 162
Farming orientation, 27
Fastenal, 47, 63–64
FBI. *See* Federal Bureau of Investigation
Fear
   definition of, 220
   impact on sales, 220–221
   overcoming, 221
Features, product, 102–103
Federal Bureau of Investigation (FBI), 48
Federal Trade Commission (FTC), 43, 186
Federal Trade Commission Act, 185
Feedback, immediate, in personal selling, 5
Feel-felt-found technique, 140
Fiction, literary, 229
Fiduciary rule, 116
Field reps, 12
Filter failure, 85
Financial advisors, conflicts of interest among, 115–116
Financial objectives, of negotiations, 158–159
First impressions, 78, 223
5:3:2 rule, 86
Fixed compensation, 198, 201
Fixed costs, 177–178
Fixed mindset, 219
Fleetio, 167
Follow-up questions, 128
Forestall technique, 139
Formula sales presentations, 100–101
Forrester Research, 9
Fortune (magazine), 220
4:1:1 rule, 86

Friendships, 59
Frowning, 108
FTC. *See* Federal Trade Commission
Fuel surcharges, 185
Fundraising
　pricing issues in, 186–187
　prospecting in, 24
　storytelling in, 113

G

Gaining commitment, 129–133
　customer-oriented approach to, 130–131
　definition of, 129
　ethics in, 140–143
　overcoming objections in, 122, 135–140
　techniques for, 131–133
　traditional approach to, 129–130, 140–141
Gatekeepers, in buying teams, 53
GE, 182
Getting to Yes (Fisher, Ury, & Patton), 150
Goals. *See* Objectives
Golden Rule, 61, 81
Google, 77
Google Alerts, 82–83
GoToMeeting, 63
Grit, 218–220
　definition of, 218
　developing, 219–220
　vs. self-control, 218
Gross margin commission, 204
Gross margins
　compensation based on, 181, 204
　definition of, 179, 181
Group Decision and Negotiation (journal), 161
Group presentations, 111
Growth mindset, 219
GrowthPlay, 27

H

Headlines, profile, 80
Honesty
　dilemma of, 165
　in negotiations, 165
　in pricing, 186
Hootsuite Streams, 82
Hot leads, 30
HubSpot Meetings, 232
Hunting orientation, 27
Hydro-Temp, 189

I

IDC, 74–75
Ideal customer profiles, 32
Implication questions, 125
Implied needs, 126
Imposter syndrome, 220
Inbound leads, 29
Incentive pay. *See also specific types*
　in compensation mix, 201
　forms of, 198–199
　time between payments, 200
Incentive pay horizon, 200
Indicators
　lagging, 91, 92
　leading, 91–92
Indirect denial technique, 139
Individual customer profitability, 188
Industry knowledge, 62–63
Influence
　centers of, 37
　spheres of, 84
Influencers, in buying teams, 53
Information dependence, 165
Information gathering, for negotiations, 157, 166
Information overload, 85
Information searches
　in decision-making process, 54
　on social media, 77
Initiators, in buying teams, 52
Innovators, 128–129
Inside salespeople, 11
　definition of, 11, 27
　number in U.S., 28
　in prospecting, 27–28, 32
　salaries of, 12
Integrative negotiations, 152–153, 163
Integrity, 61
Intelligence
　artificial, 182–184, 232
　cognitive, 225
　emotional, 224–230
Intercultural communication competence, 107
Interests
　conflicts of, 115–116
　negotiation, 151
International Journal of Communications, 233
International sales, presentations in, 106–107
Introverts, 218
Inventory managers, 53
IQ, 225
Irrelevant information, 106

K

Key performance indicators (KPIs), 90–92
Keywords, on LinkedIn, 80
Kickback payments, 170

Knowledge, 61–64
  company, 62
  competitive, 62
  customer, 61–62, 123
  industry, 62–63
  in problem solving, 123
  product, 62
  service, 63–64
  technological, 63
KPIs. *See* Key performance indicators

L

LAER model, 136–137
Lagging indicators, 91, 92
Latent needs, 54, 125
Law of reciprocity, 81
Lead(s)
  definition of, 29
  generation of (*See* Lead generation)
  prioritization of, 28–30, 231
  vs. prospects, 30
  qualification of, 28–29
Lead generation
  evaluating, 39–40
  methods of, 34–38
  in prospecting process, 28–29, 34
Leading indicators, 91–92
Lead scoring, 182, 183
Legal issues, in pricing, 184–187
Life cycle of customer relationships, 57–58
Likeability, 59
Line reviews, 52
LinkedIn
  alumni searches on, 84
  buyer-centric profiles on, 78–80
  demographics of users, 9–10
  groups on, 35
  job change notifications from, 84
  people searches in, 83–84
  profile photos on, 80
  Social Selling Index of, 91–92
  summary sections of, 80
  virtual networking via, 35
Listening
  active, 16–17, 127
  in negotiations, 151–152
  in overcoming objections, 136
  passive, 127
  in presentations, 100–101
  in problem solving, 126–128
  social, 9, 81–82
Lists
  in negotiation preparation, 156–157
  to-do, working from, 230–231, 232

Literary fiction, 229
Location, of negotiations, 160
Logrolling, 163
Loyalty, 55–56
  affective, 56
  constrained, 56
  salesperson-owned, 55–56
  spurious, 56
Lyft, 85
Lying, in negotiations, 165–168

M

Managers
  account, 27
  inventory, 53
  sales, 12–13, 210–212
  territory, 45, 93
Manipulation
  in closing techniques, 141–143
  in negotiations, 165–166
  vs. persuasion, 106
Marketing
  lead generation through, 37–38
  social media, 75
Marketing departments, in pricing, 179, 180
Marketing mix, 176
Marketing Science Institute, 5
Market research, on pricing, 180
Markup pricing, 178–179
Marriott Vacations Worldwide, 234
McKinsey & Company, 179–180
Memorable presentations, 103
Memorized sales presentations, 100
Memphis Hustle, 73
Mentoring, 211
Message consistency, 5
Millward Brown Digital, 77
The Mind and Heart of the Negotiator (Thompson), 151
Mindsets
  fixed, 219
  growth, 219
Mine-Resistant Ambush Protected (MRAP) program, 50–51
Misrepresentation, 165–166
  by commission, 165
  by omission, 165
Modified-rebuy purchases, 50, 51–52
Moneyball (Lewis), 181–182
Monopolies, 186
Morgan Stanley, 213–214
Motivation
  through compensation plans, 198–203, 208
  through storytelling, 113
MRAP. *See* Mine-Resistant Ambush Protected
Multitasking, 232–233

N

National Association of Realtors (NAR), 192
Need-payoff questions, 125–126
Needs
   explicit, 126
   identifying, 30–31
   implied, 126
   latent, 54, 125
Need-satisfaction sales presentations, 100–102
Negotiation(s), 148–173
   checklist for, 156, 157
   deception in, 165–168
   definition of, 150
   ethics in, 164–168
   guidelines for conducting, 162–164, 171–172
   online, 161–162
   planning for, 156–162
   pricing in, 180–181
   principals and agents in, 150
   as process, 151–153
   styles of, 151, 153–156
   substance of, 151–152
   team, 160–161
Negotiation agendas, 151, 160
Negotiation agents, 150
Negotiation interests, 151
Negotiation options, 152
Negotiation positions, 151
Negotiation principals, 150
Networking
   definition of, 34
   traditional, 35
   virtual, 34–35, 63 (*See also* Social media)
New-business developers, 27
New-business salespeople, 12
New-task purchases, 50–51
Nielsen, 92
Noncompeting salespeople, lead generation through, 37
No-need objections, 134
Nonprofit organizations
   definition of, 13
   pricing issues for, 186–187
   sales roles in, 13
   storytelling in presentations of, 113
Non-sales selling, 8
Nonverbal communication. *See also* Body language
   definition of, 108
   in presentations, 108–109
Northwestern Mutual, 3
Note taking
   in active listening, 128
   in negotiations, 151–152
Nuedexta, 170

O

Objections
   definition of, 133
   overcoming, 122, 135–140, 141
   types of, 133–135
Objectives
   of negotiations, 158–159
   of sales calls, 130–131
Omission, misrepresentation by, 165
One-way communication, 74, 127
Online negotiation, 161–162
Open-ended questions, 126
Opportunity costs, 25
   seller's, 177
Optimization, price, 184
Optus, 14
Orientations
   customer, 60
   farming, 27
   hunting, 27
   product, 60
Outbound leads, 29
Outside salespeople, in prospecting, 27–28

P

PandaDoc, 232
Pandemic, coronavirus, 109, 110
Passion, 219
Passive listening, 127
Pay. *See* Compensation plans; Salaries
Performance
   sales, ethical behavior in, 65
   social, 221
   task, 221
Performance horizon, sales, 200
Performance indicators, key (KPIs), 90–92
Performance management
   artificial intelligence in, 184
   sales managers in, 211
Performance measurements
   in compensation plans, 208
   in social selling, 81–82, 90–92
Pernod Ricard USA, 61, 121–122
Perseverance, 218
Persistence, 218–220
Personal brands, 69
Personality, of salespeople, 13, 210, 218
Personal selling
   advantages of, 5
   challenges of, 5
   definition of, 4
   in digital era, 8–10
   ethics in, 15–16
   factors influencing use of, 6–7

Personal selling—(*Continued*)
　forms of, 4
　importance of, 4–5
　in promotion mix, 4
　strategic role of, 6–7
Personal strengths, matching to prospecting roles, 26–28
Persuasion
　definition of, 100
　vs. manipulation, 106
　in presentations, 100
Pharmaceutical sales, 100, 170
Photographs, in social media profiles, 79–80
Pilot Flying J, 48, 68
Pitney Bowes, 9
Place, in marketing mix, 176
Planning. *See also* Call planning
　for negotiations, 156–162
　for presentations, 102–105
　for prospecting, 39
Pomodoro Technique, 231–232
Positions, negotiation, 151
Positive attitude, 40, 226
Positive visualization, 228
Postpone technique, 140
Post-purchase evaluation, in decision-making process, 54–55
Postural feedback, 223
Posture
　in presentations, 108
　and self-confidence, 223
Power movements, 223
Practice
　in development of grit, 219
　of presentations with role play, 104–105
Predatory pricing, 185–186
Predictive analytics, 181–184
Presentations, sales, 98–117
　definition of, 100
　formula, 100–101
　international and intercultural challenges in, 106–107
　memorized, 100
　need-satisfaction, 100, 101–102
　nonverbal communication in, 108–109
　preparing for, 102–105
　reasons for failure of, 105–107
　storytelling in, 113–114
　team, 111
　virtual, 109–111
Price, definition of, 176
Price discrimination, 184–185
Price fixing, 185
Price objections, 135
Price optimization, 184
Pricing, 174–194
　CRM in, 187–188
　legal and ethical issues in, 184–187
　in marketing mix, 176
　markup, 178–179
　in negotiations, 180–181
　in profitology, 177–179
　research-based, 179
　role of, 176
　strategic, 179–181, 187–188
　tips for working in, 193
Primary objectives, 131
Principal-agent theory, 208
Principals, negotiation, 150
Prioritization
　of leads, 28–30, 231
　of prospects, 28–29, 32
　in time management, 231
Privacy, in videoconferencing, 162
Problem definition, in negotiations, 162–163
Problem questions, 125
Problem recognition
　in decision-making process, 54
　in presentation preparation, 102–103
Problem solving, 122–129
　creativity in, 128–129
　customer role in, 123–124
　as job of salespeople, 17, 122–124
　listening in, 126–128
　vs. products, focus on, 123
　questioning in, 124–126, 128
　styles of, 128–129
Proctor and Gamble, 101
Product(s)
　belief in, 224
　in marketing mix, 176
　vs. solutions, focus on, 123
Product comparison sheets, 88
Product demonstrations, 103
Product features, 102–103
Product knowledge, 62
Product objections, 135
Product orientation, 60
Product specification (spec) sheets, 87–88
Product users, in buying teams, 52
Professional assessment, 27
Professional Perspectives. *See also* Executive Perspectives
　from account executives, 142, 167
　from acquisition territory manager, 93
　from director of sales, 189
　from real estate agents, 209
　from sales account manager, 14
　from sales consultant, 112
　from sales-development program, 66
　from sales operations analyst, 41
　from VIP-owner concierge, 234

Profiles
 buyer-centric social, 78–81
 ideal customer, 32
 of negotiation partners, 157–158
Profit
 aligning compensation with, 181
 definition of, 176
Profitability
 analysis of, 187–188
 definition of, 176
 individual customer, 188
Profit margins, 178–179
Profitology, 177–179
Promotion, in marketing mix, 176
Promotion mix, 4
Prospect(s)
 definition of, 30
 vs. leads, 30
 prioritization of, 28–29, 32
Prospecting, 22–45
 challenges of, 24–26
 definition of, 24
 developing strategy for, 38–40
 ethics in, 40
 importance of, 24
 inside sales in, 27–28
 lead generation in, 28–29, 34–38
 matching personal strengths to roles in, 26–28
 process of, 28–34
Prospecting plans, 39
Psychology of selling, 216–239
 emotional intelligence in, 224–230
 empathy in, 229
 grit in, 218–220
 self-confidence in, 220–224
 time management in, 230–233
Publicly traded companies, 145
Public relations, in promotion mix, 4
Purchasers, in buying teams, 53
Purchase types, 50–55
 buying teams affected by, 52–53
 decision making affected by, 49, 53–55
 descriptions of, 50–52
Purchasing agents, 52
Purchasing authority, 31, 52
Purchasing processes. See also Decision making
 buying teams in, 52–53
 and customer engagement, 49
 in digital era, 36–37, 49, 74–75

Q

Questions
 closed, 126
 follow-up, 128
 implication, 125
 need-payoff, 125–126
 in negotiations, 151
 open-ended, 126
 in overcoming objections, 138
 problem, 125
 in problem solving, 124–126, 128
 situational, 124–125
 summary, 128
 trial-close, 131
Quotas
 definition of, 24
 incentive pay based on, 198, 199
 in relative commission plans, 203

R

Rapport, storytelling and, 113–114
Real estate sales, 192, 209
Reciprocity, law of, 81
Recommendations, in social media profiles, 80–81
Recoverable draw, 199
Referrals
 definition of, 35
 ethics in use of, 40
 lead generation through, 35–36
 from social selling, 92
 storytelling about, 114
 warm, 92
Referral technique, 140
Regional sales managers, 211
Rejection
 fear of, 220–221
 rates of, in prospecting, 25–26
Relationship management. See also Customer relationship management
 definition of, 229
 in emotional intelligence, 226, 229
Relationship selling, 48. See also Customer relationship(s)
 definition of, 5, 48
 strategic role of, 6
Relative commission plans, 203
Research
 on ethics, 65
 on pricing, 180
Research-based pricing, 179
Resilience, 218–220
Results tracking, in prospecting strategy, 39
Retention, vs. acquisition, time allocated to, 26, 39
Retirement savings, 116
Revenue
 definition of, 176
 from social selling, 9–10, 76
Ride sharing, 85

Ritter Communications, 41
Robinson–Patman Act, 185
Robocalls, 43
Role conflict, 60
Role play
   definition of, 104
   practicing presentations with, 104–105
Rule(s)
   fiduciary, 116
   5:3:2, 86
   4:1:1, 86
   Golden, 61, 81
   70:20:10, 86
   Telemarketing Sales, 43
   10,000-hour, 219

S

Salaries. *See also* Compensation plans
   average, 11–12
   base, 198, 201–203
   by job title, 12
   in salary-only compensation, 201
Sales analysts, 12
Sales analytics, 7–8
Sales and Marketing Executives International (SMEI), 15–16
Sales assistants, AI-enabled, 184
Sales-development representatives, 28
Sales directories, 37
Sales enablement, 85–86
Sales EQ (emotional intelligence), 226–229
Salesforce (company), 8, 109
Sales managers, 12–13, 210–212
Salespeople. *See also specific types*
   average salaries of, 11–12
   importance of, 4
   number in U.S., 8
   personality of, 13, 210, 218
   strategic role of, 6–7
   successful (*See* Success)
   types of, 11–13
Sales performance. *See* Performance
Salesperson compensation plan choice, 199–200
Salesperson-owned loyalty, 55–56
Salesperson service, 63–64
Sales presentations. *See* Presentations
Sales promotion, in promotion mix, 4
Sales representatives, 11–12
Sales roles
   matching personal strengths to, 26–27
   types of, 11–13
Sales support, 12
Secondary objectives, 131
Securities-based loans (SBLs), 213–214
Securities Industry and Financial Markets Association, 116

Self-affirmations, 222
Self-awareness, 226–227
Self-confidence, 220–224
   strategies for improving, 222–224
   in task and social performance, 221–222
Self-control, 218
Self-management, 226, 227–228
Seller's opportunity cost, 177
Service knowledge, 63–64
Service offering, 54–55, 63
Service surround, 63
Sherman Antitrust Act, 185
Signals, buying, 131
Silence
   in listening, 127–128
   in response to deception, 168
Situational questions, 124–125
"Slick" data, 103–104
SMEI. *See* Sales and Marketing Executives International
Smiling, 108
Social awareness, 226, 228–229
Social CRM, 82–83, 91
Social listening, 9, 81–82
Socially surrounding buyers, 83–84
Social media. *See also* Social selling
   content curation in, 84–89
   demographics of users, 9–10
   minimizing distraction of, 233
   virtual networking via, 34–35, 63
Social media marketing, vs. social selling, 75
Social media profiles
   buyer-centric, 78–81
   management of, 96
   photographs in, 79–80
Social performance, 221
Social proof, 77, 80
Social responsibility, corporate, 214–215
Social selling, 72–97
   content curation in, 84–89
   credibility in, 78–81
   definition of, 9, 35, 74
   demographics of social media users in, 9–10
   growing social network in, 81–84
   as organizational strategy, 76
   performance measurements in, 81–82, 90–92
   reasons for using, 74–78
   revenue influenced by, 9–10, 76
   vs. traditional sales, 74–76
   value creation in, 77–78
Social Selling Index (SSI), 91–92
Social-to-real-life conversions, 92
Solutions. *See* Problem solving
Source objections, 134, 137–138
Southern Grit, 23

Spheres of influence, 84
SPIN selling
   call-planning template in, 32–33
   definition of, 32, 124
   types of questions in, 124–126
Splitting the difference, 172
Sports, college, 186–187
Spurious loyalty, 56
SSI. *See* Social Selling Index
Standards of conduct, 15–16
Standing-room-only close, 141–143
Story-sellers, 114
Storytelling, in presentations, 113–114
Straight-line commission, 203–204
Straight-rebuy purchases, 50, 51
Strategic concessions, 164
Strategic pricing, 179–181, 187–188
Substance, of negotiations, 151–152
Success, in sales
   emotional intelligence in, 224–230
   empathy in, 229
   grit in, 218–220
   self-confidence in, 220–224
   skills needed for, 16–17
   time management in, 17, 230–233
   tips for early career success, 20–21
Success stories, customer, 88–89
   characteristics of, 89, 90
   definition of, 77, 88
   gaining commitment using, 132
   sphere of influence and, 84
   video-based, 77
Success-story technique, 132
Summary-benefit approach, 131
Summary questions, 128
Supplier-solution decisions, in decision-making process, 54
Supreme Court, U.S., 186
Surgarai, 149
Sympathy, vs. empathy, 229

T

Task performance, 221
TD Bank, 95–96
Teams
   buying, 52–53
   negotiation, 160–161
   presentation, 111
   selling, 111
Technological failures
   in presentations, 105
   in videoconferences, 162
Technological knowledge, 63
Telemarketers, vs. inside salespeople, 11

Telemarketing Sales Rule (TSR), 43
Tennis Australia, 112
10,000-hour rule, 219
Territory managers, 45, 93
Testimonials, buyer, 77–78. *See also* Success stories
Text messaging, negotiation via, 161
Time allocation
   to customer acquisition vs. retention, 26, 39
   in prospecting strategy, 39
Time-chunking, 231–232
Time management, 230–233
   challenges of, 230
   definition of, 230
   importance of, 17, 230
   strategies for improving, 230–233
Time objections, 134–135
Todoist, 232
To-do lists, 230–231, 232
To Sell Is Human (Pink), 8
Total value proposition, 63
Trade shows, 36
Traditional competitive bargaining, 165, 166
Traditional sales
   ABC approach to, 130
   gaining commitment in, 129–130, 140–141
   markup pricing in, 178–179
   networking in, 35
   overcoming objections in, 140–141
   vs. social selling, 74–76
   strategic role of salespeople in, 6
Training programs, 211
Trial-close questions, 131
Trigger events, 83–84
Trust, 58–64
   character-based, 59–61
   competence-based, 59, 61–64
   definition of, 48, 58
   dilemma of, 165
   in negotiations, 165
   in social selling, 75
   storytelling and, 113–114
Trusted advisors, 58–59
Truth, in negotiations, 165
TSR. *See* Telemarketing Sales Rule
Tuna, 185
Twitter, 9–10
Twitter Lists, 83
Two-way communication
   in personal selling, 4
   in social selling, 75

U

Uber, 85
Universities

Universities—(*Continued*)
  fundraising by, 24, 186–187
  searching for alumni of, 84
Up-selling, 95–96, 188
U.S. Department of Defense (DOD), 50–51
U.S. Department of Justice, 170, 185
U.S. Department of Labor, 28, 116

V

Value creation
  in customer-value proposition, 63, 102
  in social selling, 77–78
  in traditional sales, 6
Value technique, 140
Variable costs, 177–178
Vice presidents of sales, 212
Videoconferencing, negotiations via, 161–162
Virgin Atlantic, 185
Virtual meetings, 63
Virtual networking, 34–35, 63. *See also* Social media
Virtual presentations, 109–111
  customer engagement in, 109–110
  definition of, 109
  eliminating distractions in, 110–111
  storytelling in, 113
Visualization, positive, 228

W

Walking away, from negotiations, 158–159, 172
Walmart, 186
Warm referrals, 92
Webinars, 89
Websites, lead generation through, 36–37
Wells Fargo, 15, 19–20, 213
Wharton School of Business, 92
White papers, 87
Writing, contract, in negotiations, 164, 172

Y

Yourself, selling
  meaning of, 16
  skills needed for, 16–17
  through storytelling, 114
YouTube
  branded channels on, 77
  demographics of users, 9–10

Z

Zayo Group Holdings, 175
Zoom, 63
ZOPA (zone of possible agreement), 158–159